To Kim Wood,

To wield steelhead
hook-ups & screaming
runs!

[signature]

Steelhead Dreams

The Theory, Method, Science And Madness
Of Great Lakes Steelhead Fly Fishing

Steelhead Dreams

The Theory, Method, Science And Madness
Of Great Lakes Steelhead Fly Fishing

Matt Supinski

Frank Amato PORTLAND

Acknowledgements

Thanks to Anne Miller and Bob Linseman for their painstaking edits and guidance on the text and to all the professional steelhead biologists and masters: Ed Rutherford. Paul Seelbach, Leo Mronzinski, Gary Whelan, Tom Rozich, Jory Jonas, Tammy Newcomb, Thomas Coon, Jim Dexter and Thomas Stauffer of the Michigan DNR, Les Wedge, Fran Verdoliva, Bill Culligan, and Steve Mooradian of the New York DEC, Kevin Kayle of the Ohio Department of Fish and Wildlife, Neil Ledet and Brian Briedert of the Indiana DNR, Brad Eggold, Dennis Pratt, and Robert DuBois of the Wisconsin DNR, Tracy Close of the Minnesota DNR, Jon George, John Bowbly, David Reid and Fred Dobbs of the Ontario MNR, Tom Trudeau of the Illinois DNR.

A very special thank you to Larry Halyk, expert steelhead and fly fisher, fly tier and biologist with the Ontario MNR, who has contributed greatly to understanding the current status of Ontario steelhead rivers. John Valk, Jeff "Bear" Andrews, Mike Yarnott and all the steelhead fly masters that are featured in the book and have contributed their beautiful patterns, John Nagy for his photographic and fly contributions, Ray Schmidt and Rick Kustich for their innovative direction and writings, Tom Pero for having produced the great *Wild and Steelhead & Salmon* Magazine, to the Caledonia Historical Society, Alan Smitly Historian at the Northville Library, Bara Lowe Gotts and Hugh MacCrimmon for allowing me to use excerpts from their book *Rainbow Trout in the Great Lakes*.

Thanks to Gary Phillips for the painstaking photography of the fly plates, rocks of Lake Superior and other photos, to Brian Hanchen for his illustrations and photographic contributions; and Jeff Bacon, Steve Kuieck, Scott Smith, Fran Verdoliva, Dave Barber, "Vicki" Oliphant, Brian Fleischig and Mike Bennett, for their outings on the river, and Shawn Perich for his hospitality and guiding.

A very special thank you to Steve Stallard, friend, steelhead salmon expert fly angler, tier, photographer, guide, who has the "cutting edge on everything salmonid," and contributed heavily to this book. Dennis Pratt for his pioneering steelhead work on Wisconsin's Bois Brule and for his description of steelhead lifecycles. To Roger Greil and the folks at Lake Superior State University for their outstanding Atlantic salmon program, and Roger and Jo Greil's friendship and hospitality during my vagrant house visits. Thank you to: Orvis, Airflo, Loop, Patagonia, Rio, Clacka Craft boats, Chota, Daiichi, Nikon and Fuji.

Special thanks to Nick Lyons who helped me get my start in writing (something I'll be learning for a long time), and to Kevin Muse and Bill and Crispin Battles at *Fly Fish America* for their support.

Finally, to all the fabulous steelhead, salmon and trout clients I have had the privilege to guide during the years.

Dedication

To my wonderful family who have patiently tolerated my fishing lifestyle; my wife and fishing and photography partner Laurie, my son Peter. My parents Antoni and Natalia introduced me to these magnificent fish and encouraged the freedom and spirit to pursue my writings and dreams; and to my great and supportive in-laws, Joyce Moshier and my late father-in-law Ed.

Photography: Matt and Laurie Supinski unless otherwise noted.
Title page photo: John Nagy
Fly Plate Photography: Gary Phillips
Illustrations: Brian Hanchen
Design: Jerry Hutchinson

Softbound ISBN: 1-57188-219-7
Hardbound ISBN: 1-57188-258-8

Frank Amato Publications, Inc.
P.O. Box 82112, Portland, Oregon 97282
(503) 653-8108
Printed in Hong Kong
1 3 5 7 9 10 8 6 4 2

CONTENTS

Chapter 1

Steelhead Dreams

My addiction to steelhead manifests itself through the mystique of the Great Lakes waters where the fish now thrives. It is in the phantasm of the night that my dreams long to know where my wandering voyager might be. I continually lust for its return home to the rivers whose waters flow through a steelheader's heart and soul.

Nocturnal visions take me to enchanted moonlit nights. Here, rays of silvery light dance on the ripples of the charcoal-colored, big-water surf. I feel gentle breezes filled with the eerie cries of flocking seagulls. A rhythmic incandescence beacons proud and timelessly from a lighthouse port, inviting safe haven to mariners. The night is marred by unforgiving and violent storms—they are common to our giant, ocean-like basins. Respect for them comes from fear. Many a good soul has vanished while caught off guard angling for the water's salmonids. The ballad of the *Edmund Fitzgerald* echoes and haunts the beauty of these capricious lakes as foghorns bellow on ocean-going freighters from Duluth, Minnesota to Toronto, Canada.

Looking down from space, its shoreline is ablaze in a Christmas-like phosphorescence from half of North America's population. Once tainted by toxic pollutants that robbed them of life-giving oxygen, the waters are slowly healing. New, exotic organisms like the zebra mussel and the predatory lamprey are changing the ecosystem for better and worse, only time will tell its final outcome. Since the Pleistocene Epoch of ice ages, which covered the entire area in a polar ice cap, the glacially-cut lakes and their aquatic life continue to evolve.

It is in the magic moment of first light that a steelhead angler's dreams and fantasies, hopes and expectations are fulfilled as he feels the refreshing current and jolting strike of a player steelhead.

In the antediluvian darkness of the Great Lakes frontier, my passion for *Oncorhynchus mykiss* transcends and turns to thoughts of deep waters and swift rivers. My pursuit takes on a surreal lining where these silver and gray orca-like predators hunt baitfish and sip insects many miles on the offshore thermocline before plying their way through the rushing waters of their natal rivers. There they soothe themselves in the river's creases and seams. My obsession to be a part of their secret world and understand this magnificent, aggressive aquatic nomad often leads me on an impervious journey into a world where man has no place.

Yet, as the ecological balance of the ocean and Great Lakes frontiers becomes more uncertain, I believe steelhead need man as much as we are consumed with desire for them. As a chief predator, man should form a stewardship and be guardian to protect the environment these fish desperately need for survival.

From the powers of God and nature has evolved an Adonis of a fish, adorned with the blush pastels and rich red tones that even Monet's talent could not achieve.

Our journey to understanding this prospering Pacific transplant must begin humbly in awe.

Early Beginnings

The Great Lakes have been part of my spirit since birth. I was born and raised on the majestic Niagara at the Falls. Here, at this Seventh Wonder of the World, billions of gallons of azure water cascades downward 150 feet into a violent, thunderous crescendo. The Great Lakes, with enough water to flood the U.S. to a depth of 10 feet, siphons through this narrow river and gorge and creates a spiritual sanctuary which Indians worshiped as a god. The various tribes offered life sacrifices to the Falls. In the story of the Maid of the Mist, a lovely Indian maiden was launched to her death in a canoe—her reincarnation and legend still lives. The famous Niagara daredevils, like the aerial tightrope walkers, and the men in barrels and sealed contraptions, risked death, and often met it trying to conquer the Falls. My respect for its rushing waters came at a very early age. I was mesmerized by its strong flow, often hypnotized. I stared at it

for hours along the Niagara Park railings. As youngsters, we played in its side eddies and backwaters, often thinking we were little daredevils. We took excursions to the Canadian tourist district where Ripley's and Houdini's museums told the tales of catastrophic encounters with the mighty waters. Soon our boyish confidence and heroism turned tragic. A neighborhood playmate was swept into the violent rapids on a floating wooden door, which we often used as make-believe pirate ships. He plunged tragically over the falls to his death. I still have flashbacks of the horrific photos that *Life* Magazine sadly captured back in the 60s.

As I began to fish and hunt at around six years of age, I heard tales from the old-timers of large rainbows being caught in the gorge. These were probably descendants of the 1874 West Coast importing of steelhead eggs by Seth Green at the Caledonia Hatchery. Using worms and spinners I fished hard and long in hopes of a hook-up. Years went by with my desires filled with colors of the rainbow and silver. Pictures in *Field & Stream* were all I had to fantasize about.

My first encounters with the mighty "steelhead rainbow" occurred on trout outings with my father in the Zoar Valley of Cattaragus Creek in New York's Southern Tier. The Cattaragus has many tiny, gravel-laden brooks and springs that hold wild and stocked trout. I was still fishing worms on a fly rod. My first equipment was my pride and joy—an automatic retrieve Perrine reel, Garcia fiberglass rod and an intermediate line, K-Mart's top shelf. My fly selection was limited to a few McGinty's, Black Gnats and Royal Coachmans, though my Mickey Finn streamers took many a good brown trout.

On a magical day which is forever etched in memory, my humble baptism to the "steelhead" rainbow occurred. While fishing several "no name" creeks on the traditional April 1st opener, I creeled a few small rainbows and browns of about 9 inches from a gorgeous stream cascading over rocks and boulders. The water gushed cold and clear with the bounty of spring's snowmelt running. As I moved from one pool to the next, I kept a first-water advantage upstream from my dad. I always was the "creel hero" in quantity but rarely in quality. Dad worked his lethal streamers

In the vodka-clear waters of the Muskegon River, this spring female steelhead displays a pastel-colored collage that even Monet's brush would envy.

The author with a 21-pound Michigan winter-strain steelhead taken from the Muskegon River on January 26th. Air temperature (4 degrees F), wind chill (-20 degrees F), and water temperature (34 degrees F). The fish was taken on a cerise egg pattern in the primary lie of the "gut" of the run. This large alpha male fought and jumped extremely hard despite the elements. Some of the biggest steelhead are taken January through March before spawning actually occurs.

Jeff Bacon photo

masterfully on his fine cane rods and picked up many good-sized fish I had missed.

After hiking up a steep gorge, I rested at the tailout of a pool. A bright, silvery flash in the shallow gravel caught my attention. There it was. My Holy Grail of fish. I was astounded and nervous. The large rainbow I'd yearned for was virtually within arm's reach. The lone female digging her redd kept me spellbound for minutes. I was not sure whether to fish for it or admire it. However, my testosterone-driven pubescence triggered my hunter/gatherer instinct and I planned her capture. Cutting off half of my leader to only the stiffest butt section, I carefully secured my Mickey Finn streamer and placed some split shot several feet up from the fly. My hands shook while I perspired in the cool April afternoon. My first casts were off target and the fly swept past the fish much too high in the turbid flow. Adding more lead, I was able to get a better drift. The second cast revealed a flicker of interest as the fish's fins perked up and she made a swipe at it, only to refuse. After making several more attempts, I don't know how many, since the world and time as I knew it stopped, I felt the lightning-bolt jolt of the strike as she hammered my streamer. The hen immediately cartwheeled through the air as I stumbled backward, holding on for dear life. With a quick snap the line went limp. This was due to an emotional lockup. I was holding it too strongly. My beast vanished

into the swift pool. I was in tears. Yet tragic as it was, I felt touched emotionally by a feeling I couldn't explain. To this day, after uncountable hook-ups, I still experience the same exhilaration. The same rush. The same fix. I was impassioned forever by the brief dance of that first steelhead.

I never mentioned it to my father for I feared his disbelief. In the car I was silent all the way home. The scenario of the hook-up and the jump kept playing over like a broken record. Subliminally I rehearsed for my next encounter. Days and nights went by with me plotting feverishly. I was rabid for my next encounter.

In the late sixties, I witnessed the feverish Pacific salmon invasion of the Great Lakes. With the successful planting of coho salmon in Lake Michigan's Platte Bay by Howard Tanner and the MDNR, all the Great Lakes states and Canada were quick to jump on the bandwagon. With the unprecedented explosion of alewife baitfish due to the invasion of the lamprey (which parasitized on lake trout), the lakes became void of a top food-chain balance keeper. I recall going on a family beach outings to Lake Ontario as a child where the stench of dead alewives several feet deep on the beach was nauseating and overpowering. As a boyish prankster, I thought the dead alewives were kind of neat and loved to jam them down girls' bathing suits. The new Pacific salmon predators soon eliminated this eyesore, devouring the choice food form.

Almost overnight, tackle shops and marinas became ablaze with shiny, fluorescent Pacific West Coast tackle with colors I'd never seen before—chartreuses, oranges and pinks that were as exciting as the holidays. Charter-boat fleets were being launched like allied naval armadas to put enthusiastic anglers on the king and coho salmon that were drawing accolades of mythical proportions. In an almost anticlimactic way, steelhead were being reintroduced in good numbers from Lake Superior to Ontario.

State Department of Natural Resource fish agencies were telling sportsmen that once they migrated from the big lakes to spawn, the salmon would not feed or take a bait or artificial offering. Snagging became legal and commonplace—an idea which later created a monster of doom that won't go away. As a fly fisher, I would have nothing of those barbaric ways. Armed with my newly acquired Fenwick fiberglass 9-weight rod and Pflueger Medalist reel, I would fish as a purist. I soaked craft-shop yarn of bright colors in anise oil and petroleum jelly. I used Christmas tinsel as "Flashabou." Dyed sponges imitated the egg sacs of the "long shanks" (our nickname for the spin-casting snaggers).

Misadventures came quickly. Bad knots, dull hooks, frozen reels, and the inability to strap enough lead on my line to keep it down in the strong Niagara gorge flows kept me going back to my basement fly-fishing laboratory. I still was nil for a landed steelhead; my first hook-up encounter hung over me like a dark cloud.

My late Uncle Mike lived in Silver Creek, at the mouth of Cattaragus Creek. We made our monthly trips to visit him (which I anticipated for days) so I could fish a river that was sporting some of the best salmonid runs in the state. In school—on the days that I actually made it in, rumors of a fresh run of fish taking priority and making me play hooky—I daydreamed about my next hook-up. It would come on the "Cat." I was sure of it.

On a particularly frigid autumn day in November, with periodic snow squalls, I had my dad drop me off at a place on the Indian Reservation where a steep river gradient created riffles through a classic riverbend—it smelled like steelhead water. For seasons now, I'd been following around a spawn dunker in a green van like a groupie at an Aerosmith concert. He was a ragged and weathered curmudgeon who always caught fish. He rolled his spawn bag artistically through runs and the tailouts of pools with a long, glass fly rod. I watched carefully and learned his dropback technique, surely this will work with my well-marinated yarn ball and gaudy wet-fly dropper. I watched "Mr. Green Van" land two chrome silver fish that morning, gaff them on his stringer and leave—he was done for the day.

As the snow became heavier, it was my turn. My dad who was enjoying his Polish vodka and herring in cream sauce back at my Uncle Mike's house was probably thinking of me and the cold. With my K-Mart pre-polar-fleece layering of five sweat shirts and sweat pants piled on so thick that every vein and capillary screamed of suffocation, I was chilling progressively like a crackling cold Sauncerre wine. Sinking enough lead to moor a tugboat, I penetrated every inch of the pool. One snag after another was the rub.

As the snow thickened, paranoid thoughts took me to my worried Dad and exaggerated tales of Indian skinheads on the hunt for a scalp. I propped my rod up on a twig and waited to be rescued from the storm by my dad on his Polish army militia horse—at that time a '69 Buick Skylark. Suddenly, a gust of wind blew hard and knocked my rod off its prop. I scurried to retrieve it before it headed for Lake Erie. As I lunged to grab it, the rod bent and throbbed. Magically, the wind turned warm and soothing as

the steelhead gods announced their presence. The magic continued and produced an audience, as my dad coincidentally pulled up the dirt river road in full view of my encounter.

In a slow-motion state of karma I battled and turned the big red-cheeked male steelhead with perfection, having rehearsed every moment many times in my mind. I subdued the hard-driving runs and leaps time and again. With confidence in my knots I grabbed the net and my nemesis was finally at hand. My thoughts, testosterone, and heartbeat were bordering on circuit overload.

As the fish gulped air while it laid amongst the beautifully colored rocks of the shoreline, my father yelled for me to "club it" for the cooler. Instead I did something that was new and totally confounding to me—I let it go! A sense of nausea engulfed me for a brief moment for this ludicrous move. For years I've introduced many a trout proudly to my mallet priest and stuffed them in my creel with fresh green ferns. But I could not with this first steelhead.

For the first time I was in an emotional state—about a *fish*? What had gotten into my accomplished fish-slaying persona? Could it have been that I lusted and craved for this fish for so long that I had a compelling urge to honor it by letting it go? For the first time, a true sense of sporting ethics manifested itself in

The austere volcanic rock cliffs of Lake Superior's Steel River on Ontario's north shore, provides the perfect backdrop for Canadian author/guide Scott Smith's tight loop cast. The Steel's unique in that it has a wild reproducing summer steelhead run. The rivers of the north shore run swift on heavy spates and require respect by the wading angler. Perhaps no other area of the Great Lakes resembles the panoramic vistas of British Colombia than the rivers of this desolate and pristine region.

my young life. The voices of indecision in my head haunted me. As a growing young man, struggling with the irresponsibility of youth and the hard-pressing integrity of early manhood, I faced a new code of conduct foreign to me. As I looked hard into that first steelhead's eyes I let go of a lot more than a fish that day. In a sudden feeling of honor and respect, I grabbed its tail, pointed the fish's nose into the swift current and watched it charge back into the river on its mission to survive. That day it seemed my life was forever changed. The Bible talks of "taking off the old man and putting on the new man." I was transformed into the new sporting steelheader. For years my visionary quest for steelhead had been an obsession. I had dreamt of its silver leaps, its hard violent runs stripping line off the reel like nothing I've ever experienced. It gave me an unprecedented sense of conquest when I finally slipped the net under one. To a fish that gave me everything it had, I fairly and respectfully gave it back its life.

Now, uncountable numbers of steelhead later, each time I let go, the satisfaction I receive transcends the sport of fishing. When I hold this precious voyager captive in my hands, I feel its power. I see the beauty of God's work each time I stare into the savage beauty of its face, admire its spectacular color or glance through its translucent tail as shiny silvery scales peel off its body like freshly minted coins.

In the quiet moments after releasing a steelhead, I am captivated by this wild thing which gives such pleasure. My quest for the enigmatic steelhead, which took on conquering youthful aspirations in Moby Dick-like proportions, ended then as they end now—serenely.

Today, when I wet a line in a steelhead river, I see, feel and hear more than what the fish offers. The gleaming riffles, a morning steam on the river, the panoramic spectacle of a sunset, and the soothing feel of rushing waters on my waders all tranquilize me. The song of migrating birds, the stealth-like stalk of a heron, and the soaring eagle eyeing prey, let me know that others share my passion for the river. Even when it is raining miserably, or blistering cold winds and snow squalls pelt me, I feel a sense of honor that I can still stand in a steelhead river when others think I'm crazy.

At a young age, I was a man of the river. I am even more so today. Yet I long to be more mature, more patient, more forgiving, so much more respectful. As I grow older, my steelhead dreams are filled with the longing, the hope, the yearning for another encounter with my silver-finned friend. Each day my memories grow fonder of the camaraderie of friends and rivers. I revel in the exchange of flies, good Scotch whiskies, cigars and fly rods, and relish a gourmet lodge dinner. Occasional dunkings while clumsily wading, along with other embarrassing misadventures keep us laughing—we need more of this.

If steelhead fly-fishing was easy, it would not draw us so strongly. We choose these fish because they elude and mock us. They humble us when we take this "fly guy" stuff too seriously.

As our passion for the fish grows stronger, we become forever immersed in the challenge, pursuit, and lifestyle of steelhead waters.

A perfect Michigan-strain female winter steelhead with the iridescent pink, purple, and bluish-green colors only a woman could lavishly display.

Chapter 2

The Legacy and Science: The Verve to Survive

What are "steelhead?" Where did they come from, and how they live their lives are questions often asked by steelhead fly fishers—both experienced and novice. The steelhead trout, originally had a native range from the southernmost boundaries of Baja, California to Alaska and Russia's Kamchatka. The species went through considerable taxonomic uncertainty and confusion due to the 33 species of trout described in David Straw Jordan and Barton Warren Evermann's book, *The Trout of Western America* (Circa 1923). Much of these "spotted trout" were rainbows, with local dialect and regional idiosynchrosies influencing their classification. When Dr. Gairdner, a Hudson Bay Co. physician at Fort Vancouver on the Columbia River, sent Sir John Richardson–a premigrant steelhead for investigation, Richardson placed the trout in the *Salmo* genus and honored Gairdner by giving it the species title *gairdneri*. Eventually *Salmo shasta, Salmo kamloops* were named based on the river system or watershed where they were found. Through professional courtesy and the law of nomenclature, the initial finding by Richardson and Gairdner stood forthright, the steelhead trout became widely accepted as *Salmo gairdneri*.

In 1989, the American Fishing Society shocked many with it's new classification for all Pacific salmonids: genus *Oncorhynchus*, giving steelhead the species *mykiss*. Fossil records based on 20 million years showed a major branching that split the North American salmon/trout populations into two distinct populations Atlantic (*Salmo*) and Pacific (*Oncorhynchus*) population. DNA and chromosomal protein testing verified the split.

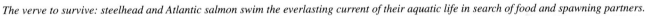

The verve to survive: steelhead and Atlantic salmon swim the everlasting current of their aquatic life in search of food and spawning partners.

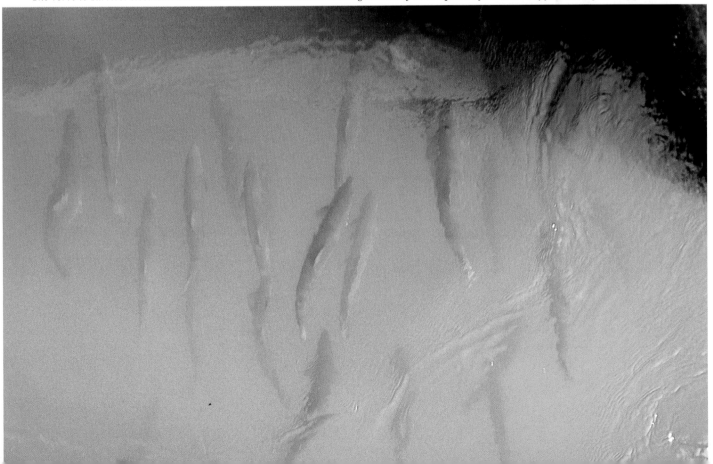

The transparent, spotted tail and minted coin-like scales with their tint of pink are characteristic of a freshly migrated steelhead from the big lake. As sea lice often coat the Pacific migrators' bodies, Great Lakes fish might have a small lamprey predator attached to their skin. Through their incredible jumping ability, they are often able to shake off the unwanted harbinger of death.

In the North Pacific in 1792, a rainbow trout found in Russia's Kamchatka Peninsula was given the Russian species title of *mykiss*. Since this preceded the Gairdner classification it was honored the predated priority status.

So the differemce between a steelhead and a rainbow trout is logically simplified as one being ocean-bound (or Great Lakes as their inland ocean) and the other being a stream resident. Both are *Oncorhynchus mykiss* and differ from Pacific salmonids (which die after spawning) in that steelhead can reproduce multiple times in their lifetime. Do some steelhead remain in rivers and never run to oceans or lakes and vice versa for the resident fish? Yes, this is true especially in rich watersheds with great diversity in food abundance and habitat. The name "steelhead" comes from the dark gray, steel-like upper body against the silvery bottom versus the greener and highly colored resident *mykiss*. In very tight genetic strains of steelhead, which most have become, the urge to escape and swim the big-water basins is a drive too strong to ignore.

The Great Lakes Steelhead Invasion
(Excerpts from *Rainbow Trout in the Great Lakes* by Hugh MacCrimmon and Barra Lowe Gots)

Rainbow trout were first brought to northeastern North America privately in 1874 and 1875 when Seth Green incubated eggs at the Caledonia Hatchery in New York. The stock was obtained from Campbell's Creek on the McCloud River system in California through J. B. Campbell (Green, 1880; Wales, 1939). By 1880, the Caledonia Hatchery held "California trout" ranging in age from fingerlings to five-year-old fish (Kendall, 1924) and, by 1885, nearly 9 million fry had been distributed (New York Fish Commissioners, 1886).

Pioneering fish culturists such as Seth Green of Caledonia, a fish hatchery in New York, were instrumental in bringing the "California Trout Experiment" to the East Coast and west lakes.

In 1876, Daniel Fitzhugh, Jr. transferred the first eggs of the western "red-sided", or Shasta trout, from the McCloud River to Michigan. He probably incubated them at the Northville Hatchery, situated on the middle branch of the Rouge River, in Wayne County, operated by N.W. Clark (Smedley, 1938; Westerman, pers. Comm.) In 1878, his son Frank, as brood stock for the hatchery purchased yearling trout from the McCloud River. The U.S. Fish Commission leased the hatchery beginning in 1880 and shipped eggs there from Crooks (now Greens) Creek, California, where it operated a facility between 1879 and 1888 (Wales, 1939). The first Great Lakes planting of steelhead took place in Michigan's AuSable River, a tributary of Lake Huron.

Subsequently, eggs shipped to Michigan in 1882 were sent to a new hatchery at Paris on the Muskegon River (Westerman, pers. comm.) and all rainbow trout stocks from the other hatcheries were ultimately transferred there. The U.S. Fish Commission provided Crooks Creek stock to the Pennsylvania, Minnesota, and Wisconsin Fish Commissions first in 1880 and to the New York Commission between 1881 and 1883 (Wales, 1939; Lingbiel, pers. comm.). All of the early plantings in northeastern North America, therefore, were fish of McCloud River stock from either Crooks or Campbell Creeks.

After 1898, the U.S. Fish Commission collected eggs from the Willamette River and later the Rogue River system for the Clackamas Station, Oregon. Eyed-eggs were shipped to Duluth, Minnesota and Northville, Michigan (Ravenel, 1899, 1900). Subsequent sources of steelhead eggs included, the Puget Sound area, Columbia River, and Banker Lake of Washington State (Bower, 1909) but precise details on shipments to eastern North American hatcheries are not known.

The Lake Ontario watershed was the second Great Lakes basin to be stocked with rainbow trout when, in 1878, progeny from the first brood stock of the Caledonia Hatchery were planted in headwaters of Caledonia Spring Creek and Genesee River tributaries in New York State (Green, 1880). By 1884, some of these fish had moved downriver into the lower Genesee River and Lake Ontario.

The Caledonia Hatchery in New York produced the second planting of rainbow steelhead in Caledonia spring creek and the Genesee River which empties into Lake Ontario.

Ontario did not become actively interested in the steelhead rainbow trout until 1900 when the Canada Department of Marine and Fisheries procured 75,000 eggs from Bath, New York, for their Ottawa Hatchery. In 1912, this Agency imported rainbow trout from the United States to their hatcheries at Port Arthur on Lake Superior and Southampton on Lake Huron. The Ontario government began a rainbow trout program in 1914 by obtaining Lake Superior steelhead eggs for incubation at the Mount Pleasant Hatchery.

Initial plantings of rainbow trout fry into the Lake Erie-St. Claire watershed were made in 1882 from the Northville Hatchery, Michigan, into Clinton, Huron, and Rouge River systems and in an unnamed Ontario tributary of Lake St. Claire near Sarnia (Clark, 1882). Early plantings in Pennsylvania tributaries of Lake Erie seem to have been initiated no later than 1895, and perhaps as early as 1881 (Shiffer, pers. comm.). New York authorities did not introduce rainbow trout into Lake Erie watershed until 1899, when fingerlings and yearlings were planted in the headwaters of the Cattaraugus River (New York Commissioners, 1900). With the exception of the recovery of a single specimen from the Grand River (Lake County), harvests of rainbow trout had not been recorded from other Ohio waters by 1911, despite an active commercial fishery for other species in Sandusky Bay near the mouth of Cold Creek. Between 1913 and 1918, about 19,500 fry and older fish were planted by Federal authorities in the Cuyahoga River System of Ohio, mainly in headwater areas.

Lake Huron's Au Sable River of Michigan was the first watershed in the Great Lakes basin to receive rainbow trout when, fish from the Northville Hatchery were planted there in 1876 (Smedley, 1938). Beginning about 1880, progeny from the brood stock established at the same hatchery (Smedley, 1938) was stocked repeatedly in the Au Sable River. Attempts to establish the species in the Canadian waters of Lake Huron and Georgian Bay began some time prior to 1900 when fish were brought privately from Sault Ste. Marie to a pond on the upper Nottawasaga River in Dufferin County. In the fall of 1903, John Miller, owner of a small hatchery near Owen Sound, imported eyed-eggs of McCloud-Klamath stock from Manchester, Iowa. The following spring he planted young fish in the Sydenham River and small tributary below Inglis Falls (MacKay, 1962).

In 1912, the Canadian Government planted 47,000 rainbow trout fry in a small lake and creek, tributaries of the Saugeen River, in Bruce and Elderlie townships. As early as 1912, adult fish averaging three pounds were taken during spring migration into the Maitland River (Bellinger, pers. Comm.).

Rainbow trout were introduced into Lake Michigan watershed by the State of Michigan in 1880 when plantings of fry from the Pokagon and Grand Rapids hatcheries were made into the Boyne, Paw Paw, and Kalamazoo rivers. Although rainbow trout were shipped to Indiana from the McCloud River in 1882 (Wales, 1939), the first planting of this stock into the Lake Michigan watershed was not until 1889 with the release of yearling fish into lakes of the St. Joseph system (U.S. Commissioner of Fish and Fisheries, 1988-89).

Documentation on the earliest presence of rainbow trout in Lake Michigan streams is generally lacking, although Yaestin (1907) reported that the North Boyne River, Charlevoix County, had supported no other trout species but rainbows for the previous 15 years. By 1909, major runs were occurring in the Pere Marquette, Pentwater, Boardman, and Muskegon rivers (Bower, 1909).

Wisconsin began its experimental plantings in 1963 with releases of 9,200 rainbow trout into Door County streams. Between 1964 and 1967, plantings of over 189,000 fish were made directly into Lake Michigan between Sheboygan and Rawley Bay (Daly, 1968). The substantial rainbow trout fishery which occurred in Lake Michigan through the next two decades was sustained largely by the natural recruitment of anadromous fish spawning in numerous streams in Michigan, but apparently not in Wisconsin, Illinois, or Indiana. However, the fishery experienced a decline which coincided with the arrival in 1936 of the sea lamprey (Applegate, 1950) and, also, a period of abundance of the alewife, *Alosa psekdoharengus*, beginning in 1949 (Smith, 1970). Not only did rainbow trout numbers diminish to a low level but by the late 1950s the presence of migratory fish in Lake Michigan became a rarity (Lloyd, comm.; Cartier, 1969).

Steelhead were common in the western end of Lake Superior by 1902 (Bean, 1902), and in 1903 the species spawned in most suitable Minnesota tributaries to the Brule River (O'Donnell, 1944). By 1910, rainbows had migrated as far north as the Steel River in the Thunder Bay District of Ontario where a small specimen was caught (Ontario Game and Fish Comm. 1912).

By the 1940s, the steelhead invasion spread throughout the entire Great Lakes system and the seed for the legacy was planted.

Reception of the Pacific Steelhead in the Great Lakes

As some states and the Province of Ontario began the saturation of Pacific steelhead trout, the species quickly established itself in its new inland ocean waterways with amazing success. Perhaps key to their quick acceleration, besides the food-rich inland "oceans" of the Great Lakes basin, was the vast, open biological niche in rivers and streams of the various lakes due to the loss of indigenous species. In an excellent work by former Michigan Department of Natural Resources fisheries biologist Leo Mrozinski entitled "History of Steelhead in Michigan," he cites logging degradation and soil erosion as cause for the demise of the natural brook trout and grayling on rivers such as the Pere Marquette and Au Sable, allowing the opportunistic steelhead fry and smolts to dominate the river system. Even though another exotic, the European brown trout, was stocked in 1883 on the Pere Marquette, juvenile steelhead outcompeted the brown and brook trout for food and choice stream lies in a significant way.

Similarly, the Lake Ontario streams of New York and Ontario saw the collapse of a magnificent Atlantic salmon fishery

A wild, mature late-winter female which took a hot pink Marabou Spey deep drifted through boulder-strewn pocket water where moving fish stop to rest.

in many of its rivers which like the salmon was wiped out and extinct by the late 1800s due to overharvesting, dam build-up along rivers, and habitat destruction.

Mrozinski also cites the Michigan Fish Commission's Thirteenth Bicentennial Report of 1897 which states: "the rainbow trout is permanently established in popular esteem and continues to grow in favor, and it is our intention to propagate them on a much larger scale as soon as facilities for carrying the necessary breeders are provided."

The report continues, "In the Lower Peninsula, steelhead rainbow trout show a special adaptability for the deeper parts of our larger trout waters, being more inclined than brook trout to drop downstream and frequent and inhabit the deeper and warmer sections where food is more abundant. Specimens of seven and eight pounds, equal to the largest of Lake Superior char, have been taken, while four or five-pound rainbow no longer attracts special attention!"

Mrozinski goes on to cite that by December, 1913, the Michigan Fish Commission had sufficient brood fish at the Paris Hatchery on the Muskegon River to provide close to 4 million rainbow eggs, predominantly of McCloud river strain and was expected to collect an additional 5 million from the big run of the Pine River off the Big Manistee. This was the beginning the "wild" fish era in Michigan.

However, the sentiment towards the new steelhead rainbow was quickly changing in certain areas. Mrozinski goes on to state: "Around 1900, some resentment toward the steelhead rainbow began to develop. By 1908, although there was growing enthusiasm for the fish, there was still considerable opposition to the further introduction of steelhead rainbows into our streams. The rainbow was looked on by many as inferior to the brook trout and for driving them out. Permits were sold to spear rainbow and steelhead trout in 1917, 1918 and 1919, as 343, 358 and 555 permits were respectively sold."

During the mid-1900s, wild steelhead stocks of the Great Lakes received their deadliest setback besides the spears—the dreaded sea lamprey. As a result of the opening of the Welland Canal, allowing the upstream passage of ships from the Atlantic Ocean, the deadly lamprey parasite attached itself to salmonids like the natural lake trout and new steelhead and sucked the protein-rich life out of them in a matter of weeks. On the bittersweet side of the unleashing of the lamprey, millions of alewife baitfish swam into the upper Great Lakes setting the stage for a comeback of salmonids.

As the Pacific salmon experiment in Michigan's Platte Bay saw great success in reducing the alewife population nuisance, U.S. state and Province of Ontario agencies again focused more attention on restoring depleted steelhead stocks.

In this modern era of Great Lakes fisheries management, because of the high esteem in which all segments of anglers hold the steelhead, every U.S. state and Province of Ontario is beefing up hatchery steelhead programs. In addition they are also focusing on wild, genetically unique steelhead strains in their rivers and streams. Through great research and planning, the legacy of Great Lakes steelhead might survive forever.

The Verve to Survive

The life force of a steelhead is a powerful one. Like all ocean-going (in this case, Great Lakes) salmonids, it must persevere many natural- and man-induced obstacles to survive. From its birth in the gravel redd of its natal river to the end of its adulthood, which can span as much as a decade, it will traverse thousands of miles in search of prey and endure the harsh rigors of procreation—contributing its precious genetic make-up to the next generation.

A wild yearling steelhead getting ready to smolt. Within weeks it will begin to turn silvery, and on that magical night will migrate downstream to the big lake in the safety of darkness. The only biological difference between rainbow trout and steelhead is this single life phase.

To capture one's prey, in this case the fish for the fisherman, one must know its ways. To conquer the enemy is to study its whims and weaknesses, strengths and predictabilities. To a fly fisher, the steelhead is more a subject of noble admiration than a foe, its elusive ways on the days we are skunked, the times we are humiliated by them and the uncertainty of when the "bite" will be on, all serve us to better understand them. To the modern steelheader of the new millennium, comprehension of the complex life and behavior of steelhead is the key to angling mastery.

Naturalized Great Lakes steelhead have retained the anadromous life history patterns of their Pacific Coast ancestors (Bette et al. 1981). Anadromous describes the "fresh water to salt water" (and the reverse) migrations of ocean-bound fish, the term potamodromous describes the Great Lakes ocean-like basins where fish move freely in freshwater environs. As a steelhead fly fisher, I have observed and pursued both Great Lakes and Pacific steelhead. I firmly believe that due to the less complicated physiological demands on potamodromous steelhead, they often have a unique predisposition. Since they forgo the metabolic complication of the salt/freshwater transitions–which taxes the renal system regulating the amount of salts in the bloodstream each up and down river migration–our Great Lakes fish seem to have greater mobility and urgency in migration, spawning, habitat preference and attitude when striking the fly.

Since the Great Lakes steelhead fishery has established many wild strains of fish in its short 100-year evolutionary history, it, for the most part, has relied heavily on hatchery planted fish. The problem with the hatcheries is the potential for disease and the fine line crews face when rearing what should be done in the wild instead of in the cement confines of a hatchery. Thus, the hatchery often becomes sign of man's encroachment on what should or should not be. For the time being, the Great Lakes fishery needs the hatchery system and probably will continue to need it into the future.

Factors such as less-than-ideal river nurseries for wild smolt creation, degraded riverine habitats, unfavorable water temperatures from development and agriculture encroachment, and the fact that they are thus highly utilized for recreation, will always make them vulnerable. Some wild strains have found ideal niches in the Great Lakes, such as Michigan's Little Manistee strain and Ontario's Ganaraska and Thunder Bay strains. In order to satisfy the hungry appetites of sporting anglers, we plant and utilize literally every marginal piece of Great Lakes tributary for some kind of steelhead program so we often introduce these habitat-specific fish into waters in which they don't belong. Hence, the Great Lakes fishery is far from the snow-capped vistas of the pristine and wild *Oncorhynchus mykiss* Valhalla of British Columbia. Here in the Great Lakes they are enjoyed by many and in great numbers. Through sheer magnitude we have created a steelhead dynasty. Yet it is our challenge to spread and create quality through wild fisheries.

The lure of wild steelhead is strong in the Great Lakes. Many steelheaders flock to the pristine northwoods waters of Michigan's Pere Marquette and Lake Superior's Thunder Bay in quest for wild fish. Are wild fish truly superior to their less elite hatchery cousins? Many insist upon this. Yes, they have learned to become wary and dance in the air like leaping white mustangs when hooked. Though many believe, as I do, that once a hatchery fish of wild genetic stock heads to the open waters and feels the freedom, it too acts as wild as those born in the gravel. There is a fascinating story from Tom Trudeau of the Illinois Department of Natural Resources where a micro-tagged Skamania summer steelhead, that was stocked off the harbors of Chicago in Lake Michigan, somehow found its way down the Illinois River into the Mississippi River and was captured in a fisherman's basket net in Baton Rouge, Louisiana. Trudeau also states his micro-tagged steelhead are routinely captured as far away as Lake Ontario. The urge to wander is strong and wild, even in hatchery-raised fish.

From the Gravel Cradle

Once successful spawning has occurred, the eggs cling to the gravel and begin their incubation period. A few hours later, cells within the egg begin to divide and multiply and the same natural mystery occurs at this point as in the life of all living things. The exact blueprint for the individual steelhead is already set within the developing embryo, continuing the special traits which allowed its parents to survive to spawn. During the steelhead's life, nature will select for the fish with those traits necessary for survival and "death" will come to those without them. Newly fertilized eggs are delicate and subject to trauma with movement. After 24 hours or so, they harden by absorbing water. Development times vary depending on water temperatures. At 56 degrees F, 20 days are required. At 46 degrees F, 33 days, 80 days or more are needed in 40 degrees F.

Once the eggs reach the "eye-up" stage, hatcheries can count and ship the eggs because they are more rugged. Once the steelhead hatch, they are known as "sac fry," their yolk sacs hang from their bellies and provide the essential nutrients necessary for life. Freshly-hatched fry cling to the rocks and boulders, quickly learning to fight the current, dodge ominous predators like minnows, sculpin, smaller trout, and the chinook salmon fry which hatched earlier and now have voracious appetites.

It is some time during this early life stage that steelhead may memorize the exact location of their spawning bed. When its yolk sac is almost fully absorbed, the fry breaks loose of the gravel, swims up to take a quick gulp of air at the surface to fill its swim bladder, then half swims/half drifts laterally to the shallows near the stream bank. The free-swimming fry then gradually drifts downstream along the riverbank in search of its next home. It looks for an area out of the main current, possibly a root tangle, submerged weed bed, or a tag alder branch lying in the water. When it finds a spot, the fry begins to feed on extremely small food items such as plankton and insects as they drift by or on small invertebrates attached to underwater debris.

Freshly hatched steelhead "sac fry" absorb their embryonic yolk sac for nourishment until it is gone. Then the hunt begins for minute aquatic invertebrates.

The giant Michigan mayfly—Hexagenia limbata and recurvata– is a strongly imprinted food form on Great Lakes steelhead. As steelhead smolts begin their late-June descent down their natal rivers toward the open waters of the big lake, they encounter massive hatches of these mayflies and gorge profusely on them. Since these mayflies exist in abundance in the silted river estuary lakes, the smolts imprint on this food form strongly and will inhale a Hex nymph instinctually upon their return to the river as spawning adults.

As they progress from fry to parr and then finally to the smolt stage, natal imprinting on food forms plays a strong role in their lives. (Steelhead fly-fishers need to learn these food forms.) Their exposure to different types of food forms are stored in the memory of the fish and will one day be remembered as the fish run the river to spawn as adults. As they grow, they learn to feed in little schools along the shoreline where safety is often provided by their running up on the bank in an inch or less of water to avoid predators. Their eyes are focused on the sky for diving kingfisher birds and herons. Amongst themselves, competition over holding spots and feeding lanes begins creating an aggressive predisposition for natural dominance. Beautifully banded and colorful parr marks soon develop as rainbow markings appear.

I have always been fascinated by the large array of egg and nymph patterns preferred by adult-migrating river steelhead. Fly anglers use tiny mayfly, stonefly and caddis nymphs with a high degree of success. On a trip to New York's Salmon River with David Barber, former owner of the Fish Inn Post and guide out of Altmar, he excitedly showed me

Blue Winged Olive Nymphs that took good numbers of fall steelhead on the Salmon. I have heard of many interesting nymph patterns from other fly-fishers. This sent me on a quest for scientific data to study the many pattern preference theories of fly fishers.

Feeding, Imprinting and Steelhead Flies

Les Wedge of New York State Department of Environmental Conservation and Lake Ontario fisheries supervisor, introduced me to eye-opening research done by James H. Johnson, Senior Aquatic and Terrestrial Ecologist for the DEC. His work, "Comparative Food Selection by Coexisting Subyearling Coho Salmon, Chinook Salmon and Rainbow Trout (steelhead) in a Lake Ontario Tributary," drove home a powerful message on how natal imprinting on food forms may dictate adult responses to fly patterns later in life and during various

Midges provide important nourishment to steelhead fry in the rivers. Where the natural reproduction of steelhead occurs, schools of small fry will dimple the shoreline during midge hatches. Here they learn the important behavioral skills for feeding, hierarchical dominance in schooling behavior, and how to avoid aerial and subsurface predators. With the Great Lakes invasion of the zebra mussel which strips the water of plankton, midge larvae are increasingly important in the baby food stages of yearling steelhead.

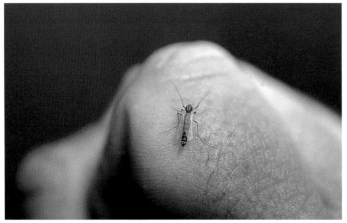

A Great Lakes steelheader's fly box—full of nymphs, egg patterns, black leeches, attractor wets and Marabou Speys. Due to the extreme abundance and diversity of food Great Lakes rivers possess, the angler must literally "match the hatch" or pique the natal instinct of the steelhead who has so much from which to chose.

Stoneflies contribute greatly to the diet of steelhead fry, smolts and adults, particularly in the spring when early black stoneflies hatch during the spawning drive.

months. The study stream, Orwell Brook, was a tributary of the Salmon River on the Tug Hill plateau in Oswego County, New York. In 1978, stomach contents of 370 subyearling coho and chinook salmon, and 140 steelhead, were examined from May through October. Aquatic invertebrates, mainly Ephemeroptera (mayflies) and Chironomids (midges), predominated the foods taken during the first month after emergence.

The fact that 54 percent of the diet of subyearling steelhead is aquatic insects can possibly explain the strong desire a steelhead have to take a fly. As Johnson continues, "Subyearling rainbow trout fed more heavily on aquatic invertebrates (48 to 64 percent) than did either species of salmon. The primary aquatic components eaten by the trout were Ephemeroptera (mayflies), Chironomids (midges) and Trichoptera (caddis), Hymenoptera (ants/bees), Lepidoptera larvae (moths), Coleopterans (beetles), Homopteran (cicadas) and Hemiptera (stinkbugs/ladybugs), were the chief terrestrial, aquatic and invertebrates taken."

In another study Johnson studied four tributaries of the Salmon River, he found yearling steelhead have a strong drive to eat salmon eggs. "Yearling steelhead fed most heavily on salmon eggs (99.1%) in October, along with stream resident brook and brown trout." This feeding on protein-rich eggs is most likely conditioning for survival during the harsh Tug Hill plateau winters.

Smaller mayflies, like blue-winged olives and Sulphurs, are devoured by steelhead fry, yearling and smolts and comprise a major portion of their diet.

Dietary composition as a percentage of dry weight of stomach contents of 140 subyearling steelhead collected from Orwell Brook, New York from July to October 1978.

TAXON	July	Aug.	Sept.	Oct.
AQUATIC FOODS				
Turbellaria	...	...	...	1.01
Oligochaeta	...	0.13	0.11	...
Hirudinea	...	...	0.70	...
Hydracarina	0.16	0.25	0.14	...
Collembola	0.95	...	0.35	0.07
Plecoptera				
Leuctridae	0.23	...	...	...
Perlidae	...	...	...	...
Perlodidae	...	...	...	0.70
Unidentified	...	...	1.75	0.84
Ephemeroptera				
Baetidae	5.43	23.42	10.08	3.37
Ephemerellidae	5.69	...	1.72	1.19
Ephemeridae	...	...	...	1.41
Heptageniidae	...	...	3.72	2.50
Leptophlebiidae	...	1.19	0.18	2.25
Unidentified	12.29	7.85	1.84	1.48
Trichoptera				
Glossosomatidae	0.62	...	0.18	0.84
Helicopsychidae	...	...	4.48	...
Hydropsychidae	2.17	1.42	2.19	8.05
Hydroptilidae	...	...	...	0.21
Odontoceridae	0.77	1.58	7.01	4.36
Philopotamidae	...	...	...	0.70
Unidentified	0.93	0.32	2.63	1.05
Hemoptera				
Veliidae	...	...	...	0.42
Coleoptera				
Dytiscidae	1.09	...	...	...
Psephenidae	6.58	...	...	...
Doptera				
Ceratopogonidae	0.05	0.52	0.11	0.63
Chironomidae	20.61	9.24	16.71	6.31
Dixidae	0.53	...	...	...
Simuliidae	2.48	1.69	1.40	...
Tipulidae	0.19	...	8.81	2.25
Gastropoda	...	...	...	1.09
White sucker (larvae)	1.55	...	...	...
Total	62.30	47.61	64.11	49.87
TERRESTRIAL FOODS				
Arachnida	1.33	4.75	3.38	8.43
Coleoptera	...	22.15	1.96	3.47
Dermaptera	1.55	3.16	0.53	...
Diplopoda	...	...	0.87	...
Diptera	2.26	4.73	3.78	5.13
Hemiptera	2.33	1.36	9.89	6.95
Homoptera	6.50	2.74	4.96	9.28
Hymenoptera	13.71	0.95	5.29	15.46
Lepidoptera	10.02	10.97	5.23	1.41
Neuroptera	...	1.58	...	...
Total	37.70	52.39	35.89	50.13

To the steelhead fly fisher and fly tier this is very fascinating stuff. It's no wonder that a Great Lakes steelheader's fly boxes are jammed full of unique nymph and egg patterns. A yearling steelhead's ability to imprint on food forms plays a substantial role when success with realistic fly patterns of indigenous aquatic invertebrates and salmonid eggs.

The Drive to Smolt

The period when young trout transform themselves from the spotted rainbow colors of their youth to silvery, gray-backed adolescents who emigrate to the ocean or Great Lakes, is perhaps the most important phase of a steelhead's life. The genetic signal to emigrate downstream towards big water, to smolt, is the single difference between a rainbow trout and a steelhead. More scientific research has been done by fisheries biologists working on their masters and doctoral candidacy on this phase of a steelhead's life than any other. For a steelhead fishery to exist, smolting must occur and be successful.

Dr. Paul Seelbach of the Michigan Department of Natural Resources Institute for Fisheries Research is a front-runner in steelhead smolting research. "Dr. Steelhead," as he is known, has conducted very valuable research on Great Lakes steelhead, particularly with wild and hatchery smolt survival and successful establishment of river fisheries. With his computer modeling and utilization of genetics, he envisions a future with managing wild strains along with successful plantings of wild-stock hatchery smolts, which attain higher survival and a greater survival yield to the adult population.

Seelbach has found that parr spend 1 to 3 years in their natal streams before emigrating to the lake as either smolts or parr. Emigrating parr are age-1 juveniles that have not yet undergone the physiological smolt transformation and are generally thought to be migrating downstream because of limitations in stream habitat (Lieder et al. 1986; Loch et al 1998). In ocean-going populations, emigrant parr do not survive to adulthood (they are thought to lack tolerance for sea water; (Loch et al., 1988).

In the freshwater Great Lakes however, emigrant parr may survive and contribute significantly to certain populations. Adults return to spawn after 1 to 4 years in the lake and may repeat spawn in subsequent years.

Since most steelhead juveniles spend up to two years in their natal streams, some will smolt early to the big lake if conditions for survival become harsh. Jon George, a noted Lake Superior steelhead biologist for the Ontario Ministry of Natural Resources, states, "Several tributaries of Lake Superior (e.g. Portage Creek at 80%) have a dominance of one-year, stream life steelhead juvenille smolting. (extremely rare and I do not believe this has been documented in any other region of the Great Lakes." Obviously this is an important life strategy when in these systems. Some tributaries, especially small streams along the Nipigon to Marathon shoreline, may become intermittent in the summer. Steelhead fry are forced to move to lake shorelines and live in rock embankments and appear to nursery well in these locations.

After a breathtaking battle, this steelhead was beached then gently slipped back into its natal waters to continue upstream on its spawning migration. The appreciative angler thanked the fish for the pleasure it gave and bids the fish adieu.

The potential survival of steelhead in the Great Lakes is directly related to the number of smolts and their lengths, as has been shown for numerous ocean salmonid populations (Chapman 1958; Ricker 1976; Wedemeyer et al 1980, Ward and Slaney 1988). Ward et al. (1989) found that survival of steelhead increased from 10% to 23% as smolt length increased from 160 to 200 mm. Seelbach began to realize that "one must plant smolts that are physiologically ready to imprint and to then migrate quickly from the river" to achieve high survival rates. "Most of the large yearling smolts stocked, however, had spent just 2 months in the river and this group had a smolting percentage of 48.2. The yearling and fall fingerlings that survived 12-20 months in the river had a percent smolting ranging from 0.5 to 2.9. Fall yearling smolts had spent 8 months in the river and the percent smolting was 7.1." It is obvious fall planting fish in the fall exposes them to the harsh conditions of winter and stream predators.

Michigan's great success of steelhead program's combination of approximately 50% wild and 50% stocked fish has achieved high productivity according to Seelbach, planting larger spring yearling smolts increased smolting approximately 50 times more than for fall fingerlings and yearlings.

In another Seelbach study, with collaborators James Dexter of the MDNR and Neil Ledet of the Indiana DNR, they found that 50% of the mortality in downstream migrating smolts occurred in the final 6-8 km of the journey. This was perhaps due to the larger, warmwater estuaries of the Lake Michigan rivers where walleye, pike, bass and a host of other predators–such as seagulls and cormorants–devoured the descending smolts in a chow-down gauntlet. Seelbach and Gary Whelan studied the contributions of wild and hatchery plants to the fisherie's populations by using scale samples from fish that showed unique growth patterns.

Nature has helped cloak the massive downstream migration of the susceptible smolts by having them imprint on to the photoperiod of darkness. Thomas M. Stauffer's (Michigan Department of Natural Resources Fisheries Institute) research on the Black River of Lake Michigan in the late 1950s noted, "the major portion of downstream migrations occurred during the time of darkness or reduced light. Annual downstream migration occurred at approximately the same time as it did in West Coast streams with most fish migrating during late May through June." On Michigan's Betsie River, Tammy J. Newcomb and Thomas G. Coon of MDNR, set up visual observation, time-lapse videography and mark-recapture to assess smoltification. They found, "smolts migrated past the monitoring site in a consistent nightly pattern. The greatest number of smolts passed over the Homestead Weir between dusk and midnight. Over 80% of the smolt passage occurred before 2:00 A.M."

In their book *Trout*, Judith Stoley and Judith Schnell (1991, Stackpole Books) discuss the survival from egg to adult. "Under normal conditions, average survival from egg to smolt stage is 3%. Survival from smolt to adult stage in the Great Lakes can range anywhere from 6 to 29%. So, survival from egg to returning adult would be about 0.18%. Given an initial deposition of 4000 eggs by a female steelhead, this means on average 7 individuals would survive to return to spawn from an average redd in the Great Lakes."

As darkness of night did everything it could to provide safe passage, the rigors of survival in the big lake are yet to come for the noble little swimmer.

The Big-Lake Hunting Ground

As the smolt enters into the deep waters of the big lake–which lacks the substantial food-bringing currents of its natal rivers–it must now maximize its time and energy to put on weight and hunt prey so it will become big and powerful for its survival and return to the

As steelhead smolts imprint to the photo period of darkness to begin their downstream migration to the big lake, they feast on the June/July hatch of the giant mayfly, Hexagenia limbata.

spawning ritual. As they arrive in the near-shore areas, their mothers and fathers, cousins and uncles all look at them like they do all other baitfish—as prey. There is no love lost here, as they must constantly dodge their salmonid kin's jaws until they gain weight and size. Many smolt will stay close to shore eating smaller baitfish and aquatic invertebrates. In their favor, most larger schools of salmonids will be migrating outwards toward the deeper, cooler water hunting grounds in the June-July period, thus leaving the smolts less hampered by their acclimation to their new home.

In their formative years they learn to adjust their optic system to the new dark-water environment, regulate their air bladders to the varying depths they will encounter and begin hit-and-miss baitfish-attacking behavior that someday will sustain them. The rainbow's "can do", aggressive behavior to feed quickly helps them to overcome these learning curves.

Certain preferences are known for the big-lake steelhead lifestyle. They prefer water temperatures in the 48- to 55-degree range, although they will tolerate much higher if sufficient food forms are present. They have a penchant for surface or topwater cruising and feeding. Also, they have slower and more hesitant attack speeds on baitfish as opposed to their Pacific salmonid cousins, like the chinook and coho. Individual roaming fish eventually arrive at schooling sites based on their preference for certain conditions and thus are located by charter captains.

In the fall, winter and spring, steelhead cruise the coldwater shorelines where their diet is composed of herring, alewives, smelt, bloater chubs, sticklebacks and other baitfish. They also

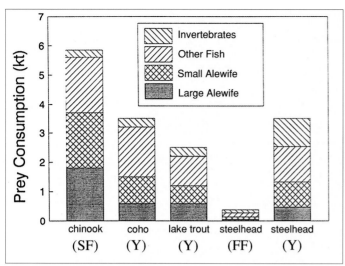

Exhibit Chart 1B. Prey consumption (kilotonnes, kt) per million fish stocked for three previously modeled salmonids (Stewart and Ibarra, 1991) and steelhead in Lake Michigan. Prey consumption estimates for yearlings (Y) were lowest for lake trout and similar for coho salmon and steelhead. Chinook salmon, stocked commonly as spring fingerlings (SF), exhibited the greatest predatory effect on prey. Diet of steelhead was more evenly distributed among the four diet categories. Predation by steelhead fall fingerlings (FF) was low due to high post-stocking mortality.

show a preference for freshwater *Mysis* shrimp. To maximize hunting, the steelhead have learned to focus on the low-light periods of dawn and dusk for cloaking, as their gray backs blend into the waters as they hunt. This dawn-and-dusk hunting behavior could have come from evolutionary genetic imprinting to target the Pacific Ocean's vertical migration of squid which happens at the same time and is a primary source of food for ocean steelhead. It is no wonder that these periods seem to correlate with the most productive times for steelhead angling.

In the summer, as offshore waters warm, steelhead search for cooler waters. Showing an instinctual preference for feeding areas

Surf casting is quickly becoming an effective way to target summer, fall and spring steelhead off of smaller rivers and creek mouths in the Great Lakes. When rivers run low and their outlet channels become buried, steelhead cruise the shoreline troughs and outflow current breaks and are receptive to streamers resembling baitfish or fluorescent attractor wets. The ambient sound of the surf creates a soothing and relaxing mood well worth the angler's efforts.

Steelhead binge feed in the warm and cold thermal bars of the "scum line," where aquatic invertebrates, terrestrial insects and baitfish gather along with other floating debris.

which accommodate their slower, curious prey-attack speeds, they arrive at optimum surface-feeding areas known as the scum line. The natural interaction of water currents and offshore air streams forms sharp thermal bars where warm and cold waters meet. This creates a trough of baitfish, terrestrial insects and other aquatic invertebrates on the water's surface where the steelhead feed at an pick-and-choose, unhurried pace. The words "scum line" refers to the various debris (i.e. bottles, trash, logs, etc.) that accumulates along these currents.

In an outstanding work done on steelhead growth and foraging entitled, "Modeling Steelhead Population Dynamics in Lake Michigan and Ontario," Seelbach, Wedge et al, developed computer-generated biogenetic models for *Oncorhynchus mykiss*. The study was a result of the fear Great Lakes biologists had for the potential predator-prey imbalances from the high stocking levels of salmonids. They found that steelhead consumed much fewer alewife baitfish than chinook salmon (63% versus 14%) and thus concluded, "a larger invertebrate component in the diets of adult steelhead." (see Exhibit 1B.) They also noted that their two-year river internship where food forms change because of regularly based on seasonal availability, wild steelhead consumed much fewer baitfish than hatchery fish. Savitz and Bardygula (1989) studied salmonids and prey fish in a large aquarium and concluded, "Unlike more aggressive chinook and coho salmon, steelhead had trouble capturing fish in open water and often relied on trapping prey in corners or along physical structures of the aquarium. Therefore, the evidence of steelhead foraging along the invertebrate-rich scum line offshore (Haynes et al. 1986) may represent specialized foraging behavior." (See Exhibit 1B.)

In contrast to the schooling, predatory attacks of salmon, steelhead seem to be more solitary roamers in the big lake, often cruising the upper-water strata. Their elusiveness often confounds charter fleets so they are less vulnerable at times to the charter harvest. They have been known to roam in and out of all the barrier-free areas of the Great Lakes system and are often caught at incredible distance from their natal inland seas. We can only imagine the incredible journeys they undertake.

Homeward Bound

With no GPS (global positioning system), radar or navigational aids, once the urge to return to their natal rivers arises, they are determined to run the river. With the help of their genetic imprinting to daylight photoperiods and keen olfactory system that can detect a scent in 3 parts per million of water, the chemical makeup of their native or stocked river draws with them incredible accuracy to the place of their natural birth or stocking. Other biologists suggest factors such as stellar navigating and the earth's electromagnetic fields might guide this nomad home. Like prodigal sons and daughters they return and provide great sport for the appreciative angler in waiting.

In their synthesis of Great Lakes steelhead life history patterns, Biette, et al. (1981), concluded that in most populations, over 97% of the returning adults spent 1-4 years in the lake, over 50% of the returning adults were virgin spawners, and only a very few fish spawned more than once. Yet unique areas in the Great Lakes exist with extremely variable stream habitat conditions which favor greater repeat spawning. Jon George of the Ontario Ministry of Natural Resources on Lake Superior's Thunder Bay writes, "The north shore of Lake Superior is a cold harsh climate with sterile environments in the nursery streams. To compensate for low production and longevity, the wild steelhead have repeat spawning encounters yearly, often as high as 70%. This allows the populations lots of buffering capability and large individuals that can spawn in the faster glacial flows of spring and move large gravel in redd construction. It is also not unusual to have a fair number of third and fourth time spawners and 5 and 6 time spawners are present." Similar findings of high-repeat spawners were found on the north shore of Lake Ontario in the Ganaraska wild strain. From 1975 to 1991, the repeat spawner index for female rainbow trout in the Ganaraska River was 58 to 90%; male mortality was much higher in both Superior and Ontario. Thus in rivers with harsher environs, nature favors strong, wild fish that are more able to repopulate on a continual basis.

In another excellent work done by Paul Seelbach on the population biology of steelhead in the Little Manistee River of Lake Michigan, he studied the ages of autumn and spring migrators. He states, "Lake-age-1 (jack or skipper) males were more prevalent in the autumn than in the spring. The numbers of wild adult steelhead returning to the stable-flowing cool waters of the Little Manistee were among the highest reported for the Great Lakes. Spring runs in the Ganaraska River (tributary of Lake Ontario) are also quite large, averaging 12,000-14,000 fish in recent years (Kargas 1987)." It's no wonder the two most utilized wild strains for stocking programs in the Great Lakes come from these two rivers.

In a work on homing return accuracy done on Southern Michigan rivers, Seelbach, Dexter and Ledet concluded, "homing instinct of Little Manistee steelhead to their upstream stocking sites was as high as 77%." Skamania summer strain showed higher lake-catch mortality as a result of straying from their stocking sites perhaps due to their longer period on the big water. (They spend up to 3 years in the Big Lake—bred on the West Coast to be 3-salt steelhead.)

Since nearly all Great Lakes steelhead spawn in the late winter and spring, the early returning summer and fall steelhead spend from 4 to 8 months in the river prior to spawning. These early-running genetically-driven fish are perhaps the hardest fighting and aggressive fly-taking steelhead since their metabolism is not caught up in egg and milt production. Once they achieve their aggressive disposition of the initial upstream run, they settle into a stream lifestyle more appropriate to a trout; seeking cover and finding comfortable holding lies.

The diverse biological river life and competitive nature of the resident inhabitants forces the steelhead to fit in as the spawning urge slowly develops. The need for hierarchical dominance causes the holding steelhead to investigate food forms and exhibit behavior from their parr-smolt life phase—and thus look opportunistically at fly patterns.

Because of their faster metabolism, summer steelhead have been known to eat terrestrial insects in the rivers and chase all types of food from leeches, tadpoles, baby snakes and frogs. Fall fish lower their holding metabolism to coincide with the onset of winter, yet often feed on riverine baitfish and insects because they compete with stream trout. Who grabs the first bug or shiner is a matter of competition rather than the need to eat (sort of like a group of hunting dogs fighting over a rawhide bone). As a result of this perked-up state of interest, holdover steelhead have been known to go fully "on the bite."

Startling proof of feeding by holdover steelhead was revealed during the winter of 1999 on Michigan's Muskegon River. Jeff Bacon, a knowledgeable river guide and friend, enjoys strike indicator nymph fishing for stream-resident rainbows and browns during the winter months using scud, caddis and midge larvae patterns in the size 18-22 hook range—tiny stuff! One Saturday in January, I saw him hook and land a beautifully colored 9-pound female steelhead on a size-18 olive/tan scud with 5X tippet and a four-weight rod. The fish swallowed the fly. Other accounts of winter steelhead feeding on midges and tiny caddis larvae have started to circulate.

The author proudly displays a magnificent, broad-shouldered February male steelhead taken from the gut of a pool below prime gravel. The turn of the century, 1999 and 2000, saw tremendous growth rates in Great Lakes steelhead due to extremely abundant baitfish populations in the big lakes as a result of warmer-than-average waters.

Steve Stallard Photo

Once late winter arrives and the daylight photoperiod increases, the urge to spawn in the steelhead is seen through the hunt for gravel areas. The males seek territorial dominance by holding and protecting pocket water and tailout lies above and below prime spawning areas. One of the largest buck males I've taken in the Great Lakes, a 20.9-pound wild Muskegon fish caught on February 9, 1999 in 35-degree water on a cerise Egg Omelet fly, was caught in the gut of a deep run below the hottest spawning gravel in the river. This fish was holding down the love nest waiting for the female entourage to arrive. It was a magnificent broad-shouldered, crimson-cheeked, kype-jawed beast that fought incredibly hard with aerial jumps, uncommon in frigid water—truly an alpha male. After its release, we saw the same fish well into May. It was very nervous, impossible to view for more than a few seconds, but obviously found a way to survive the angling pressure. I'm sure it sired many females, passing its regal genetic bloodline into the next generation. This is the beauty of catch-and-release steelhead fishing.

Spawning

Spawning in the Great Lakes can start as early as late January and February for the summer-run strains. The majority of Great Lakes fish spawn in March and April with Lake Superior, Huron and Ontario north shore tributaries seeing spawning runs peak from May to June.

Spawning is driven by various natural signals. Signals such as the natural maturation of the sexual glands, based on the timing and the runs of the various strains (i.e. summer/winter strain), are crucial. Late-winter and spring water temperatures generally result in a steady increase in metabolism. When water temperatures approach the 35- to 40-degree range, the signal to seek gravel and sexual mates kicks in. An increasing daylight photoperiod is a stimulus for both holding river fish and late-winter/early spring fish still in the big lake. Warm spring rains and snow melt that raise the flow of rivers are often a green flag for the spawning run, usually signaling the official starting gun for the spring spawning run.

In the preliminary stages of late winter, holdover males will stake out and seek territorial dominance of holding water near gravel. Nature seems to provide well for the larger, precious egg-carrying females by allowing them to hold over in the big lake through winter, growing fat and healthy. The females tend to deepen their silver color during spawning, with beautiful shades of rose, lime green and purple along with an occasional rosy pink broadside rainbow band. The males develop strong-jawed kypes, with deep red-crimson gill plates and deep, red-banded bodies; occasionally a top and bottom band is found. During the sexual drive, all colors in the spectral rainbow appear and the fish are truly nature's artpiece.

Steelhead arrive at gravel spawning areas by their innate preference for strong tailout flows over gravel bottoms. Spawning beds vary with flow. Near-shore areas are preferred over strong currents. Mainstream deep channel beds are selected during low water and drought conditions. Larger fish seek deeper gravel beds because they hold better in stronger flows and because of their important need for concealment. Because of pheromonal attraction, the first series of gravel areas selected by the females digging redds usually attract frequent visitors and set up multiple spawning areas. During heavy angling pressure or low river flows, considerable nocturnal spawning occurs.

Dawn and dusk, along with inclement weather spurs the females to dig gravel with their tails. A large female can excavate a redd up to one foot deep and 1.5 feet wide. Here they deposit their eggs in the deepest part of the pit. As the females dig, males jockey and spar back and forth for hierarchical dominance with the larger alpha males eventually gaining the right to mate with the females. As the couple slowly drifts backward over the pit, the female shoots her eggs down as the male squirts its milt over them. Since the bottom of the pit lacks considerable current, the eggs and milt quickly adhere and lodge in the filtered gravel.

Once females drop the eggs, they dig and push more gravel with their tail which eventually covers up the redds. Males continue to seek out other females and larger alpha males service a host of females. Males face a large mortality rate during spawning because they expend a lot of energy fending off other males, taxing their scarred and battle-weary bodies. A 20-inch female can produce an average of 3,500 eggs; a 32-inch female, approximately 12,000 eggs.

Once the ritual is complete and the last of the wandering males are gone, the drop-back migration of the tired and wary fish begins. Some fish will begin feeding in the river system once spawning is complete. Others wait until they reach the big water. If they make this harsh transition back, they will change their spawning colors back to their silver-and-gray lake attire. Those that survive the treacherous spawning run already begin to feed in preparation for next year's migration upriver. With new life seeding safely in the gravel, survival of the species is secured and the circle is complete.

Several males court a female and jockey for dominance to help propagate the species.

Chapter 3

Mastering the Rivers

Steelhead rivers and streams are in a constant state of change. Their ever-evolving ecosystems and hydrodynamics present some of the greatest challenges a steelhead fly fisher will encounter. No two rivers are the same. They behave differently and fish uniquely. As a result of natural conditions brought on by heavy floods, droughts, erosion, river rechanneling, natural obstructions and latitudinal climactic weather factors, these natural forces will dictate the migration routes and holding lies of river-ascending steelhead.

Man-made influences such as fishing pressure, regulations on waters, stocking sites, natal imprinting to hatcheries on riverine systems, and dams built for hydroelectric operations—with or without fish ladders for upstream movement—compound nature's impact on riverine systems. The old saying that "10% of steelhead anglers catch 90% of the fish" usually holds true since successful anglers study the rivers they fish. They monitor changes which affect steelhead from year to year. Some keep very accurate records, which I encourage all to do.

However, keeping records of your catch rate from key holding lies and locations is only the tip of the iceberg. Your notes will tell you a fish's preference for a particular area but the enigma lies in the reasons why and the factors that allow for the preference of a steelhead to take up position or migrate through certain runs, thus becoming vulnerable to a fly-fisher's presentation. This is where the study of river systems takes on its greatest importance and relates to how steelhead behave in each river niche they occupy.

Deep forests of pines and hardwoods along full-flowing, spring-fed and tailwater rivers, characterize the steelhead waters of the Great Lakes. Though our vistas lack the snow-capped mountains of the West Coast, our aesthetic beauty lies in the charm of our rivers. Laurie Supinski plies boulder-strewn pocket "throat" water in search of fall steelhead on Michigan's Muskegon River.

Jackpine River

Steel River

Cypress River

Michipicoten River

Devil's
Track

Little Two
Hearted
River

Tempurance River

Chocolay
River

St. Mar
River

Knife
River

Baptism River

Two Hearted
River

Ontonagen
River

Big Huron
River

Ocqu
Ri

Bois Brule
River

Peshtigo River

Platte
River

Big & Little
Manistee River

Oconto River

Betsie
River

Riffle
River

Kewannee River

West Twin

East Twin

Pere Marquette
River

Sheboygon River

White
River

Muskegon River

Milwaukee River

Grand River

Kalamazoo Rive

Root River

St. Joseph River

Little Calumet
& Salt Creek

Trail Creek

Blue-Ribbon Steelhead Rivers of the Great Lakes

1. Humber River
2. Credit River
3. Bronte River

Beaver River
Bighead River
Wilmot Creek
Ganaraska River
Stony Creek
Sandy Creek
South Sandy Creek
Nottawasaga River
Saugeen River
Au Sable River
Oak Orchard Creek
Maitland River
Niagara River
Salmon River
Oswego River
Grand River
Genesee River
Sandy Creek
Big Creek
Eighteen Mile Creek
Clinton River
Cattaraugus Creek
Elk Creek
Chatauqua Creek
Huron River
Grand River
Walnut Creek
Rocky River
Conneaut Creek
Chagrin River

Steelhead fly fishers tend to make unique observations on the rivers they love, often to the amazement of biologists and researchers who study the steelhead's behavior and habitat with overwhelming scientific data to support their theories. The enthusiastic and often overzealous theories steelhead fly fishers make are a result of the angler's daily craving to understand the uncertainty of the sport of steelheading and to give some relief to the method of their madness from the absurd, double-digit hook-up days, to days and weeks of depressing bedlam on the river. A steelhead mentor once told me that a good river will change on you like a vintage wine, or a special lady—growing more complex with time. Often just when you think you have a river figured out, you are humbled again by its whimsical, melancholy changes. Thus, persistence and analysis are strongly favored attributes of a steelheader's profile.

West Coast Versus Great Lakes: A Dichotomy and Fusion

The West Coast heritage of reading waters has become a more established practice as opposed to the emerging school in the Great Lakes. This is due primarily to the Pacific region's greater historical documentation and practice of the sport, the fly fishing methods applied, favorable weather conditions for steelhead, and their larger river systems. When I read through the pages of Trey Combs' *Steelhead Fly Fishing* (Lyons & Burford) and his legendary *Steelhead Fly Fishing and Flies* (Frank Amato Publications), I was captivated by the long-standing West Coast traditions that parallel the legacies of the men of the Catskills and their rivers. Their passion for the art of the fly, the study of its rivers and the incredible personalities of the devoted steelheaders, evoke the traditional method we in the Great Lakes have yet to incorporate. The bottom line? We are living and writing the history of the Great Lakes tradition as we speak—and fish. We are, as the English fly fisher G.E.M. Skues put it, "the live knowledge." In his book written at the turn of the 20th century, *Modern Tactics for Chalkstream Trout*, Skues evokes the empiricist in us all to live and breathe the river, which only reveals itself through intimate observation and experience. By studying the trout and the daily changes and opportunities a river can give, we separate the "dead" knowledge of outdated books and stories from the living contemporary environment. To the steelheader of the Great Lakes or elsewhere, these are powerful words of wisdom that keep us focused on our challenge, especially with the severe changing seasonal conditions often found in the Great Lakes. Keep in mind our steelhead have had a short 100-year history in a new ecosystem that is molding new behavioral patterns through the forces of natural selection.

However, our two different fisheries are as much alike as they are dissimilar. Because of the natural and man-made factors that influence the rivers, we must all learn to read water in an elementary way and then at an advanced level, regardless of where our rivers may be—British Columbia or Michigan.

Negative stereotypes have haunted the Great Lakes steelheader since the fishery was conceived in the late 1870s. The riverine fishery was for the most part keyed in on the annual spring spawning migration. Our barbaric attitude started very early in the 1900s when resentment for the steelhead rainbow ran high among anglers who accused the exotic rainbow of driving out the native brook trout. In 1917, permits were sold to spear the steelhead in Michigan, with some hoping to eradicate them.

Further ethical setbacks occurred in the Great Lakes fishery with the dawning of the Pacific salmon invasion in Platte Bay of Lake Michigan in the late 1960s. The fisheries managers made the mistake of condoning and encouraging by legislative action, the snagging of the salmon. This spawned the "art" of lining and snagging migrating salmonids. This practice rears its ugly head even today in all angling techniques well after the final banning of the technique in all of the Great Lakes ended in New York's Salmon River in 1995.

Fishing for salmonids on spawning gravel, which is now a firmly established tradition in the Great Lakes, has trained even the most seasoned anglers to sight-fish for steelhead rather than learn to read the water and fish for them blind in the more traditional West Coast sporting sense. Our trend seems to be to follow the crowds and go along with the other fishermen—where the spawning steelhead are. Great Lakes plug and spawn fishermen perhaps read water more effectively than fly fishers who tend to sight-fish egg patterns and nymphs to gravel concentrated spawning fish. The effectiveness of shallow-water fly fishing has become too convenient with minimal exerted effort in presentation. To become effective year-round steelhead fly fishers, we must focus on the elements of riverine systems and understand the when, why, and where of how a steelhead takes the fly.

Classic Great Lakes River Components

Riverine components effectively join together on all river systems, regardless of their size, to produce the holding lies, migratory areas, and water quality that steelhead seek. Since, for the most part, potamodromous steelhead enter their natal rivers for the ultimate purpose of procreation, their strong hormonal drive will keep them focused on utilizing the river's structure despite how uninviting at times it may be (i.e. floods, cold water, waterfall obstructions, etc.). However, since spawning is predominately on the minds of steelhead entering river systems, the Great Lakes and West Coast experience considerable "in-and-out" river hopping by steelhead in the lower estuaries and short tributary systems. This unique behavior in some fish is being studied by biologists with continued interest, for it reveals a fish with very fickle and curious tendencies. This usually occurs in very short, both low- and high-gradient tributaries, with easy access to the big lake. Streams such as Wisconsin's Root River, Minnesota's North Shore, Erie's Ohio and Pennsylvania south shore rivers, Indiana's Trail Creek and New York's Tug Hill Plateau Creeks like the Sandy and Stoney just to name a few, seem to share migrating steelhead in spurts with other nearby smaller Great Lakes tributaries.

River Classification

For reference when discussing tactics and presentation methods, I have classified Great Lakes and West Coast steelhead rivers into the following orders.

Class I
- Moderate gradient, fairly stable flows emanating from underground springs, tributary networks and/or tailwater influence
- Large to medium-sized rivers and streams
- Classic steelhead riverine structure: riffles, pockets, pools, tailouts, riverbends, etc.
- Considerable mileage of water available for upstream migration
- Good supply of gravel and cold to cool water with good prospects of natural wild steelhead reproduction
- Rivers cut through rocky moraine, thus giving it a boulder, rock, and gravel streambed

Class II
- Low-gradient systems with great fluctuations in flow
- Plains, farmland or prairie rivers and streams, large, medium and small-sized river systems
- Minimal riverine structure

Dry-line nymphing for skittish spring steelhead requires a stealthy approach when water levels are low and clear. The steep-gradient French River of Minnesota's Lake Superior north shore had outstanding runs of wild steelhead. When the fishery declined rapidly, catch-and-release regulations and accurate data-gathering devices were put in place to restore a unique genetic population of steelhead. Today the French, and other Minnesota rivers like the Knife, are staging a steady comeback thanks to the efforts of biologists like Tracy Close.

- Fairly short distances of accessible river mileage (with some exceptions)
- Minimal spawning gravel and predominantly warm-water conditions not suitable for natural wild steelhead reproduction
- Run often colored due to clay, soil runoff from agricultural areas

Class III
- Steep gradient systems with strong flows fluctuating on heavy spates (i.e. spring floods)
- Medium to small river systems
- Forbidding impassable structure such as waterfalls and rapids
- Usually entering lakes from steep rock or slate/shale shorelines
- Usually good supply of gravel, wild steelhead propagation occurs but is slowed by harsh flows and weather conditions—multiple adult spawnings sustain these mostly wild populations

By addressing the important stream components of gradient, size, flow, structure, and their ability to propagate wild steelhead, almost all of the Great Lakes rivers can fit into one of these categories. Some may have unique characteristics that can be applied to two categories.

Examples of Class I systems would be the hallowed, classic Great Lakes steelhead rivers and streams that have become very popular for fly anglers because of their production of large steelhead runs, aesthetic beauty, potential for wild steelhead production, and importance given to them by state and provincial fishery managers. Fisheries such as New York's Salmon River and Cattaragus Creek, Michigan's Muskegon, Pere Marquette, Manistee and Au Sable systems, Wisconsin's Bois Brule, Ontario's

Saugeen, Maitland, Ganaraska and Steel rivers are some examples of Class I steelhead waters. Their long-standing reputation for producing steelhead for nearly one hundred years, not to mention their aesthetic qualities, makes them ideal destinations.

Class II waters are mainly low-lying systems on Great Lakes farmland plains, which include large and small tributaries that are often void of water during drought and silted conditions and high during heavy precipitation. Due to their low gradients, siltation and widely varying water temperatures, natural reproduction is a problem. They flow primarily through the plains of Wisconsin, Ohio, Indiana, Ontario and New York regions, though examples are found in each region. Riverine gradient and low flows are the primary forces here, coupled with the rich soil that these ecosystems drain. Wisconsin's Root River, Indiana's Trail Creek, Michigan's Grand and New York's Oak Orchard creeks characterize Class II streams. Wild steelhead reproduction is marginal to non-existent on these waters.

Class III rivers are unique systems found in geographically specific areas like Lake Superior's North Shore, Pennsylvania, and New York's Erie shoreline with other Great Lakes exceptions. Waterfalls, rapids, and difficult migration waters characterize steep river gradient. The flows are usually strong with well-oxygenated gravel, so spawning does occur and wild fish populations exist. Yet spawning is done through repeated encounters and smolt rearing usually done in estuaries or lakeshore bays. Rivers in Minnesota like the Baptism, Knife, and French along with Ontario's Mink, Jackpine and Cypress rivers exemplify these austere river systems.

As mentioned, unique river systems exist that have attributes of all three classifications.

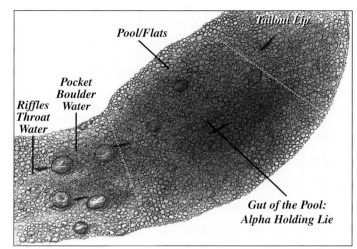

Classic steelhead-river gradient structure.

A very happy Rusty McKay with a silvery-pink summer Skamania steelhead taken on a Marabou Spey. Bear in mind, we were wet-wading and the air temperature was in the 90s on the St. Joseph River in August. With the introduction of the summer steelhead, Great Lakes steelhead anglers can pursue their art 365 days a year.

Three come to mind immediately—one being a true river, the other nearly Great Lakes channels.

The St. Joseph River—which originates in Michigan, flows through Indiana and then returns to Michigan before emptying into Lake Michigan—is a phenomenally productive world-class steelhead fishery that receives excellent runs of summer (Skamania) steelhead and Michigan winter-run fish. The river has minimal to non-existent natural reproduction and is stocked heavily by Indiana and Michigan. Though a large river system flowing for hundreds of miles, it is predominantly a Class II river with low gradients, agricultural runoff and marginal water temperatures and gravel bottom. Yet, in certain áreas (below the dams at Berrien Springs and Niles and in South Bend), it takes on the character and structure of a Class I steelhead river. Its tributaries like the Dowagiac River can be characterized as Class I water. It's also unique in the Great Lakes in that a series of five fish ladders built at hydro-dam sites allow fish up to Indiana, with fish-viewing windows for the public built on the ladders. For the most part, is the Columbia River of the Great Lakes.

The Niagara River below the falls and the St. Mary's at Sault Ste. Marie, Michigan and Ontario are as mentioned river channels that drain vast amounts of water in relatively narrow areas. The St. Mary's drains Lake Superior into Lake Huron through the often violent and dangerous rapids. It boasts excellent runs of steelhead, along with Atlantic and Pacific salmon with some Class I riffles, pocket water and pools.

Similarly, the mighty Niagara River with its thunderous rapids and whirlpools also typifies the classic West Coast-style steelhead waters with excellent runs of steelhead and some natural reproduction like the St. Mary's. These streams can fall into the Class I and III stereotypes, exhibiting qualities of both.

Though one can dissect all the rivers in our Great Lakes system and find unique qualities that might be cross referenced, the three major classes describe the geographical influences that shape and mold at least ninety percent of the Great Lakes.

Almost all steelhead rivers exhibit a series of changing water structure based on river gradient and hydrodynamics. From its source to its big lake mouth, steelhead river segments can be dissected beginning from top to bottom in the following fashion:

Riffles or Rapids/Throat water

Pocket Water

Pools/Gut/Flats

Tailouts or Lips

This progressive movement of flow can be found in segments in higher gradient rivers or it may be spread out over miles on lower gradient rivers. For instance, a pool and flats combination, often called eddies, can stretch for miles on some larger river systems. Hydro-dammed rivers behave uniquely, since their highest river gradients are at the dam sites, in effect making the dams the riffles or rapids.

Steelhead behavior in migrating riverine systems is influenced by the following:

•Water flow, temperature, and clarity

•Weather conditions

•Time of day and season

•Riverine structure

•Abundance of fish in the river and competition

•Natural or man-induced migration burdens

Dynamics of the Water

Perhaps no other variable shapes a steelhead's riverine predisposition and sporting attitude than the importance of hydrodynamics: the study of flow. Since the rainbow trout's evolution took place in high-gradient, fast-flowing rivers and streams for millions of years, the steelhead rainbow prefers a steady current; other salmonids like the brown trout favor slower currents and slack water. Thus, the yearning for current tugs at the big-lake-wandering predator and causes upstream migration.

Once steelhead enter their natal river of wild origin or hatchery planting, olfactory imprinting causes migration to

Mike Dzienny with a brilliantly-colored, deep-girthed winter female. The steelhead took a large Hex nymph on a bottom drift-fishing method using running line. The fish was caught in the flat of a pool adjacent to a warm spring-creek tributary.

A beautifully-colored winter female that fell for a shrimp pink Clown Egg pattern.

occur quickly—as much as thirty miles a day, or it is staged and plotted. The speed of migration depends on the urgency and time of the year the run takes place, along with the unique behaviors of various strains of steelhead.

Ideal conditions for upstream migration often occur during major river spates (i.e. heavy rains, spring runoff, etc.) With these conditions, water color is often muddied or tainted with natural elements such as soil, peat or mineral components which alter the clarity of rivers. Reduced clarity, combined with flow, will cloak the advancing steelhead and allow for constant around-the-clock migration by groups of fish.

In high-water conditions, steelhead utilize the buffering comfort and reduction of flow that shoreline areas provide. Riverbends, boulders and the mixing of brackish water and the stronger river flows will create creases and seams that steelhead ease gently in and out of for metabolic comfort and rest.

The thermometer has long been a steelheader's best friend. Water temperature will dictate rate and distance of migration as does flow. Optimum migration usually takes place from 45-58 degrees Fahrenheit. However, these ranges are utilized by less than fifty percent of the steelhead migrators. Winter and early-spring spawning fish move in waters 34-40 degrees due to their strong hormonal instinct to spawn and procreate. Summer-strain steelhead have learned to migrate at a good pace from 60-72 degrees—primarily on the St. Joseph and Manistee rivers of Lake Michigan and the Salmon River of New York. Thus, we have a water temperature range from 34-70 degrees which will

allow the four-season steelheader the opportunity to catch fish. Low-water conditions or droughts will hamper steelhead migration or cause steelhead to drop back into lower estuary pools for security and comfort. In Class II river tributaries, low waters will drop steelhead back entirely to the big lake. Minimal water flow migrations will take place from dusk to dawn, with daytime hours spent under cover in deep pool structure often impenetrable for fly presentation.

Ideal water conditions for productive steelhead fishing usually occurs after rising river levels have fallen and the fish establishes strategic holding lies. For consistent steelhead angling success, a series of river spates (rising waters) followed by stable flows allows for upstream migration of fresh fish in intervals, then they begin establishing holding and taking lies.

Water clarity is particularly important to wild steelhead, which were born and raised in clear, stable-flowing Class I rivers. These fish are reared in clear, classic trout stream waters and learn to feed on midges and other food forms as parr and fingerlings prior to smolting. Hatchery fish stocked in often-murky Class II waters spend relatively little time in their early smolt environment and are much more tolerant of cloudy and silted waters because their migrations mainly occur from their genetic and hormonally driven upstream spawning migrations.

Fluctuating water flows not only determine holding and moving behavior, but have a powerful effect on where steelhead will dig redds for spawning. Steelhead are very particular about the water they use. A moderate to strong flow is needed over gravel areas, usually at high river gradients. This will ensure keeping the eggs silt free and provide dissolved oxygen in good quantities. When river levels are high, spawning will usually take place on gravel gradients near shore. When flows diminish and river channels shrink, the more direct, middle-of-the-river channel will be selected. High waters afford shallow redds to be dug. When low water or drought conditions exist, deep-water spawning will occur in heavy flows for concealment and to maximize river channel velocity.

Though all steelhead are the same species, distinct differences in their preference for certain waters and their flow are shown in wild and hatchery steelhead. Because of natal imprinting and conditioning, wild steelhead that were reared in very fast river systems can tolerate the current much better than hatchery fish. Because of the short smolt and riverine rearing periods of stocked steelhead, often the natal imprinting to ascend a particular river is not as strong nor are they as resilient to obstacles such as strong flows, rapids and waterfalls. Hatchery fish tend to "shop around" for river systems that are much more favorable to ascend—thus the greater roaming and straying of hatchery stocks to rivers other than the river of their origin.

River system interactions with the Great Lakes they drain into play an important role in determining whether there will be a major migration or a gradual trickling in of individual fish. Onshore and offshore winds create distinct advantages for steelhead to hone in on a particular river during their migrations. River and lake flow interactions often create conditions for steelhead to migrate—particularly in short-distance Class II waters—even when their migration switch is not turned on.

A common scenario occurs in almost any season when offshore winds create an upwelling effect where the cool deep Great Lakes waters replace the outgoing warmer beach waters and draw in steelhead almost like a surfer riding a wave. If river temperatures coincide with shoreline temperatures and the outflow from rivers is strong enough, curiosity and a general liking of current will draw the fish up river. This is particularly important for summer Skamania steelhead that often encounter warm beach temperatures in the 70s during July and August. These warm surf temperatures often act as a blockade to entering rivers even though the river temperatures might be comfortable for migration.

Hard-pounding waves from onshore winds often create great turbidity and discolored shorelines for considerable distances into the lake. Offshore temperatures are conducive to steelhead hunting baitfish in relatively shallow shoreline waters, predominantly in the fall, winter, and spring. The discolored waters are uncomfortable for steelhead. If a clear-flowing river system is emptying into this murky water, the clear plume of water is often detected by schools of steelhead and draws them up river systems quickly.

Power lines and tight-looped lines mix as Brian Fleischig casts to steelhead on Ohio's Chagrin River in view of Clevelend's downtown skyline.

These sporadic migrations draw steelhead up river systems just as quickly as they will cause them to drop back down to lake waters. They do not seem to be permanent migrations of the kind exhibited by the hormonal genetic spawning drive which forces the steelhead up rivers in a non-stop, never-look-back fashion.

The riverine water dynamics are often completely discarded when bullish, sexually driven steelhead ascend a river for the clear intent of spawning. Since almost all Great Lakes steelhead spawn in the spring, there are considerable wait-to-the-last-minute migrators who are on a quick mission to do their thing. At these times, fish will often tolerate low flows, warm waters, and hot sunny weather, since they are very persistent about their duties. These fish are usually the exception rather than the norm.

Water dynamics are intriguing in that they reveal the uniqueness of steelhead personalities and preferences.

Targeting Player Steelhead

As a cardinal rule, steelhead migration and holding behavior will follow the path of least hydrodynamic resistance. The ideal sporting fish for a fly fisher is a "player" steelhead. This is a fish that is most likely to take a well-presented fly with enthusiasm—a sporting acrobat that tests the skills, proficiency, and coordination of the steelhead fly fisher.

When scouting for players you are looking for a fish that has not been subjected to the trauma of typical Great Lakes steelheading pressure. This can include encounters with boat motors, plug pullers hammering gaudy-colored hardware at them, or the pounding boots of the gauntlet of wading anglers hovering over spawning gravel near dam fish ladders.

This fish usually slips into its natal stream from the big lake under the cover of darkness and with cautious savvy. A quick thaw or freshet of melting snow or rain will discolor the water to the fish's advantage—providing both protection and a feeling of security for it to travel. Under rising water conditions steelhead will travel comfortably for many miles, from pool to run, stopping only occasionally to rest briefly. This green-backed, mint-silver beauty is the ideal specimen and is a candidate for becoming a player.

Once the water lowers, it will find a holding pool or run to its liking and establish its territory. Given the player's aggressive nature when seeking prey in the big lake, this fish's search-and-destroy programming is fully in gear. The first spinner, spawn-bag, or fly that comes its way will get nailed with a vengeance.

The most important factors that influence the making of a player, other than the lack of angling pressure, are water temperature, current dynamics, sunlight, and changing stream topography. Water temperature is perhaps the most crucial variable. At 33 degrees and below, all movement, for the most part, ceases. But well-presented, bottom-hugging nymph, egg patterns or slow-moving Speys and leeches fished in a staggered fashion—i.e., much slower than the current—will still get a firm strike from a player. From 35 to 38 degrees, activity rises markedly. Fish become interested in presentations and will become players as long as the offerings are placed relatively near them—they are still conserving energy and move very little. The magic temperature zone starts at around 38-40 degrees F. Temperatures at or above this reading will signal aggressive behavior, movement, and migration—not to mention vigorous leaping and fighting behavior when the fish is hooked.

Sunlight can be both a positive and negative factor for the steelheader. When cold-water conditions prevail, a good bright day can warm the runs and pools, and often provides an emergence of black winter stoneflies and midges. Swimming and crawling nymphs often arouse steelhead from dormancy and can create some excitement. Fish are often found in the shallow waters near the bank or in the riffles. Unfortunately, sunny days and snow bounce shadows around, spooking fish and sending them for cover. The worst condition is very low, clear water that is above 44 degrees F. If conditions like this exist, wait until dawn or dusk to fish. Gin-clear waters can make for some very spooky fish. Persistence and endurance are the keys to success.

When you've activated a player by a chase or swirl to your offering, stick with the fish. Change pattern sizes and tippet diameters until you finally get a strike. When fishing for a player, an angler must leave no stone unturned, no waters uncovered. Using the countdown method, break down the entire run in graphic squares, the steelheader hunting players should fish each quadrant thoroughly until every cast has been met with exhaustion or a jolting hook-up. Due to their savage and untamed cocky behavior, player steelhead strike the fly aggressively. Usually the first appropriate well-presented fly pattern elicits a reaction, especially in ideal water flows and temperatures.

Holding Versus Moving Fish

One of the "great debates" in steelheading involves the behavior of steelhead in holding and moving waters. Opinions vary greatly and literature is often contradictory on this intriguing subject. Since I am not able to find any clear-cut scientific studies on when player steelhead are most likely to strike the fly and whether it's when they are holding or moving, I am left to fuse the theories based on observations of great steelhead fishermen and conclusions of my own.

A twenty-pound January male taken during the calm of the evening when water temperatures reach maximum levels. The gut of a particular run was worked several hours before this fish struck. It could have been that the fish was indignant during that period or it just slipped into the run at dusk from downstream. Steelhead migrate at low-light levels of dawn and dusk.

Gary Phillips Photo

In Trey Combs' classic, *Steelhead Fly Fishing and Flies* (Frank Amato Publications), he recognizes migrating steelhead to be much more likely to strike the fly than holding fish. Years later in his book *Steelhead Fly Fishing*, he writes in length about the nuances of holding water, including fly-taking opportunities and the behavior of steelhead in them.

Legendary West Coast steelheader, Lannie Waller wrote eloquently and knowingly in *Wild Steelhead and Atlantic Salmon* magazine (Winter 1995) in a piece entitled "The Bite Is On—Isn't It? Why a Steelhead Takes the Fly." He speaks of the "mystery grab"—when no one knows when the bite will be on. He sites behavioral and natural factors such as weather, water dynamics, etc. that form a complex union of indicators for favorable steelheading. Waller says, "In my opinion, moving steelhead will often stop to take a fly, though I much prefer a holding fish in what Atlantic salmon anglers knowingly call 'a taking lie.' I think that such a fish is more likely to respond then because it does not have travel on the mind."

Combs' and Waller's theories are well put and validate the steelhead hook-ups and places in the river where they occur.

Much of what has been written about steelhead angling behavior stems from West Coast experiences, but I personally believe that the West Coast ecosystem shapes steelhead behavior differently from the Great Lakes ecosystem, the physiological adjustments necessary for migration from salt to fresh water creating the differences. In addition to the West Coast's more conducive water temperatures during the runs, varied water system dynamics with longer watersheds, West Coast steelheading is an angling tradition similar to Atlantic salmon-style fisheries.

It is my opinion that the Great Lakes steelhead behave much more opportunistically. This may result from the less-complicated physiological transition from their freshwater ocean-like basins to the freshwater riverine systems at the adult and smolt stages, thus allowing for more repeat spawners and river encounters. Also, the relatively short migration distances on Great Lakes river systems often tends to keep their aggressive food-striking behavior more in line with their big-lake hunting behavior. In effect, the Great Lakes have a smaller "window of opportunity" when angling, which usually coincides with the most ideal and vulnerable conditions to catch steelhead. Usually this occurs in the fall and spring. Winter and summer runs are more challenging and require greater effort and specialized tactics.

With trees lined tight to the bank, a single or double Spey is an effective cast to reach holding steelhead in turbulent and unwadable waters. This is the Mays Ledges on the hollowed steelhead waters of Wisconsin's Bois Brule River. Throughout the Lake Superior region, the waters are tinted from iron- and mineral-rich geology.

All steelhead have the ability to become players. Whether migrators or movers are better players than holders or vice versa is a perplexing question that I believe will never be answered. The steelhead fly fisher on a quest for an active player fish needs to be concerned with where to find and stalk the moving or holding fish and how they might react differently to the fly as a result of their river environment.

Though a steelhead angler can learn to read holding water, there is no such thing as "moving water"—the whole river is moving water. Moving water is commonly associated with fast riffles, rapids, or pocket waters known as the throat of the river.

In these areas, migrating fish will stack-up to negotiate the water intuitively and cautiously, allowing them to hold periodically for long enough to inspect a fly offering. In essence, the moving fish have become holding fish in that they hold long enough to inspect, show curiosity, then reject or strike the fly.

There are several well-established facts on steelhead behavior in riverine conditions. All the data which fisheries biologists accumulate at egg-taking weirs or fish ladders, indicates that when fish are passing through them in large migrations, steelhead angling success is usually poor. The "mystery grab" Waller talks of is a very common experience on all steelhead rivers and applies to when fish are known to be in the river systems in good numbers and for some period of time. Whether the bite is on or off is primarily due to natural weather and water dynamics affecting holding and moving fish. In West Coast rivers could it be possible that the bite is off because of the steelhead's physiological balancing of salinity and fresh water which might cause them a feeling similar to the flu?

The behavioral variables for when the bite is on or off can be endless. The saying, "the more you get to know steelhead, the less you know about them," is true. Jon George, a noted Province of Ontario, Lake Superior steelhead biologist who passionately studies the behavior of his wild fish, told me once that he wishes he had several lifetimes to study these fascinating beasts.

Steelhead Taking Lies in Relation to River Structure

Even if we optimistically look at all steelhead as potential players, we must realize that some will be more aggressive and will occupy the more optimum lies for fly presentation and the strike. The primary taking lies are often occupied by the more aggressive holding fish because they have ideal flow levels for the fish's comfort. Secondary lies are a result of the submission of females and smaller steelhead. They also exist because steelhead abandon primary lies for various reasons, including changes in water dynamics or too much angling pressure on the primary spots. I have noticed that on days during the major fall and spring runs when angling pressure is significant, we are successful when I focus my angling and guiding efforts on those places—tertiary lies—other anglers pass up, believing incorrectly that there are no fish.

If you observe other steelhead anglers or recall your successful hook-ups, you'll see they tend to come from these well-established places on the river. These primary lies are known as places for catching fish. The importance of having first-water advantage on a steelhead outing is obvious when you see all the guide boats and anglers scurrying to these prime spots at three a.m. It can be extremely competitive to say the least—we won't mention the fist fights and obscene verbal exchanges because we are now entering a new era of ethical fishing (I pray) in the Great Lakes with the snagging days long gone.

A steelhead angler battles a feisty spring male to the net. Careful easing of the fish is required in faster currents, slowly drop the rod down, as you pump the reel and gently lift the rod to gain your line.

First-water advantage at low light will usually reveal a fresh player that has moved into a primary lie and is poised for a strike. Usually after the fish are hammered by wading and boat fishermen or startled by high sunlight, their aggression is quickly dampened and they head for the protection of the secondary and tertiary lies.

Riffles and Rapids

Major gradients in rivers are revealed through these cascading areas. The flow can be turbid and complex with various undulating and undertow currents where drop-offs occur. To a newly migrated steelhead, in this new water environment, after many years of relatively currentless flows of the big lake, often presents a puzzling scenario where staging of the fish will occur. On my home rivers of Lake Michigan, I can predict with fair accuracy whether I will encounter fresh chrome player steelhead at the first major river gradients up from Lake Michigan each early morning if given the luck of first-water advantage.

When the steelhead face these water obstacles they usually drop back into the pocket waters or pools immediately below and debate their next move—how to negotiate the swift water with the least amount of physical exertion and with the best protection, this usually occurs along the shoreline. There is usually an adjustment period when encountering the first gradients, steelhead become staged.

Primary lies are found in riffles because the fish move up this system in stages—rarely do they shoot through quickly. By using the seams of shoreline, coupled with large boulders or wooded obstructions, they normally glide through these sections gracefully. Prime taking lies are found at the top or to the side of boulders and close to the bottom where current deflection is high and a good field of vision is possible.

Other primary lies are found next to shoreline troughs, where seams create good holds for moving fish. It is extremely important to fish shoreline areas in rapids and riffles before wading out too soon and spooking the fish. This is particularly important at first light or dusk.

Bridge abutments are also primary taking lies for they shield the fish from current well. Steelhead that are nosed up to the abutment and in the calm water below it are often hard to present a fly to. However, a significant seam often occurs for a considerable distance down from the abutment allowing for presentation.

Secondary lies usually do not exist in riffles and rapids. Shooting the rapids is the only alternative for non-dominant fish if all primary lies are filled by dominant steelhead. If the run is fairly fresh and the fish's competitive spawning behavior has not yet taken hold, several fish might school at primary lies in fast water and the potential for repeat hook-ups or fish encounters in one lie might occur.

The Throat Pocket Water

Almost in unison with the riffle/rapids, throat pocket water begins where there is a slight decrease in the current and drop-off begins to take place. This is the ultimate player steelhead water. This water is often overlooked by the steelhead anglers concentration on pools and tailouts. Pocket-water stages fish that are on the move. Water speeds may vary anywhere from one to five feet per second. The ultimate depths are 4 to 12 feet on large rivers and are scaled down on smaller systems. Their strong preference for rocky bottoms is usually met in pocket water. The steelhead fly fisher bottom-bouncing nymphs or egg patterns will clearly feel the ticking of the weighted system bouncing along the bottom. Great Lakes anglers often comment on the good feel of ticking gravel and how the water smells "hot" for active fish.

As with riffles, boulders or troughs in the river bottom also create pockets. Here, primary taking lies again are found at the top and the sides of the boulders. When several boulders or obstructions are aligned vertically with the flow, primary lies will often be found in the soft water behind and in front of the obstructions. The distance of these lies can range from several feet to as much as thirty feet in larger rivers. In pocket waters or throats that have little obstruction, the "gut" of the river

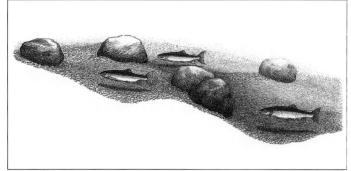

The comfortable current-shielding confines of the boulder pocket water provides ideal resting water for moving fish. This water always seems to hold fish that will target a fly so fish it thoroughly.

channel or the seams and creases along the shorelines will be utilized by the steelhead. The gut usually has the least amount of current on the bottom and relief from the flow is achieved.

One of the most common problems anglers have in fishing strong flowing riffles, rapids, or pocket waters is that they do not penetrate the bottom strike zone. Too often a fly angler rides the presentation too high, especially in cold-water conditions. If high-stick nymphing or drift-fishing methods are used, enough weight casted well above the targeted lie will allow the presentation to be seen by the fish.

If fishing a Spey or streamer fly on the downstream swing, heavy sink-tips are needed for casting and successfully mending upstream well above the fish. Due to the enormous amounts of dissolved oxygen, summer steelhead hold in pocket water. Here greased dry line and riffle-hitch methods can entice steelhead when summer temperatures are more suitable to the surface or near-surface rise and take.

It is important that pocket water is fished thoroughly, with each potential primary lie covered. In cloudy, inclement weather with good precipitation, fish will be on the move all day. If you cover the pocket water early in the morning with no luck, come back later in the day or evening, since each newly arriving steelhead at a major gradient will take up a primary lie

Throat pocket water begins where the fast currents of the riffles or rapids drop deeper into boulder-shielded pockets. Steelhead hug the current-shielding boulders and ride back on the upwelling currents.

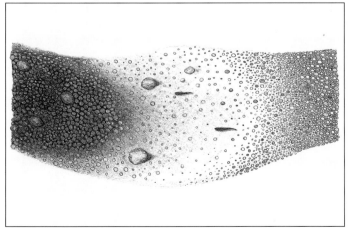

High-stick nymphing pocket water
1. After the cast is made some slack is given
2. Lifting the rod to high-stick, a vertical penetration allows the fly to sink deeper with a little current surface drag resistance
3. The high-sticker turns with the current and leads the fly for maximum penetration
4. At the tail end of the drift, many strikes occur on the upward swing

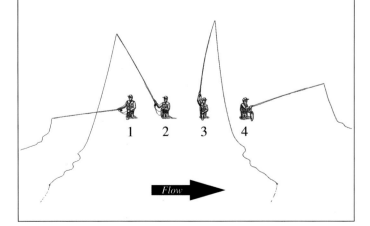

A drift boat is a favorite way to negotiate and fish long stretches of steelhead rivers often inaccessible by foot. Here on Lake Ontario's Salmon River of New York, a whole new summer fishery developed for Skamania steelhead and Atlantic salmon. Fishing traditional West Coast wet-fly and Spey techniques can prove successful due to the higher water temperatures not found on Great Lakes rivers through the deep freeze of winter.

when daylight and weather conditions have changed. Keep in mind that due to the turbulence of the surface in pocket waters, the fish's visibility through the surface is minimal—which is to your advantage. Wade these areas rarely; fish from the bank as much as possible since fish will hug shoreline.

Pools and Flats

Since a majority of Great Lakes fly fishing takes place in very cold late fall, winter or early spring conditions, anglers concentrate on pool/flats areas where steelhead drop back and hold to allow for the conservation of energy in the reduced flows. Often the bottoms of pools have the warmer temperatures not found in the shallower river areas. When steelhead are pressured from angling or when water levels drop, they abandon riffle and pocket water for the security of the big pools.

As faster pocket water drops off into pools, a deep trough or "gut" usually occurs in the virtually non-existent current. This gut provides holding steelhead with the ultimate comfort in river flow, depth, and concealment. In these troughs, steelhead can swim sideways and backward with comfort. Not having to face the current is similar to big-lake water conditions. As the pool lengthens out, a flats area of even more still water occurs. Here steelhead can take advantage of the shallow flats areas in winter when sunlight will warm the waters to a more comfortable temperature. The flats are also close to deep pools when the need for a quick escape arises.

Some pools are difficult to fly fish because they lack substantial current to present the fly. This water has traditionally been

position periodically throughout the day. If a good fish is turned in these waters yet refuses to take a fly, try different patterns or techniques. Sometimes rest the fish and come back

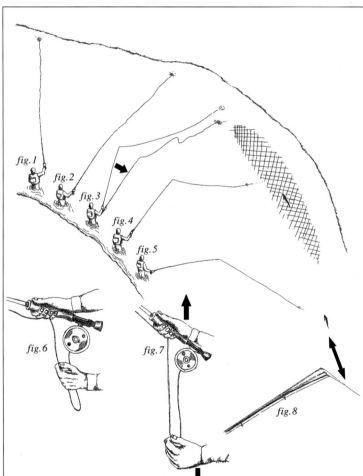

fig.1
fig.2
fig.3
fig.4
fig.5
fig.6
fig.7
fig.8

Bottom Drift Nymphing Technique

Fig. 1 - In faster, deeper water, an upstream presentation (10-11 o'clock) will allow the rig to penetrate the bottom.

Fig. 2 - In shallower, slower waters, the presentation should be at a more down-and-across drift (12-1 o'clock).

Fig. 3 - Once the cast is made, make a series of "stack mends" to allow for depth presentation.

Fig. 4 - Once bottom has been detected, a high-stick approach will allow for the vertical entry of the line in the water which will cut water drag resistance to a minimum.

Fig. 5 - Many strikes come at the end of the drift because of the longer inspection time presented to the steelhead or the appealing swing and lift of the flies as they sweep up directly downstream of the angler. Hang time—the amount of time an angler chooses to let the drift lay downstream—is also critical for eliciting additional strikes.

Fig. 6 - When drift fishing, use your rod-hand fingers as a "cleat system" to control the line tension during the drift. The "free" hand should be below the "cleat" fingers to pull-up on line, let line out during the drift, etc.

Fig. 7 - To set the hook on a fish, to lift the hooks of bottom snags and "glide" them over boulders, etc, strip down with the "free" hand and rod set to the side or upward should occur.

Fig. 8 - During the entire drift, the angler's eyes should be glued to the rod tip. A steady "ticking" of the tip signals a good consistent presentation. If the rod tip bends down slowly, it is usually a snag. Quick, sudden throbbings of the tip usually signal a strike.

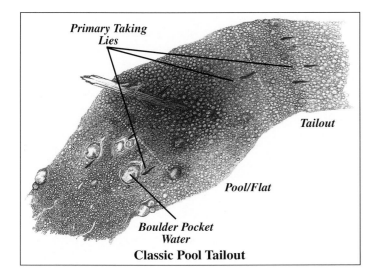

Primary Taking Lies

Tailout

Pool/Flat

Boulder Pocket Water

Classic Pool Tailout

depth is usually ideal for presenting a fly—not too deep, not too shallow. Tailouts offer a transition area where the slower-moving pool couples with the quickening flow of the lip ready to cascade over the next gradient. Individual fish can pick and choose their comfort zone based on their flow needs and metabolism. This is a great area to swing a Spey fly or wake a large dry fly.

In a large majority of cases, tailouts have a gravel bottom. If the fish are sexually maturing and close to spawning, their need for gravel and laying claim in their new territory will trigger aggressive behavior and they will strike the fly well at this time. Freshly migrated fish in holding lies, especially during difficult gradient migrations, are now feeling comfortable and will show a greater curiosity towards fly presentations.

The final lie provides concealment under the wooded debris and is important for fish that have been pressured either from anglers or because of unfavorable conditions such as falling water levels with extreme sunlight. Obviously, this is not a taking lie but one for survival.

Spring Seep and Tributary Influences

Spring seepage and tributaries are common components of steel-heading rivers, their attraction to migrating steelhead are significant. These are great elementary waters for the beginning steelhead fisherman.

River tributaries obviously attract steelhead because they are highly utilized as spawning areas and are often their strongly imprinted birth sites. Split river channels that concourse islands may also act as a tributary influence, especially if they split the river for a good distance.

Most tributaries entering steelhead river systems form significant holding pools or pocket runs where steelhead gather. Quite often tributaries are not navigable because of low, clear flows. Steelhead will usually only ascend them in these conditions when the spawning urge is too strong, i.e., they are running late on their biological spawning timetable (late-spring spawners).

Many steelhead fishermen flock to tributary pools at dawn to get first-water advantage for newly arrived, low-light migrating fish. Native fish smell the familiar water of the tributary and gravitate quickly to it, as do stray fish from different river systems. Like the steelhead, wild or planted, these strays take a liking to these newly-found incoming flows. Since arrival at tributaries may be months ahead of spawning time, staging will occur and primary lies are formed.

Steelhead halted on their upstream migration in these tributaries will show great interest in taking a fly and can become quite aggressive. Since males tend to arrive early on many of the spawning runs, early hierarchical dominance and jousting for position will cause responsive and inquisitive attention to their river surroundings.

I recall a late fall day on a Lake Ontario river where I was swinging and stripping my Bunny Spey flies through a tributary pool. On my third cast, two male steelhead chased the fly all the way to shore, only to refuse it. As they quickly turned back to the pool, I noticed that they took a "roll and tail, back-lashing pot shot" at each other before going their separate ways—a sort of bar room scuffle quickly abated.

Migration up the tributaries often occurs with rising water levels or spates, especially in discolored water. Many times, holding males will wait for newly-arrived females to lead the way either up the tributary or further up the main channel.

Some tributaries may be large spring creeks or spring flow influences which stem from subterranean aquifers and pump out

known as bobber/spawn bag water (it's also known as sucker/frog water). Bait and hardware anglers consistently catch fish here in the winter when the fly guys strike out.

Several techniques, such as strike indicator nymphing with large floating indicators on dry lines with long leaders, can be used to float flies endlessly down a flat. Deep-water jigging with Bunny Leeches on sink-tips can be rolled downstream. Or classic drift fishing with weighted rigs can be drifted slower than the speed of the current with a drop-back, lift and glide method. Keep in mind that the proper depth penetration and consistent bottom presentations are needed to fish these areas.

Finally, the fish occupying these holding lies are often sluggish holders or pent-up fish off the bite because of low water conditions or extremely low temperatures. Strikes to the fly will come slowly, often after considerable angling time. When concentrating on pool/flat scenarios, patience, optimism and a good deal of angling time are necessary. It is important to keep in mind that steelhead do not prefer the deeper holes that chinook salmon do, depths over fifteen feet are usually considered unfavorable.

Tailouts

The classic pool tailout is perhaps the most productive steelhead water during all seasons in the Great Lakes rivers. Active and holding fish will occupy this prime lie since it incorporates all elements of water-flow dynamics from which the steelhead can choose depending on its migrating, holding or concealment mood.

When a classic pool tailout is coupled with a larger wood debris obstruction, you will find four primary lies; three are taking lies, one is solely for security. The first taking lie occurs at the gut of the tailout, preferably over gravel, where the fish is in full view of the main current in a comfortable flow. In this water, a fly can be easily presented and the fish usually have a strong response for taking them.

You'll find the second taking lie where a seam is created by the obstruction of the wooded debris. The steelhead uses it to deflect the water, and as a spot where it can keep an eye on the mainstream flow. A fly presented close to the obstruction can pique the fish's curiosity and cause it to take the fly.

One of the most powerful taking lies in the tailout occurs at the tail or lip of the pool. Often fish that have surpassed the fast gradient below the lip stop to rest in the deep carved-out trough in the center of the tailout, or they rest in the shoreline areas. Many player fish are taken from these areas since water

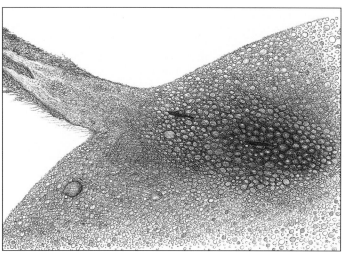

Tributary Influences:
At early and late light periods, steelhead hold close to the
tributary influence. The most secure spot for a large alpha male
or female steelhead is in the gut of the tributary pool.

alkaline water from 46 to 58 degrees all year long. They cause a natural staging place for steelhead when main river system temperatures are less than ideal. This occurs for summer steelhead that often enter river temperatures in 60- to 74-degree range and immediately seek cool, well-oxygenated water. They often ascend these rivers regardless of how low or clear they are due to their cool, comforting water.

Most spring-influenced tributaries hold temperatures from 45-58 degrees year round, prime temperature range for steelhead. Winter steelhead prefer it when river temperatures drop in the low to mid 30s. The warmer spring influence will cause considerable staging in these areas so concentrate fishing efforts there.

When targeting river tributaries, a topographical map is often your best bet. The best indicator for locating true spring-creek

influences is the presence of green plants such as watercress, Elodea, Chara and duck wort. Since most springs originate in calcium carbonate bedrock, their waters run alkaline, which the plants love. Also, in winter, warmer ground around the spring tributaries will be barren of snow. Nearby roads with names such as Mineral Spring Road, Sulfur Springs Drive, etc. are a dead giveaway for the presence of spring tributaries.

The importance of springs cannot be emphasized enough, they play an important role in a steelhead fly fisher's success. However, all spring influences are not as noticeable as stream tributaries. Some just percolate through the gravel and sand and seep unnoticeably. Usually larger river gradients which cut through rocky moraine have the dual function of supplying steelhead with the gravel they like and springs which creep out of the cut bedrock. Look for these elevation changes on your maps.

Riverbends

The ultimate steelhead holding water combines riffles, pockets, pools, flats, tailouts etc. with a riverbend. I can think of no more optimum area for holding fish than these areas. Whether a river makes a broad or narrow turn, it deflects water and causes considerable holding water for a good distance (i.e., river bends to the right, deflects from the left). It allows for a series of creases and seams on the inside, which make prime holding water for moving or stable fish. As the bend cuts sharply on the opposite bank, it also creates a substantial drop-off or undercut bank at the tailout, which is also a highly sought-after, primary taking lie.

In riverbends which do not have the classic structure, fish will still hold in good numbers because of the river deflection. When riverbends narrow, the flow becomes concentrated and accelerated. Here you'll find fish in the bottom central gut of the run or hugging the shelves. Almost all riverbends harbor deep pools and holding water with often steep, glacially-cut or eroded banks. When one riverbend is followed immediately by another, fish will zigzag deflecting creases and seams in a predictable fashion. This

The spectacular Salmon River of New York State is one of the premier—and most heavily fished—steelhead rivers in the world.

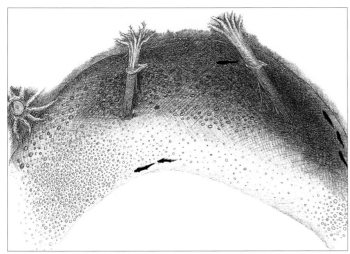

Classic riverbed steelhead lies.

behavior creates primary lies which can be relied upon from year to year.

Dam Sites

Many Great Lakes rivers harbor single or multiple dams, with or without fish ladders. Many anglers fish these upstream blockades to migration. There are steelhead fishermen who dam-hop since they are so effective at reading these waters, producing high catch rates. Besides, it's pretty dam easy to locate a dam and catch a lot of dam fish!

As with all hydrodynamic functions there can be productive and primary taking lies as well as unproductive areas at dam sites. When the initial bullish, hell-bent migrators are confronted with a dam, they will do everything in their power to conquer it. This results in their repeated and often unsuccessful attempts to jump a dam. This generally occurs at low dam sites. However, strong fish that have learned to use the upwelling, undertow currents to project them aloft, can often negotiate dams, which are marginally breached. Most of these fiercely concentrated fish are not concerned with taking a fly and rarely show interest. When the unrewarded and exhausting jumping ceases, the fish will begin to drop back and stage. The flats and tailouts of dam sites usually produce prime taking lies for frustrated holding fish.

When fish ladders are present, usually on one side of the dam, it might take considerable time for the steelhead to find its way to it—some never will. Often fish that only migrate alongside the river where the ladders are make the ascent. Since most states and provinces of Canada do not legally allow angling in front of a fish ladder, due to the concentrations of fish there, you are better off concentrating on downstream areas where frustrated steelhead will become aggressive players.

High flows at dam sites can be both productive and unproductive. When the water is running high and a strong run is on, the sheer numbers of staged aggressive fish allow for multiple hook-ups and fabulous angling, usually at the start of a run. This hot action can turn off as quickly as it starts when fresh fish are insistent on jumping or migrating.

Low flows are usually more consistently productive since fish tend to concentrate in pockets and seams of holding water at this time. Because of the water's clarity, varied presentations can be tried.

If dams generate hydroelectric power, keep in mind that hydro turbines dictate the river's flow and holding lies. Observe

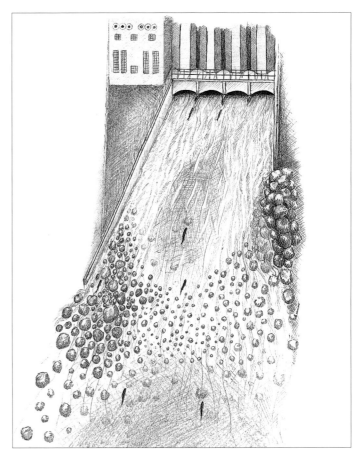

Dam site steelhead lies.

where the foam and current lines shape up and which turbines are open or shut. Slack waters behind dams do not concentrate fish. Occasionally a stray steelhead will roam these still waters out of curiosity and might be caught if it happens to bump into your line.

Any berm walls or other structural elements of the dam might hold congregating fish or create seams and holding lies. By studying the intersection of current and foam lines, one can often find, with accuracy, the holding water conducive for the take.

When steelhead negotiate fish ladders or dams, they exert a tremendous amount of energy and must rest to regenerate that energy, which is limited. If migration is primarily for spawning, the fish are not motivated to eat and replenish their stored fat and energy reserves. They possess a finite amount of power. If their energy is not conserved adequately, they will die. Usually dam sites harbor larger pools, brackish waters or impoundments directly above them where resting and holding water exists. If fish migrate in less-than-optimal water conditions—like the summer Skamania steelhead—their need to find cold water with dissolved oxygen is paramount for survival, so they will quickly seek out coldwater tributaries for comfort.

Hierarchical Domains in Holding Lies and Pools

Because of the aggressive nature of steelhead and the fact that a river possesses both optimal and less desirable waters, it makes sense that there would be competitive territorial behaviors exhibited when fish enter rivers. Since steelhead are forced at birth to battle the onslaught of man and nature with odds against their survival, the stream-smart, aggressive, and cocky fish that has reached adulthood is further developed in the unique environment of the freshwater Great Lakes ecosystem. Since it is at the top of the food chain and has no natural predator other than the occasional lamprey or man, this "king of the water's" attitude is quite apparent when hooked. When a silver torpedo takes to the air with violent headshakes, its pompous nature is quite apparent.

Though little has been written or researched in the scientific community concerning steelhead sociological behavior other than during the spawning process, how and where fish take up primary and secondary holding lies and utilize the varied river structure must surely be a consequence of individual personalities and dominance.

In *Steelhead Fly Fishing*, Trey Combs addressed this subject eloquently, with observations based on the various behaviors exhibited by the different genders caught in particular holding lies. His theories that dominant fish select and guard the primary lies while subordinate fish may be forced into less desirable lies holds true, especially when compared to angling success at the various sections of a river. The core of his theory is that large males often hold in the deepest, most comfortable lies in the gut of a pool while smaller fish hold in the stronger-flowing tops and bottoms of runs and pools.

When comparing notes, this holds merit and is true for the "big buck", twenty-pound-plus alpha males I have taken in Lake Michigan tributaries. My two largest, wild Michigan strain fish came in the winter months of December and February, when holding is the primary behavior at 34 degree water temperatures. Each struck in the deep gut of a pool at the bottom of the pocket water on classic riverbends. Here, the current flow and depth was ideal. Conversely, I have also taken smaller males and females from this identical lie, often in multiple hook-ups from the same spot in one hour, signifying that more than one fish will hold in a certain primary lie. One could also conclude that no larger, more dominant fish was around at the time, so inferior smaller fish took big daddy's lounge chair, just like your dog does when you are not sitting in it.

Thus, it makes complete sense to theorize that larger fish are more dominant and get prime holding territories. Yet, I am not completely convinced that a twenty-pound male is necessarily dominant over a twenty-pound female simply because of gender. I have witnessed an almost "step-back, watch out" attitude from males of all sizes when a large female moves into spawning position. It surprises me how gentlemanly the would-be suitors become as the sexual drive kicks in.

Silver females that I have caught in the fast water known as the throat or in the pool tailout have always been very fresh fish, usually in the six- to twelve-pound class. My larger females over 14 pounds came from the gut of classic riverbend pool in the same lies as the alpha males. Is it their dominance that puts the larger males and females in the deeper, slower waters, or could it be that smaller fish can tolerate and even prefer the faster flows where they are often caught? Could the pocket water or tailouts, which are known to have freshly migrating fish, be productive because of the sheer numbers of fish moving through them rather than these fish showing a preference for the flow? Or are they banished there by the larger, gut-lying big bullies? Unless someone does an underwater camera survey of these classic lies

A Christmas Eve 20-pound steelhead taken on the inside seam of riverbend pool. This dark, super-inflated male must have eaten well in the big lake, note the fatty deposits and stretch marks on its skin. We tagged the fish with a floy tag and named it "Jimmy Houston." Four months later, "Jimmy" was caught four miles downstream by Steve Stallard and released again.

from season to season, generation to generation, we will never know for sure. One thing for certain is the old saying, "steelhead and morel mushrooms are where you find them." Hierarchical enigmas will forever intrigue the steelhead angler.

Another dilemma arises when pools and runs fish well one year and poorly the next. On my home pool on Lake Michigan's Muskegon River, I have seen a pool fish remarkably well followed by several years of poor fishing—only to be followed by another excellent season. Atlantic salmon fishermen firmly believe that moving fish will not stop in a pool if it is void of fish. Thus, the pools that angle the best are usually a result of a few pioneering migrators stopping to pitch tents with the rest of the campers following in suit. Is there a pheromonal attraction elicited from pooled-up fish, even before the prime spawning times, which causes the desired congregating? Or can it be that the pools that attract steelhead and fish well in a particular season might have the ultimate qualities of flow, depth, temperature, shelter, structure, etc. for pooled-up holding to take place?

My gut feeling is that coincidence plays a meaningless role in steelhead migration. When studying why my home pool fished well in certain years and poorly in others I began to research current flows, water temperatures, depth and structure. Not surprisingly I found that my pool fished terrifically with higher flows and at deeper depths. In the drought years when flows and depths were low, the pool fished poorly. One year when the flows and depths were identical to the years it fished marvelously, the pool did not fish well despite good numbers of fish in the river. I was perplexed. Coincidentally, that year I noticed I was not getting bottom snags from what seemed to be a large tree trunk near the gut of the primary lie. Because of my hunger for mystery, I donned my scuba equipment and found no previous debris in the area where the lie was. Instead, I found heavily silted-over tree trunks and branches at the tailout of the pool, fully exposed which never existed there before. Was it the security that the tree afforded or a combination of all three factors: flow, depth, and security coming together to form the perfect situation? With the greater flow and depth, the pool becomes a gathering place. In the opposite scenario, fish quickly move through it. As a probing angler you can draw your own conclusion or this may remind you of similar situations that make you go, 'Hmm! Steelhead have a funny way of doing that.'

In conclusion, I feel that the behaviors associated with this hierarchical dominance in holding lies can only be applied when steelhead are allowed to behave in a natural and unmolested setting, as is often the case in Combs' hallowed rivers of British Columbia. In B.C., fly fishers practice catch and release for the most part and the rivers are relatively untamed.

Because of our Great Lakes "whack 'em, and stack 'em" philosophy of hammering the runs with heavy angling and harvest pressure, the large dominant steelhead holding in the perfect primary lie are usually caught quickly by the aggressive nature drift boat and jet-sled warriors that relentlessly pound the prime areas. True, natural steelhead behavior is not manifested on most of the popular Great Lakes rivers because of this philosophy.

I have fond memories of having Great Lakes streams and rivers to myself, I reveled in the way steelhead responded. Curious, striking aggressively, the pecking order in the lies—all was evident when the river was unmolested.

As Bob Dylan sang, maybe we should just, "sit and watch the river flow." Maybe we need to give the steelhead and rivers a rest once in awhile.

A chrome fall steelhead that struck a tangerine McFly Foam Clown Egg.

Weather Conditions
The Impact of Barometric Pressure and Light

The Great Lakes experience incredible variations in seasonal weather forces, we are often at the mercy of Mother Nature's whims. Storms, floods, droughts, and icy temperatures all have a strong impact on rivers, steelhead behavior and migrations. As steelheaders we have learned to live with inclement weather and have found that it often coincides with good or bad steelheading. I've experienced blistering snow squalls while fishing Salmon and Sandy creeks where I've had both incredible and miserable fishing. I've also had bright, calm sunny days where the fishing was equally as mixed.

I have discussed how water flows and temperatures influence steelhead to strike or sulk, migrate or hold. But there are days when conditions appear to be ideal and yet we get skunked.

Although once again there is not much data regarding weather conditions and the steelhead's eagerness to strike the fly, as anglers we often keep accurate diaries and journals on our forays. The dynamics of flow, clarity and temperature are usually hard indicators for judging steelhead-fishing success. But there are factors that often go ignored by steelhead that have a strong influence on their behaviors. Barometric pressure and light levels are two of the most important.

Barometric pressure theories vary widely from one steelhead expert to the next. I can only expound on my years of observation and the opinions of others that seem to share my beliefs.

It is a given that barometric pressure plays a strong role in anadromous and potamodromous salmonid migrating behavior. Since water is an ideal conductive medium for pressure, it definitely impacts aquatic vertebrate and invertebrate life in many ways. Hatches of insects are often surprisingly disappointing when big changes in pressure occur. This explains why they are so sporadic and unpredictable when different weather patterns occur.

Steelhead have a very sensitive air bladder system which adjusts to the various depths of a lake or river. It is logical to assume then that changes in pressure impact the fish positively or negatively. We often see steelhead porpoising on rivers or gulping at the surface looking as though they are taking invisible insects. It is commonly understood that this behavior is linked to the adjustment of their air bladder. They may gulp oxygen when exhausted after a long-fought battle with an angler or from the rigors of spawning.

A very chilled Dr. Don Cusamano with a heartwarming winter steelhead.

The stable atmospheric pressure at sea level is based on millibars at 29.92. This is a mean atmospheric pressure. Generally, low- to high-pressure systems are based against a variance from the other atmospheric system around them and generally range from 28.00 to 3100 mb.

Barometric pressure often indicates weather systems present or moving in lows and highs. In reviewing my steelheading success, coupled with barometric pressure at the time, I'm led to believe that seasonal preferences exist and are related to water temperatures and the fish's behavior at that particular time of season.

If we take a look at how weather has impacted steelhead migration for thousands of generations, we can hypothesize that migrations normally took place when low systems presented inclement weather with heavy rains and cloudy low-light conditions ideal for upstream movement. High pressure usually signaled sunlight and dry conditions, allowing for falling water which has the opposite effect on migration. *Which* barometric conditions are best for steelhead on the bite is still debatable. A strong indicator is any marked, quick change in barometric readings—falling lows or climbing highs—will usually put the bite off. These marked changes dictate the migrating urge on low-pressure systems and the holding and seeking of cover on high-pressure changes. Steelhead in these two conditions are often preoccupied with the task at hand and are less likely to show interest in the fly.

Seasonal variations occur in relationship with water temperatures and conditions. Each season shows steelhead preferring certain barometric conditions and weather patterns. Often a series of weather patterns or barometric pressure systems are favorable to producing good fly-taking in steelhead.

For instance, fall steelheading begins anywhere from September and lasts to December. Water flow and temperature are very crucial, since the urge to spawn has not yet manifested in any strong persistent upstream migration. Autumn flows are usually low from the summer periods. Critical to a run is a strong runoff or river spate from rains on a low barometric pressure system. A lake tributary low and clear and void of steelhead will become teeming with fish after rains virtually overnight. Thus a low-pressure system which triggers the run and remains constant, at say 27.92 for instance, will put fish on the move and probably off the bite. If a high-pressure system gets in after the low front, and holding lies exist, the bite will be on big time, since the fish will assume primary taking lies and the pressure could stabilize, at 30.16 for example.

Comparing all of my seasonal record keeping and my clients' angling success with the computerized records of the National Climatological Record Keeping Center in Tennessee, a stable barometric pressure reading in the low 30.00s seems to be the magic number for the steelhead bite in the fall, winter and spring. This reading can take place under two different conditions. I recall a March 22, 1999 date with Dick Barch, devoted steelhead angler, on the Muskegon River with cold sleeting weather and steelhead heavy on the grab, deep-mouth hookups and violent fights—chromer steelhead in "the ultimate knock-your-rod-off" mood. The barometric pressure that morning was 30.01 and steady.

On April 7, 1999, with client Jim Leopardo and gang, fishing the same run under clear and cold weather conditions with similar water levels and temperatures, but with a dense fog, the fish went on a similar violent bite. Many trophy steelhead in the 12- to 18-pound range chased after our small Speys and hammered Hexagenia Nymphs—it was gangbusters. Barometric pressure under the high frontal system that morning was 30.16. The 30.01 of March and 30.16 of April were both the daily high-pressure readings at the time, yet under two different weather systems: one cloudy and icy, the other clear and sunny. It is interesting to note that as the day progressed on April 7th, the fishing success dropped dramatically as the pressure fell to 29.81, in fact it virtually shut down. Could the drop in pressure cause the fish to move and ignore our flies? It's possible.

Several constants seem to be critical for steelhead angling based on my records. A relatively stable, somewhat high pressure in the low 30.00s seems to produce the big steelhead bite. Also any sudden deviance from a stable reading tends to result in poor angling. Is instability a signal for certain behavior—moving or sulking? Are a series of fluctuations coupled with a stable high the magic ingredient for success?

Steelheaders are always on a mystical quest for the "magic bite," we put up with a lot of crappy weather, frequent ugly days and the rare good days. Some go to fortune-tellers, palm readers, carry good luck charms and flies, or wear garlic around their necks in superstition. Though all of this has an element of good-hearted humor and merit, one thing is for certain, it sure as hell makes sense to pay attention to barometric pressure.

When the fly fisher is presented with falling barometric pressure and inclement weather, target the "moving water" of pockets and tailouts with gaudy and bright marabou Speys and streamers. If given the good fortune of stable high pressure, concentrate on all the primary holding lies with a complete arsenal of methods and fly patterns. (Note: many outdoor watches are now made with barometric pressure gauges—invaluable!)

Though consistent high-pressure patterns are ideal for the bite, consistently low barometric pressure readings—from 27 to 29 mb—can also produce equally outstanding fishing. If the low-pressure system has been stable for some time, the bite is often fantastic. However, if given a choice between a consistent high or low—the high pressure seems to produce more hook-ups. Consistency is obviously a strong component of success, particularly in fall, winter and spring steelheading, however, summer steelhead respond positively when strong and stormy barometric pressure systems occur. Since they are often exposed to less-than-ideal high-pressure systems with hot sunshine, warm and low rivers, a strong low-pressure system signals relief and brings cooler rains, darkness, etc. that are ideal for the bite.

As for light levels affecting a steelhead's predisposition to strike the fly, one must look at the way a steelhead views its world, its behavior at varying light levels, and seasonal water temperature interactions.

When you look at the basic components, a steelhead's eye functions much like a human eye in that it has receptors in the back of the eye that transmit light and color. Rods transmit light energy for vision. Cones relay spectral color. Rods are very sensitive and specific to the varying amount of light available from dawn to dusk and alert the brain which triggers active or passive behavior.

Though not as light-sensitive as a brown trout or other *Salmo* species, steelhead or rainbows have evolved from western Continental Divide waters where they have more sunlight days than Scotland's Loch Laven district and its brown trout. However the Pacific Northwest and a good portion of the Great Lakes sees inclement stormy and cloudy weather for a good deal of time when steelhead enter the rivers in fall, winter, and spring. It's not uncommon to have thirty continual days of overcast clouds and fog from lake-effect climatic conditions in Michigan. Similarly, the Pacific Northwest often sees the same. One can conclude that steelhead prefer low-light conditions since they coincide with the majority of their seasonal migration and they normally function aggressively and with curiosity when it comes to striking the fly.

The optimum steelhead fishing times of dusk and dawn coincide with their habitual behavior of feeding in the Great Lakes. Steelhead in the big-lake environment will target schools of baitfish at low-light levels so their advances are more cloaked.

Also, as a result of their Pacific lineage, behavioral patterns shaped on the West Coast to the morning and evening vertical drift of squids—the primary food source of Pacific steelhead—may have something to do with their feistiness at dusk and dawn. In the Great Lakes, we have a similar migration of *Mysis* shrimp.

Low-light periods correlate with the coldest water temperatures, which are very important to summer steelhead and early fall fish that often encounter hot spells and less-than-desirable water temperatures.

A steelhead's willingness to take the fly during these low-light periods is quite evident when you research anglers' journals. Because there is less boat traffic and man-induced noise, the fish feel more secure. Low light does not bounce shadows and refract bright sun rays, both of which startle fish.

Steelheaders lend some credence to the solar/lunar calendar in the *Farmer's Almanac*. Their "best days to fish" calendars based on these cycles seem to be of high value to generations of

After a long day probing for winter steelhead with no success, a fat chrome hen strikes at dusk, making Bruce Barbour a very happy steelheader.

anglers. How exactly they affect steelhead is a big question, one that will probably never be answered. Since migratory fish respond to the changing diurnal cycle, it is logical to assume that steelhead migrations are affected by variations in the duration of daily sunlight.

During cold weather, strong light improves angling conditions by warming the water and rousing the steelhead's dormant metabolism. Often a two- to three-degree change in the water temperature can motivate the steelhead to strike the fly.

Also of importance to note, changing barometric pressure systems and varying light levels may impact the steelhead angler psychologically, causing them to fish less effectively. When it's cold, windy and/or wet, we tend to gripe about the less-than-ideal conditions and often lose focus and, more importantly, confidence in our presentations. For obvious reasons, wind can make fly fishing difficult, if not impossible. High sun and glare makes reading water trickier for the novice steelheader. Low light often means not seeing what you are doing.

In summary, the complex interaction between the natural and man-influenced variables impacts steelhead fishing and steelhead behavior. To achieve steelhead-river mastery one must become intimate with all of the variables and adjust accordingly. When your success is achieved through your ability to understand opportunities and capitalize on them, the rewards are all the greater.

Chapter 4

Seasons: Autumn

A bright harvest moon ushers in the cool crisp nights along the shoreline. The foliage is ablaze in crimson and gold against the tea-colored Great Lakes rivers as if to decorate for the arrival of their long-gone prodigal sons and daughters that frolicked and fed in their nursery waters as tiny parr and smolts. With each passing fall, I look at the trees with a new respect.

Great Lakes steelhead rivers are synonymous with forests. When I liked a particular river it was perhaps its banks that drew me. In autumn, the broad-leaf maples, oaks, and sycamores are overwhelming with tones from reddish-orange to soft pastel yellow. Salt and pepper birches and the old, enduring greenery of the towering pines fill the color spectrum in this magnificent autumn gallery. It's as if Mother Nature has put on a final fireworks display to announce the transition from the bountiful life of summer to the harsh and unforgiving winter to come. Fall steelheading brings me close to the startled excitement of a flushed grouse as I hike the river's paths looking for pools with silver linings. I see deer turn from their summer carelessness to a frightened awareness as the first shots of the gun season are heard. I occasionally find a wounded deer that couldn't be tracked by a disgruntled hunter sipping its last gulps of water while it sadly lies on its side in the grips of mortality. Since life as we know it evolved from the sea, all of creation seems to be drawn to waters in a mystical magnetism.

The life-to-death saga unfolds beautifully in the fall runs of chinook and coho salmon. Here, they fulfill the journey's highest

On an autumn morning, as the stream and fog cast a pastel-colored collage against the rising sun, an angler's rod is bent with a steelhead hook-up. This scene occurs daily from New York's Salmon River to Michigan's Big Manistee.

priority of procreation in their gravel birthplace, which then becomes their grave as they leave their genetic programming for future generations. In a final sacrifice to the gods of nature they donate their decaying carcasses back to the food chain to nourish the newly created life and feed these parentless offspring.

Encountering fall steelhead with a fly rod is an exhilarating experience. These paragons of sporting superiority are unmatched in their tenacity—except for perhaps the noble leaper, Atlantic salmon. It is the electricity of the aggressive take, the strong hard drives, the exhilarating, cartwheeling leaps, and their uncanny ability to leave the angler's line trembling, that creates the addictive narcotic requiring repeat encounters.

It is in the autumn months that the steelhead fly fisher of the Great Lakes can successfully pursue their sport in a true West Coast fashion—fishing traditionally established methods.

Yet I wonder if there is such a thing as tradition anymore. We are still evolving our own Great Lakes sporting legacy which began barbarically with treble snag hooks, moved humbly forward to spawn sacks and sponges, lead and yarn, and evolved further still to methods with sink-tips, classic steelhead flies and two-handed rods. I believe reference to tradition should be left purely for subjective gratification, much like the fisher who insists on fishing solely with a rod built of fine Tonkin cane.

If I had but one season to enjoy our Great Lakes steelhead it would be forever autumn. In this season we find the fish moving into rivers under ideal water temperatures, with normally consistent flows, and with their savage attitude to strike the fly never more firmly intact. Coupled with the fact that the fish's spawning urge—which often distracts it from its playful curiosity—is not eminently apparent, we see our steelhead behave the way it does in its big-water environment—as an aggressive hunter and predator, fearless and confident. Given these flexible angling parameters, fall steelhead can be pursued with various fly fishing methods based on personal preference.

How and Why Fall Runs Occur

One of the most common questions asked by steelhead anglers is why fall upstream migrations occur, even though the spring spawning drive is still many months later.

One must first understand that fall runs will not always occur in a particular year nor will they always be significant in numbers. The duration and numbers of fish in a fall run is directly related to water temperatures, flows, weather factors and healthy steelhead populations with a good mixture of year classes in the big lake. I have witnessed incredible runs one season, followed by virtually non-existent runs the next year.

Growing up in the Great Lakes and catching my first steelhead—which was in the fall—I read every article in sporting magazines about fall fishing. Today I look back with humor on some of the material that was written to describe the fall fishery. Most writers alluded to the fact that steelhead run up fall rivers to "gorge themselves" on the caviar of spawning salmon. Today I find it hard to believe that steelhead swimming around in one of the Great Lakes will intentionally swim many miles up a river because once they get there they will have tons of salmon eggs to feast on. Though steelhead love to eat loose salmon eggs once in the river, unrelated conditions brings them on an upstream migration.

One of the most significant factors for a successful fall run is the "window of opportunity" brought about by water temperature and flows. This occurs uniquely in each of the Great Lakes based on weather factors and water temperatures of the lake and its adjacent rivers. Once the big-lake shoreline water temperatures

cool down to the upper 50s through the low-40s, steelhead move into the shore area from their big-lake environment. Shore anglers fishing from beaches and piers often catch them.

If river temperatures coincide with beach temperatures and there is significant flows emanating from the tributaries, the window of opportunity for migration is ideal. Since steelhead have evolved to show preference for flow and currents they will nose their way up river systems creating a fall run. Just how long the run will last or the amount of fish that will choose the river depends on how long this ideal window is open—meaning consistent temperatures and flows. For instance, if an ideal window exists for the first week in November due to mild and seasonable weather, and is quickly followed by frigid cold weather which lowers the tributaries' water temperatures to undesirable levels in the low to mid-30s, a run can shut down as quickly as it begins. I recall the fall run of 1998 when El Niño weather patterns created balmy and above-average weather for November and December. This kept the ideal conditions consistent for as long as eight weeks. The fall run that year was outstanding and thousands of steelhead migrated up river systems throughout the Great Lakes.

Temperature factors seem to be more important than flow, fish will tolerate low flows given the proper temperatures. This was very apparent in Ohio Lake Erie tributaries in December of 1998. Fishing the Chagrin River near Cleveland with guides Mike Bennett and Brian Fleishig, we had unbelievable double-digit hook-ups on the river using tiny size-18 Bead-head Nymphs, strike indicators and light 5X tippets. This incredible fishing was due to the extremely low and clear waters. Since droughts ran rampant throughout the Great Lakes in 1998, any pool that had enough water to harbor the Chagrin's steelhead held considerable numbers of fish from five to fourteen pounds. It was an incredible sight to see fish stacked up in pools like at hatchery raceways. The very cold nights and warm days balanced the river temperatures in the preferred ranges for steelhead—45-56 degrees F.

Genetic makeup is another factor which sends steelhead up rivers in the fall. Since our Great Lakes fish are comprised of many strains from Pacific West Coast stocks, some rivers and strains show a greater predisposition to run in the summer and

With beautiful fall colors as a backdrop, a happy steelheader lands a broad-shouldered wild winter-strain Michigan steelhead taken on a steelhead orange Glo Bug. Fall steelhead are ravenous feeders on Pacific salmon eggs, and hunt for them relentlessly. Curt Collins with a Muskegon River fall steelhead.

fall because of the large river systems often negotiated. Through evolutionary molding, successful fish needed to get a head start on river migration to make it to higher headwater spawning areas by late winter or spring. This genetic signal varies from strain to strain and within individual fish, and there appears to be no rhyme or reason as to when a specific fish will migrate during non-specific spawning drives.

Secondary factors, which are much more theoretical yet may have some significance on fall runs, are schooling behavior and pheremonal attraction. Since the Great Lakes are giant fishbowls with salmonids roaming and hunting in schools or individually, the strong communal bonding of these schools often sends the whole pod upriver, especially at spawning times. The fall run of chinook and coho salmon is a significant hormonal drive and is spawning-specific. Often when an angler encounters a school of coho salmon on a spawning run up river, they will catch the miscellaneous steelhead and brown trout mixed in with them. This may happen as a result of the communal bond of the schooling groups that have hunted baitfish together for extended periods of time. Though the biological clock of the Pacific salmon sends it up the river to spawn, the occasional steelhead, brown, coaster brook trout, etc., will go along for the ride.

The concept of "eating caviar" may have some validity in triggering an upriver migration, but it is difficult to prove scientifically and can only be considered hypothetically. Since pheromones are elicited by all animals, the pheromones given off by significant numbers of lovesick and sexually active salmon might trigger steelhead to run rivers, as they are attracted to the powerful scent of the upstream orgy. On arrival, the steelhead gladly partakes in the egg-eating at this Roman-style orgy.

Finally, it is important to note that even when the window of opportuny for ideal fall migration exists, there must be significant populations and year classes of steelhead in the big lakes. The Great Lakes steelhead populations are directly related to the harvest numbers of charter captains working the big-lake waters. In the early and mid-1990s when significant declines in chinook and coho populations occurred due to BKD (bacterial kidney disease) and other infections, charter boats targeted the "scum line" fisheries which develop at considerable distances from shore. These are areas of thermocline demarcations where upwelling waters funnel significant food sources and concentrate steelhead populations near the surface. In the years when charter fleet harvests were high, steelhead runs dropped significantly in the Great Lakes tributaries. In the mid- to late 1990s, when the baitfish populations surged and the chinook and coho populations were significant, the charter fleets stayed relatively close to shore and targeted the easier salmon, thus accounting for the significant steelhead runs of 1998 and 1999.

Phases of Fall Steelheading

Since fall-running steelhead are not biologically driven like spawning salmon, there are wide variances from fish to fish regarding migration. In some short Class II low-gradient river systems, migration can be rather quick due to the lack of strong current and fairly flat and structureless waters to negotiate. On Class I waters with stronger flows, classic high-gradient structures and considerable distances in the watershed, migration can be slow or staged at the convenience of the steelhead. Since there is no hurry to get anywhere at this time of year, the steelhead exhibit curious behaviors, particularly when it comes to striking the fly.

Though all steelhead might be *Oncorynchus mykiss*, the more you fish for them, the more you realize that they have quite varying personalities, particularly when comparing strains, year classes

and genders. Early fall migrators that ascend the river rapidly and show great tenacity to strike are often the two- to three-year-old class, chrome-colored "jacks" or "skippers." These are usually sixteen- to eighteen-inch fish that spend only one summer in the big lake before coming up the river in the fall. They behave opportunistically and feed heavily on the salmon eggs, nymphs and food forms available. They are often the first fall steelhead caught by fly fishers targeting chinook and coho salmon near gravel beds. These jacks will hammer an egg or nymph pattern readily in the pockets and gravel runs in the salmon spawning grounds. They are also quite vulnerable to streamer and Spey flies fished with down-and-across swings or stripped aggressively streamer style.

Many rivers and streams in the Great Lakes which host fall runs usually exhibit gender-specific migrations. For instance, on my home river, the Muskegon, on the eastern Lake Michigan basin, our fall run is made up predominantly of males, with the occasional female. Some tributaries that drain into Lake Superior and Erie show a strong predominance of females in the fall run. In rivers such as Michigan's Au Sable, the run is evenly divided. The factors that account for these variances are uncertain and may have no merit. Perhaps the male steelhead in the fall migration are more dominant in their territorial holding and taking lies, and thus more apt to get caught. From an evolutionary and biological standpoint, it would make sense for the females to winter over in the big-lake environment, getting fatter and stronger to endure the rigors of spring spawning and to protect her precious cargo of eggs.

Fall runs usually appear when salmon spawning has peaked or is tailing off. Look for good migrations when Indian summer conditions bring warm temperatures and significant precipitation raises water levels.

Fall runs can be quite significant in some river systems and may be small to non-existent in others. In Lake Michigan tributaries with consistent subterranean ground flow levels and wild reproduction (such as the Little Manistee River), studies have shown that as much as 60% of the season's spawning run is in the river by winter (Seelbach). On several Class III waters with steep gradients, winter shelf ice and often-low fall trickles, 80% to 90% of the run will occur when snow melt and rains make the waters negotiable and tolerable in spring (J. George). These waters usually exist in the harsher climate areas, such as

A purple Spey fly against an autumn background.

Lake Superior's North Shore or in some of Lake Ontario's and Lake Erie's tributaries.

Since wild strains dominate these systems, they have evolved in the short 125-year history of the Great Lakes steelhead era to run these rivers at maximum spawning success times and often with individual fish demonstrating repeat spawnings.

In the initial phase of the fall run, steelhead will quickly take advantage of the egg-eating opportunities near salmon spawning beds, and can usually be found in the pockets and pools directly below the salmon redds in relatively shallow areas. Since the initial phase of fall steelheading can take place as early as September or October, it is often common to have warmer weather with coinciding stream water temperatures. Under these conditions the need for dissolved oxygen drives the steelhead into these faster runs; thus they feed opportunistically on the eggs and dislodged nymphs and larvae from female salmon digging redds. Because of the large male chinook salmon's aggressive need for territorial dominance, steelhead know better than to get too close to the spawning activity. I have seen many a fresh flesh wound on a fall steelhead which got a little too close to a pod of large-toothed, aggressive spawning males.

Once salmon finish spawning for the season the steelhead will seek deeper flows and holding waters to winter-over in the river. They will usually drop back into the pools and flats, and slow their metabolism to coincide with the falling water temperatures. The large majority of fall-run fish will stay in the river all winter until the coming spring spawn. In some Class II short tributaries, they may bounce back down to the big lake or hop-scotch around several other tributaries before spring arrives.

As the steelhead holds over through the winter, the chrome and steel colors of the fresh-run fish will darken considerably, particularly in the males where they are darker green with a bright crimson cheek-to-tail stripe.

The Ultimate Autumn Steelhead Lie: The Tailout and the Invasion of the Zebra Mussel

I've always managed to catch fall steelhead in the tailouts of pools. Often I come upon the fish by chance after my fly presentations swing out of a deeper pool. Sometimes I target these areas specifically.

It wasn't until the startling invasion of the zebra mussel in our Michigan rivers in 1999—which caused the Muskegon, Manistee and Au Sable rivers' water to become so impeccably clear—that I learned the true importance of this river lie.

For years, our waters flowed with natural peat and tannic stains from the bogs and forests that surrounded them, until, almost overnight, they became shockingly clear. The tiny, exotic zebra mussel—which was brought to the Great Lakes from Russia's Caspian Sea in the ballast of oceangoing freighters—can filter up to 20 liters of water a day. Not only do they rob the life-giving plankton from the ecosystem, they act as one giant water purifier.

Michigan rivers have suffered a three-year drought (1997-2000) due to a lack of snowfall and summer precipitation (thanks to El Niño and La Niña). Our rivers were not only running critically low but also amazingly clearly. *Seeing* dozens of the once-elusive fall steelhead skittishly hiding and running around our rivers was kind of cool at first—sort of like looking at fish in a giant aquarium. It was a confirmation of sorts to see fish holding in lies where they should. It was also frustrating to cast to a run for hours, only to lift the anchor on a drift boat and go over several dozen chrome steelhead in the 12- to 14-pound range that had been there all the while you fished your flies.

In a short amount of time, it became quite apparent that fall steelhead worshiped the outside bend of a pool tailout. Time

after time, we would ride over fish with our drift boats spooking them, yet they always returned to the same tailouts.

If you watch plug-pullers, they consistently set up their plug-trawling boats on the pool flats just before the tailout. The reason for the fall steelhead's preference for this area started to become logically clear.

The outside bend of a tailout had perhaps the least concentrated flow in the river—its comfortable seams were ideal, in the perfect 45- to 55-degree autumn water temperature range. Its bottom structure consisted predominantly of rocky boulders which were the start or finish of a gradient cutting the rocky moraine of the river channel. Many underground springs occurred here, attracting the steelhead.

If the tailout was paired with large wooded debris, the fish found the ultimate holding water along with a primary lie.

In the long run, the infestation of the zebra mussel in the Great Lakes steelhead fishery has caused us to change our tactics. Now we must use 18-foot leaders down to four-pound-test fluorocarbon tippets. The fish have become extremely nervous. Chances are if you can see them, they can see you—and you'll be hard pressed for a hook-up.

Early morning and dusk hours are the time to fish. Long casts and Spey rods will allow 100-foot-plus presentations in the big rivers, increasing your odds of a hook-up in the normally low and clear waters of autumn. Petite Speys (sizes 10-14), like those tied by John Valk on the clear Grand River on the Canadian side of Lake Erie, are becoming increasingly popular.

Will our steelhead fisheries take on the complex characteristics of spring-creek fly fishing? For the most part it already has. One thing is for certain, it will only challenge us to become more competent at our art. The dry fly is looking more and more likely as the future fly of choice—could it be "good-bye Glo Bug?" Only time, and natural selection, will tell.

Tactics for Fall Steelhead

Providing that water temperatures remain in the desired range of 38 to 58 degrees freshly migrated chromer steelhead or holding fish that have been in the system will take the fly aggressively throughout the entire season. By fishing various presentations, the fall steelheader can pursue the fall run well into the winter months.

Fall steelhead love the slow currents of a tailout. This is a great place to swing a Spey fly near the surface where a large surface window is available to these fish. When coupled with large wooded debris and a deep hole, all holding needs are met.

This enormous fall steelhead—caught by Norm Rosenberg on Michigan's Muskegon Rivers—slammed a chartreuse Tasmanian Devil as the guide was grilling chicken for afternoon lunch. Who says sunny afternoons are slow?

There is no question that a fresh fall chromer will provide the most powerful battles, with spectacular aerial leaps. It would be wise for the steelheader to target these fish at first light in the faster-moving throat/pocket waters, pursuing holding fish later in the day or evening. Moving water is usually in high-gradient areas with narrow river bends, this congests the migrating fall fish,that usually arrive at dusk and early evenings. At first light they occupy holding and taking lies and are quite aggressive for the angler who has first-water advantage.

Steelhead detect scents as low as 3 parts per million, thus bringing them back to their gravel place of birth or their stocking site. The nose of a steelhead is like the eye of an eagle—sharp, focused and constantly on the hunt. Fresh chromers often fall victim to spawn-bag fishermen because of their extremely aggressive and curious nature and the powerful scent of the spawn. For consistent day-in, day-out action, one should start off with high-stick, bottom-bouncing drift-fishing techniques using egg patterns varying in styles from traditional Glo Bugs, Clown Eggs, Nuke Bugs, Pom-pons and Crystal Omelets, in tangerine, baby pink and chartreuse.

Since I don't consider myself a purist steelheader (whatever that actually means), I've often experimented with various scents applied to egg patterns. They work remarkably well and will increase your chances of steelhead hook-ups dramatically. Since I practice catch-and-release and do not use the scent in fly-fishing-only waters, I have experienced no catastrophic damage from this practice—though I respect the opinion of anglers who find this offensive.

If I've piqued your curiosity, you may want to try bottled liquid pheromone mixtures geared specifically for salmon and steelhead. WD-40, anise oil and shrimp scents work well also. Though steelhead will take egg patterns without scent, you are more likely to be successful when matching the food with its proper scent. Aquatic insects have no scent other than the water in which they live and usually require no such scent-induced applications.

A down-and-across wet-fly swing, with either a single- or two-handed rod, is equally as effective for fresh migrating fish. Floating, intermediate or sink-tip lines can be used based on the various water depths and flows encountered. The trick is to cover the holding lie at the peak of the presentation. At this point, the fly swings broadside into the taking area at the proper depth and speed. Proper mending to produce depth penetration and casting well up from the lie are important to target the strike zone. Cover every possible taking lie of the pocket/throat water from top to bottom.

Fall steelheaders often make the mistake of using wet flies, Speys or streamers that are way too small. Fly fishers can learn a great deal by observing the plug-puller. The West Coast technique of plug-fishing Wiggle Warts and Hot-N-Tots is very popular in the Great Lakes and is extremely effective in the fall. Since the freshly migrating fish still have their aggressive search-and-destroy mentality, they will slam plugs that appear to be too large—up to five inches long. Dynamic colors like orange, gold, pink and chartreuse, combined with blue, purple and black, can be quite deadly. The powerful attraction of these plug-angling methods have had me perplexed since young adulthood.

Fresh fall-run steelhead go through many phases in terms of what they will strike. At times, the bait-fisher using spawn does extremely well; during that time fly fishers can duplicate this with yarn and possibly scent. The plug-puller and spin-fisherman may do extremely well at specific times while the bait-fisher has poor fishing. The key is to duplicate the bouncing, throbbing action a

plug can achieve in a stationary environment, which eventually antagonizes steelhead. My early angling development started me down the road to solving this enigma.

New-Age Great Lakes Spey Flies

Scotland is a place of open spaces, stark mountains, raging winds, steady rainfall, and glacier-carved valleys. It's also home to the noble sporting traditions of Atlantic salmon fishing and upland bird shooting. For the connoisseur of distilled spirits, the Macallan Distillers age highly aromatic and peaty single malt scotches in sherry casks.

The Valley of the River Spey is also the birthplace of the deadly Spey fly—the most reliable flies gillies have used for centuries.

As stark as the land surrounding the river, the first Speys were lackluster in appearance. Traditionally, bronze mallard wings were tented over wool of dark and earth-tone colors; palmered by hackle from a heron or Spey cock saddle, a local farm-raised capon. Ribbing of French tinsel fastened the feathers. Hooks developed on the River Dee rounded out the pattern with their fine-wire, long-shanked silhouette.

In long, deep pools and soft eddies and river flats, the Spey fly responds to even the subtlest currents, breathing life unto itself. When lethargic salmonids hold in clear pools, the Spey fly agitates, thus provoking a strike. Today's Speys, tied with time-honored materials, synthetic reflectors, and motion-stimulated materials like rubber hackle, are lethal.

As a teenager, I chased fall steelhead in the icy, greenish-blue waters of the Niagara Gorge. On many trips I met with failure and frustration—the steelhead were very finicky at times. The exasperating hike down the Devil's Hole section and, worse yet, the straight 150-foot ascent back up, allowed plenty of time for contemplation. In a strange parallel, I think back to Albert Camus' *Myth of Sisyphus*. Sisyphus rolled his stone uphill, only to have it fall back down, and thus he would repeat the process, all the while contemplating his eternal damnation. My absurdity revolved around the steelhead's unwillingness to accept my fluorescent yarn flies in the clear pools. As I walked back up, I felt a lot like Sisyphus, as I rolled my personal stone of fishing frustration, which bore down heavily on my sporting ego.

After several trips to the local bait shop where I perused the dusty fly boxes that had long been forgotten, I eyed several old

Fall and winter marabou Speys and Buggers against a backdrop of snow.

trout streamers and wet flies. Much to the surprise of the tackle shop owner, who was gloating over his new display of fluorescent lures that drew business to his shop, I bought a few tattered, motley-looking brown and dark-blue wet flies. I still recall the puzzled look in his eyes as I asked about the price of the flies. I'm sure he was ready to throw them out.

After bringing a mint-silver steelhead to the snowy bank the next day, I ran to the tackle shop with the tattered blue fly dangling from the 12-pound male's mouth. Looking back on this experience, I see a curious boy searching for solutions often overlooked by adults mired down in their comfort and complacency.

Fourteen years later, after moving to Indiana, I was poised for another challenge: summer-run Skamania steelhead. Most of northern Indiana's steelheaders were spinner and spawn-sac fishermen; I had no legacy from which to work. Because the streams lacked current, I sought patterns that were motion-stimulated, tied with materials like marabou, Ultra Hair, Flashabou and rubber hackle. Some flies were tied in hot pink and orange for aggressive fresh-run fish, while others were tied in black and dark purple for fish that had been spooked and tormented by the hardware bombardiers. The breathing quality of the flies was responsible for taking 20-pound Skamanias, much to the amazement of my hardware-throwing counterparts. One other fisherman had success: the nightcrawler dunker. Why? Motion without movement. Pieces of the puzzle were slowly moving into place.

After moving to Grand Rapids, I was impressed with Michigan's west coast and the Upper Peninsula's peaty, tea-colored rivers. Most appealing was the fact that wild steelhead took small stonefly, caddis and *Hexagenia* nymph patterns. I pursued this methodology avidly, using 4X tippets and size-12 flies to fool highly stressed and spooked wild steelhead.

On a November day on the White River, I was brought back to the origins I had all too quickly forgotten—Stimulator flies that probed the heart and mind of steelhead.

Steve Stallard, an excellent steelheader, fly-tier, and angling companion, showed me a box of new black, purple and electric blue patterns. Inspired by a Trout Unlimited lecture I gave upon my arrival in Michigan—which was received with much cynicism by the local naturalistic-imitation school of steelheaders—Stallard showed me a box of impressionistic patterns. With them, he had landed 12- and 14-pound male steelhead that attacked these "new wave" flies. Meanwhile, I watched in amazement as I fished my stonefly and Hex nymphs, enjoying a relaxing and fishless afternoon. The next day, I returned to the same spot, armed with Stallard's patterns. I had my hands full, fighting aggressive steelhead at dusk. Because of the experience, I believe that the Spey patterns presented motion stimulation and novelty. It was a case of showing the fish something different.

Stallard's flies combine classic patterns and materials with new-age synthetics. The flies only *resemble* what the fish eat, rather than specifically imitating something from their diet. Because the flies don't duplicate nature, Stallard calls the patterns forage "concepts and "impressions." "There are times when attractor materials like Flashabou, Krystal Flash, etc. just don't cut it," Stallard says. "That's when the fly fisher must go back to the stark basics in color—let the fish decide. MWM (motion without movement) is the key to the new-age Great Lakes Spey fly's success."

Materials used for the patterns may consist of expensive and exotic items like Spey hackle and jungle-cock, as well as more common materials like marabou, tinsel, dyed Angora goat, blue-eared pheasant, bunny strips, possum, silk, turkey-butt, mallard and teal wings, schlappen, Flashabou, Krystal Flash, and dyed Indian saddle hackle.

Beautiful purple, blue and silver sheen on an Atlantic salmon resting in the turquoise waters of Michigan's St. Mary's River after a hard-fought battle.

Further exploration into "motion without movement" came from fly patterns inspired by famous West Coast fly anglers like Mel Krieger and Bob Hull who experimented with rabbit strips to produce moving, undulating patterns like the Steelhead Bunny and String Leech. These flies can be worked with slow pulsating and rolling action, driving fall steelhead crazy, just as Wiggle Warts do for pluggers. Colors for classic fall steelhead wets, Speys, and leech streamers, should incorporate varying color motifs. Orange, yellow, and gold is one effective combination. Pink and chartreuse with natural tones is another. Electric blue, purple, and black is one of the most effective. Be creative and use time-honored materials combined with flashy modern synthetics. Realistic baitfish imitations are

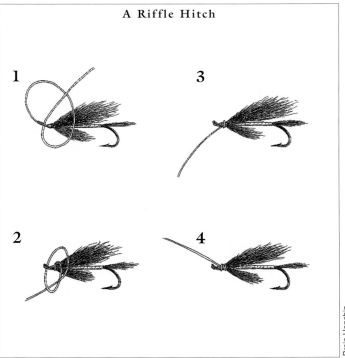

A Riffle Hitch

1

3

2

4

Brain Hanchin

often very effective on extremely fresh fall-run steelhead. Since their baitfish feeding instinct is still strong, white, silver, gray, and blue alewife and smelt streamers work well, as do white rabbit and marabou leeches.

I came up with a series of marabou Speys that, when tied effectively, can do all the damage of a plug-pulling Hot n Tot and Wiggle Wart drop-back fisher to get explosive strikes. The Metallica Spey marabou Spey series incorporates marabou tied sparsley in two-color combinations (one strand of marabou), the sparseness of marabou creates more movement. Long, thin strands of electric red, blue, purple, orange and silver Flashabou dangle and shimmer off the tail several inches back and provide amazing movement. When tied with a riffle-hitch knot, the pattern wiggles sideways like a plug. The hot marabou color combinations include black and purple, fire orange and lighter orange, hot pink and white, and chartruese and black.

Fusion Steelheading

Finally, as far as the motion without movement frontier is concerned—and my yearning to eliminate all boundaries in presentation to maximize steelheading success—I have come up with the notion of fusion steelheading. With this technique, I am aware that I am going out on a limb and begging for criticism since many purists will scoff at this approach, not considering it to be fly fishing. If you take a good look at the various methods used in big-game fly fishing today, you will constantly see barriers being broken. Are large, glass-body, Mylar, epoxy baitfish streamers really flies or duplicates of Rapala lures? Are shooting heads really fly lines? Do anti-reverse and large-arbor reels replicate big-game trolling reels? I believe tradition is nothing more than one's subjective feelings or orientation decided upon purely for the sake of personal emotional gratification. We are constantly breaking tradition each time a new product comes out in the high-tech fishing business.

My fusion steelhead techniques employ methods like using the gyrating, flashing, and spinning Cheaters (Spin n Glos), designed by Beau-Mac Company of Washington State. Under the direction of Mary Lou Beaupre, they make an incredible array of prismatic Cheaters that create movement when added to steelhead wet flies, Speys or Bunny Leeches.

When spin Cheaters are coupled with egg patterns, particularly the Egg Omelets that use rabbit tails, the results can be impressive. This presentation should be fished classic drift-fishing style on shooting lines. If you go a step further and apply scent to this drift rig, you will include all variables a steelhead targets: motion, movement, olfactory signal, and color.

Other fusion techniques include incorporating odd materials such as hula-hoop rubber legs into your leech patterns, with the addition of rattling optic eyes, and glow-in-the-dark materials like glow yarn. These concepts cover virtually the entire spectrum of presentations a fly-fisher can make.

The concepts of fusion methods originated from my life-long desire to use the fly rod, fly reel, line other than pure monofilament, and lure which on presentation is considered by all broad classifications to be a fly. When hardware and bait fishermen are successful, particularly in high, off-colored waters, fly anglers often fail and flail away at the water. With fusion techniques, you can be very effective, often outfishing the competition.

If a fall steelhead fly angler chooses to incorporate fusion methods, they have one powerful weapon in their angling arsenal that the hardware and bait fishing steelheaders cannot duplicate effectively—the ability to realistically produce the natural's imitation and deliver it on a fly-line system that is essential for the best presentation.

Silver, pink and gray adorn this beautiful Skamania summer steelhead.

The motion-without-movement and fusion methods are geared toward a fresh-run fall steelhead's aggressive behavior and once conditions for permanent holding behaviors arise, the winter-over fish's attitude changes markedly towards hibernation, caution, and refuge. Here is a fish that has survived the hammering of plug-pullers with their hefty, brightly colored offerings, wised-up to the smell of freshly fished spawn, and has been bombarded by wading and boat anglers in search of the charismatic fall leaper.

Steelhead hold in the currentless bottom of dark pools and tailout flats and become a little more selective about when they choose to pick a fight with an angler. Strong drifts of aquatic insects such as *Hexagenia* nymphs, caddis, stoneflies, midge larvae, and even freshwater scuds, often rouse the holding steelhead and put them on the bite. The fish seem to behave more like a resident rainbow trout—as opposed to the bull-in-a-china-shop disposition of the fresh-runner—the stream-feeding behavior of their early natal upbringing takes over.

Dry-line nymphing with a strike indicator (See Chapter VIII Presentation and Tackle) is a very effective method. The drift presentation must be natural and drag free. Strikes are often subtle with nothing more than a gentle mouthing of the fly. The new Thill balsa fly indicators are excellent in all river classes because they are highly visible and can tolerate split-shot in heavy applications if needed. Now is the time for the steelhead fly fisher to tone down fly size and color and use lighter tippets.

Fly sizes should match the natural as much as possible. Water clarity will often dictate size as off-colored waters allow gaudier and larger patterns in sizes 6 to 10, low and clear flows require tiny nymphs in sizes 12 to 18.

A fall nymph sampler should consist mainly of *Hexagenia* nymphs, green caddis, claret stoneflies, Gartside Sparrows in all tones, along with shrimp imitations and tiny bead-heads with sparkle dubbing in various colors. Micro and pom-pon eggs in hot pink still arouse the steelhead's genetic urge to eat fish eggs.

The ability to read water, understand the fish's behavior, and make natural presentations are all crucial to fall steelheading success, but the dumb luck of being in the right place at the right time also plays a part and is the humbling factor we can never control. Fall steelheading is a lot like panning for gold—you have to pay your dues. But its rewards are priceless.

Chapter 5

Seasons: Winter

Great Lakes winters are harsh and unrelenting. Yet oddly, the long, frigid months are met with celebration by the true lovers and natives of the lakes' basins. Its blistering-cold lake-effect snow squalls and the sub-zero wind chills are incapacitating. Winter floors us with its ability to rob millions of people of the opportunity to function at the socially accepted modern-day frantic pace. Blizzards close workplaces and schools and suffocates traffic commutes. Skiers, snowmobilers, ice fishermen, and dog-sledders are all in their sporting glory. Hunters pursue rabbits with a passion. For many, like me, winter is the season of the elusive steelhead. It has been that way for centuries in the Pacific Northwest, but in our brief Great Lakes centennial, the steelhead have become the sporting demi-gods of our cold, icy rivers.

Every winter steelhead must be earned—the hard way. Flogged by brutal weather extremes and river conditions, icicle steelheading is a cult sport for the hardcore fly-fisher. Throughout the Great Lakes, "these crazies" (as some anglers call them) don polar fleece, heavy neoprene waders, hand warmers, and a flask of cognac in their hunt for that magic hook-up with a winter fish. If you're sitting at a bar in Baldwin, Michigan on the Pere Marquette or watching the lake-effect snow pile high and deep in a Pulaski, New York diner near the Salmon River, you'll recognize winter steelheaders by their weathered red faces and the wild look in their eyes.

Winter steelheading weeds out the fairweather anglers. It draws a thrill-seeking adventurer—an angling animal that can't

A winter wonderland abounds as a Moravian starburst of the sun warms the ice-cold waters, stirring the sulking steelhead ever more toward the afternoon "bite."

be caged. You learn to love the exhilarating cold. In a primal way we do it because we can. When our health is strong, even though we battle the cold and flu seasons, our passion and desire for a steelhead hook-up is insatiable. Usually by February, cabin fever and post-football-bowl-game depression are raging. With a feeling of "I can't take it anymore, get me out of here," we go in search of a winter steelhead river. The first numbing of the fingers and icy blast of wind in the face tells us we're back in our element.

Each time I try to describe the winter experience, I get caught up in the peculiarities and nuances of the ritual. The act of catching a steelhead is the end that justifies the means—in winter steelheading, however, the "end" is often never achieved.

One outcome can be controlled. At the end of a day on the river we can bask by a glowing fireplace sipping warm coffee or sampling heart-and-soul-warming cognac as we puff on a fine cigar or a new pipe tobacco blend. These moments are precious when spent in the company of angling friends, spouses, growing children, and hospitable guides and innkeepers. Often with a special dinner soon to be enjoyed, the ritual of this cozy gathering, along with the good night's sleep we always seem to have at a river lodge, all of this stems from our love and pursuit of steelhead. This winter celebration of being alive while nature lies dormant is etched forever in our fondest memories.

The Nature of Winter Fish
Without question, the steelhead is one of the only coldwater salmonid game fish still at the top of its sporting challenge at this

A ripe winter steelhead taken on a pink Comet Egg in the lower Muskegon on a February day. Though the water temperature was 34 degrees the fish fought and leaped like it was late spring. Freshly migrated fish often do not turn down the metabolic engine until being in the river for some time.

Steve Stallard Photo

time of year. The gusto with which it strikes a fly is still present despite chilling water temperatures hovering near the freezing point. Even though winter-run Pacific Northwest steelhead run their rivers under the more comfortable water temperatures and conditions more common to their environment, these transplants run the harsher environs of the Great Lakes rivers and streams with abandon.

Since my addiction to coldwater steelheading grows stronger each year, I've come to realize that just when you think you've figured out winter fish your baffled by a new event that throws all your theories into the garbage bin of "dead knowledge."

One of my most humbling encounters with these winter fish took place on January 7, 1999. After a fierce winter blizzard dumped up to 40 inches of snow and air temperatures tumbled into the sub-zero range, my thoughts were far from steelheading. Sun-tanned goddesses in bikinis, warm turquoise waters with sand, and taking a sail in the tropics with Captain Morgan were my daily fantasies.

Dozing off in my reclining chair after shoveling 3 1/2 feet of snow from our deck, I snapped forward as the phone rang. On the other line was an overly enthusiastic graduate student from Indiana University and his friend who were dying to go on a guided winter steelhead trip. "When?" I asked. "Like tomorrow," virgin winter steelhead apprentice Ramon Zabriskie replied. "You've got to be crazy," I replied in a nice yet discouraging way. "We don't care about the weather, we're ski bums and fly-fishers from Park City, Utah and we've gotta hook one of those beauties we saw in *Fly Fish America* magazine." That month my mug was on the cover holding up an 18-pound winter steelhead with plenty of snow around me. That shot would continue to haunt me and send me on more bonechilling fishing days than I've ever imagined. After Ramon's relentless insistence, he bantered, "I don't give a damn about the weather and you shouldn't either for Christ's sake, your supposed to be a winter steelhead guide." I felt my manly pride being challenged and shot back, "You're on, but it's going to be a hell of a cold and expensive boat ride."

As soon as I hung up the phone, I planned the dreaded logistics. Obstacles were numerous, yet I was not about to be accused of being a wimp again. Since the sub-zero cold denied us use of the jet boat, we would row the McKenzie drifter. Since the landings had not been plowed for weeks, finding a place to launch the boat in 40 inches of snow was a problem. I loaded up the space heaters, glued myself to the weather channel and hoped for a break from the NOAA (National Oceanographic Atmospheric Association) computerized "weather nazi" on my radio band. He (it) is a monotone Teutonic simulated voice. Sounding like it was stuck on rewind, it blared, "Extremely cold sub-zero veather vit heavy snowfall." It sounded like a cross between Arnold Schwarzennegger and an old German hotellier I once worked for. I was dreading going to work the following morning.

At 9:00 a.m. Ramon and Frank showed up, exuberant as ever, despite driving all night with no sleep. They were pumped. I was nervous. "We'll launch the drift boat down a steep slope at the Croton Dam on a tow rope and let it tumble to the river, that's the only way we can get it in." I sounded captain-like to my new rookie recruits. The air temperature on my thermometer was -2 degrees F., wind chill was estimated at -34 degrees. I was nuts. I warned them that for their safety at the first sign of someone getting hypothermic or any adverse weather change we'd go right off the river. "No problem," said Raimon, "We're happy to be here."

Since the Muskegon is a tailwater, it remains open and ice free all year. We tumbled the driftboat down the slope and giggled as it hit the water. "OK, here's the scoop," I commanded.

"The only boat landing we could get a reasonable chance of taking out at is twelve miles downstream. I've got one spot about four miles down from here that I know has some holding fish. But in 33-degree water I'll bet a thousand bucks we ain't gonna get 'em to hit. Besides, we have about five minutes before all of our tackle, anchor rope and the feeling in our hands and fingers freeze up. And I ain't taking anyone to the hospital for frostbite—you guys got that?" I barked. "Aye, Aye captain," responded Ramon.

I rowed my butt off to the honey hole to keep warmed up. Upon arrival at the winter steelhead pool, I started to rig rods with pink egg patterns and Hex nymphs and lots of lead as the virgin Hoosier steelheaders' teeth were chattering. With one rig ready, I handed it to Frank. "Cast right there, in the gut of the run, bounce the bottom very slowly and if you feel it stop, drive the hook home. If it starts talking back, get the line on the reel and let the fish rip your drag—got it?" As I proceeded to tie Ramon's rig, despite my fingers already numbing up, I heard a yell after Frank's second or third cast. "Holy bajesus, look at that huge fish jump downstream," Frank excitedly proclaimed. As I looked up, I saw Frank's rod throbbing. "That fish is on your line, man! It's yours!" I yelled. Because his hands were numb, I don't think Frank felt it. It was a chrome fish of about twelve pounds and it was dancing around in the air like a fall- or summer-run fish. "You gotta be kidding me!" were the first words that ran through my mind. After a careful coaching on how to battle the fish, we coerced it to the net. It was a fresh-run chrome female with rose-colored cheeks. We lifted it up for photos as steam poured off the water and then kissed it goodbye. Frank was delirious. I was befuddled. Raimon was screaming, "It's my turn, it's my turn!"

Before I could get my bearings, Ramon was already chuck-and-duck bombarding the run below where we drifted down as we chased Frank's fish. I was still in a daze as I noticed slush on the water's surface. Ramon immediately yelled out that he was snagged on the bottom. Just then the fish gods, after recovering from their laughter over the previous hook-up, decided to show up again. The snag began to move. With hard strong runs, we knew we had a big steelhead on. It ripped deep into a 20-foot pool and charged downstream, upstream and dove under the

A good steelhead guide like Jeff Bacon doesn't let a few feet of snow stop a trip when the river is full of fish—even if he has to push his drift boat down the steep, unplowed boat launch.

boat. After a twenty-minute battle, Ramon hoisted a 16-pound, dark buck male that hammered a large Hex nymph. As I slid the net under it, I was further dumbfounded. Pictures, high-fives, and adrenaline going crazy, it was a sight to see. Here were three grown men acting like giddy schoolboys. "See, I told you we could catch 'em," Ramon screamed. "You're the best guide in the world!" he bellowed. In shock, I shook my head in disbelief. Before rowing the eight miles to the take-out, I cut lines, lit the heaters, and took a first water temperature on my digital thermometer, 33.2 degrees. Air temperature is -5 degrees, wind chill is out of control, and who gives a damn—we are outta here!

Looking back at that memorable day, all of my previous theories on winter fish and behavior where crushed. In all of my previous information on steelhead striking behavior, an air temperature of 33 degrees was a red flag for non-activity and hopeless angling. Yet despite these water temperatures we saw active, aggressive steelhead taking the fly. An important note on that day: conditions were sunny and clear with a high-pressure barometric reading of 30.18.

The two fish that were caught were quite different. The first, a chrome female which leapt and fought near the surface, was definitely a fresh-run fish that occupied the end of a tailout on the outside riverbend—prime fish-holding water. The second, a dark male who was in the river for perhaps months, struck like a dead log in the gut of the pool, then came to life with strong runs on the bottom. These two totally different responses of the fish, considering each was in 33-degree water, is directly linked to their metabolic rate of activity. The fresh chromer was still semi-migrating or newly migrated and stalled, it had not yet learned to turn down its metabolic thermostat for survival. The darker fish was already in its winter, slowed-down metabolism, thus the strike felt like a slow tree snag. As in the fall, we were presented with an active, somewhat moving fish and a subdued and holding fish, both in a state of suspended activity. The fact that both fish struck the fly shows they still maintain their aggressive strike response.

Besides an ideal barometric pressure reading, which appears to indicate the strong possibility of angling success, another factor that cannot be overlooked is the non-existent angling pressure while we were there. From January 1st to almost the 10th, the Muskegon accommodated no anglers since boat and shore anglers were unable to use access points. Not to mention the downright nasty sub-zero-degree air temperatures, and the fact that the fish were spared from their daily bombardment. I firmly believe that steelhead become more aggressive in a wild, natural setting and are much more territorial and show a greater curiosity when left unmolested. These are some of the reasons first-water advantage at dawn is lethal.

In conclusion, because of this new information on water temperatures, I believe steelhead will respond favorably to a winter steelheader's presentation in waters as low as 33 degrees, when its coupled with a stable, high pressure and a lack of angling pressure. Of course, as water temperatures increase from 33 degrees to 40 degrees and above, metabolic activity and migrating behavior will increase.

As far as moving and holding winter fish, I say with confidence that perhaps 80% of the fish will be in the dormant holding stage when water temperatures are low, so it is wise to fish deep holding lies.

Sunlight on a winter day is also correlated with success, whereas during fall and spring fishing it can be a deterrent. Since fall and spring fish have water temperatures more conducive to moving and spawning, these fish usually occupy more shallow and vulnerable lies.

Winter steelheaders swear by Mad Bomber hats, polar fleece and propane heaters which allow them to practice their passion in even the most brutal elements.

The author with a deep-crimson January male taken in front of Gray Drake Outfitters on the Muskegon River with fusion steelheading techniques. Note the extreme clarity of the water, a result of the zebra mussel invasion which makes steelheading a spring-creek style experience requiring exact presentations, small flies and fine leaders.

In winter, sunlight will penetrate deep pools holding the dormant fish. Sunlight also might heat up the water a degree or two, which affects the steelhead's metabolism.

Biological drift or migration of aquatic insects also arouses the steelhead, especially when they have been eating since their pre-smolt stage food forms are knocking on their noses. Given the steelhead's curious predisposition, something is bound to happen.

The Ideal Winter Water

Since winter fish are doing everything possible to lower their metabolic rate, the relatively current-free and usually warmer stream bottom is where you'll find them. The long, deep pool and flats of its tailout is often known as "frog water" or bobber water by the spawn sac fishermen. Plug-fishing techniques are ideal in these areas, since the plugs can shake, rattle, and roll in the same spot for long periods of time, rousing a sulking steelhead to hit. Usually the "gut" of the pool or run will have the deepest, slowest, darkest water for a steelhead weathering out the winter months. If the gut of the pool is over gravel, all the better. Depths of six to twelve feet are ideal.

The flats of the pool are the slower sections just before the tailout lip. They may be much more shallow and often hold good numbers of winter fish because of their very slow current. On sunny days, the water heats up much more quickly than the gut does and creates a luxurious pool that allows steelhead to slide down and sun themselves. Steelhead are attracted to gravel, for future procreative purposes and the fact that they are silt-free areas which do not irritate the steelhead's breathing apparatus, but flats will often accumulate undesirable silt and are thus not tolerated for long periods of time. When underwater debris and large boulders are found in the pools and flats,

steelhead hang out in these waters for their concealment and current deflection abilities.

Since the steelhead has a predisposition for flowing waters, seams and creases play a very powerful role in winter. In these border areas of lies, which have stronger and slower flow demarcation lines, the steelhead may ride in and out of them according to their metabolic preference. Seams and creases are created by defraction of the water's hydrodynamics. They are more prevalent in riverbend and pocket/throat water areas where the bank deflects currents and causes eddies. They are also found where pocket/throat water has stream bottoms with boulders or wooded obstacles creating dividing and undulating currents. Quick, gravel drop-off shelves are also excellent lies for winter steelhead, and can be very tricky to detect in fast water. Since they act similarly to the undertow of waterfalls, fish often cruise the shelves sideways in total comfort.

Spring creeks and underground springwater seeps are highly sought after by holding winter fish since groundwater flows are usually in the prime water temperature range of 47 to 58 degrees. If an adjacent pool/flat correlates with these creek inflows, the dynamics come together to form the ultimate lie. Often streambottom seeps of springs are hard to detect. When one pool is producing well in the winter mornings, drop a thermometer down to the bottom and take a reading.

Finally, for obvious reasons, dams and hydroelectric warmwater discharging areas collect steelhead in good numbers. Dams halt upstream migration. Even if they have fish ladders, most of these structures are too difficult to negotiate or are often closed by DNR agencies in the winter months. Dams also create undertow and undulating currents, which steelhead glide on, holding secure in the current with no effort exerted on their parts. Warm-water discharges create ideal temperatures and attract baitfish, which allow the fish to feed if they have the urge—especially for newly migrated steelhead.

Perhaps the greatest advice for a winter steelhead fly fisher is to become intimately aquainted with one river or hire a seasoned river guide. Since you are pursuing an elusive fish in less-than-ideal conditions, understanding each peculiarity and nuance of a river will make your outing much more productive and satisfying.

Becoming a true steelhead fly fishing expert has its foundation in mastering the demanding winter fishery.

Cold-Water Tactics

Without doubt, the greatest challenge for the winter steelheader is to keep the fly presentation on the bottom and moving as slowly as possible despite the fast-moving currents. A good rule of thumb is to slow your presentation down to as slow as one-fourth the speed of the current at the taking lie. By using "lift and glide" drifting techniques such as when the angler fishes extremely slow frog-water pools and flats, the fly cannot fall to the bottom and create a dead presentation. Thus, moving-water and dead-water presentations must be applied with the various methods that can be used.

Today's Great Lakes steelheader has a lot of help with multi-tip sinking heads and lines, fast-cutting shooting and running lines, and long, one- and two-handed rods for high depth presentation. A cornucopia of added lead and weighted rigs can be applied in addition to all shapes and buoyancy of strike indicators. Fly fishing technology has created so much to help the winter angler practice his or her art. Nature's forces, steelhead's attitudes, and pure luck are the only uncontrollables.

Active Water

Since rivers and streams vary in their depth and flow, actively moving water with significant currents will usually exist in the throat, upper pool, and extreme tailout sections. Three presentations can be applied to these areas: classic bottom drift fishing, down and across; one- or two-handed wet-fly sink-tipping; or high-stick, strike-indicator nymphing.

Perhaps the most successful, and scorned, technique is the highly utilized bottom-bouncing drift method (i.e. the dreaded "chuck-and-duck"). Here the fly angler can penetrate all the deep holding bottom lies and slow down or speed up the rate of presentation by the addition or subtraction of weight in the form of split shot, slinky rigs, or wrap-around lead. Drift-fishing techniques also allow the angler to use a very thin running or shooting line, which does not freeze up at the guides as quickly as traditional line. With the added weight, the brutal winds on blustery days pose less of a challenge.

When classic drift fishing in winter, several mistakes are often made by anglers. To penetrate a deep holding lie, the presentation must be casted well above the desired targeted area. Too often our initial casts are made at the desired location causing the drift to bypass the area downstream. Since winter strikes by steelhead are usually subtle, having too much slack in the line will make strike detection difficult as the drift bounces and thumps along the bottom. By using a long rod and high-sticking it (raising the rod hand directly vertical sky-high), your line will cut the water current much better and allow for more snag-free drifts. Another common error is that many anglers pick up the drift too early. Allow the drift to extend fully downstream, sometimes tailing it for a few seconds as a lethargic fish is given ample time to make up its mind to strike.

Some people consider winter steelheaders to be "lunatics and mad people" addicted to rivers and in constant search for their steelhead fix. Guide Jeff Bacon dodges icebergs on Michigan's Muskegon River as he bellows, "Fish on!"

Classic down-and-across, slack line with wet-fly presentations, or one- or two-handed rods are also effective, though much more concentration and effort is needed to achieve the desired drift. Since Great Lakes rivers can range from the fast currents and great depths of the mighty Niagara River to the gentler flows of the Pere Marquette, this science entails using the correct sinking line or tip in various lengths and sink rates of feet per second to achieve quick penetration which are markedly slower than the current drift. The art comes in the angler's ability to achieve maximum time at the desired depth on each cast and to cover all the holding lies thoroughly. Easier said than done—especially in harsh climactic conditions. This is where the purist fly-fishers will find enjoyment in fly presentation, though the number of fish caught or that even view the presentation will be much less than the drift methods. This results mainly from the time needed to execute the presentation successfully. It's a quality versus quantity thing.

Since the classic wet-fly swing works much better in fall, summer, and spring conditions when water temperatures are more conducive to fish moving and taking a fly, the winter angler must reduce line tension and employ slack-line techniques. By careful line mending, both up and downstream, along with controlling lateral line speed, the fish will see a broadside view of the fly moving very slowly to correspond to the steelhead's lethargic nature.

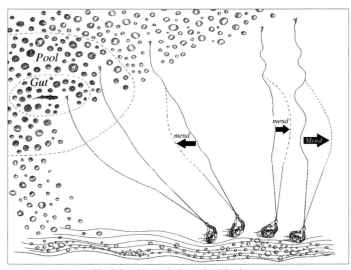

Slack-line deep-drift method for heavy hook/long leader floating line or sink tipping.

The slack-line drift begins with the angler positioning themselves upstream of the targeted taking lie. The cast is made across and slightly upstream, much further up the opposite bank than the targeted lie actually exists, this will allow the line to curve-sweep into the strike zone. Once you make the cast, make a powerful upstream mend while giving slack to allow for a deep vertical presentation. Throughout the drift, adjustments are made both up and down stream to keep the drift deep and in the strike zone for an extended duration.

Creating slack for penetration along with keeping enough tension for strike detection is the key. Also, a sink-tip that is too heavy will hang up on the bottom and hamper strike detection. Since subtle takes are often associated with winter fishing, anglers must look for any noticeable or odd movements the line makes. Confidence and a sixth sense are also highly desirable. Keep your leaders short for quicker penetration of your fly. Often strike detection comes by coincidence, such as when a fish cartwheels in the air with your Spey fly startling you or you think you're stuck firmly on the *bottom* and then it starts to move. With practice, the slack-line technique can be mastered and is especially effective in winter when you know exactly where the fish are holding. In this

Battling a wild winter steelhead on Michigan's hallowed Pere Marquette River in the flies-only/no-kill stretch below Baldwin.

scenario, repeated presentations can be imparted until a strike is elicited. However, for general winter hunt-and-peck searching presentations, classic drift fishing by bouncing the bottom will be much more effective.

Finally, high-stick, floating-line nymphing with strike indicators is perhaps the easiest method. Using long leaders and just the right amount of weight, coupled with a buoyant indicator of balsa, one-fly or two-fly rigs can be fished deep with adjusting mends to slow down the presentation. Keeping a sharp eye on the floating indicator is the key to the slight nibbling takes of winter fish.

Fishing Frog Water

Since this very slow, almost dead, moving water is heavily pursued by plug fishermen, fly anglers either overlook or strike out in these areas. The key is to create motion without movement (MWM)—like a steady pulsating plug—which gives the fish plenty of time to look at the offering. Since the water lacks current, the fly offering will fall to the bottom. This water is where the steelhead fisher tossing bobbers and floating and suspended spawn sacs cleans up. The fly fisher can as well, never underestimate your capabilities.

Strike indicator, floating-line nymphing is the logical choice for this type of water. The indicator can be adjusted up and down your leader and you can experiment with the weight necessary to produce the same float and drift a spawn-sac bobber-thrower produces. By using flies with added MWM materials like Flashabou, marabou, possum, and bunny strips, the flies may be manipulated by throwing mends in the line or lifting and gliding the presentation in an almost "jigging" motion.

With the classic, wet-fly swing (down-and-across method), rolling and curling marabou or bunny leeches and Spey flies with rod-lifting mends and glides will impart the same jigging motion needed for slack water.

Overall, winter presentations require a great deal of positive thinking, enthusiasm and persistence from the steelhead fly fisher. Employing the various techniques mentioned and experimentation will often produce results when others have given up.

Remember that winter is the time when plug and spawn fishers shine, often laughing at fly fishers desperately flailing away. Rather than being intimidated, infiltrate their haunts inquisitively. Hang out at the same doughnut shops; pick their brains and watch where they fish. Often their success is a no-brainer; sometimes it's dumb luck. But, often the winter steelhead tells us something about the where, when, what, and why of their winter lifestyle.

A Winter Fly Box

Winter steelheading has very distinct phases or transitions. The beginning of the winter season usually marks the tail end of the fall migration by the third week in December. Weather factors can be downright nasty and full of winter's wrath or they can be balmy and mild with folks wearing T-shirts and shorts like during the El Niño winter of 1998. Remember that in "typical" Great Lakes winters, the number of winter steelhead in the river is directly related to the numbers in the fall migration. And fresh fish migrating all winter if mild water temperatures and increased flows occur.

More weather-related transitions occur at the end of winter when the pre-spawn drive can begin with the first winter thaws and extended daylight hours in late February and March. Winter steelheading must be analyzed in terms of active and dormant stages.

Eggs, eggs and more eggs—steelhead can't get enough of them. Everyone has their favorite colors and times of year they work best. Guide Sean McDonald goes through the painstaking process of selection on Michigan's Big Mainstee River.

Fly pattern selection must reflect these weather transitions. It must be specific yet flexible (oddities occur more in winter steelheading than during any time of year). This is due mainly to the elusive and often uncompromising nature of sulking winter fish. Steelhead are turned on by flies of all sizes from minute to big grocery bag flies. When icicle steelheading, the steelhead really show their individual personalities and preferences.

I categorize Great Lakes steelhead fly patterns into three groups: natural, impressionistic attractors and seducers, and fusion. The natural fly patterns are far more successful than the impressionistic attractor patterns. This is especially noticeable in the potamodromous migration of Great Lakes steelhead as opposed to the physically-taxing anadromous adjustment Pacific fish must make. I believe the urge to feed is much stronger in the potamodromous steelhead of the Great Lakes thus calling for naturalistic imitations. This holds particularly true for naturally reproducing wild fish which have imprinted to riverine aquatic invertebrate food forms.

It was long believed that steelhead lose the urge to feed once on their upstream migration, but this notion is changing. In an article entitled "Steelhead on the Grab" (*Fly Fisherman*, February 1991), Dick Pobst and friends from Michigan performed stomach sampling of fall, winter, and spring steelhead; they found that 35-40% of the fish sampled contained salmon or steelhead eggs, caddis larvae or tiny black stoneflies in their bellies.

A startling revelation regarding winter steelhead feeding came about in January of 1999. Since the fall run of 1998 was exceptionally strong with many large 12- to 14-pound males, I was curious about their dormant winter behavior. I often fish the lower river areas closer to Lake Michigan because winter fish

seem to prefer the deeper, slower holding water found there; this area is also fished heavily by plug and spawn fishermen. One winter afternoon as I was taking out at the boat launch, a hardware charter guide was cleaning a very large dark male of about fourteen pounds. I asked the man if I could take the stomach entrails, a request he found to be quite humorous. "What the heck are you going to do with that stomach, fry it up like sweet breads?" he laughed. "I'm planning on looking for signs of feeding activity," I replied. "Everyone knows that these fish stop eating once in the river," the plug guide remarked. Boy, was he wrong.

To my astonishment, this big-shouldered, dark brute's stomach was packed full of food. Large clumps of black sludge in his belly turned out to be hundreds of tiny size 22 black midge (*simulium*) larvae. Furthermore, his stomach contained numerous green caddis larvae and tiny gray shrimp (scuds). Why the hell would a big fish in 34-degree F. water focus on such tiny food forms? After careful thought and seining of the bottom of pools and holding water, I found the biological drift of the daily emergence of midge larvae to be extremely significant. The fish fed by simply opening his mouth as a whale feeds on krill. I have since used black midge larvae patterns tied on very stout shrimp/scud hooks down to size 16 and have had remarkable success. Shrimp and green caddis patterns tied on the small hooks have yielded similar success for many anglers who fish the spring creek-like tailwater rivers of Michigan's Muskegon and Manistee.

These discoveries show steelhead behaving like stream-resident rainbow trout during the winter holding stages. The steelhead's urge to feed is still intact. It appears that the longer a fish is in the river, the more likely it will show interest in river food sources, just as a resident trout would.

The first stage of winter steelheading involves fishing to both freshly chrome migrating fish and holding fish that were early fall arrivals. Target lies like the faster, narrower throats and riverbend tailouts with light attractor marabou, bunny, or traditional Speys and wets in orange and gold, chartreuse and black or in hot pinks, black, and purple. Hot pink and white combination marabou Spey flies are great for winter fish.

Natural patterns such as nymphs and eggs should mainly be fished in the afternoon hours or at dusk since water temperatures are highest in the deep pool and flat areas. Attractors in the morning and naturals throughout the day are a good bet.

Stage two is the winter dormancy period when water temperatures are at their lowest and the metabolic activity of steelhead is at its most lethargic. Gartside Sparrows in green and tan, little black stoneflies, hare's ears, and green caddis are excellent. Filo-plume, possum, and marabou *Hexagenia* nymphs are also important in steelhead diets since their downstream emergence in June coincides with the annual smolting of steelhead young. Egg patterns in hot pink, cerise, and creamy pink are excellent in winter months. I believe the hot pinks arouse the spawning drive in steelhead as the colors correlate to the bright reds of the males.

The third stage of winter is the transition of winter into spring during late February to March. By February we usually see a fresh run of predominantly chrome, pink, and purple fat females with hard and not yet matured skein. These "green" females are quite aggressive with attractor Speys and wets in pink and silver tones. Many of these fish will strike white streamers that imitate the baitfish they have just been feeding upon. Patterns matching the naturals, particularly the little black stone, are important since this species is hatching at this time. Large, dominant males will become active on sunny afternoons, striking pink and red Speys, wets, and Egg Omelet patterns.

A late-winter steelhead outing is complete with this spectacular deep-bodied silver female taken by Chicago angler Bill Donath.

Fusion methods, already described in the autumn chapter, work particularly well during seasonal transition stages. Where two-fly rigs are legal, fish attractor patterns as the top fly with a natural nymph or egg pattern dropper. Adding a flashing, spinning Cheater to an attractor or egg pattern, like the Omelet, that incorporates bunny strips and Flashabou for movement will really show the fish a lot of options and cover a lot of water. In winter, we knock on the doors of the steelhead. We ask them if they would like to come out and play. The more doors we knock on, the more chances for a positive response.

One dichotomy exists in fly presentation among steelheaders for very cold and clear, deep, winter water conditions. Some swear by tiny naturals, others go to large clown-style egg patterns and extremely gaudy Speys, wet flys, and streamers. In my personal experience, I have had luck with both and have caught dormant holding fish on each. Here is where the unique personalities and metabolic variations in winter fish can explain different fly preferences. Could the large, gaudy egg or Spey fly be what is needed to bring the fish out of its sulking winter hibernation to strike the fly? Can some fish acclimate more comfortably to their cold riverine environment and feed regularly like my midge-feeding big buck male? Until we can interview a steelhead through telepathic means, these answers will never be known.

In the meantime, we must continue to fish our patterns confidently and be willing to experiment. Showing the fish something different will always be an important part of steelheading.

Battling Winter Elements

The following tips will make your days on a winter steelhead river more pleasurable:

• Dress in layers. Use both wicking material like capilene that draws moisture away from the body and insulating polar fleece.
• Use a wind-breaking, waterproof, Gore-Tex parka.
• Warm hats hold body heat (I swear by the Mad Bomber Hat).

• Use two pairs of gloves: one for fishing (fleece, fingertips cut) and one for holding fish for photographing (wire mesh or neoprene varieties). Dry hands thoroughly after exposing them to water.
• Carry hand warmers and heat packs.
• Take doses of cayenne pepper tablets which are known to aide in blood circulation.
• Use 5 mm guide weight neoprene boot-foot waders lined with Thinsulate. They circulate warm air better and don't cut off circulation in your feet.
• Good amber-colored polarizers are suggested.
• WD-40, ice-out spray and new high-tech fly-fishing goops, like loon's stanly's ice-off paste, have some merit when it comes to keeping rod guides and anchor system ice free.
• Some reels ice up easier than others. Ask your fly shop and check out the different brands
• Have a cell phone or GPS for emergencies.
• Avoid excessive alcohol consumption, although a wee nip from a flask of your favorite elixir is good for the spirit and attitude—don't overdo it. Alcohol actually cools the body.
• Carry a wading staff—avoid wading if possible.
• If you start to lose feeling in your extremities, it's time to get your butt back to a fireplace or hot tub.
• Learn to respect Great Lakes winters so you can live to steelhead-fish another day.
• Bag Balm is great for weathered and cracked skin. Super Glue used carefully can seal weathered finger cracks.
• Spey fishing and slack-line sink-tip techniques keep your body parts moving and keep you happy and warm.
• Carry tire chains, jumper cables, salt and a tow-rope in your car or trunk.
• Have propane space heaters available in your boat.
• Listen to a local NOAA weatherband report before venturing out.
• Watch the barometer: if it's falling or rising with rapid fluctuations, don't waste your time—go home, read, tie some flies, spend quality time with your significant others or start writing about your steelhead forays.

In conclusion, cherish each winter day out on a steelhead river whether you catch a fish or not. Life and steelheading are gifts, and should never be taken for granted.

As the first warm rays of sun melt the deep freeze of winter and stirs the spawning drive of the steelhead, the first leapers appear at dams and waterfalls throughout the Great Lakes region on their upriver migration. A large male steelhead's seen here trying to jump the Rockford Dam on Michigan's Rogue River.

Chapter 6

Seasons:Spring

My passion for spring and its steelhead was a gift bestowed upon me once again in boyhood. I recall with fondness the sound of pounding waterdrops as the first warming rays of sun melted the crystal, spiked icicles which hung ominously from the gutters on my garage fishing den. Here I created my secret little getaway. I hung my rods and reels proudly and rehearsed my thoughts in preparation for battle with the fresh-run steelhead of the season to come. Sharpening hooks, checking old fly lines and packing my vest full of fly boxes optimistically stuffed with new and time-honored patterns, I learned the ritual of preparation that became an important part of my adulthood angling.

Spring's resurrection of new life coincided with the excitement of the Easter holidays which gave me many school-free days to ply my favorite runs and pools in my home steelhead waters. The smell of the fresh-baked Easter ham and sausages, the aromas from the pot of boiling beet soup and the visions of my mother painting beautiful, intricate designs on her Polish Easter eggs will forever enhance my appreciation for springtime.

To love this season is to experience its subtleties. Its charming nuances revealed themselves graciously upon my arrival to the pristine forests and rivers of the Michigan northwoods. Here, for the first time, I heard the drumming of a mating male grouse at dawn that sounded like an old Harley motorcycle starting up. I smelled the fresh scent of pines and cedars. I witnessed the amazing crawl of newly emerged black stoneflies maneuvering through the remaining patches of snow like miniature mechanical robots from a Star Wars epoch.

Wildflowers and mosses carpeted the forest floor in a brilliant display. In awe, I admired the spring nesting of bald eagles and heard the vivacious chirpings and songs of the many migrating birds in the forest's bountiful foliage. I relished finding precious morel mushrooms—those epicurean treasures that hide in the ravines of aspens and poplars. White and pink trillium sprang up like Easter lilies once the forests and ferns were painted in a deep tone of hunter green.

However, as with all of my eye-opening encounters with natural beauty, it was my pursuit of spring-fed Michigan rivers filled with their legendary wild steelhead which allowed me to experience all of this. Many of us never do. It is for all of this that I am humbly and forever thankful.

Fragile spring violets adorn the woods near steelhead rivers of the Great Lakes.

The precious and delectable "morchella," the morel mushroom of Michigan's northwoods. They can be found in early May after a good spring rain in the woods surrounding Great Lakes steelhead rivers. Many Michigan steelheaders take an afternoon break to hunt for this delight. Gastronomique.

The Big Run

To a large majority of Great Lakes steelheaders, spring is "the time" to pursue these magnificent sporting fish. Since the fish are on their annual spawning migration, they are adorned with spectacular colors ranging from the king crimson red cheeks and stripes of the male bucks, to the subtle pastels of the rose, lilac, and lime casts on the silver scales of the fertile females. Carried in their plump bellies are the precious cargo, eggs that will produce new life and generations.

Steelheading in the spring is less difficult strategically than during other seasons since they are found in large concentrated numbers in very shallow spawning gravel. These conditions create sight-fishing opportunities for anglers with polarized sunglasses that are familiar with gravel spawning sections of streams and rivers.

Perhaps the most controversial and ethically challenging issue of the Great Lakes steelhead fishery is the fact that anglers are allowed, with the exception of a few nursery waters, to pursue actively spawning fish on gravel redds. We have been severely ostracized by Pacific West Coast anglers since this practice is considered taboo and unethical.

The fact is that this commonly accepted form of angling is and will always be implanted in the Great Lakes tradition. This has been a difficult pill to swallow for some, and is highly applauded by others. Ethical and "don't give a damn" anglers, meat fishermen, catch-and-release stewards, and fisheries managers will forever grapple over whether it's ethical to fish over redds and will never see eye to eye. Perhaps not until steelhead fisheries become extinct will this method cease.

In every corner of the Great Lakes I have fished and traveled, I have seen great differences in attitude, philosophy, and "grips with reality" from anglers and fisheries management. Fish, like the steelhead, drive the passion of men and women who angle for them, and I have yet to find a utopian environment where all who use the resource are satisfied. The rising trend of catch-and-release fishing—which is for the most part a self-initiated subculture—has created a battleground between fly anglers and the meat harvesters. I have witnessed great strides in recent years by fisheries managers, as in the case of New York's Salmon River, where the Department of Environmental Conservation (DEC) has regulated two flies only, "no kill" angling zones and other progressive mandates to create spawning nursery waters.

I have high hopes that the steelhead ritual of spring spawning will be more protected in the years to come. I hope that what is right for nature, and not what is most beneficial to political and economic greed, will eventually drive fisheries management and will be internalized by the growing numbers of conservation-minded angler.

I respect everyone's right to harvest "legal" spring spawning fish. However, the ethical question of whether one should kill ripe females full of the precious eggs that guarantee the future of our mighty steelhead hangs over us like a dark cloud? Should spawning fish be targeted indiscriminately? Should males be harvested instead of females? These are perplexing questions that *are not* and, if we remain complacent, *will not* ever be addressed.

Personally speaking, I have much hope and faith in the future generations of anglers and conservation managers who are much more ecologically friendly and sensitive since they have witnessed the rape and destruction of steelhead fisheries brought about by their forefathers' greed, blatant ignorance, and short-sighted attitudes. With the aid of this new generation's morality, nature will cure our insensitive human practices. As has happened with the demise of the West Coast fisheries, my fear is that ecological protection and intervention by humans will be too little

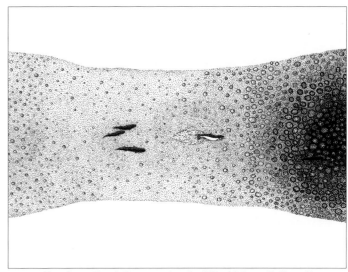

Female steelhead digs spawning "redd" with her tail. She will dig a hole as deep as 12 inches to deposit her eggs which the male will fertilize with its milt. Behind her lies three courting males jousting to be the dominant suitor. The larger alpha male will usually chase off the inferior fish by biting their bodies.

late too little. I pray that this will not be so in our marvelous Great Lakes steelhead ecosystem.

The Gathering of the Spring Run

As daylight hours increase, the first thaws begin and the inclement mix of snow and rain ushers in the new season. Steelhead start their hunt for gravel areas with highly oxygenated waters and good, strong flows. All strains of Great Lakes steelhead were developed from West Coast, Pacific stock which influences their spawning times and water condition preferences for spawning. So, the spawning can occur as early as February or as late as June depending on the steelhead's location in the Great Lakes basin, the river, variable water conditions and temperatures, and of course the genetic preference of the strain.

If Great Lakes weather conditions are normal, the first spawning runs occur in mid-February with the Skamania summer steelhead in the tributaries of the southern shores of the Great Lakes, on Indiana's Trail, Salt and Little Calumet creeks, the St. Joseph River and Wisconsin's Root River. The Skamania, which was genetically engineered by fisheries biologists to be an early spring spawner, have been in the rivers from as early as June of the previous year and are biologically ripe and fertile for the spring mating. Due to their hormonal time bomb, they are not usually affected by the cold water temperatures—33 to 36 degrees F.—they usually encounter at this time.

Certain Great Lakes strains have been created in our short 125-year history and show distinct late-spring preferences for spawning migrations. The Little Manistee strain of Lake Michigan shows a distinct preference for April to mid-May spawning. In waters such as the north shore of Lake Superior with their genetically unique wild steelhead, reproduction may come as late as May and June because winter grips that area much longer and the strain has evolved accordingly. The north shore rivers of Lake Huron's Georgian Bay and the St. Mary's also sport late runs at the same time. Established West Coast strains such as Washington's Chambers Creek strain, which is highly utilized by New York, Pennsylvania and Wisconsin for their stocking programs, shows a preference for fall and winter migrations, coupled with early spring spawning. There are always examples of unusually early and abnormally late spawners in all strains.

Spring steelhead devour green caddis rockworm larvae with a vengeance and Great Lakes rivers are loaded with green caddis. When females dig the gravel to make a spawning redd, they release many caddis larvae into the biological drift of the river.

a cloaking system for the moving steelhead. Barometric pressure variances and stability previously discussed (in Mastering the River) will dictate frontal weather movements or mild calm weather.

If you've been lucky enough to time your spring steelhead trip with all the conditions coming together perfectly, you still may face secondary obstacles. Usually spring is prime-time steelheading with double-digit hook-ups—what many steelheaders live for. The fact is that most popular steelhead streams are crowded with other anglers and boaters, and this can be a maddening experience. Many have experienced the bumper-car-like drift boat rides down the Pere Marquette in Michigan and on the Salmon River in New York where you drift hopelessly through the gauntlet of bank fishermen all looking for that magic hook-up. Even going during the week doesn't help anymore since everyone else is thinking the same thing. As a steelhead guide, I've often seen better angling on weekends since all the die-hards thought that it would be crazy to fish on weekends. Keep in mind that though conditions may be ideal, the steelhead will be extremely wary and downright scared during this circus-like scenario. Once they hear the first tromping footsteps of the dawn angler, the clanking of a boat anchor or speedboat fury of a river guide, you can bet they are scurrying for cover. Often your best angling happens late afternoon to evening as the last car trunk is slammed shut.

Timing and conditions vary on the different river classes and must be carefully weighted in with the natural and man-induced factors. On Class I rivers, which are fairly long and have a high gradient, migration will be spread out and staged for a considerable amount of time, lengthening the optimum period of the run. The river's source also plays an important role in its fishability at the time. If the river watershed is composed primarily of precipitation and snow melt, it can rise and fall very quickly. These rivers may remain high for considerable time or fall so low as to be unfishable. They also tend to go from cold to warm and clear to muddy much more quickly than Class II rivers with low gradients and agricultural run off.

Ideal springtime steelhead rivers are usually Class I systems which tend to have controlled spring-fed water flows, like Michigan's Pere Marquette and Wisconsin's Bois Brule. Though they can muddy up after severe rains, they will usually stabilize more quickly. Tailwater rivers with controlled releases and stable flows, like Michigan's Muskegon, Manistee, Au Sable and New York's Salmon River, provide clear, stable flows with the consistent water temperatures that are ideal for spring steelheading. These rivers also have tremendous amounts of spawning gravel since the dam and reservoirs above act as giant silt traps.

When with a guide, a steelhead fly fisher must discuss what type of fishing they want to do and what it takes for them to feel successful. If one insists on sight-fishing to spawning fish on or near gravel, conditions must be just right. If you choose to fish the entire river system for moving fish, then ideal conditions are less important. With all the various fly-fishing methods in existence, success is now more likely in all weather and river circumstances. Along with a growing number of sporting steelhead anglers, I prefer the latter alternative. The exhilaration one experiences from the lightning-fast strike on your well-presented fly in a deep dark run marks the pinnacle of the steelheader's sporting experience.

Finally, in the Class III river systems, characterized by very steep gradients and either low or extremely violent flows, timing is very critical since the steelhead will use the river's brief windows of opportunity for spawning. Dropping back down to the lake will occur if conditions fluctuate or become undesirable. This is often the case on Lake Superior's north shore tributaries along

Spring steelheading is a combination of fishing to winter holdover fish that are sexually mature and ready to spawn, and newly arrived chrome arrivals that show a greater interest in eating the fly. Winter holdovers usually strike in a more aggravated territorially way.

Timing the Run for Success

How well you understand general river characteristics, as well as water dynamics, weather-related conditions and steelhead strains, will determine your success timing a run. Though the calendar is a general guideline, keep in mind that being in the right place at the right time helps greatly. Dumb luck however has no place in spring steelheading since conditions can be interpreted and tactics adjusted to the various situations.

For most Great Lakes steelhead (with the exception of the summer Skamania steelhead previously noted), several key factors are needed to trigger upstream spawning migration. Water temperature is perhaps the most important factor for successful spawning and migration, with optimum readings being between 38 and 55 degrees F. Increased water flows from annual snow melt or spring precipitation allow safe passage into shallower spawning grounds from their downriver winter holding lies or their big-lake environment. The off-colored flows of spring act as

with others on Lake Ontario. Your best bet is to know an honest guide or fishing biologist who can save you a hell of a lot of money and wasted time. I kindly suggest to all steelheaders that *numbers* of steelhead caught should not be your sole reason for enjoying your steelhead outing. If it is, you're in for a lot of disappointment. Chill out and enjoy the sporting life and the beauty of this season.

Springtime Tactics

Since the urge to spawn and hunt for gravel is strong, the fish's motives are much more clearly defined than a holding fish in the deep of winter. Since water temperatures will be close to ideal, and allow for optimum fish metabolism levels, virtually every tactic known to the steelhead fly fisher can be applied.

As with the other seasons, two approaches are best. The first, and most preferred, approach, though controversial by ethical standards, is to sight-fish for spawning fish on or near gravel. Spawning steelhead will either be highly vulnerable to presentations or totally indifferent to them.

When steelhead take the fly on gravel spawning beds, they do so based on two basic behavioral drives. The first stems from agitation—either through territorial protection or an induced strike—which is generated from consistent multiple presentations. The second behavior comes from the actual response of "eating." This response can take on many striking forms. Food is not foremost on the minds of spawning anadromous or potamodromous salmonids. But in the case of freshly migrated spring steelhead that have moved in from big water to spawning gravel in a short period of time, the urge to eat is quite strong and they strike out of instinct. In the prime of the spring run, a fresh, chrome female out of the big lake will smack aggressively and without hesitation the first well-presented egg or nymph pattern she sees—especially if her nest digging has not begun. Also, because of a steelhead's imprinting on various invertebrate food forms, fly impressions of caddis, stonefly or mayfly nymphs and larvae can trigger memories causing them to strike. Finally, some fish show a stronger urge to eat than others. This is perhaps more true for the less dominant, younger year fish which most likely will not contribute to the spawning because aggressive, larger alpha males and females will chase them away. Frustration might lead to alternative behaviors such as feeding. One fact does remain, all steelhead are genetically programmed to eat fish eggs—all fish do it. Thus a well-presented egg pattern in the natural colors of steelhead roe is often lethal.

When targeting steelhead on or near gravel, one should understand the fish's behavior on gravel. The fish can go from extremely excited and frantic to downright cautious and spooky. Early dawn and later dusk usually find the steelhead most responsive and active. Since hardware, bait, and fly fishers pound steelhead in this prime season, they spend a great deal of the low light and night periods spawning. This instinct for self-preservation is very obvious on hard-fished rivers like the Salmon in New York and the Pere Marquette in Michigan. Many guides and anglers point out the freshly-dug gravel beds that weren't there the previous day and comment that the fish have bedded up and left. This is usually not the case since fish seek deep holes, pockets and

When fighting powerful steelhead on streams with wooded debris, the angler must know the limitations of his or her tackle and turn the fish away from obstructions to avoid break offs. Here a large spring male steelhead stubbornly comes to hand on the beautifully pristine northwoods Platte River of Michigan.

wooded debris during the time when the sun is high and the gravel is a dangerous, shallow area in which to be.

For significant activity on gravel beds to occur, a female fish must be actively fanning her redd. Often several females will pursue a single large bed. Male suitors dash in and out of the redds, with dominant males chasing off submissive, smaller fish. Since gravel beds are usually in the high-gradient tailouts between pools and pocket water, this dodging behavior from dark water to exposed gravel beds will be ongoing.

If spawning fish are left unmolested, they will not spook as easily and will bed up at all times of the day. Before the legal spring opening, I've seen active fish spawning in the bright sun of the afternoon. Since water temperatures often rise in the afternoon on cold spring days, the slight increase in water temperature will drive holding fish to shallow gravel, especially when water temperatures go from 34 to 40 degrees F.

On some rivers, certain gravel areas are used year after year. Fish will leave the area when water volume and direction of the river course are changed by obstructions like downed trees. The nest will continue to attract ongoing spawning migrators since it becomes "the place to be," for reasons which may range from pheromonal attraction to just the right flow and holding conditions. I've often noticed that sometimes perfect gravel areas or areas which produced well in previous years may be void of fish some years. The unique ability of the spawning steelhead to arrive and linger at the prime mating sites is directly related to where the females choose to start digging their redds.

When spawning fish become cautious, weather changing from a sunny day to a dark thunder or snowstorm will put fish back on gravel. The comfort of the dark skies and pounding snow or rain droplets distort the water's surface to close the fish's visual window. Wild fish are much more cautious than hatchery fish. Hatchery fish learn the game of survival very quickly when given enough of an angling "pounding." I've often witnessed a large male swim almost to my feet to check me out when I get too close to the redds.

Prime gravel areas exist within comfortable distance of dark pools and pocket holding water with wood debris. Some of these prime spots lie directly beneath branches of downed trees where an angler has no chance of a presentation! Thanks to Mother Nature giving them "street smarts," they carry out the spring spawn despite the many anglers who harass the fish during their procreation.

Fishing over spawning gravel areas requires two techniques: sight-fishing to individual fish or blind, dark-water hunting to holding fish. When sight-fishing, the most important factor to consider when presenting the fly is flow analysis. The successful steelheader will judge current speed and depth and adjust tackle properly. The goal is to present the fly dead-drift in a one-foot-wide drift directly to fish holding firmly on the bottom. Fish on spawning gravel rarely move great distances to take a fly, although there are exceptions, especially when fish are highly agitated.

A very effective technique for fishing to skittish fish on gravel is using dry-line, strike-indicator nymphing methods. The strike indicator, which allows the nymph and split shot to hang down at a 90-degree vertical angle, picks up very slight "mouth-and-spit" strikes and allows the nymphs or egg patterns to dead drift. The angler can either watch the strike indicator for a take, or watch the fish if it's visible for sudden mouth openings, head shakes, fin quivering, or sudden body movements to either side all of which may indicate a take to the fly. Proficient dry-liners use their peripheral vision to watch the indicator and for fish movement—a highly-efficient technique born of much practice. Use a long leader with weight attached to the tippet or built into the fly.

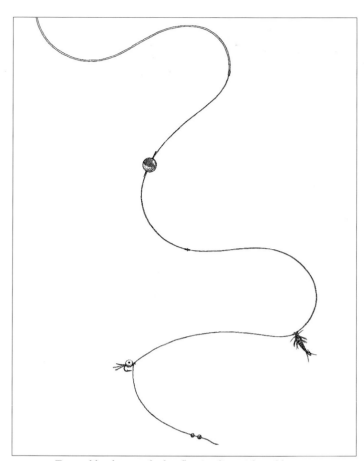

Tapered leader attached to floating line with nail knot or loop-to-loop. Butt section with float should be short, tapering quickly to a thinner-diameter leader for 90° right-angle presentation of nymphs. Split shot should be at end of rig "panfish style" and adjusted with strike indicator to effectively fish various depths.

Mending the dry line is essential for depth penetration and to slow down the presentation when high-sticking. Since the fish are not visible, the deep pocket water near the gravel can be explored with greater confidence with this method.

The Politics of Gravel

We cannot ignore the dark aspects of fishing gravel spawning beds. We also should not be hypocritical by condemning those who do fish gravel. I believe many of us (especially fly fishers) have or will fish these areas where the "tiny-fly guy" does so well. Let's look at the subject practically and analyze the ethical outcome of the various fishing methods.

Paramount to this ethical debate is the subject of "lining" or "fly-snagging" fish on gravel. Lining fish occurs when anglers fish flies on long leaders over gravel. The theory holds that since a steelhead's mouth has a fairly large (3- to 4-inch) circumference and is opening and closing in the act of breathing, a leader will sweep in front of the mouth of a fish, and your chances are good because of the high concentration of steelhead on the gravel bed. When the leader gets caught in the mouth and the fish moves to avoid it, the angler will feel the tightening and strike the fly which is threaded like a needle to the outside of the mouth.

Many anglers feel that fishing a long leader is the culprit and endorse shorter leaders attached to weight. In my humble opinion, I believe this nonsense is like trying to cure cancer with an aspirin. If you are fishing to a high concentration of fish in the very susceptible lies of spawning gravel, long leaders, short leaders, fat leaders, and skinny leaders are going to line fish—period!

Spawning spring steelhead on a gravel redd.

Laurie Supinksi with a muskegon river drop-back, spawnedout spring steelhead that devoured a gray drake spinner on the surface while she was targeting trout with her four-weight. Many drop-back steelhead remain in food-rich rivers into June to devour insects and baitfish like resident trout. Late May and early June offer the best chance for steelhead on a dry fly.

Exactly how many fish are "lined" on gravel will remain a mystery. The days when the fish are off the bite and have been "beaten" hard by fishermen, a good number of fish will be lined. When the bite is on, the opposite will occur.

The tradition of fishing for gravel-spawning, spring steelhead in the Great Lakes has taken place for approximately 125 years. As sportsmen, we must apply our ethical knowledge toward this murky issue and deal with it rather than debating it in a non-productive, accusatory way.

Spring Players
Fresh Fish and Drop-Backs

If gravel fishing is not your cup of tea, you can try a more refreshing approach for newly migrated fresh-run fish or post-spawn steelhead dropping back to the Great Lakes. Since the urge to eat is quite strong in the fresh migrators—which were eating several days earlier before entering the rivers—their aggressive attitude towards a fly will elicit hard, jolting strikes. Post-spawn, drop-back fish migrating back to the big lake will be in search of food to replenish their exhausted fat supply and boost their metabolism.

The early black stonefly adult which hatches in Great Lakes springtime.

When targeting fresh migrators coming up for the spawn, focus on areas *near* spawning gravel since the fish are moving quickly to these sites. Pocket-water throats and riverbend tailouts are prime targeting areas for these fish. Since they are relatively new to the riverine environment, they are quite wary, often seeking cover. As water temperatures rise in the later springtime days of May and June, these player fish will chase classic wets, Speys, and streamers with a vengeance.

Drop-back steelhead come in two varieties: movers and clingers. The movers migrate down the river system quickly and often do not feed until they reach the big water. The rate of drop-back will coincide with existing water conditions. High, and conversely low, flows will accelerate the migration. Moderate flows pace the fish and allow them to face upstream for occasional holding positions so a fly presentation can be made.

Clingers are individual fish that remain in the river system for several weeks after the spawning ritual. They are usually younger year class males and females and usually later migrating fish (May and June spawners). Tailwater steelhead rivers like Michigan's Muskegon, Manistee, and Au Sable and the Salmon River in New York will usually have more clingers because of the incredible abundance of food which these drop-backs find too irresistible. Sucker spawn, chinook salmon fry, and aquatic insects, especially mayflies, are all in super abundance during drop-back periods and the fish will chow down.

Each year on my home river of the Muskegon in Michigan, the gray drake hatch coincides with the last of the drop-back migrators. Dry-fly fishermen take several four- to six-pound steelhead on the gray drake and *Isonychia* spinner fall at night each year. Since the river has both resident brown and rainbow trout, the steelhead rises to the gray drake spinners are often quite noticeable to the resident fish. Steelhead feed much more clumsily and splash water a lot more than the tight, energy-efficient gulp of a stream trout. The clinger drop-backs will miss the fly and must be drummed up to it. They're quite fond of the fast-swimming *Isonychia* emergers and often smash an emerging soft-hackle pattern on the swing.

A Spring Fly Box

A thousand and one patterns come to mind when it comes to fly fishing for spring steelhead. Gravel patterns and patterns for fresh player/drop-back fish are the most important for spring steelhead.

Nymph fishermen can really excel in the gravel. The most common patterns are black stoneflies, green caddis, Hexagenia nymphs, Hare's Ears, and Pheasant Tails. There are perhaps hundreds of variations on each of these patterns using different materials, colors, and hooks (see color fly plates).

Nymphs using the filo-plume of the underwing of pheasant, partridge and grouse are used in Hex patterns and the famous Gartside Sparrow nymphs. Estaz nymphs and beadhead scud and caddis patterns tied in a myriad of colors also produce.

Of course, egg patterns always do well. Tie them in a wide size range from large clown eggs for dirty high water to tiny micro and nuke eggs for clear water conditions. Sucker spawn yarn is also very effective since large numbers of red horse suckers will be spawning by late spring—the steelhead and trout gorge on this.

With rivers that contain good natural populations of chinook salmon, the fry will be everywhere and a good chinook parr pattern will be necessary.

For fresh migratory/drop-back fish, a good selection of classic steelhead wets, Speys, and streamers in chartreuse, gold, and orange work best. Chartreuse egg patterns are also highly successful on fresh player fish. Baitfish-imitating streamers in white and green with pink hues also stimulate the predator response. Large Hex nymphs tied with fluffy marabou, filo-plume and other undulating materials also bring good takes.

Large, soft-hackle emergers of the gray drake and *Isonychia* variety do well for drop-backs, along with the natural mayfly spinner imitation. White streamers in all color tones imitate the various baitfish and chinook parr of the various river systems.

Variations on a theme, creativity, and an open mind will enhance your spring steelhead fly selection. But keep your foundation of the proven patterns that consistently produce from year to year.

Jointed Hex Wiggle Nymphs look up at the angler almost like curious little mice. They are extremely effective during all seasons of Great Lakes steelheading.

Chapter 7

Seasons:Summer

In my former career as an hotelier for many years, I always chose jobs with my highest priority in mind—they had to be within a close enough drive to chase trout, steelhead or salmon on my days off! I was very fortunate to have worked on the West and East Coasts of North America and in Europe, taking me to salmonid destinations most people only dream of. But when the call came for an offer to open up a hotel in Indianapolis, Indiana I was quite concerned. I envisioned all my fishing exploits revolving around small farm ponds and Hoosier prairie streams with smallmouth bass, if I was lucky. Endless flat fields of corn were a far cry from the snow-capped mountains that adorned the steelhead rivers of British Columbia. However, Indiana did have forty miles of shoreline on the steelhead factory of Lake Michigan. There was a glimmer of hope.

Before saying yes to the big-buck job offer, I had to make a quick call to the Indiana DNR office in Michigan City which was about a two-and-a-half-hour drive from Indy. I heard some tight-lipped talk of summer steelhead along what they call the Gold Coast shoreline. Dan Brazo, one-time head biologist of Indiana's Lake Michigan program really got me excited. "It's the best-kept steelhead secret in America. We raise a million Skamania summer steelhead and they pour into our creeks and the St. Joseph River by the thousands—twenty-pounders too," Dan exuberantly lauded. I was psyched up to say the least. I took the job, and began my pursuit for the silver tarpon of Lake Michigan—Skamania steelhead.

The dog days of summer and a 100-degree heat wave which gripped the Midwest in my first summer in Indianapolis, made it

The magnificent leaping of summer Skamania steelhead can be compared to the antics of Atlantic salmon and tarpon.

Brian Hanchen Photo

A chrome mint summer Skamania steelhead taken on a black-and-purple leech from Lake Michigan's St. Joseph River. On the often off-colored Class II waters in agriculturally-rich regions of the Great Lakes where siltation run-off is a factor, black-and-purple marabou or bunny strips combined with metallic blue and purple Flashabou provide high visibility and movement.

Brian Hanchen Photo

really tough to get enthusiastic about Great Lakes steelhead. I read every local fishing rag, snooping for information on this, literally, hot summer fishery. Fly fishing was yet to be explored on these small creeks that looked more like Louisiana catfish ditches. The creeks always appeared off-color—a sort of limy green, mocha color. These muddy ditches soon revealed their secret when I dipped in my thermometer on a sweltering July day and found them running at 59 degrees—aha! Limestone-fed spring seeps. Ignoring the discarded refrigerators, shopping carts and tires that provided the streamside ambiance and structure, not to mention the sewage treatment plant that was pouring liquid with a funny smell, my quest for Skamania steelhead began. I was about to enter into a new era of my steelhead apprenticeship amidst the backdrop of smoke-bellowing steel mills, nuclear power plants, and the Chicago skyline not far across the lake.

My first step was to seek out a guide. Not surprising, I found none. Paging through an article in a fish and game publication, I came upon a man known as "No Net Joe," CEO of Joe's Guide Service (aka Joe LeMarche). It was around the 4th of July when I called him. We'd had some serious thunderstorms and rainfall, which cooled the weather and dropped the air temperatures from the oppressing 90s to almost unseasonably low 60s. On the phone Joe told me, "the fish were pouring in the creeks by the thousands." Yeah right, I thought. Joe was not a fly fisherman, he preferred light noodle rods with light-line bobber techniques using spawn sacs, Gummy Bears, licorice sticks, spinners, and marshmallow worm rigs. Being an ex-Indiana DNR creel clerk, he should know where the fish were. He was a very kind man. We booked the date and I was pumped-up, yet still skeptical.

Our outing began with an early morning rendezvous at a doughnut shop, one mile up from the Bethlehem Steel Mills along the Lake Michigan shoreline. The creek was gushing with chocolate-colored water after the recent rains and I was a bit concerned. Joe said not to worry. Before we left, he popped into the carryout for several packs of Gummy Bears—that's candy to the non-familiar.

As I waded into the creek, I was astounded to see wave after wave of steelhead pouring through the creek system while waking the water like pods of walrus, occasionally they would even hit my shins and calves. "This is amazing," I shouted to Joe as he rigged up his spin outfit with chartreuse Gummy Bears. By the way, the Gummy Bears also provided Joe with snacks as he diligently fished them. In a pool the size of a pick-up truck, I had my first hook-up with Mr. Skamania. It hammered a hot pink leech and jumped seven times with wild bronco-busting runs before it beached itself. Adrenaline pumping and out of breath, I looked into my prey's eyes and thought this fish was not of this world. I've never had a fish fight as hard and with such acrobatic moves as the Skamania—it had a suicidal, maniacal personality. As more hook-ups came that day (I counted 31), I was progressively falling victim to Skamania Mania as the locals called it, and became addicted for life. Needless to say, I hunt them passionately today and will for as long as I'm able.

Understanding the Nature of the Beast

In 1971, Bill Hollingsworth, Indiana Fishing Chief, secured summer steelhead eggs from the Skamania fish hatchery on the Washougal River in Washington State. He raised 100,000 smolts out of a makeshift hatchery using a fairgrounds aquarium, little did he know that Indiana was to create a dynasty run of steelhead unprecedented in the Great Lakes.

In order to create a summer fishery along the fishless and warm Indiana southern Lake Michigan shoreline, Hollingsworth, biologist Bob Koch, and Neil Ledet persisted until the mother-lode run of 1981 brought Indiana worldwide attention when lean, hard-muscled, silver torpedoes in the 12- to 23-pound range as four-year-old fish showed up. Record books were shattered that July with three fish over 23 pounds taken. In 1993 the Great Lakes and World All Tackle was broken by Kyle Johnson with a 31-pound, 4-ounce monstrosity taken off of Illinois waters. It was estimated at 8 to 10 years old and a Skamania released by Indiana. Today, summer steelhead are pursued and treasured in most of the Great Lakes states and Province of Ontario, and create a year-round fishery for the avid four-seasons steelheader.

To know summer steelhead is to master them. Michigan experimented with Oregon strains of summer fish from the Rogue, Umqua, and other systems with limited success, only to discard them from their hatchery program for lack of returns and potential genetic problems with their wild Michigan-strain fish. Virtually all summer steelhead in the Great Lakes, other than the wild runs of Lake Erie, Superior's and Huron's north shore, are of Skamania origin. This "designer steelhead" which originated from the Skamania fish hatchery on the Washougal River had specific criteria to meet for their development of the strain. As a result of declining runs of the once-famous summer steelhead of the Washougal which Bill McMillen, noted West Coast steelheader, wrote so eloquently of in his book *Dry Line Steelhead*, the Washington Fish Commission decided to make some changes.

The author holds a perfect summer Skamania specimen, that hammered a pink marabou Spey fly on Indiana's Trial Creek.

To create a "super strain" of summer fish, the first selection standards were to choose early running fish—those that made it back to the Skamania hatchery, which was at the headwaters of the river, in April, May and June. This ensured an early running steelhead migrating on photoperiods of daylight and certain water temperature variables. It also was a race horse, galloping quickly back to its natal starting gate. This selection had both good and bad implications. On the positive side, there was no mistaking the early returning fish, for they migrated quickly, keeping this selection trait clean. On the flip side, it was bad for the anglers since the steelhead did not stage along the river system like natural fish do, providing holding and taking lies for the fly fisher.

The next criteria was for early spawning fish—those that hit gravel and reproduced in January and February, as opposed to late March or April. Finally, and perhaps the most impacting of all the selection traits, was choosing 3-salt steelhead (fish that spent 3 years in the ocean); females would be 30 inches or more in length, males 34 inches or larger.

This super selection created gargantuan steelhead that spent a full three years in the ocean where they fed like garbage disposals, coming back to the river with big broad shoulders on a sleek and tubular body. These "genetic Frankensteins" as Michigan steelhead biologist Paul Seelbach put it, spend an extra year out in the big water and come back so cocky that when you hook them, you can almost hear them bellow, "How dare you!"

What differentiates the Skamania from other Great Lakes strains, both hatchery reared and wild, is this bold and brassy predisposition to take the fly with reckless abandon, which I believe

stems from their longer time in the big lake away from man and fishing pressure. Also, according to close friend Roger Greil, Lake Superior State Aquatic Laboratory Atlantic salmon expert, "They are so far away from the sexual drive which turns off the bite," and makes these fish monsters of the rivers.

Unfortunately, this noble fighting warrior is subject to the hostile environments of warm rivers and streams and life-threatening low water levels unable to house them. Large, chrome fish that succumb to the 78-degree water temperatures and lack of oxygen, is the tragic side of the Skamania fishery in the Great Lakes. In the traditionally cool Great Lakes summers of the past, their survival was not a problem. During the monumental heat waves of the '90s, the Skamania suffered tragic losses.

Most believe this is a put-grow-and-take fishery, mortality by anglers and Mother Nature is to be expected. This is quite sad when we're dealing with such an impressive beast as the Skamania steelhead. I regret that, for the most part, nothing can be done, other than planting them in rivers and streams with cool spring flows or bottom draw tailwaters. A return to the cooler summers of the past may be wishful thinking as global warming rears its ugly and uncertain head at this new millennium.

Timing the Summer Runs

Summer steelhead normally begin their migration up their natal rivers any time from June through September. The months of July and August usually see the bulk of the migration. Summer steelhead have been known to migrate as early as May and well into the fall on extremely warm spring and summer days.

There are three migrating signals for the summer run. Photoperiod on length of daylight is critical to all spawning-run migrations. Since the summer-runs don't spawn until February or March, the longest daylight periods of June will start the schooling up process when the steelhead are far offshore.

Perhaps most critical to these genetically designed fish is the state fisheries department's operations for capturing fish to be stripped of eggs and milt in hatcheries for future stockings. This factor will single-handedly alter the genetic migrating signal. If

The breathtaking leaps of a silver summer Skamania steelhead break the transposed sky on the waters of Lake Michigan's St. Joseph River.

early running fish are captured for broodstock in June, the timing will allow for the traditional June-through-August runs. If fish for egg taking are not harvested until middle August, as was the case of Indiana's trail creek in years past, the early running tendancy to run in May and June may get diluted. This would eventually push the summer-runs into fall migrators.

There is also the impact of natural selection molding the future of the runs. Since these fish are being selected to run against their instinct and brings them into life-threatening warm and low water conditions, there is a self-preservation drive to negate their genetic design and remain out in the cooler, big-lake water, to run in the fall when river conditions are more accommodating. Fisheries managers have documented fresh-run summer steelhead in October and November which have either had late weir-harvesting genetics or simply defied their programing and did what was best. The greatest potential for the fall migration of summer steelhead comes from wild fish, which are few in the summer steelhead world, except for a few north-shore Great Lakes tributaries. Here the genetic signals can be altered through generations of spawners and a niche can be carved out.

Perhaps the most notable factor that can produce later-running summer steelhead is possible interbreeding with Great Lakes winter-run strains that enter the rivers in the fall through winter.

Finally, one of the most reliable of all migrating signals is the alignment and correlation of water temperatures, which can be monitored on the Internet using satellite temperature readings for the Great Lakes and the general weather forecasts. The gradual heating of the offshore water, coupled with long daylight photoperiods, starts the urge of the schooling runs to target the shoreline and the natal river, stream, and creek basins of their origin during the May-June time period. The critical link for the summer migration is once again the "window of opportunity" between river temperatures and river-mouth beach temperatures. When they both line up with ideal water temperatures (57-68 degrees), a massive upstream migration will take place.

Since river-mouth beach temperatures can run very warm from June through August, averaging in the 70s and reaching as high as 78-80 degrees in extremely hot summers, these temperatures can be a serious red flag to upstream migration. Perhaps the single most important element necessary for upriver movement is the magic of offshore winds. When these winds occur, especially over several days with strong wind velocities or for extended periods with lighter, constant velocities, they will blow the warm coastal waters out into the lake and create an undertow of cold offshore water. All Great Lakes beach-goers have seen this phenomenon. One day bathers bask in the comfortable waters only to find the waters on the same beach to be toe-numbing cold the next—temperature drops from the mid-70s to the upper 50s are common.

Summer steelhead use this fluctuation in the water temperature and pile up in rivers in good numbers. Temperature, rather than water levels, is the single most important factor for migration. During the phenomenal returns in June and July of the

This Skamania steelhead was captured after jumping three times consecutively. Skamania, with their insane leaping ability, have been known to jump into boats, crash into people's private parts and stomachs, often knocking the wind out of them.

heat-stricken summer of 1999, steady southerly offshore winds off the tributaries of Indiana created massive runs of 14- to 27-pound summer steelhead in creeks that were barely dried up. Fifty hook-up days were common. Offshore winds coupled with cooling conditions from a thunderstorm and deluge of rain sending rivers out of their banks are ideal conditions if they come together. Once the waters recede, the fish will be spread throughout the entire watershed.

Keep in mind that ideally the offshore wind should align with the direction and place in the lake into which the river is emptying. For rivers like the Big Manistee and St. Joseph in Michigan, an east wind is essential. The Salmon River in New York would need a south to southeasterly wind, the Root in Wisconsin, a westerly.

Target the months of July and August and watch for the critical offshore wind opportunities and cooler summer weather.

Targeting the Great Lakes Summer Run

Before beginning your quest for summer steelhead, inquire about the current run status of the river you're going to fish. Since all Great Lakes states and the Province of Ontario have experimented with summer strains over the past years, summer-run programs and strains stocked have changed drastically. Consulting your area fisheries officials will give you the most current and most accurate information.

As a general reference, Indiana, Wisconsin, Illinois, Michigan, and New York are planting the largest numbers of Skamania-strain steelhead. Wisconsin's Root, Sheboygan, Manitowa, Oconto and Kewanee receive the greatest Wisconsin returns. Indiana's Trail, Little Calumet and Salt creeks runs are massive. Perhaps the greatest returns in North America occur on Michigan and Indiana's shared St. Joseph River. Michigan's Big Manistee also has excellent runs below Tippy Dam in Wellston. The Salmon River in New York has been concentrating and expanding its summer-run program.

The Province of Ontario has experimented with summer runs and has created some wild summer-run fisheries, like the Steel in Lake Superior's Thunder Bay and other Georgian Bay streams of Lake Huron. The Grand River of Lake Erie is recently producing some August to September running steelhead, which promises to be an exciting new fishery. Lake Ontario's north shore sees limited runs on the Credit and Wilmott systems.

Paramount in your pursuit for summer runs is the hunt for cold water and preferably good flows. Before embarking on a stream or river, it's best to hire a reputable guide who has experience with summer steelhead. If there are none, local creel clerks and biologists or your local fly shop can steer you in the right direction.

Obtain topographic maps of the river you're going to explore, look especially for spring-creek flows and seeps that will congregate fish because of the cold water that often hits a warm mainstream flow. I was amazed when exploring the Skamania streams of Indiana and the St. Joseph how many roads were entitled Mineral Springs Road, Big Spring Road, Sulfur Springs

Silver and gold: a summer steelhead taken and the reel that brought it in.

Road, etc. This is as good a hint as you will ever have. Look for alkaline-loving vegetation like watercress, Elodea, duckwort, etc. in these tributary streams. Any significant, or even minimal, cold discharge will attract Skamania at its creek mouths.

Since the fish move through the system quickly, any obstructions curtailing upstream migration will congregate fish. Especially important are cool, oxygenated hydro dams. There are five hydrodams on the St. Joseph with fish ladders and all of them concentrate fish.

Deep holes with structure and wooded debris are your option because they are the only safe refuge for large fish. Since their spawning drive is many months away, they have no desire, or need, to be near gravel areas.

Highly-oxygenated pools, tailout riffles, and pocket water are excellent places to look for summer steelhead. Since these large fish require a lot of oxygen for their massive bodies, they will risk being seen to venture out in shallow riffles, particularly in the morning.

I recall a brutally hot day on New York's Salmon River with guide Dave Barber, former owner of the Fish Inn Post in Altmar, New York. Temperatures soared to near 100 degrees and his "buffet barge" (as he calls his Willie drift boat) nearly crunched the large Skamanias holding in inches of water as we dredged the shallow riffles going down river. The riffles produced life-giving oxygen for the steelhead.

With Skamania steelhead there is a tremendous amount of straying to other rivers. Wisconsin fish may end up in Michigan, Indiana fish slip into all of the Lake Michigan tributaries, and many Salmon River fish from New York end up in Ontario streams. Since they are stocked as relatively larger smolts and migrate quickly, they don't necessarily feel loyalty to any one river. Cold, flowing streams within a fairly short distance of the big lake will attract these wandering nomads quickly if the conditions for migration are right.

Streams that were stocked at one time—like the Pere Marquette, White, Betsie, and Boardman of Michigan, along with the Lake Erie streams of New York—still get remnant wild runs of these fish in very small proportions. Anglers stripping black Woolly Buggers for trout often get a big surprise when a ballistic, silver bullet manhandles their four-weight rod sending the angler into shock.

Phases of the Run

As with the other seasons, there are two phases of the summer fishery: the fresh run and holding stage. The fresh run is obviously preferred by the fly angler since these fish run up the rivers and attack your fly with reckless abandon. Usually the aggressive drive will be full blown for about the first 72 hours of upriver migration before the need to conserve energy and to adjust to the often oxygen-depleted, warm rivers. Some of the hottest action occurs in the pre-dawn hours along the river mouth pier heads where fly anglers stripping streamers in fluorescent colors can do very well.

Unlike other winter-run strains which are usually not as responsive to the fly during a major upriver migration, the Skamania are highly vulnerable to your fly offering while they move upriver quickly, negotiating as many as 10 miles of river in several hours.

The holding stage can be the most difficult to penetrate. Once the excitement of the fresh run ceases, and water levels have dropped and river temperatures are reaching the critical-for-survival stage, the fish will park on cool springs, deep holes, and other places for survival and then begin to act like sulking August Atlantic salmon. They become aware of their new home which lacks the cold-water comfort, depth, and smogasboard buffet of

their big lake environment. They will be stubborn or not hit at all, even when provoked by attractor patterns. Very early morning and late evening can elicit activity from these fish since their photo imprinting to these periods coincides with the feeding and baitfish-ambushing behavior of the big-lake environment. This biological timeclock is well programmed.

Major weather changes and frontal systems will rejuvenate these pooled-up fish, especially if a cold front with precipitation occurs for an extended period. With these weather systems, the urge to move will manifest itself again. Unlike the fall, winter, and spring steelhead, in their cold-water environments, that turn off with major barometric changes, summer steelhead seem to be invigorated by these drastic barometric changes since their sole purpose seems to be migration driven by the need for cool-water relief.

Fly Tactics and Patterns
for Summer Steelhead

With each passing summer run, I am beginning to better understand these magnificent fish. Though it seems the aggressive Skamania hit just about anything, I've begun to see a more clearly defined trend in their selectivity preferences. Focus on three colors for targeting fly selection: hot fluorescent, the power of black, and terrestrial insect impressions.

Hardware and bait anglers have long hammered fresh-run Skamanias with hot orange, red, pink, chartreuse, and electric blue crankbaits and spoons. Silver in combination with these colors works well also. These colors stimulate the aggressive drive of the fish yet correspond with nothing natural. They simply provoke the attack mechanism of the new arrival. Fish Bunny Leeches, marabou and traditional Speys and streamers in these colors. Use Flashabou coupled with rabbit strip and marabou, which give the angler maximum visibility. Don't be afraid to fish these colors in relatively large sizes up to 2/0. The best presentations are made with sink-tips on single- or two-handed rods. Use classic steelhead wet-fly techniques swinging down and across, with aggravated, intermittent fast strips to agitate the fish. When you're stripping big leeches and Speys, Skamania prefer a very fast pace. Fresh-run fish are of course much more aggressive than holding, sulking fish.

The correlation between terrestrial insects and the summer fishery was perhaps my most interesting finding. I was finally able to test and duplicate it with confidence in the summer of 1999. Through research by Great Lakes biologists, it was known that steelhead fed in the summer months in the far offshore waters of the Great Lakes. Air and water current interactions form thermal bars there. Normally water currents run south to north while consistent winds are normally westerly. Where warmer shoreline waters meet colder offshore waters, thermal bars are created.

Landborne terrestrial insects ride the high, thermal air currents blowing offshore. The bugs get sucked into these high, thermal currents and eventually land out in the big lakes. When the cold and warm waters interact, hydrodynamic wave and current action congests a wide variety of floating bugs, debris and schools of baitfish along a seam known as the "scum line." Aquatic water boatman, shrimp, and other macro-invertebrates create a chow line for the steelhead who are very surface oriented and prefer to eat other food forms because of their lower attack and efficiency speed. Charter captains like Dick Swan and Mike Gnatkowki began to explore these scum-line fisheries when bacterial kidney disease (BKD) put an end to the chinook salmon fishery. It was obvious that bugs and buggy-looking foods were foremost on the mind of summer steelhead that freshly migrated from these scum lines to the river environments.

Back in the early 90s, I created a Woolly Bugger-style fly known as the Electric Candy Cane. It incorporated marabou for the tail along with alternating bands of chenille along the hook with rubber legs and schlappen. Though initially tied with black and red bands, the chartreuse/yellow and black bands seemed to work much better for fresh-run fish. Could this yellow and black banding be impressionistic of bees and hornets and the yellow and black potato bug that carpet beaches in the summer? That was my guess. One of the hottest flies for the summer of 1999 was a black bead-head bee pattern, tied with alternating bands of yellow and black vernille with a few turns of grizzly hackle. With their increasingly buggy-looking motifs, the flies and streamers I began using looked more like "A Bug's Life," than classic steelhead flies. Incorporating peacock herl, tarantula legs, etc., a close circle of Michigan steelheaders came up with unique, buggy-looking imitations that were deadly. Well-known Michigan steelhead guide and friend, Seann McDonald, could not believe it when he hammered the Skamanias one July morning on the Big Manistee at Tippy Dam on a bee imitation—exciting stuff.

Finally, the last piece of the puzzle is the power of black. Black has always been a proven pattern color for Atlantic and Pacific salmon, steelhead, and trout for generations. Classic patterns revolve around it. Many insects like beetles, wasps, etc. are black, plus it's a very easy color to see when waters are tainted, which means fresh migrations of aggressive fish. They are also less alarming to the fish and extremely lethal when tied with motion materials like marabou, rabbit strips, schlappen and Spey hackle.

Great Lakes lower river basins abound with black leeches and are traversed by steelhead smolts on downstream migrations. Also, since holding summer fish nose right up to the bottom of the river's pools and runs, they view a wide array of small dark sculpin, tadpoles, and leeches not to mention large hellgrammite and stonefly nymphs in dark tones. Black Woolly Buggers, leeches, stones, sculpins and anything wiggly and black are the ultimate summer steelhead starting point.

When holding fish have set up residence in summer rivers, they will get a "second wind" if they find ideal habitat with cold waters and good flows. Through stomach samples, I have found crayfish, tadpoles, frogs—you name it! While fishing the backwater spring seeps on the St. Joseph in the summer of 1998, many fat chartreuse-colored leaf worms in the overhanging trees dropped into the river. No wonder a chartreuse chenille-bodied Woolly Worm produced so well. The parasitic lamprey, particularly unique to the Great Lakes fishery, attaches itself to the salmonid and literally sucks the life out of them. When small they are blackish-brown like leeches. Could the aggressive response toward them by steelhead be an act of self-preservation—maybe?

Author plays a leaping summer steelhead on a Spey rod as the fish cartwheels down the St. Joseph River.

~ Steelhead Dreams ~

Chapter 8

Presentation and Tackle

Though we both chase the same fish, Pacific and Great Lakes steelheaders approach their sporting passion from fundamentally different perspectives. Pacific anglers utilize the classic steelhead wet-fly swing and present flies on the surface. Great Lakes anglers are for the most part preoccupied with depth penetration of their fly delivery on or near the river bottom, which correlate to the harsher weather extremes they encounter. Thus a major philosophical schism has occured between the more puristic approach by the west coast angler and the unorthodox techniques of the Great Lakes steelheader. In an almost Halfordian/Skues-like controversy (the great English dry-fly versus the nymph ethical debate of the 1800s where Halford's proper dry-fly methods condemn the bottom-dredging of Skue's nymph techniques as barbaric and non fly-fishing), the Great Lakes steelheader has been dismissed by the West Coast stoics as lead-tossers, gravel rappers, and charlatans of the "classic" West Coast greased line, dry-fly, riffling hatch, and wet-fly techniques. Complicating this even further was the past presence of legalized snagging in the Great Lakes salmonid fishery which features undesirable techniques, such as "gigging, lifting, and ripping"—ugly hook-setting techniques.

I have opened Pandora's box on our controversial Great Lakes past hoping to lead the way to a bright, shining future. There is a silver lining in that some old-timers and progressive young anglers are committing themselves to ethical sporting principles. I am optimistic that our present and future direction is along a healthy road.

In the past and also today, anglers focus on depth-presentation techniques. The Great Lakes region differs considerably from Pacific West Coast environs. There is no disputing the fact that Great Lakes autumns, winters, and springs are more severe than the more pleasant climates of the West Coast with their ocean-current and jet-stream-related weather patterns. Massive snowfall, frigid temperatures, fluctuating barometers, and frozen rivers rage, for the most part, during the prime times of our steelhead runs of winter-strain fish of California origin. With such adverse conditions, which really limit fly presentation to bottom-dredging nymphs, yarn, and wets, steelhead anglers have prided themselves on their fine-tuning of depth penetration techniques. Obviously, to the practical-minded angler, dry-line, greased wet-fly techniques were non-applicable since the steelhead would not move like they do in 50-degree water. These water conditions can be found in mild West Coast winters—rarely do they exist in the Great Lakes.

It is because of these environmental differences that presentations in the Pacific and Great Lakes areas differ. Though bottom-bouncing drift techniques continue to be the basis for spawn drifters on the West Coast under harsh river conditions, the classic West Coast steelhead fly fisher chose not to use this technique. Inversely, in order to fish the tributaries of the Lake Superior shoreline in a blinding snowstorm with rivers running like a 33-degree slushy, a steelheader must have a headstrong predisposition to hook and play a steelhead. These conditions do not allow for the leisurely choices a steelhead angler under more pleasant conditions would have. Thus, inclement weather conditions, and the nurturing reinforcement of steelhead hook-ups, has led the Great Lakes angler into using bottom-drifting techniques.

Decisions, decisions...which fly will pique the interest of a summer steelhead?

In the early years, both West Coast and Great Lakes steelheading were heavily emersed in "machismo," with anglers of legendary status competing to see who could catch and kill the most steelhead. Harvesting mass numbers of fish was "the thing" back in the days when double-digit fish were hung on poles and proudly displayed. Since these were the days of plenty, only a few stuck to hard conservation efforts and catch-and-release—and most were fly anglers. The angling climate was very competitive. The "river legend" or "steelhead slayer" pursued very effective techniques to enhance their ego. In our brief 100-year steelheading history, the steelhead slayer was the role model, the ultimate fisherman. These weathered, hard-core steelheaders were known to catch fish under the worst of conditions. The best presentation was an accurate bottom-bouncing, dead-drift, keeping the fly or bait moving more slowly than the current, and drag free, on a slip weighted rig. The convenience and effectiveness of this technique was too powerful to resist. Nurtured in this angling climate, the Great Lakes steelheader rarely explored other West Coast methods since their technique was so effective. This "if it ain't broke, don't fix it" mentality endured for many years and is commonly accepted today.

Most of the fly-rod drift rigs used monofilament as their main line. There was no fly-casting—just a spinning/bait-rod style lob. Though effective, there had to be a more aesthetic "fly-fishing" type approach. Enter Bruce Richards and Ray Schmidt.

Developing the Running Line Revolution

In the early 1970s, things were brewing on the Manistee River systems of Lake Michigan's Eastern Shore. Bruce Richards, developer for 3M's Scientific Anglers line series, along with one-time sales representative for the company and now legendary Michigan river guide, Ray Schmidt, developed a fly fishing technique incorporating the bottom drift fishing method so popular with the hardware and bait fishermen.

Schmidt, starting a new career as a fly-fishing outfitter, decided to dedicate himself to the pursuit of flies-only, even as the bottom-bouncing, baitfishing steelheaders laughed their way back to the boat landings with limit catches of winter steelhead. As Schmidt and company tested the classic West Coast steelhead flies and techniques with limited success, they realized there must be another way. The baitfishers were so successful with their bottom drift fishing techniques. Using lead and long leaders to hold their spawn sacs (either fresh steelhead or salmon eggs tied in wedding veil mesh) or live wigglers (the natural nymphs of the giant mayfly *Hexagenia limbata*) on the slow currents of the river bottom, they'd get their presentations right in front of the lethargic winter steelhead.

Bruce Richards of Scientific Anglers writes, "With holding winter fish in deep pockets, pools, and fast water, conventional full-sinking or sinking-tip lines can't effectively present a fly "drag-free" to steelhead in these places. The buoyancy of full floating line often creates individual uplifting and drag induced frustrating scenarios. A small diameter shooting line with a long monofilament leader with split-shot above the fly is the most effective delivery." Soon Schmidt and others (like myself, a young experimenter and others throughout the Great Lakes, who were modifying similar fly systems based on bait-rig techniques at the same time) further focused on creating yarn-fly egg imitations to imitate spawn in various colors and also to create exact duplicates of the Michigan wiggler. By further developing the art of bottom drift fishing by fine-tuning the cast, depth penetration and control of the drift to desirable holding and moving steelhead lies, Schmidt and Richards developed a fly fishing system

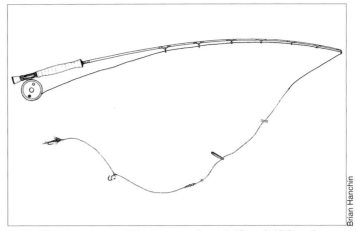

Shooting or running line is put on the reel. About 9-10 feet of 8- to 10- pound fluorocarbon is nail-knotted to the running line. A "slinky" (parachute cord with lead) or pencil weight is eyed through the leader in "slip sinker" fashion. A small ceramic bead is placed before the two-way swivel for proper weight rotation. One or two flies in tandem are placed below the two-way swivel.

that became effective and put fly fishermen into a dimension of big-game steelhead fishing where they failed before.

Conventional fly fishing uses the line weight to cast the fly. With the shooting/running lines, weight is propelled to cast the line. Many will agree that this is not fly fishing—and rightfully so. Yet one still fishes with a fly rod, fly reel, fly line, and fly. As Bruce Richards says, "It is a legal and effective technique, what we call it doesn't matter."

Over the years, this Great Lakes technique has become something of an artform with the many new running lines being manufactured and perfected. Unique weight rigs such as slip sinkers, slinkies, etc. and exact flies with MWM (motion without movement) help us continue to evolve the techniques. The bottom penetration legacy and tradition has been firmly established in the Great Lakes since the late 1970s.

Coming Full Circle: Personal Choices and Style

As seasoned Great Lakes steelheaders mastered the sport of the bottom drift, *once the novelty of the running line experience wore off, they searched for other more sporting and aesthetic techniques.* Curiosity drove them to the more sporting and hallowed "true fly fishing like" practices that west coast anglers employed for decades. West Coast manufacturers, writers, and steelhead experts saw great market potential in the rapidly flourishing Great Lakes steelhead fishery and started promoting their methods and techniques to an eager listening audience. By marketing and educating more fly fishing-like techniques, a growing number of Great Lakes steelheaders quickly adapted the classic wet-fly and slack mending techniques using impressionistic patterns with growing success.

The lethally effective technique of bottom drifting was easy to execute, not to mention it took a lot of fish under stubborn conditions. With this "apple of Eden" temptation just a quick rig or adjustment away, sufficient stream times and traditional techniques were, and still are, not given proper attention by "quality" anglers—why grab a muzzle-loader rifle when you've got a machine gun?

Personal choices and philosophies of the Great Lakes steelheaders is entering a new phase of steelheading. To put away the lead and adapt to more classical steelhead methods takes some maturing on the part of the steelhead fly fisher. The question, "Is this all there is, there must be something more?" comes to the steelheader who has caught his or her thousandth steelhead and is looking for even more thrills from the sport. With this desire to enhance the sport in steelheading, degree of difficulty becomes a challenge and new passion.

One of the chief obstacles to taking on new challenges is the fish numbers game. "Hooked 57, landed 31", "landed 14 over 10 pounds", these self-gratifying endorsements are always heard when effective steelheaders discuss their victories at the end of a day. There is something manly about bellowing these victorious proclamations—for those that know my enthusiasm, I have been one of the most guilty in this respect. We will never become filthy rich hooking steelhead, so when we steelheaders and guides bellow such accolades, we are often looking for admiration for our dedication in mastering the sport. For it often takes a Thor-like invincibility to battle all the weather extremes to conquer nature and the elusive steelhead.

This bragging stage in a steelheader's development is an important part of reaching the next level. For many, the numbers game is "it"—the end-all to the entire experience. As long as the numbers angler does not deplete the resource by misdirected ego gratification, over-harvesting and greed—go enjoy! One must remember that angling—if one doesn't practice catch-and-release—and hunting are "kill sports." If one looks at the personality profiles of the notorious killers, henchmen, and barbarians, and the massive decimation of human life they incurred, you will often see a softening of their beastly personality as the carnage numbers went out of control. The art of killing takes on little gratification if it comes about too easy. Torture then becomes psychological. Cats like to play with their prey, but human animals eventually get bored with blood. This is the silver lining that has the potential to save mankind, along with our declining world fisheries. There is no shame in an angler harvesting a beautiful steelhead and preparing it with white wine, herbs, fresh morel mushrooms, giving the family a true gastronomic feast. It is only when we abuse this right that we bastardize our sport and existence. Excess is the chief problem of all of man's destructive vices.

We are now in a stage of development in our steelhead fishing where we can make choices. With tremendous modern-day fisheries management creating a 365-day, fall, winter, spring, and summer season for Great Lakes steelhead, we must make personal decisions on our angling style. Ask yourself questions like: how many fish do I want to catch; how do I want to fish for them; when do I want to fish for them; and so on. We can match our personal fly fishing identity, with how we choose to derive pleasure from the sport of steelhead angling. These are truly exciting times. The new millennium will take the Great Lakes steelheader out of the dark shadows of lead dredging and allow us to experiment with a myriad of techniques, both classic and cutting-edge. Though bottom-drift fishing will forever be our technique, we can explore the other methods at our disposal. In this new, unfolding modern era of Great Lakes steelheading, a flicker of hope is revealing itself.

I recall a recent, cold spring evening when the fresh runs were in in good numbers and everyone was "banging 'em." This "silver lining" voiced itself in the bar where everyone was sharing fish stories over warm libations. A noted "fish-pig" (one who cannot get enough hook-ups in a day and has little or no appreciation) named MoJo (an alias to protect this newly transformed ex-fish killer) proudly proclaimed, amidst the loud bustling and bragging bar talk, came out with the sweetest words I've heard in years: "Awe, you guys whacking all those big numbers of fish on gravel, that's easy—been there, done that. I caught a chrome 15-pound female on my two-handed rod with a beautiful chartreuse

The cracked and weathered hands of a steelhead guide tie on yet another pattern in the eternal search for another hook-up.

Spey I designed—I called the pattern Mojo Rising, cool, isn't it? I only needed that one hook up and I was done, dude—bet you guys can't do that. I worked every good-looking run and pool for hours with perfect drifts until it clobbered the fly. It was awesome!"

It was at that moment I realized there is a steelhead god. The future was bright. Mojo, with all his crude and crusty ways, his tainted "fish pig" days, had come full circle.

Tactics for Bottom-Drift Fishing

A highly specialized technique initially developed on the West Coast by bait fishermen using spawn, anchovies, and shrimp , is a highly effective Great Lakes technique for steelhead where water temperatures are cold and fish are sluggish. The principle is to get the weight to tick the gravel bottom and slow the fly's presentation to slower than the current and drag free (see rig diagram for bottom-bounce drift fishing, page 34). Longer, softer-tipped fly rods usually work better for this highly tactile approach to fly delivery and strike detection. The rig consists of a nine- to eleven-foot six- through eight-weight rod (depending on the size of fish and water volume), a good drag system reel and proven running line. Eight feet of 10- to 12-pound monofilament or 0X to 1X fluorocarbon are tied directly to the running line with a nail knot. Using what's called a "slip sinker," add lead to the main leader so that it swings freely up and down the line. Though some anglers use three-way swivels and tie the lead in with direct connection with the line, I firmly believe that the "slip rig" allows your presentation to drift more freely and naturally and lessens the mouth detection of a steelhead when it cautiously picks up the weighted offering. The use of Slinkies (parachute cord packed with buckshot and clamped on a snap swivel), a two-way swivel with a tag of split shot or pencil lead with an eye running up and down the leader also works well. A two-way swivel is then tied in the main leader once the slip-lead rig is in place. This swivel stops the downward movement of the weight. From the two-way swivel, one or two flies can be added two to three feet apart and the rig is ready.

To execute the cast, caution and thought must be fully given to its method. Since weight is propelling the line, the caster must allow for the backcast to fully "tug" and load up before casting forward (similar to a bow and arrow or sling shot load). It is wise

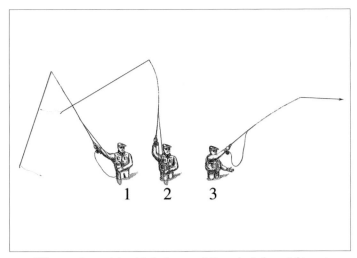

When casting weight with the bottom-drift method, the weight must load-up the rod tip then execute a high "hook shot" over your head. As the tip of the rod is loaded in the back, the forward release comes from your "pounding-a-nail" snap of the wrist.

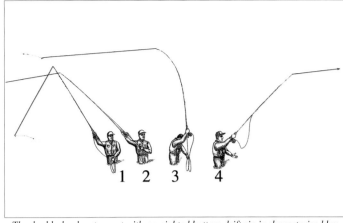

The double-haul water cast with a weighted bottom-drift rig is characterized by:
1. Angler swings toward backcast with singlehaul
2. Lets line out on back cast as rig touches watrer for a split second to load the tip
3. Second haul and snap of the wrist sends rig hurling forward
4. Rod tip and line all points to direction

to hold the elbow up at shoulder length to allow for more clearance at the terminal end above the head (you've heard of chuck-and-duck). Since the weight is heavy enough to cast the rig, muscle has no place in the delivery. Finesse and the fine-tuning of how weight responds to your casting technique takes time and patience.

For more advanced casters, a double-haul cast is highly desirable and can cover great distances. A simple haul lifts the line out of the water, an amount of line is allowed to slip through the hand on the backcast and another haul propels the line forward. When the rod is allowed to fall back to the three o'clock position, and letting the rig touch the water in back of you for a brief moment to load the rod tip (some call this a water cast), tremendous catapulting distances can be achieved.

Adjusting the line drift depends upon depth and speed of the current. Once the presentation hits water—if you are working a deep and fast run—several seconds of slack line should be given to your rig before you "get tight with it" and start to feel the bottom bounce. On deeper holes, the farther you cast upstream, the more time allowed for the rig to penetrate the strike zone. Shallower runs mean more down-and-across casting.

One of the biggest obstacles to bottom-drift fishing is snags. Several factors are a given: You will lose flies and rigs when drift fishing. The better you know your river and its bottom strata, the better off you'll be. By using a high-stick drift method, where the line runs through the fingers of your rod hand and your other hand holds and directs the surplus of the line, snags can be avoided by as much as 90%. With the high-stick method, you get a more vertical presentation of the mainline, which avoids horizontal snagging. At the slightest feel of a slow, downward-moving snag, strip the line and your rod tip with your other hand. Timing is the key—if you wait too long, the current will hang you.

It is important that you target the lie you wish to fish and cast far enough upstream so your presentation approaches the strike zone. As you cast out and your rig hits the water during the slack-line descent adjusting period, your reel hand should be stripping line off the reel to have sufficient line to let out at the end of the drift. To drift-fish effectively, one must drift the lies from top to bottom. As the drift becomes 75% complete,

anglers often run out of line and thus make an ineffective drift. As much as 60% of the steelhead takes occur at the bottom end of the drift because steelhead follow the fly down stream, or it may be that the drift is finally ticking the bottom correctly and penetrating the strike zone. With practice, you will learn the subtleties of the drift.

Adding and subtracting weights is always necessary to adjust the speed of the drift. The drift should be two or three times slower than the current. With the gliding techniques, lifting and adjusting the rod tip will help the presentation bounce along the bottom, mainly on downstream presentations or where the creases and seams of the current run out of water speed. Using somewhat of a jigging technique, you can place your offering exactly in the right holding and taking lies.

High-Stick Dry-Line Nymphing

This is a very effective technique when fish are in shallower runs and lies, or fish are holding in winter frog water (sluggish, slow deep flats). A complete, drag-free presentation is desired, with the nymph or egg patterns flowing naturally at the dead-drift speed of the current. The key is to use the floating line to present a "right 90-degree angle" drop technique with the leader and flies by using a strike indicator of some kind. This is basically sophisticated "bobber fishing" with fly tackle, but it is very effective on spooky steelhead in pristine water conditions which require light-diameter fluorocarbon leaders.

Positioning oneself for dry-line nymphing is crucial. Before attempting the technique, study the lies and holding pocket areas you wish to penetrate. Position yourself slightly upstream, begin the cast and then throw upstream slack-line mends in order for your nymph or egg offering to hit the target zone. High-sticking will allow you to control the line drag on the water and adjust the line mends up or down, depending on the speed of your presentation. High-sticking also allows maximum vertical depth presentation on fast-moving waters which drag floating lines.

Strike indicators vary between manufacturers so it's a matter of personal preference. Floating indicators include putty, greased-up yarn, umbrella yarn wrap, and foam or balsa wood/cork indicators like Thill and Corkies. Some high-stick nymphers forgo floating indicators for fluorescent leader butt section indicators.

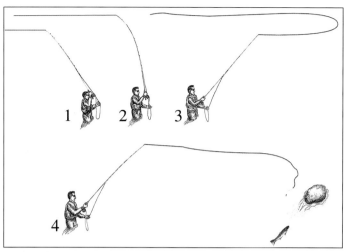

High-stick nymphing is often initiated by a tuck cast where the rod is abruptly stopped at 1 o'clock to curl the delivery for quick depth presentation.

Critical to success in floating strike indicator fishing is judging the proper depth of the water to be fished. This determines the length of line between your floating indicator and split shot weight. If needed, split shot can be added to the leader above the fly, between the two flies if fishing a double rig, or directly on the bottom, with more leader added from the last fly and shot pinched at the vertical bottom end. In the direct right-angle approach, the fly or flies must be presented no higher than a foot from the bottom since steelhead most likely are hugging the river bed between rocks and boulders. The margin of error in setting depth adjustments is very small, so be precise.

Besides strike indicator dry-line nymphing, true classic dry-line nymphing and wet-fly techniques, pioneered by Bill McMillan in his famous book *Dry Line Steelhead* (Frank Amato Publications), are preferred by traditional steelheaders. They are often very effective techniques in extremely clear water where split shot and strike indicators spook wary steelhead. By using the rolling mends of slack line and above-and-across positioning, the angler can manipulate the floating line with great accuracy. With the expansive sweeps of the fly controlled by the mends, the fish will be tempted to strike the nymph or wet fly.

Critical to McMillan's dry-line presentation are long leaders with larger and heavier 2/0 hooks providing the weight to carry the fly down to the bottom. Flies are dressed sparsely with materials like Spey hackle and silk to avoid water absorption.

I greatly enjoy using classic dry-line techniques in the early fall and late spring where the brief period exists to try this true method of steelhead fly fishing.

Classic Wet-Fly and Greased-Line Techniques

Perhaps the most pure, traditional approach to classic steelhead fly fishing is the wet-fly swing. It is an effective and uncomplicated approach which many Great Lakes steelheaders have enjoyed since the onset of the fishery more than a century ago. At the turn of the 1900s, when thousands of Pacific West Coast steelhead were being stocked in the great trout streams of the Great Lakes, many a brook trout angler swinging a pair of wet flies encountered a jolting strike from a 10-pound steelhead rainbow fresh out of the big lakes. Under conducive water temperatures—45 to 65 degrees—the crosscurrent wet-fly swing suits the playful and curious mood of a fresh-run steelhead quite well. The beauty in the

Along the berm wall of the St. Mary's River at Sault Ste. Marie, steelhead and Atlantic salmon cruise the crystal-clear waters that empty out of ice-cold Lake Superior.

many colors and materials the fly fisher can use in their wet-fly offerings makes the technique even more alluring to those that want more out of their sport. Nymphs, such as the *Hexagenia* patterns, are also effective on the swing.

Though I've seen children casting a small Mickey Finn catch nice steelhead by luck, the key to wet-fly steelheading is to have command of your presentation. By manipulating the line through proper mending techniques (both up and down mends) and depth penetration, fly speed can be adjusted to stimulate a steelhead to take your fly. Various casts get the line to settle on the water differently and will allow the angler a controlled cross-current swing.

The parachute (or puddle) cast invented by Charles Ritz is effective here; cast the forward delivery higher than normal, and drop the rod butt to produce a jagged, loose drop. The check cast is stopped similarly to the parachute cast, delivering coils of slack line near the fly penetrating the water. Zig-zagging the tip of the rod adds greater snake-like coils, an angler can choose the loose delivery method.

When swinging the fly, some anglers hold the line straight to the reel; others use several feet of slack line in the hand. Usually the steelhead hooks itself on the downward swing and is quickly in the backing, screaming the drag. Keep the drag set moderately for shock absorption. By holding slack line, you give the fish extra' time to turn on the fly, similar to the Atlantic salmon fly hook-set, where the biggest problem occurs when not enough time is given for the fish to draw the fly into the corner of its mouth.

To start the wet-fly swing, the angler is positioned slightly above and across from the lie. By using one of the slack-line casts mentioned, place a series of upstream mends to allow more slack as the fly gets to the strike zone to maximize depth penetration. With a large downstream mend, the angler must then get tight to the presentation to feel the strike and allow the hook to be set. With trial and error, you will learn to adjust the speed and depth of the fly by learning the river's hydrodynamics under its high and low flows. Another beautiful aspect of the wet-fly presentation is that each square foot of a pool or run can be systematically covered by the angler working down the water and meticulously covering each quadrant thoroughly. In this "panning for gold" manner, the angler is bound to turn up a player fish.

When steelhead anglers discuss "greased line" techniques it is like having a philosophical discussion on divinity and the existence of the supreme almighty. The crux lies in the writings of A.H.E. Woods and Donald Ferris Rudd (pen name, Jock Scott) whose treatises have been interpreted and dissected to the point of "paralysis by analysis". Since I'm not going to dive into the interpretive stigmas that have been well documented by Deke Meyer in his book *Advanced Fly Fishing for Steelhead* (Frank Amato Publications) and Jim Vincent in a thought-provoking and highly enlightening article for *Wild Steelhead & Salmon* Magazine (1996, vol. 3 no. 1) entitled "Steelhead on a Greased Line," I will attempt to share the most basic, applicable concepts with the Great Lakes steelheader. Since the peak of the Great Lakes steelhead runs occurs out of the optimum water-temperature range for surface takes (50 to 65 degrees), the greased-line approach has little relevance in the Great Lakes except for on early fall steelhead and early summer-run fish. The window of opportunity is very small (one or two weeks) and other limiting factors inhibit surface orientation by river-bound steelhead. In early fall, steelhead rivers usually have great numbers of spawning Pacific salmon which encourage bottom-drifting eggs targeted by the steelhead. Early summer-run river temperatures average from the mid-60s to the uncomfortable 70-degree range where summer steelhead bury their head on the cooler spring flows near the bottom.

The fundamentals of the greased-line approach are to present the fly "broadside" and drag-free in or slightly below the meniscus of the surface. The mending is more of a folding technique to allow for less exaggeration in the drift. The fly, as Deke Meyer describes, is tethered to the rod by a line forming a "clothesline" shape. In the days of old, most fly lines where intermediate sink so they needed to be greased for floating. The complication is allowing the fly to drift downstream sideways, employing enough tension yet balancing it with enough slack to provide a dead-drift as the fly materials react life-like in the undulating current.

To "lead the fly" as Woods specified, the rod is held off to the side and pointed downstream towards the fly—the fish often hook themselves with this method. Greased-line tactics are great fun for trout and steelhead, for both surface and subsurface conditions.

The real keys to fishing classic wet-fly and greased-line methods in the Great Lakes is to time your use of this tactic with favorable water temperatures and river flows and fish each productive stretch of water thoroughly and slowly—repeating the cast and covering the water thoroughly. Remember to let your fly "hang" at the end of your drift for a brief period since the steelhead's curiosity is often piqued by the wet-fly motion-less in the current, especially at nearshore lies. A positive mental attitude believing a steelhead is waiting for your fly is necessary. Forget about the evil temptation of the split shot and yarn so close at hand in your vest pocket. Stay the course and you'll be rewarded.

Deep-Drift Wet Sink-Tipping

The Great Lakes steelhead fly fisher should become quite proficient in this application. By getting the fly down deep and moving slowly, one can practice the art of the wet fly even under our most harsh and unfavorable steelheading conditions, which are found on a majority of our fly-fishing outings. Trey Combs, pioneering author of groundbreaking books such as *Steelhead Fly Fishing and Flies* (Frank Amato Publications) and *Steelhead Fly Fishing* (Lyons & Burford), was instrumental in perfecting this technique. Together, he and West Coast steelhead fly-fishing artisan Lanni Waller, fine-tuned the technique for one- and two-handed rod presentations in the winter. The key is to control the sink-tip by using custom-made lines which have belly sections of sufficient diameter in either floating, intermediate, or running sections that can control the rate of drift and movement by a series of slack- and stack-mending techniques. Since most winter steelhead are in a holding lie such as the gut of the pool or deep tailout flats, its metabolism is quite slow. Thus, a slow-moving fly, with MWM (motion with movement) materials such as marabou, rabbit strips, and Flashabou needs to creep slowly in front of the steelhead's face because its slow metabolism keeps it from moving to strike the fly.

With so many excellent sink-tip lines of various sinking rates, an angler need no longer cut and splice sections of the line. The winter steelhead fly fisher can now carry various spools and attachable multi-loop head tips to meet the demands of all water conditions.

Efforts should focus on slowing down the fly's swing as much a possible and keeping it over prime holding lies for as long as possible to tempt the fish to strike. With this in mind, one must also have enough tension on the line to feel the often-lethargic strike and set the hook. With cold water, a steelhead often just mouths the fly, as opposed to the aggressive takes that occur in warmer waters.

Scientific Anglers was first to pioneer the various levels of sink rates and length. Their level IV, V and the Deep Water Express in the 10- and 13-foot sink-tips are more popular. The Jim Teeny series, Jim Vincent's Rio Products, and Airflo all offer excellent assortments that can get downright confusing. Your best bet is to consult your fly fishing pro shop or contact the manufacturers themselves. Most manufacturers have Internet web sites that detail their products. With various line combinations, the angler can approach the river and use slack-line techniques in the river's uplifting push, allowing for deep penetration in the roaring, winter river.

When winter sink-tipping, you must first target the lies you hope to penetrate as you hold your fly over them for as long as possible. By focusing on the cast and envisioning your fly moving and gliding slowly through the pockets, seams, and guts of the run, your presentation will become more effective. To be successful at this technique, one must learn the river's flow and bottom structure.

Once your targeted lies are singled out and studied, choose your angle of presentation and make a slack-line cast. With a series of large upstream mends, the line is well upstream of the fly. Tight mending or stack mending close to the fly allows for the greatest depth penetration. By adding slack to the line, your fly will penetrate the bottom. The amount of slack line is dictated by speed of flow and depth. By leading your fly to the outside of the target areas and allowing the fly to drop horizontally and vertically, your fly will slowly swing into the strike zone. Make constant mend adjustments throughout the drift. Once again, envisioning your fly and how it is behaving in relationship to your line and the drift is crucial.

Feeling the weight of the sink-tip line means you are getting down. Pointing the rod tip high and upstream of the sinking line, and then following the swing with the rod, allows for maximum depth penetration and tension control to detect strikes. Keep your leader short (3 to 5 feet) from the sinking line to control the fly and depth better.

Winter strikes by a steelhead can be very subtle. Occasionally a migrating chrome fish will strike hard and hook itself. Most Great Lakes winter and coldwater steelhead normally just pick up the fly to stop it, before spitting it out. Setting the fly in a downstream sideward motion, with a quick striking style, allows you to maximize hook-ups. Remember, as you go heavier in grain sink rates, you lose strike-detection feeling because of the dampening of the strike by the line. Quite often you are striking too late, after the fish has spit the hook out. Add your cold, numb hands and fingers and the challenge is even greater, demanding greater concentration on the drift and on any subtle peculiarities in the way your line behaves, which may signal a take. Many successful winter anglers often say the line just "felt right" for a take. Practice makes perfect definitley applies to mastering this technique.

Spey Style: Two-Handed Rod Revolution

With its bold new angling era, the Great Lakes steelheading world is poised for the invasion of the two-handed Spey rod. Since a majority of our angling has involved single-handed, high-stick, bottom-bouncing noodle-style rods, the appeal of the two-handed rod need not be from only a novelty standpoint. The fact that the Spey rod covers more water, more efficiently with a long line is the great benefit of learning to use these rods and their techniques. The single-handed fly-rodder spends a lot of time picking up line, double-hauling and mending, whereas several quick and efficient swoops of the Spey rod are more time efficient and less

Spey casting a deep run, this winter steelheader is in natural camouflage of black-and-white and coonskin against the salt-and-pepper snowy background.

physically exhausting than single-handed rods—particularly on larger rivers.

With a more refined efficiency of presentation desired by a growing number of steelheaders, "faster and lighter" European-style two-handed 7- to 9-weight rods—rather than the more traditional 10- to 12-weight Spey-style models—hold a greater appeal to the modern-day steelheader. With the contemporary lines designed for all types of conditions and the Spey presentations pioneered by Hugh Falkus, Mel Kreiger. Mike Maxwell and Jim Vincent, the two-handed Spey rod will become a staple technique in the Great Lakes steelheader's presentation arsenal.

Spey-casting originated on Scotland's River Spey to overcome its steep banks and trees that made backcasting impossible. The true Spey cast uses the entire bend of the rod and strong tip section in a series of time-released motions which can be described simply as an "over-extended and hind-side roll cast." Where the roll cast is flipped or turned over in front of the angler on the water, the Spey cast is delivered perpendicularly to either side of the caster.

Mike Maxwell, the legendary dean of the Spey cast on the Pacific West Coast, is quite adamant about the differences between the true Spey cast and the overhead cast. Muddled somewhere between is the misconception that the roll cast is some sort of Spey cast. A true Spey cast is artistically presented in a series of rod manipulations of the line to deliver a constant

Great Lakes steelheaders can increase their coverage of large river systems, like on New York's Salmon River, with two-handed rods and Spey or overhead casts.

With the two-handed rod, a "push/pull" hand motion of the fore and back or side cast as in the double Spey is crucial to the technique. It is critical to keep the rod tip high to control the direction of the cast and to lift line off the water. Directing the fly in a "pole position" allows the angler to probe the targeted areas. One of the greatest assets of the Spey rod is its ability to lift and mend great lenghts of line, allowing the angler to remain close to shore yet deliver to both drifts covering the far bank and close-to-shore shallow lies. Here is where the steelheader often fails. Overzealous wading frequently spooks many near-shore steelhead. As the Spey casts allow for a full downstream extension prior to the pick-up, "hang-time" strikes are often accomplished.

Single Spey

Spey casts never allow the fly to go behind the angler, creating a change of direction from the downstream starting position to the across-and-upstream delivery.

When the line is downstream at the end of the fly's swing, the single Spey starts with a steady and smooth lifting of the rod, by pushing with the lower hand and pulling with the upper hand. The line sails backward in a crescent-shaped snap at a sideward angle. The splash down, or anchor on the water, is a pivoting point for the Spey-caster whose left rod hand is on his chest while his upper body is locked in the pole position. From this pivot point, the caster uses a strong push of the forehand and pull of the backhand to unleash a powerful load of the Spey cast. The chief difference between the roll cast and the Spey is the fact that the initial "push/pull" of the cast creates an "aerial" roll cast to land in a pivot point on water only to be unleashed forward—sort of a two-step roll cast.

energy transfer of the line to execute the final cast. Spey-casting uses the water's tension to load the rod.

As a result of tradition comes transition. The "new" Spey-caster maximizes the use of the full-flex taper design of the true Spey, with the European "tip flex" fast rods, to execute effective casts that deliver the fly proficiently. Overhead, switch, single and double Speys, snake roll casts, and even the dreaded roll cast are employed by the seasoned Spey fisher to effectively probe and penetrate steelhead lies. The goal of the Spey-caster is to put the fly in the right spot, keep it there as long as possible, and control the drift.

The "anchor"—where the water loads the fly line—should be at the 2:30 position off the angler's right hip as in Figure 2 as the powerful "push/pull" snap of the wrist is delivered.

Double Spey: Critical to this cast is to lift enough line off the water as in Figure 2, not overpower too much line upstream in Figure 3 and have a good lateral to the hip "anchor" water load in Figure 4.

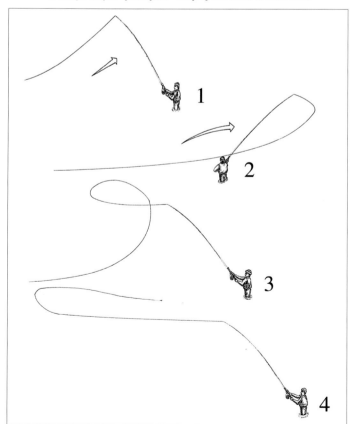

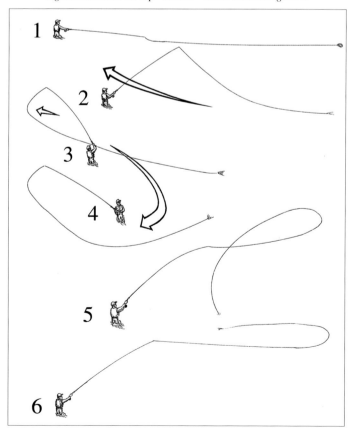

Double Spey

Most commonly used, the double Spey incorporates an upstream back-hand roll cast and a sideward power/push/snap to deliver the final cast.

With the fly anchored below you, the rod and line are swept upstream in a back-hand roll cast as the right hand leads the rod (in an over-the-right-shoulder double Spey) and the left hand is held firmly to the right side of the chest. As the fly and line lay in the water downstream with an upstream triangle of rod and line formed, a quick sideways sweeping D-shaped cast is made to the downstream, right side of the angler. This allows the direction change to take place for the final step. With a fluid push/pull of the forward cast, the right hand is held high above the head, keeping the rod tip high and stopping it to execute delivery. The tight loop Spey then sails up and across the river.

Critical to success is to not overpower your rod. The bend of the rod, tension of the line on the water, anchoring of the right foot and the locking of the upper body all allow the cast to unfold.

Switch Casting and Overhead Methods

To change direction, the rod is simply pointed at the fly and the index or middle finger cleats the line. Sweeping the rod tip upstream, at a side-arm shoulder angle, the angler takes the line from downstream to upstream, loading at 10:00 and 2:00 (2 and 10) depending on which hand is dominant on top. When the line is loaded upstream at the 10/2 position, the "snap" arches the rod parallel to the bank or downstream. With switch casting, we are bordering on complete overhead Spey casting, since the line never touches the water.

The overhead cast is becoming increasingly popular with each new year. With the stiffer butt and lightweight European tip-flex rods, the overhead is comfortable in the hands of the non-Spey caster and is quite easy to execute. It also allows the angler to cover more water than the stripping-and-hauling single-handed-rod caster.

To execute the cast with a floating or sink-tip line, clamp the line between your index finger and the balance point of the rod handle. If you have excess line on the water, you might want to hold some loose coils in your line hand to prevent friction from the water. With a forward roll cast to help load up the pick-up, begin the backcast and straighten out the loop as the line loads your rod. With a power push/pull snap, drive the cast to 10 o'clock. As the line accelerates forward, release the clamped index finger and the line will fly out quickly, especially if you have a sink-tip shooting rig, which can burn your finger with the rapid thrust.

The snake-roll cast is another popular cast for modern Spey-casters using European action rods. It is accomplished by lifting the line off the water and completing an airborne circular roll cast to generate the energy and lift the line as you execute a final, single forward Spey cast on the last delivery.

Controlling the Spey line is similar to the wet-fly swing. If the rod is dropped at the downstream angle, more drag and less fly penetration will occur. By lifting the rod high and upstream, along with strategic mends allowing for slack, the fly can be guided deeper. Eventually your magic wand will direct the fly as you learn how the various lines, sink-tips, and river currents react with each other.

When fishing 15- to 30-foot sink-tips on Spey-designed lines, one will greatly benefit from the overhead Spey cast's ability to pick up the line and cast it accurately and with great distance. The traditional single and double Spey casts are more difficult with a sinking line.

Other Spey Rod Advantages

The surging runs of a fighting steelhead on a two-handed rod are magnificent. As Mike Maxwell puts it, "the angler can fight the fish quickly and humanely" with a two-handed rod even in the strongest of currents. With the added length of a Spey rod, the fish will have a leverage advantage, which makes them fight stronger and seem bigger.

Some very light 11 1/2- to 12 1/2-foot 7- and 8-weight Spey rods are also excellent for high-stick bottom-drift fishing, one-handed style. Due to their very flexible tip section, they can detect subtle strikes on nymphs and egg patterns in very cold winter water when the steelhead are lethargic. My first experience with this technique was on a bitter cold March day. The rod was G. Loomis' GLX 11 1/2-foot 7- or 8-weight Europa. Rigged with running line, I swear I could feel every rock my lead weight was ticking on the bottom. The incredible distances I could cast and control the line single-handed was impressive. When my fresh-run 14-pound mint green female smashed my pink egg pattern, I swear I could feel her think about the grab, inhale the fly, and close her mouth and shake her head. A good rod will do that for you. Orvis, Scott, Sage, Thomas & Thomas, and Winston now make one- or two-handed rods for high-stick bottom drifting.

Selecting a Great Lakes Steelhead Rod

With many rod companies manufacturing excellent graphite and cane steelhead rods, one can literally write a book on this subject matter. I will try to simplify rod selection for the unique conditions in our Great Lakes fishery.

As a general guideline, graphite fly-rod manufacturers make 9- to 10-foot rods for 6- to 8-weight lines for steelhead. A few custom 5-weight light-line rods are built for steelheading. Words such as "fast, soft, full, tip, light-action" are tossed around by steelheaders describing their favorite rods. The feel of a particular rod is a preference akin to selecting red or white wine in a restaurant. A full-action rod is slow, bending all the way to the butt, like most traditional canes. A fast or "tip-action" rod has a stiff butt and light tip. The fast/tip action is practical because it is quite versatile in its performance.

In Great Lakes steelheading methodology, bottom drift fishing and classic wet-fly presentations are the two main venues of the sport. The faster tip-action rods are excellent in the subtle transmission of the bottom-bounce "ticking" and they load better than full and soft rods. Also, since a majority of our wet-fly swing and slack mending techniques occur in colder waters, the various weighted sinking, sink-tip, and shooting lines are used where the stiff butt, fast-tip rods excel in punching out a double-haul in nasty, inclement weather. A longer 9- to 11-foot rod also mends the line better and controls the drift. Thus, if you had to purchase just one rod for all Great Lakes conditions, a single-handed 10-foot 8-weight rod with a tip flex and light weight (4 to 5 oz.) would be ideal. Five- to 7-weight rods work equally well although they do not throw a 400-grain sinking line under unique conditions as easily as an 8-weight can.

The top steelhead rod manufacturers all have different philosophies in their rod building and create 8-weights that feel like six weights and vice versa. Without a doubt, the trend is toward lighter rods that cast a load easier and allow the fish to perform to fighting excellence.

When I asked Orvis rod designer Jim LePage how he designs rods for steelheading he said, "ask the steelhead fishermen." LePage expounded on the philosophy of a dedicated rodmaker. "Designing rods, as you may know, has in the past simply been based on historical databases of designs. Looking at its action can duplicate a great casting rod. It can be adjusted up or down in line weight, while still maintaining its action by changes in taper, wall thickness, or material used. With our new flex index action rod that can handle an overhead cast of 100-plus feet of line while the Spey-caster is looking for a more moderate-action rod that loads further into the butt. LePage states, "With the new concept of the rod flex system, our index system offers a consistent method of both purchasing and analyzing our rods. It gives those fishermen who have purchased from Orvis an opportunity to pick up another rod similar to an action that they have liked in the past; it gives the experienced fly fisher the opportunity to pick an action/flex that can work for a given situation or casting technique. I would say that this system has been a huge benefit to consumers and dealers when shopping for a rod."

West Coast rod designers, such as Sage, G. Loomis, Winston, Scott and Powell, have been intimately involved in the evolving West Coast steelhead fishery and are designing outstanding rods geared specifically for the steelhead market. A new wave of mid-priced, high-quality graphite rods are being manufactured by St. Croix, Reddington, and a host of others that perform and cast just as well as the high-priced boutique rods. Thomas & Thomas is now making excellent "boutique" rods for steelheading.

Perhaps the best way to select a steelhead rod is through a trusted fly fishing shop. To correctly choose the right rod, the following information must be conveyed: a) the type and size of rivers you are to fish, b) the average size of the steelhead you'll be seeking, c) style of fishing preferred—bottom drifting or sink-tip wet style. Your operating budget, value for brand identification, and the old "Why? Because I like it!" closes the deal.

As far as two-handed rods, without a doubt the lighter, faster stiff butt, tip-flex Speys allow the angler all of the options outside the traditional Spey-casting mode. Since many of the Great Lakes rivers are not as large or lined with as steep cliffs as those in Europe, full flex rods are not as much a necessity to lay out 100-plus feet of line. However, if one enjoys the traditional feel of these rods, just do it and enjoy.

Steelhead Reels

If you ask a steelheader about the most exhilarating moments during their battle with a fish, you'll often hear about the leaps, the driving surge of the runs—and the screaming reel. In the steelheading business, the reel is serious stuff—perhaps even the most important piece in a steelheader's arsenal. Once thought of as just a place to store the line, the new high-tech reel manufacturers are making the reel perform on command in the heat of battle. Smooth and flawless drag systems, large arbor rapid line retrieves with lightweight design, allow the steelheader to adjust to all of the fish's sudden movements: charging, driving, and leaping.

Because of their quick line retrieval, large arbor reels are invaluable for controlling the driving runs of a steelhead in battle. Loop reels from Sweden are pictured here. Their new Evotec model has a reel rim drag setting that is unique.

What often happens to too many experienced and novice steelheaders alike—a break off! Steelhead use their cunning tenacity to charge and run for cover of logjams and boulders, cutting leaders to shreds.

system we have been able to consistently build an action to a known load and flex through a mathematical equation. This allows us to cut down our development time by starting with, for example, a mid-flex 7.0 in 10-foot 7-weight rod. After that, it is time for the subjective tests that we all need to confront in the design of any rod for any fishery."

Early steelhead rods were bamboo, with some excellent designs by Wes Jordan in the early 1900s. Today's modern steelhead graphite rod needs to be able to mend more line than typical rods, so rod length (usually over 9 feet) is important. A tip that recovers quickly, while still being capable of handling large amounts of line, is always a challenge. Many times the rod that can easily mend large amounts of line does not have the sensitivity many steelhead fisherman like for detecting strikes. Moving to higher-modulus materials has made it possible to achieve the strength, sensitivity, and lightness needed to produce a rod that feels good in the hand, is sensitive for strike detection, and has the strength when mending large amounts of line.

The above information is true of both single- and two-handed rods. In addition, two-handed rods are now being produced for anglers that are overhead casting large lengths of line and not Spey casting. These are two totally separate applications and rod actions are often totally different depending on the region for which they are being designed. Typically, West Coast steelhead fishermen using two-handed rods are looking for a fairly fast-

Steelhead and big-game reels have been taken over by high-tech designers who are very good at what they do. Though there are many excellent reel companies, the personalities behind the reels are unique. Enter Steve Abel. Steve established his own automatic machine shop (Abel Automatics) in the Ventura County community of Camarillo. As a young man, he worked at various machine shops and served as a deep-sea diver in New Orleans and the Suez Canal.

Initially, Abel made precision screws using a screw machine he found abandoned and in disrepair on a nearby farm. He got it in working order and began banging on the doors of local machine shops and light-industry businesses looking for work. He made a living doing what he did best and loved most: machining products. He quickly graduated to small, precision, aerospace, computer and medical parts and more. The business expanded.

Today, Steve Abel machines or manufactures fly fishing reels, fly-rods, sportsman's luggage, a precision golf putter, a home cigar-rolling kit, and fly-fishing and cigar accessories. First came the fly reels. Steve had grown up fishing from the local piers and beaches, first in Oceanside near San Diego and later in the Camarillo area so it was not a great surprise that once his machine shop was on solid footing he began machining fishing reels. At first, he made fly feels for himself, friends, and family. But in 1987 he designed and constructed a reel that industry experts said must be marketed. The reel was originally made in one size (a size that roughly corresponds to today's Big Game #2) and the response was instantaneous—and highly positive. The first advertisements for the Abel reel broke in March 1988, and the reel immediately became one of the standards of the industry.

There are many "Abel-level" reel designers. Billy Pate, Ted Juracek, Bauer, Ari T. Hart, Staub, Peerless, Bogdan, Charelton, Hardy, Loop, Orvis, and many more, make state-of-the-art reels. The bottom line for the Great Lakes is functionalism. Due to the harsh, frozen climate the steelheader endures, and the thin running line that we use for "so called" fly-line, the reel must perform consistently.

Reel-making Michigander, Craig Harris, having chased steelhead for a good portion of his life and being involved with the manufacturing of tackle for seven years, has a number of thoughts concerning steelhead tackle and techniques.

According to Craig, a good reel for steelhead fishing must exhibit the following characteristics:

- The drag must function properly when the air temperature is below 32 degrees F.
- The drag must function properly when the river temperature hovers around freezing level.
- The drag must function properly, all day long, after the reel has been submersed in water of any temperature, especially water near the freezing mark.
- The reel cannot either freespool or lock-up/freeze-up after being exposed to menacing weather conditions.
- The finish on the reel must protect the reel from the rigors of steelhead fishing, including rocks, sand, boat gunnels, water loaded with ice and sediment, pickup truck beds and clients who attempt to destroy all tackle provided.
- The reel should have easy-to-change spools.
- The reel must be lightweight because casting fatigue becomes a major issue when one makes hundreds of casts a day chasing very selective steelhead.
- The reel should require little maintenance. Exhaustive maintenance takes time away from the stream. Selection of fabrication materials is critical.
- The reel must be operable when the fisherman is wearing gloves. Knobs must be big enough for grown-up hands.

- There should be nothing on the reel that could catch either line or tippet. Knobs should be "skirted."
- Last, and most important, the drag must exhibit a very low start-up inertia characteristic. High start-up inertia invariably means the drag will initially stick as the fish starts its first run, thus parting the tippet. Low start-up inertia allows the drag to instantly engage and apply constant drag pressure. A drag that intermittently sticks and slips will mean many lost fish.

With the onset of Harris-like production of moderately-priced quality steelhead reels came the large arbor revolution by Bauer in 1995. Large arbor reels are very popular with steelhead fly fishers because of the demands of a powerful, fighting fish. With increased line-retrieval speed, the reels respond very quickly to the rapid changing of direction that a steelhead can make during a run. A common occurrence when fighting steelhead is when they charge the angler and create slack which allows the fish to shake the hook free. With large arbor rapid retrieve, slack line can be quickly eliminated to keep tension on the rod.

One of the top pioneers of large arbor reels was Loop from Sweden. Kurt Danielsson of Danielsson Innovation developed Loop fly reels in Sweden in the mid-1980s. Danielsson, a design engineer of international repute in the steel-rolling industry, brought his skills to designing a superior fly reel for salmon and trout fishing. The result was the contemporary large arbor fly reel. In 1985, Loop reels were introduced to the U.S. market by Sage and were distributed by that company and several others until the late 1990s. In 1998, Danielsson joined Ron Larson of Roseburg, Oregon, Goran Andersson, Christer Sjoberg and Tony Karpestam of Loop Tackle Design in Sweden to form a U.S. corporation dedicated to distributing Loop reels and other top-quality fly fishing products.

Loop's greatest contribution to the large arbor market was its fast retrieve, low start-up inertia, great line capacity, a very smooth and consistent drag system, and low total weight.

Another outstanding, revolutionary reel, known as the Evotec, was created in 1999. The unique feature of this reel is that its drag system is engaged by turning the side of the reel rather than a knob—the drag can even be palmed. Featuring six drag settings—which go from zero to maximum in one third setting—I have personally been amazed by this reel's durability after withstanding hundreds of 10- to 22-pound Skamania summer steelhead on the St. Joseph River during the record-breaking run of summer 1999. Unlike other large arbor reels, the Evotec does not overrun when wet and can stand winter freeze-up conditions. The new Evotec light-weight 8 eleven is the lightest and most rapid retreive line storage reel available on the market today.

Ted Juracek's Tibor Everglades and Riptide reels are also excellent large arbors. After experiencing some difficulty in entering into the big-game reel market, Orvis has made a serious comeback in 1999 with the introduction of the Vortex reel. The Vortex, and soon-to-be-released Battenkill, large arbor reels allow the maximum take-up of line per revolution of the spool—whether the spool is full or the fish is out 200 yards—more than any other reel on the market.

The Vortex has the largest drag area of any reel out there using a drag constructed of Rulon against composite cork. It has a patented spool release mechanism, which allows for quick and easy spool removal with no loose parts to disassemble. A unique hook holder is built into the reel foot, along with a large-radiused foot for those anglers who prefer to wrap their leader around the reel foot and back into a guide. Large arbors allow line to come off the spool in larger coils avoiding line memory coiling problems. The Vortex is the lightest of the large arbors on the market.

Though large arbor reels were the turn-of-the-century craze, an angler need not have one to be an effective steelhead fly fisher. Many companies make excellent mid-priced reels. Reddington makes an excellent large arbor reel at an affordable price.

Choose the style and price range that work for you. Remember, rod and reel does not maketh an accomplished steelheader. Reading the water, making effective presentations, and adjusting tactics are what it takes to be a successful steelheader.

Lines for Great Lakes Steelhead

Virtually every fly line, or fly-line style, manufactured today can be applied to various Great Lakes steelheading presentations. There are four basic lines available to the fisher. Shooting or running lines, sink-tips, full-floating and custom Spey lines are the most applicable for the fishery.

A great majority of our presentations deal with cold weather and water temperatures. Since we employ bottom drift fishing techniques, we are very serious about our running/shooting line orientation. Before the explosion of manufacturers making these specialized lines, Great Lakes steelheaders simply used heavy monofilament on fly reels. Many still swear by this system today. However, mono tends to have memory and coils quickly in cold weather. Besides, it just doesn't look like a fly line or fly fishing for those aesthetically self-conscious fly fishers casting amidst the hardware and spawn-tossing crowd.

Since a weight of some sort attached to the leader before the fly is the chief vehicle which loads the rod for the cast, many argue that this method is "not really fly fishing," as Bruce Richards of Scientific Anglers will say. Richards, who pioneered the use of shooting lines for Great Lakes steelheading says, "I agree that this isn't fly fishing. In true fly fishing the weight of the line delivers the fly. The fact that we are using a fly rod, reel, line, leader and fly makes it fly fishing to most people. It is legal and effective, what we call it doesn't matter."

Originally designed for attaching sinking shooting heads, the running/shooting lines are now marketed in the Great Lakes solely for bottom drift fishing. Scientific Anglers, Orvis, Cortland and many others offer these lines in diameters from .025 to .031.

I am greatly impressed with several of the boutique shooting lines, such as Airflo's Poly Shoot and Clear Running lines, along with Jim Vincent's Rio Products shooting lines in lime and clear monocore tones.

Once the scourge of winter fishing, iced-up guides need not be a problem any longer with products such as Loon Outdoors' Stanley's Ice-Off Paste. Now there is no excuse not to fish even on the coldest days.

Airflo's PolyShoot running line was originally designed as a low-stretch, low-friction ultra-thin running line for shooting heads. Airflo's high-durability PolyShoot is fast becoming the line of choice for deep-water, dead-drift applications—without the use of a shooting head.

The ultrathin diameter line cuts through water like a knife and the low-stretch core ensures instant bite detection and solid hook-ups. The "crack-free" Airflo thermopolymer coating replaces the traditional PVC offering, greatly increasing durability with significantly less memory.

PolyShoot is available in Intermediate Salmon (0.030") and Trout (0.025") as well as new Floating formulations. The PolyShoot works extremely well under icy conditions and can be casted great distances while high-stick, bottom drift fishing with a 10- to 11 1/2-foot rod. Iain Sorrel of Airflo likes to spray Armor-All on his line to really shoot it out.

Rio Products' new 120-foot intermediate shooting lines in .024 diameter are outstanding for bottom drift fishing techniques. They come in a lime and clear monocore. They have no memory and shoot through the guides easily, even during cold weather conditions.

Sink-tip line technology has really become progressive, with many interchangeable, multi-tip line lengths and rates of sink-tip. Scientific Anglers' various steelhead sinking line tapers and Deep Water Express were pioneers in the market. Today, Jim Vincent's Rio Products, Airflo and Teeny Line Company make all sorts of versions from fast 5-foot sink-tips to 30-foot versions. Airflo's Hi-D full-sinking lines offer thin-diameter, 7 sink rates and cast effortlessly. Airflo's depth finder sinking lines are some of the fastest sinking integrated shooting head fly lines available. The 200- to 400-grain models will cover all your steelheading needs. Increasingly popular are the floating multi-tip lines, which come with a wallet of interchangeable heads. Those multi-tip lines are excellent since the angler can interchange sinking heads of various grains without having to carry many different reel spools loaded with lines. Rio's new stiff non-hinging loops are excellent innovations to the interchangeable head systems.

So where do you start with sinking lines? Once again, visit your favorite fly shop, discuss the various conditions, size of rivers you'll fish, and rod weight and they should be able to outfit the various lengths and rates for sink tips.

As for floating lines, weight-forward models are appropriate under the often-harsh windy weather conditions encountered on a steelhead river. Orvis's new Wonderline and Scientific Angler's AST coated technology greatly reduce line friction and mend the line well, particularly in strike-indicator dry-line nymph fishing.

Clear monocore floating lines work for extremely skittish steelhead in clear water, shallow gravel lines. Airflo's clear floating SP line is the best on the market, available in weight-forward and delta tapers. Bob Linsenman, noted Michigan steelhead author and river guide, combines stealth with casting ease by cutting off the first 10 feet of a WF3F and splicing in the first 10 feet of WF3 clear line. "It shoots well, mends great, and is wonderfully effective in clear water," says Bob. "It really adds 10 feet of 'mendable' leader to your rig."

Rio's Steelhead & Atlantic salmon fly line with its tapered weight-forward floating design, is made for the specific casting needs of steelhead and Atlantic and Pacific salmon fly fishing. The long belly was developed for roll or overhead casting and single-handed fly-rod Spey casting. A bullet front taper helps deliver Bombers and other large flies. This line works well with a greased line or waking fly technique. Rio's state-of-the-art computer-driven fly-line machine allows them to step up the rear belly with slightly more diameter. This creates weight in order to load the rod butt for casting permanence and durability in this critical area. Cold-water coating covers their multifilament cores.

Finally, Spey lines have been developed, particularly by Vincent's Rio Products and Loop, that allow the angler to have all the custom tapers and heads that the steelheading Spey-rodder used to have to cut and splice together. Though there are some advantages to building your own taper, based on your casting style and preferences, the new boutique lines work just as well. The WindCutter Interchangeable Tips Spey Line was developed from the WindCutter Spey Line. Two loops and two sinking-tips are added for a multi-purpose, multi-application Spey line with loops that do not hinge. The design includes the front floating Tip 1 for light-fly presentation and Tip 2 has weight for stiffer rods or for a heavier tip needed in windy conditions. This is the best line for learning to Spey cast, as well as for sink-tip fishing. The middle section and floating tip can be removed allowing for attachment of a Rio 30-foot or 40-foot shooting head directly to the belly. This enables you to get the fly very deep while controlling its drift and swing with the floating section. The complete system includes the body and shooting line, a light forward tip, heavier middle tip, a 15-foot Type 3 (3-4 inches per second) and Type 6 (6-7 inches per second) sink-tip plus a shooting-head wallet. Rio's Accelerator Interchangeable Tips Spey Line is an interchangeable tip version of the Accelorator Spey Line, with a second floating tip for windy conditions.

Orvis's Double Taper Intermediate with its sink rate of 1 1/2 inches per second, along with the excellent Scientific Anglers, Loop, Airflo, and Lee Wulf Spey lines, round out the category.

Leaders and Tippet

Each of the four basic line types and fishing styles mentioned employ a unique set of leaders for executing the fly presentation. Paramount, is the Great Lakes steelheader's consideration for copolymer (mono) or polyvinyliden-flouride (fluorocarbon) materials to be used in the cold weather extremes of our region. The abrasion factor from bottom bouncing, knot strength, and their overall stealth for dealing with the spooky, nervous fish, often "hammered" with multiple presentations during prime steelheading time, should all be considered.

For the running/shooting bottom-bouncing rig, tapered leaders need not be used since the gradual energy transition of various diameters is not crucial in turning over the line. Here the snap and punch of the loaded rod from added weight is the driving force. From the shooting line, nail-knot a 6- to 10-foot section of 0X or 1X fluorocarbon (Maxima 10 pound or 8 pound). Before tying onto a two-way swivel, some sort of weight (slinky, two-way swivel split shot, pencil lead) is slid up this section in a Lindy lip-sinker style system. Place an orange, pink, clear or chartreuse ceramic bead between the weight and the two-way swivel to cushion the knot. From the swivel add several feet or inches (depending on water flow and depth) of 4- to 6-pound (1X to 5X) tippet. Finally, attach the fly or double-fly rig. An eye-to-eye or eye-to-hook shank method for tying the tandem fly (where legal) is all it takes.

In sink-tip or sinking-line presentations, leaders are short and usually straight tippet of 6- to 12-pound test (3X-0X). Since most interchangeable sink-tips utilize non-hinging loop-to-loop

A 20-plus-pound spring-spawning Indiana summer Skamania steelhead in Indiana. The summer-runs are usually the first steelhead to spawn in the New Year, around early February.

methods, tippets of any diameter can be attached. Where heavier 300- to 600-grain lines are used, a stiffer section of leader, 0.022 to 0.026 must be nail knotted and eventually tapered in 6-inch increments to the desired tip. When sink-tipping, you have better control of the fly and drift if your leaders are relatively short, 3 to 5 feet. Since sink-tips are basically steel gray or brown, they do not alarm fish as much as the more highly fluorescent section of floating or running bellies of the line.

Leaders for floating line, wet-fly presentations or high-stick nymphing should start out with at least 36 inches of a heavier butt (0.022-0.026) to cast heavier wets and nymphs with split shot. The tapers should occur quickly in 6-inch segments with a long 4- to 5-foot tippet or desired diameter down to the flies. For high-stick strike-indicator nymphing, I generally use leaders of at least 9 to 14 feet on bigger rivers. In smaller rivers, where strike indicator right-angle presentations are made, an ideal leader usually calls for a longer, heavier butt abruptly tapered down to a light tippet where the strike indicator is placed on the end of the heavy butt. This will cause a direct right-angle drift from the fly line and butt since the split shot and nymph hang directly down to the proper depth on the bottom where steelhead lay. This is a very effective technique when fishing small, clear steelhead rivers and streams where smaller nymph and egg patterns are used with very light 4- to 6-pound (5X-3X) tippets for leader-shy steelhead.

Excellent pre-tied leaders for steelhead dry-lining include Orvis's Big Game XT Knotless Steelhead leaders and Rio's Steelhead and Atlantic salmon knotless varieties. Climax and Airflo also carries comparable selections.

As for two-handed Spey-rod fishing, if one is dry lining or intermediate lining, the same heavier butt steelhead tapered leaders previously discussed are ideal because of their excellent turnover energy transmission. When sink-tipping off the Spey, the same short-tipped system is advised to control the fly and drift with confidence.

When it comes to tippet materials, there is a wide range of products available. As far as copolymer, nylon, resin, and mono products, Maxima material has long been the standard for Great Lakes steelhead fishermen. Manufactured in Germany, Maxima's Ultragreen™ is perhaps the best all-around tippet for abrasion and knot strength, and it has a long shelf life. The problem with many of the high-tech copolymer materials is that they have a limited date of freshness and do not handle exposure to ultraviolet light and prolonged dampness. Orvis has pioneered the use of an expiration date on the tippet spool for all of their products. Maxima often rates higher than the "pound test" stated on the spool. Many tippet manufacturers like Orvis, Climax, and Rio are manufacturing true IGFA-approved BIG GAME tippet material out of hard new formula nylon that is abrasion resistant with superb knot strength. Rio Products Powerflex® is a high tenacity copolymer with excellent knot strength and coating for abrasive resistance. A light gray color blends into the water well.

As for the new highly touted fluorocarbon (polyvynliden flouride) which is supposed to be invisible to fish and have great abrasion resistance, for a very hefty pricetag (double the cost than mono), many have been critical of the material failing to match up to its billing. They often abrade and shred against rocks and have poor knot strength.

The technological hype of fluorocarbon is that it has a refractory index of 1.42 in water (1.33) compared to nylon (1.62), which makes it invisible to fish. It is also supposed to have UV resistance and does not absorb water. I exclusively use three fluorocarbon products applicable for the rigors of Great Lakes steelheading.

Airflo's Sight-Free fluorocarbon has great abrasion resistance and knot strength in a material that can be compared with the

Steve Stallard admires a St. Mary's Atlantic salmon.

durability of Maxima. It is very economically priced, coming in 50 M spools as compared to the 25 to 30 M spools of other companies for the same price. I have used it extensively in bitter Michigan winters and the knot strength has held up well on 18-pound steelhead. Orvis's highly acclaimed Mirage is also very durable and comes in standard and IGFA-certified diameters and pound test. Rio's Salmon-Bass-Steelhead is a medium stiff nylon Powerflex derivative with a fluorocarbon coating for maximum abrasion resistance and superb knot strength.

Knots

There are many knots for attaching line, leaders, and flies, but I have found through trial and error that only a few are necessary. For attaching the leader to the line, the standard nail knot is still best. The many "quick-tie" gadgets on the market make this once-laborious attachment easy. For attaching leader to leader of various diameters, the triple surgeon's knot is far stronger than the blood knot in tensile strength and is easier to tie. As for the final tippet attachment, the water knot (four-turn surgeon's knot) has tested 100% strength on Rio's Instron testing machine.

As for leader to fly, the Duncan loop (sometimes called a Uni knot) and Trilene knot far outperform the standard clinch and improved clinch.

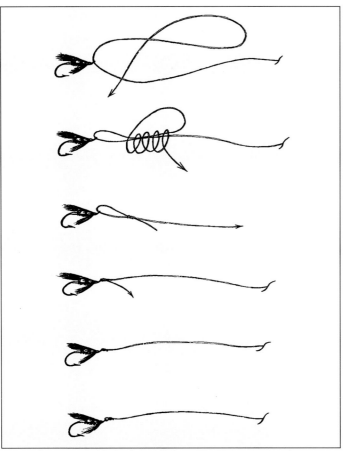

The most reliable leader-to-fly knot: The Uni or Duncan loop.

*"Steelhead Charlotte" holds a beautiful
tailed big buck male that fell for a Glo Bug.*

The Dreaded Lead

In a book on fly fishing for steelhead, it is almost embarrassing to write about lead weights. Unfortunately, they are a vital part of our bottom bounce drift fishing and strike indicator nymphing.

For even bottom gravel and rocks, slinky rigs (parachute cord stuffed with lead shot and fished slip-sinker style with a snap swivel on the main leader) are used and are preferred for their snag avoidance. A similar rig is made using a two-way swivel and tying some mono on one end and adding split shot. This is added to the main line, like the slinky, and weights can be adjusted by adding or subtracting shot. Pencil lead is used for deep currents and jagged rock shelves. Pipe lead and lead wrap-around straps along with surgical tubing lead are also used as weights. However, there are alternatives to using lead.

Many manufacturers are going environmentally friendly by using non-leaded products such as tin, tungsten, etc. Dinsmores of England has pioneered non-toxic tin "Egg Shot" which can be pinched off and on—highly recommended. Loon Outdoors, the company that uses the "Fishing with a Conscience" motto, has a Deep Soft Weight re-usable Tungsten putty that is excellent for strike-indicator nymphing.

If you must use lead split shot, avoid the bright, shiny kind—they spook fish. Bullet Weights Lead Plumb is dark and does not spook fish. Dark coated bullet weights can be fished slip-sinker style above a two-way swivel very effectively for bottom bouncing. If you have shiny lead, let it tarnish by putting it in water for several days and then let it dry.

Waders and Clothing

Since the wader business has gone as ballistic as the other gear, the Great Lakes steelheader can get severe migraines over deciding which pair to buy. Keep it simple, the ardent steelheader should have two pairs of chest-high waders. For cold water conditions, 4-mm neoprene boot-foot waders are the ideal choice. Boot foot waders, besides being easy to put on, usually have Thinsulate linings and allow warm air to circulate around the feet. Stocking-foot booties cut off the circulation to your feet, numbing them very quickly—in my opinion, avoid them at all cost!

The new wave of lightweight Gore-Tex no-sweat waders have invaded the market. They are excellent in early fall, late spring, and summer. Each year the technology gets better and these waders are going down in price. Orvis, Simms, Hodgeman, Streamline, and Ronny are the most popular.

As for socks, Thorlo's wicking underliner layering system works well and keeps your feet dry.

Studded cleats and boot chains are indispensable for wading fast water with slippery rocks. Studs or cleats are more preferable than chains, which can actually cause a cold-water spill because of their slipperiness. A good wading staff is indispensable. If you're an aggressive wader, a CO_2 cartridge rip-pull life preserver collar is recommended, it will save your life. Don't forget to bring extra clothing on every trip in case of a spill.

Dressing for the extreme cold weather elements of the Great Lakes has been made much easier with the high-tech layering system pioneered by Patagonia. They've made a science of outdoor dressing and have introduced many products such as Capilene. Polypropylene fleece in Polartec, Polarfleece, and many other brand names have helped make winter steelhead excursions toasty. Patagonia's new Regulator Insulation by Polartec is a new midlayer insulation that is as soft as fleece, but warmer, lighter and far more compressible. It also breathes very well. It is available in lightweight, midweight, and thermal varieties.

The outer shell of Gore-Tex inspired jackets and parkas are incorporating the same no-sweat technology with rain-resistant materials, which keep a blowing cold wind off your warm body. Patagonia's Salmon Steelhead Trout SST jacket and Orvis's new Tailwater Parka are among the best. Simms, Columbia, Hodgeman, and many others are creating equally good products.

Now for the hands and head. These are by far the most important parts of your body to take care of in cold weather conditions. Glacier Gloves and other neoprene gloves have engineered the fingerless flap-tip gloves for icicle steelheading. I find that neoprene tends to cut down circulation and often makes the hands sweat and freeze. The best choice is heavy 300-weight fleece fingerless gloves and rollback mittens by Wind River Products of Colorado. The fleece fits more loosely, allowing warm air to circulate and it can take a bit of wet snow and not harm your hands. Have a fishing pair like these and a non-fishing full-fingered pair of fleece gloves for when you're resting your rod. Squeeze-and-heat hand warmers are also invaluable on those days when nothing can keep you warm. Propane heaters can be taken on boats or kept on shore while wading.

As for headgear, we all know of the head's control of body heat and loss. Personally, I am in love with my Mad Bomber hat. Some swear by coonskin hats. High-tech fleece and Capilene hoods and pullovers work well, especially when you're moving at fast speeds in a boat. Leave your ballcap at home when winter steelheading—save it for the lodge and the fireplace after a long day on the river.

Finally, about alcoholic libations. If you must indulge during the day's fishing, sip sparingly on cognac or fine whiskey. Remember, alcohol gives the body a false sense of immediate warmth by dilating your blood vessels but it eventually causes you to be colder and possibly even hypothermic. While we are on the subject of hypothermia, use common sense and don't go out in minus subzero windchills—that's just stupid.

There seems to be this macho "great white steelheader of the north" mentality regarding who can be the ultimate maniac steelheader and endure the worst conditions. If you crave that, go climb Mount Everest. At least you'll make the national news rather than some small-town obituary page.

Hooking, Fighting, Landing, and Photographing Steelhead

When the "big bite" is on, the steelhead seem to jump on your hook—it's like nothing can go wrong. Yet all steelheaders know that these days are few and far between. Once again, with the cold weather extremes prevalent in the Great Lakes during peak steelheading time, steelhead are often playing the biting game with a lowered metabolism and are somewhat indifferent toward the fly. The ideal situation, of course, is a fresh-run chrome-silver fish that hammers the fly and peels line off the drag before you know what hit you. However, there are subtleties in hooking that increase your chances for a fighting encounter if you know how to recognize them.

In high-stick bottom drift fishing, the flies usually float drag-free with a slip-sinker/shot rig keeping them near the bottom.

After an intense battle, employing alternating sideways rod movements to tame and confuse the fish for quick capture and release, the steelhead's head finally surrenders to the surface.

The current carries the rig as it completes its drift and swings toward the angler. Strikes can be very subtle—tiny bumps, that often go unnoticed—especially when the water temperature is around the mid-30s. Fish often mouth or bump the presentation for a fraction of a second, setting the hook downstream and to the side will generally set the hook into the corner of the mouth securely. The down-and-to-the-side hook-set is also combined with a strip set where the angler strips line with his free hand while setting the hook with the rod hand as the rod-hand fingers cleat the line for tension. This cleat, not a "death grip," must allow line to pass through the fingers as the fish runs yet still keep the appropriate tension. With subtle cold weather hook-ups, it is wise to second strike an already hooked fish. The second strike should be lighter and used to ensure that the hook is secured properly for battle. Lethargic fish often mean weak takes and fish off. I can't tell you how many winter fish are lost by a few head wags followed by a limp line.

In the wet-fly swing or deep slack-line penetration drifts, most strikes usually occur when the fly passes broadside through the targeted lie or when it has hang time at the end of the drift. These takes are usually self-hooking from the belly of the line being drawn by the current and forcing the hook-set. Once again, a down-and-to-the-side hook-set is preferred.

In the bottom drift fishing technique and wet-fly swing many anglers commonly make the mistake of setting the hook straight up and upstream. This will usually take the fly completely out of the fish's mouth.

In strike-indicator nymphing, many times the angler is fishing to very visible fish on or near gravel. A down-and-to-the-side hook-set is once again the standard as the angler either watches the strike indicator dimple or go down or actually sees the fish intercept the fly. Steelhead have white mouths that are very easy to see. When using small dark nymphs, as is often the case in thin-water fishing, watch for sudden movements to the side or up, a quick gulping of the mouth or quivering fins as they often signal a subtle take that could elicit a hook-set.

Once the hook is set, the game is about to begin. The first seconds of the fight are usually the most crucial, and potentially disheartening if the angler is not focused. Many curse words bellow from the would-be fighter. Setting the hook backward and too hard just as the fish is taking off on a run is one of the most common errors, this is especially problematic if the fish's running downstream with the current increasing its thrust. Having the line wrapped around the reel seat or handle, stepping on the line, or having the loose coil of the line wrap around your leg are dreaded occurrences. Having the drag set too hard or having over-lapping loops in the line on the reel will quickly snap a fish off.

Your chief priority during the first phase of the fight is to keep tension on the fish in the form of a rod arc while you scurry to put slack line on the reel. Here is where the large arbor reel's quick pick-up comes in handy. Once the line is on the reel, the angler must quickly brace themselves for the moment where the line tension comes "ground zero" with the fish—which means tight. If the fish is running and the angler forgets to slow down the reel winding a break-off will immediately occur. Practice makes perfect.

Another very common problem in the initial phase of the fight is when a fish charges the angler or boat head-on, leaving lots of slack and a panicking angler. In this case, the angler is best advised to drop the rod tip at the fish and make long hard strips. A common problem which causes many broken rods in this type of battle is when the angler goes back and straight upward with the rod as the slack line wraps around the rod guides and eventually snaps off the tip as the fish finally turns away and runs. Fish aggressively "charges at you" and creates all kind of slack line, drop your rod tip in the water as you put line on the reel. The water will put tension on the line to keep the hook in the mouth.

Once all systems are go for a battle, it is time to enjoy the special fighting qualities of the sporting steelhead. Concentration must be maintained. As the fish initially bullies itself through several fast drives, the drag should properly be maintained at a lighter setting with a more downward arcing rod. If the fish is on a very strong downstream drive, as is often the case with a fresh-run player, the angler might have to run after it along the bank or lift anchor on the boat to chase it. It is futile to fight a fish against brutally heavy water. You not only risk damaging your rod and reel but also overly stress the fish to the point of exhaustion, which can eventually kill the fish. It is to your advantage to get the fish to fight both you and the current, you can do this by positioning yourself downstream of the fish.

Once the fighting fish is under control, drop the rod to one side and then to the other. This confuses the steelhead and disorients it as it turns its head. Use one hand to ply the butt section, this employs a push-and-pull sidestroke which can provide more leverage and fighting ability.

Like Atlantic salmon, steelhead have the uncanny ability to deceive anglers into thinking they are all played out and belly-up. Often last-minute surges and runs catch the angler completely off guard. I call this the "walking up to the winners circle with your pants unbuttoned" stage. Usually the angler is quite proud of his or her achievement thus far and is regaling all with their victory stories. Concentration is lost and the steelhead somehow knows it. A quick "snap" and then "how the heck did that happen?" The lesson to be learned here? Stay focused till the very end. Save the cigars, flasks, and bravissimo for when the fish is actually in the net or has been photographed and released, or harvested if one desires. That one last, surging drive often leaves many an angler in tears.

One can either land a fish by net, preferably with an experienced partner or guide, or beach-land it by the tail. On large rivers with shallow gravel shoals, beach tailing is possible. On swift narrow rivers, it is impossible and a net should be used. Always net the fish head first and wait until it is at the surface—don't go digging for it on the bottom.

If you plan to release your fish—which I strongly encourage—leave the fish in the water so it can continue to breathe. Use a fine-mesh catch-and-release type nets and carry heavy pliers to remove the hook quickly.

With the greatly welcomed catch-photograph-and-release trend, comes a lot of fumbling and tormenting of the fish in the process of taking those "hero shots." Here are the steps. Keep the fish underwater in the net. Have your cameras in order before hand, making sure they are on, have film in them and are on the proper settings (i.e., aperture, flash, automatic, etc.) Also, remember that cold weather affects a camera battery negatively. Quickly compose the picture; look at your background, don't shoot into the sun, have an aesthetic background like water, trees, etc. Have the photographer focus on you holding up a "make-believe" fish to ensure that all systems are go—while the fish is still resting comfortably in the net. Use a tailing hand glove—Normark's Steel Mesh Fish Filleting Glove is the best out there to grab a slippery tail. When it's time to take the shot, communicate with your photographer as you are holding the fish in the net ready for lift up—saying something like "ready, set, go!" Hold the fish out of the water for no more than a few *seconds*. If there is an aborted shot put the fish safely back in the water. Once photographed, revive the fish by *gently* swishing it backwards and forwards to allow water through the gills so it can regain its orientation. When the fish power surges out of your hand, it's ready to go back and fight another day. Now get out the cigars.

Tips From A Few Steelhead Guides

Following are some words of wisdom that I have accumulated over the many years of steelhead fishing and guiding that are well worth your attention.

- Pelican water-resistant cases are excellent for cameras and film.
- Take a casting lesson or practice before you book an expensive steelheading trip.
- A good hook sharpener and stream thermometer are vital.
- Buy a Radio Shack Weather Band—it monitors National Weather Service locally and offers up-to-the-minute weather forecasts.
- Try to fish for several days if possible because of the often-unpredictable nature of the sport—you're bound to hit it right one day.
- The new zip-lock waterproof bags are great for keeping extra clothing and equipment dry. Watershed Co. makes a great one.
- Study one or two rivers well, they'll keep you busy for a lifetime.
- Don't take yourself or the sport too seriously—laugh, have fun, loosen up, life is too short.
- Being courteous to others when on the river or in a boat is the best way to have it shown you.
- Internet information is only as good as the credibility of the source. Most of Internet surfers fish from their office or den—not from the stream. Rely on reputable guides, steelhead veterans and outfitters. Their pride is in their professional credibility.
- If a guide tells you it is not worth coming, then don't argue with them or find a straining outfitter who'll take you for a "boat ride"—tomorrow is another day.
- Carry a cell phone *for emergencies only*, they can save lives on winter outings.
- Be upfront with your guide—tell them your experience, expectations, limitations, how and where you want to fish, and what you want to learn. Guides are not mind readers.
- Tip a guide at your own discretion. Tips should be based on professionalism, amenities such as an outstanding meal, pleasant, jovial camaraderie, safety, and what the guide has taught you. Do not base your tip on how many fish were caught or the weather—the guide is not in control of either of these variables.
- When introducing children to steelhead, teach them about the beauty of a steelhead's life and the return to the gravel. Introducing the biological nature of the sport of steelheading is equal to the catching—and creates a future conservation-minded fisher.
- Remember well that a day on a steelhead river—with the soothing sounds of rushing water and nature's spectacle during each season—let's us appreciate our life, health, and the simplicity of achieving happiness.
- A steelhead fly fisher can greatly benefit from all the little gadgets that make the game of preparation easier. Lanyard necklaces have become very popular for holding all the tools of the trade. A great gadget company, Mayfly Hex-cessories located in Holland, Michigan, creates lanyards with the steelheader in mind. Made from beads, rope or hemp, they have easy-to-open snaps and bulldog clips. A good lanyard can hold tippet spools, line snippers pliers, a thermometer, nail-knot tool, soft lead container and hook sharpener—all essential items for a day of steel

heading. Pouch lanyards can hold fly boxes and fleece drying patches along with other essentials. A handy multi-use Swiss Army knife is invaluable and can be attached to the lanyard. A good pair of heavy-duty pliers is invaluable for crimping on split shot, removing hooks from boney-jawed kypes, etc.

Getting There: Driftboating and Jetsledding for Steelhead

There is no question that a drift boat or jet sled will allow the steelheader a greater opportunity to fish hard-to-reach river destinations which are often impossible to wade to or present a fly offering. As a steelhead guide, I utilize both my drift boat and jet sled to maximize fishing time and presentation, and cover as much on steelhead rivers as I can. Jim Johnson, an established steelhead guide and avid boat designer from Michigan says, "Steelhead fly fishing opportunities here in the Great Lakes region have rivers filled with downed trees, the occasional gravel bar, and limited public access. It doesn't take long on these waters to realize that a good boat with a shallower than average draft is a huge asset."

If a motor-propelled watercraft is within the reach of your budget, consider one of the outboard jet models. The jet pump is about 30% less efficient than a prop, but the increased shallow water performance is well worth the tradeoff in top speed and fuel economy. If your taste runs towards smaller rivers and streams where a motor is unnecessary or even illegal, then your choice of watercraft is clear—you need a drift boat. Originally adapted from the rowing dory used in the commercial fisheries of the North Atlantic, these classic crafts can go almost anywhere. As pretty as they are functional, these boats can turn and stop on a dime, enabling an experienced oarsman to avoid rocks and other obstacles with ease. Their wider bottoms provide a safe and stable platform from which to fish.

Here in the Midwest, we have developed smaller versions of the drift boat, commonly referred to as the low-side. These lower and lighter boats are quicker, float shallower, and do not get blown around in the wind as much as their higher sided cousins of the west. Although very slow under power, drift boats can be used effectively with outboards up to 10 horsepower, and work very well on small lakes with an electric motor.

Here's a quick overview of what to look for in a fly fishing boat:

- Fly-line friendliness—the fewer knobs and protrusions the better.
- Shallow draft—A boat that will float in 4 inches of water will give access to more waters than a boat that needs 8 inches.
- Lightweight—A light boat is easier to launch, requires less horsepower (or muscle power) to push, and is easier to trailer.
- Adequate storage—The more gear that can be put away, the less gear a fly line can find to get wrapped around. Look for a storage area for spare fly rods, tackle bag, cooler, life jackets, etc.
- Stealthy—A good fly fishing boat should be able to approach a quarry unseen and unheard. Look for colors and materials that deaden sound and blend into the bank or sky.
- Good visibility—You can't avoid hitting obstacles that you can't see. In a motor boat, this means moving the console forward and the passengers to the back. In a rowing craft, it means avoiding high bows or towering knee braces.
- A properly designed fly fishing boat will open up waters away from the crowds, and help you to catch more steelhead.
- Aluminum and fiberglass drift boats are the most popular with steelheaders. Excellent designs are made by Clacka Craft, Hyde, Fish Rite, Stealth Craft and Willie. Jet boats

vary in design and motors. Yamaha and Honda make the quietest and most technologically designed jet motors. Johnson, Mercury, Evinrude, and Mariner all have outboard jets—now available in four stroke models.

Landau's Steelhead Wide Guide and SEA ARK boats are the lightest. The Wooldridge and Fish Rite series of boats are very intricate, featuring luxurious designs. Many guides, like Ray Schmidt of Michigan's Manistee River, prefers Fish Rite "power drifters"—a flat stern, v-shaped bow boat with an outboard, popular on the West Coast. Rivermaster has a great new line of jet sleds.

The Surf

There is something mystical about why we are drawn to large bodies of water with thunderous waves. We can walk the shoreline for hours enthralled by the shifting sand washing up on the stone colored rocky beaches. The back-and-forth swaying of the surf acts as a hypnotic device, making us lose track of time. I like to think back to the times of the French Jesuit missionary tours of Marquette, Joliet Mercier, and LaMoyne, which hugged the Great Lakes shoreline in 30 foot wooden Montreal canoe boats. For unparalleled solitude, long soul-searching walks along the surf transcend meditation.

If a Great Lakes steelhead fly fisher is in search of chrome steelhead that are savagely uncontrollable in their big-water foraging grounds, then learning the ways of the surf can add exciting new dimension to your angling. Steelhead roam the beaches and an shoreline year round with the introduction of the summer Skamania strain. As they hunt for baitfish and other prey or look to run their natal rivers, the steelhead can be caught by the fly fisher if one takes the time to understand the fish's big-water behavior.

Since the majority of Great Lakes steelhead are of the winter strain, they will search out shoreline waters once the beach temperatures cool to the mid 50s. Many will ascend rivers as fall running fish. Often small creeks and rivulets that have downed (restricted flow) creek mouths will attract baitfish and steelhead. In the springtime, spawning steelhead will again be trekking upstream and available to the shore angler.

Summer Skamania steelhead begin to show off the river mouths by June. Here they linger off the river pier heads due to the often uncomfortably warm waters of the natal rivers. This hesitation makes them consider, day by day, whether to run the rivers. An offshore wind, which creates an upwelling effect, drawing warm beachwater out to the lake and bringing a carpet of cold undertow will drive the fish upstream.

Surfing the Seasons

Shoreline and pier fishing for steelhead has long been a Great Lakes tradition. Mostly done by spawn dunkers and hardware fishermen, fly fishers have been experimenting with tactics popularized by East Coast surf fishermen.

Fall and early winter see Pacific salmon on their spawning migration up lake tributaries, along with steelhead and browns cruising the shoreline. Spawning runs will usually stage off the tributary harbors, piers and beaches as they wait for large returning schools of potential sexual partners and optimum spate and water temperatures in the rivers.

Warm water discharges from power plants attract schools of baitfish during the winter. Feeding orgies occur when the steelhead target these fish in prime water temperatures—the warm water effluent keeps the lake ice-free.

Early spring sees the steelhead on their spawning migration. Coho, chinook and brown trout cruise the shoreline at ice-out and are vulnerable to baitfish imitations.

Perhaps the greatest appeal for the would-be Great Lakes surf fly fisher is the summer steelhead run beginning around the first

Early dawn is the best time to target "surf's-up" steelhead—particularly the summer and fall fish.
A good wave chop gives the fish a feeling of security, allowing them to cruise comfortably.

week in July and extending until salmon season. With warm water temperatures and a fish that is not ready to spawn until the following spring, the summer steelhead is savagely aggressive.

Tackling the Beach
Early dawn and dusk hours see the greatest concentrations of salmonids near the shoreline. Fishing can be fast and then dissipate within an hour of the low light period. Rainy days can produce action all day.

In the cold months of November and December, concentrate on the offshore river flows and plumes that mix with the lake's surf water. Along these seams close to the river mouths, the steelhead and browns will cruise deep, often looking for eggs. Fish with 200-400 grain sink tips using Airflo's Hi-D and Scientific Anglers Deep Water Express lines with 8- or 9-weight rods. Fish big egg cluster yarn patterns and baitfish imitations slowly. Use the gentle chop of the waves to help you impart action and keep the offering moving. Black and purple leech bunny streamers with holographic tinsel and electric blue Flashabou are hot patterns for this style of fishing. Those who can master a Spey rod will do very will in distance casting. Use a belly boat only when the surface is calm and no undertow exists.

Warm water discharges concentrate the fish close to the area of hydraulic warmth. The water from the plant usually steams and one can see where it meets the shoreline ridge of feeding activity. Winter fish are lethargic—slow, almost dragging presentations are a must. Smelt patterns and Clown Eggs (large Glo Bugs in chartreuse and hot pink) are the tickets here. Warm, afternoon periods when rod guides don't freeze up are the logical times to try.

Spring brings Great Lakes salmonids to the surface chasing baitfish. Chartreuse, electric blue, and silver baitfish patterns stripped fast and erratic often does the trick. Rainy, miserable mornings and afternoons keep fish close to shore.

Summer steelhead are your best bet for top water fishing. Mr. Bob's chartreuse popper—and a newly designed black and blue Skamania pattern—will take fish when presented with a degree of faith and patience. Otherwise, use bunny leeches in hot pink, orange and chartreuse. Hit the surf at 3:00 a.m. to make sure you're ready for dawn activity. Brief angling opportunities in the surf exist at first and last light.

Learning to double haul cast and handle stiff winds are musts for this style of fishing. Fishing from the piers is best at first light, but a boat is an invaluable tool for getting around. Experiment with various shooting tapers and sink-tip lines until you've found the right combination—your fly shop can be a big help to you here.

Beach Masters
It takes a rare breed of person to tie elaborate baitfish patterns, get skunked time after time, and walk for miles to get that margin hook-up on a big lake ballistic missile. Matt Reid and Russ Madden of Michigan are fly fishing "beach bums" that walk to the beat of a different drummer.

Madden, based in Traverse City, Michigan, uses the surf as a "means to get away from the crowds." According to Russ, "I started fishing the surf because I got sick of the rat-racing steelhead crowds of spring and fall. People out there lining fish on gravel—it was insane!"

Russ pursues the walk along the surf as "meditation"—here he finds steelhead in a true state of hunting and eating baitfish. He uses traditional East Coast surf tactics and streamers with translucent materials. Due to the extremely clear waters of the Great Lakes, thanks to the zebra mussel, he can spot fish at great distances and cast to them until one breaks out of the school and chases his offering.

Russ uses glass-body baitfish imitations and Clousers. At night he uses glo-in-the-dark phosphorescent materials with great success. He swears by clear intermediate fly lines for ultimate stealth deception. Typical bonefish-type rigs of 9 1/2 foot, 8-weight rods are ideal.

Russ says to pick your beaches carefully. "Look for cracks and ruks (deeper channels) along the shoreline that concentrate fish. Target the sand bars in the early morning or late evening."

Matt Reid, as with Madden, became involved in the surf fishery to get away from the river crowd. He wanted a shot at steelhead in their aggressive hunting state of the big lake before they the "gauntlet of drift boats and split shot."

Reid, whose baitfish streamers adorn the color fly plates of this book, is serious about his surf fly designs. He enjoys tying fly patterns of the dominant baitfish in the Great Lakes. Keeping in mind some critical aspects of surf fly design as outlined by the innovators of salt water tying, he focuses on the smelt and alewife. Creating an anti-fouling pattern with no compromise of the fly's action has been his great challenge. Super Glue or Goop can be applied to the materials near the tail tie-in point or at the hook bend to keep them in order and prevent tangles. Hook point-up concepts like the bend-back or keel hook are almost hassle free. These ride properly in the water and will usually slide over or around rocks in shallow water. As for wing constructions, today's variety of mylar, Flashabou and other reflective synthetic materials offer a lot of flexibility for color enhancement and experimentation when needed, especially with glow-in-the-dark materials. One of the most important components of a streamer is the eye. The finished fly just comes together when the eye is applied. The eyes are a very important striking trigger. Seldom do you hear emphasis on eyes in comparison to color, action or size, but always add eyes to streamers, no matter how small, or large. Both alewives and smelt have large reflective eyes. And for that reason, prismatic stick-on varieties work well. Reid applies a drop of Zap-a-Gap to attach them, but if you would like them to last more than three casts, a top coat of Devcon 5-Minute Epoxy—is highly recommended. As for threads, clear mono has appeal because it reveals the work underneath, continuing your color schemes through the head of the fly. Mono behaves a bit differently than normal thread so practice, by applying consistent tension here. Be sure to use a needle or a similar instrument to mix epoxy. Hardened epoxy on tools can usually be crunched off with pliers, so don't worry. When Reid first started using epoxy, he was surprised at how the work would always turn an amber color after time, even on unfished flies.

A beached chrome summer steelhead taken from Lake Michigan's surf on a chartreuse Mr. Bob's Saltwater Popper used for stripers.

Chapter 9

The Art of the Great Lakes Steelhead Fly and its Flymasters

ach time we present a fly to a steelhead, we delve into its very essence for existence and its savage urge for survival. With each cast, newly developed fly design, or old reliable pattern delivered with confidence, we celebrate a ritual of probing the very heart and soul for an adult steelhead's psyche. When a steelhead takes the fly we rekindle juvenile experience with food forms and ominous predators. By mimicking its adult big lake forage feeding and presenting striking colors of sexual aggression, we trigger the various instinctual drives and

personality traits steelhead seem to possess. As steelhead fly fishers, we often look at our quarry as possessing demi-god like qualities which fuels our imagination and creativity as we return to our tying vises adorned with a panache of spectral colored tying materials. With less than a century and a half of dealing with Oncorhynchus *mykiss* in the Great Lakes, our legacy of the fly tradition comes by no means in a glamorous or puristic fashion. The steelhead fly fishing tradition in the Great Lakes can be distinctly broken down into three phases.

This Great Lakes steelheader's fly patch is a colorful mix of egg, nymph, streamer and Spey patterns garnished with the fresh snow flakes that constantly fall on lake-effect Snow Belt regions throughout the Great Lakes.

Humble Beginnings

This initial phase was one of the haphazard encounter. Dating from the late 1890s through the 1960s, steelhead were predominantly encountered by fly rod trout fishermen plying their favorite cold flowing streams for brook trout, grayling, and the recently introduced European brown trout. Tales of rod breaking hook-ups with "big rainbows" circulated. These were the days of the pioneering "troutsman." They were river men from Wisconsin's Bois Brule, Michigan's Pere Marquette, and AuSable Rivers, and every Great Lakes tributary from Georgian Bay to Lake Ontario that held native trout in its headwater systems. With cane rods, English reels, and beautiful wet and dry flies, they learned to match the hatches and study the nature of the northwoods rivers with the aide of entomological pioneers like Presten Jennings of the Catskill dynasty. Many were guides taking wealthy lumber baron clients down the rivers that were slowly healing from the deforestation of the late 1800s. With beautifully, hand-carved, long canoe-style or flat bottom boats pushed by a steering pole, these pioneers took pride in their fly boxes and wallets of wet flies and streamers that once seduced the rapidly diminishing stocks of grayling and brook trout. Patterns such as the Parmachene Belle, Wickham's Fancy, the Professor, and the Mickey Finn were the pride of many a troutsman's repertoire. With their bright attractive colors they proved highly seductive to the migrating steelhead rainbows.

The steelhead rainbow of the early period was not a mainstay of the fly fishers trout fishery due to the Great Lakes U.S. States and Province of Ontario's trout season which generally ran from April through September. Since many of the high quality blue-ribbon trout waters drew runs of steelhead, the brief encounters by the troutsmen occurred in the spring. Quite often the steelhead had already spawned and left the rivers before the opener. Fall and winter runs were closed to anglers. When the spring thaw ran late into the trout opener and good spawning runs of steelhead were present, the troutsmen with their light cane and general tackle were often ill equipped to do battle with these gargantuan phantoms that lurked the river's gravel pockets and pools. A growing number of trout anglers realized that heavier tackle and leaders along with durable forged hooks were necessary to battle and land these fish. It is here that the journey to understand the Great Lakes rainbow started. River men like the late Zimmy Nolph of the Pere Marquette once showed me a wallet of black, blue, and purple wet flies, which he used along with the cardinal red tones that enticed the Pere Marquette's wild steelhead.

As the opening of the Welland Canal invited salmonid predators of catastrophic proportion like the lamprey, which attaches itself to a fish and sucks its life giving fluid, the steelhead rainbow of the Great Lakes saw a serious decline. The entire Great Lakes system was in a state of demise and decline due to the unfolding industrial and agricultural pollution of its larger cities. As the stocks of lake trout, coaster brook trout, and blue pike declined, the steelhead rainbow managed to survive and develop in its newly found freshwater environment.

Its highly competitive and aggressive personality, coupled with elusive qualities makes the steelhead a hearty survivor. I recall the words of a great steelhead and Atlantic salmon guide Tom Lee from British Columbia who in an interview for *Wild Steelhead and salmon* magazine summed up a steelhead so accurately. He says, "When you hook an Atlantic salmon, it's scared; when you hook a steelhead, it's angry".

The Great Lakes Rennaissance Evolution

The introduction of Pacific salmon into Platte Bay of Lake Michigan in 1966 marks the start of the modern era of steelhead and for all practical purposes the beginning of Great Lakes steelhead flyfishing. As coho and chinook salmon were planted by the millions in all the Great Lakes to deal with the unchecked blossoming alewife population, a renewed interest in steelhead also occurred. Heavy stockings of West Coast and already acclimated Great Lakes wild strains revitalized and rejuvenated the runs in all suitable rivers and streams. Along with the salmon and steelhead came modern West Coast tackle and their methods of hardware and baitfishing tactics. The tried and true proven fluorescent colored lures in chartreuse, orange, and red tones targeted the spawning migration of salmonids. Great Lakes fishermen soon learned the West Coast trolling methods, drop-back plug pulling from river drift boats, and bottom bouncing fresh salmon or steelhead egg sacs and put them to effective use. Light, long spin rods and jig fishing methods were also used with great success. Fly fishing took a back seat to these highly methods and many fly fishers were convinced to drop the feathers and fur and jump on the hardware and bait bandwagon. Ardent fly anglers tried copy-cat methods using colored sponge, which imitated egg clusters and soaked them in petroleum jelly and anise oil. Colored yarn from fabric stores worked well. For many Great Lakes fly fishers like myself, this is the way most of us started to experience the blossoming "big numbers" fishery.

As the Catskills rivers such as the Beaverkill and Neversink are famous for being the cradle of American fly fishing for trout, the hallowed "Century Circle" tributary rivers of Lake Michigan's eastern coast, bearing such legendary names as the Pere Marquette, Manistee, Muskegon, Platte and Betsie, produced a legacy of its own. Here steelhead anglers were creating the foundation for the Great Lakes fly fishing renaissance.

Today, I am truly honored to live in this legendary circle of rivers in Michigan's "steelhead valhalla." Having been fortunate enough to converse with and interview some of the founding fathers of the past, I can piece together parts of the empirical approach they and others like my much younger self, took to pursue steelhead on fly rods, when the odds were stacked against us.

Modern day Michigan steelhead master, Ray Schmidt, explained to me how bottom drift fishing approach, developed by him and Bruce Richard in the late 1970s, was conceptualized to compete with the deadly spawn dunkers and bait drifters using "wigglers." By developing fly patterns such as Glo-Bugs, Hex nymphs and gradually working in other nymphal imitations,

The Hexagenia limbata *is a major aquatic invertebrate hatch in a majority of Great Lakes rivers and becomes an important food form for steelhead, particularly smolts. Here an orange-tagged Hex nymph tied by Jeff "Bear" Andrews meets the natural adult.*

Schmidt and his clients began to take steelhead in selective conditions when the bait and hardware anglers failed.

In the late 1960s and through the 70s, early developers of Michigan's steelhead fly legacy were combining a West Coast fly pattern influence along the styles of the Polar Shrimp, Skykomish Sunrise and the Silver Admiral with a more naturalistic approach. George and Dave Richey of Honor, Michigan and Platte River fame, and biologist Dave Borgeson, Sr. were front-runners with these patterns like the Platte River Pink, Nasty Ides of March, Orange PM Special and other beautifully tied concoctions. They experimented with full and sparse dressings based on the heavy runoff conditions of spring, or low, clear waters of fall. Dave Richey's book, *Great Lakes Steelhead Flies* (1979) summed up their patterns and philosophy of flies. Bob Nicholson, famous Pere Marquette River guide, tells a story dating back to his early training years, when he pursued steelhead with a Royal Coachman streamer on the "Deer Lick" section of the Pere Marquette. One April afternoon as he was struggling to catch selective Pere Marquette fish, he saw two brothers, Phil and Ron Spring of Muskegon just "hammering" steelhead one after another. From a river bluff, Bob yelled to them "What are you guys catchin 'em on?" The guys simply held up a brownish looking fly and said, "This thing." Having only a slight glimpse of this Woolly Worm—like concept, his wife Krista got some tannish brown yarn and Bob palmered it with brown hackle and was soon catching steelhead. The Spring brothers' fly later became known as the Spring Wiggler, a great *Hexagenia* nymph imitation with a shell style back.

Bob Nicholson later used a rig known as the "stop light," a red and green yarn ball along with various colors of yarn wrapped in a bow-tie style.

In the evolving school of this renaissance, anglers were quickly coming up with the "fly of the week." As a fly's success quickly spurred other imitations of a similar fashion, a steady perhaps coincidental progression toward the naturalistic imitation was developing. It is at this pinnacle that the Great Lakes fly pattern development took on a marked divergence from the more elaborate and flashy stimulator wets and Speys of the West Coast. With the infusion of West Coast steelheading books, videos, and writings hitting the Great Lakes market by authors such as Trey Combs, Bill McMillon, Frank Amato and steelhead experts Lanie Waller and Jim Teeny, the Great Lakes angler was often left more confused than enlightened. In Trey Combs' *Steelhead Fly Fishing* (Lyons Burford Press, 1991) three sentences out of 491 pages mentioned the Great Lakes fishery. Most of the West Coast stoics looked at us as simply "lake-run rainbow chasers." In an almost anarchistic approach, we doggedly pursued our own patterns and vision.

The Unfolding Naturalistic School

If you asked a West Coast steelheader to show you his or her box of favorite patterns that consistently produce fish, you are bound to see beautifully tied wet and Spey style flies with attractive color combinations in the pink, purple, orange, and bright blue overtones—black is always a predominant color combination. On the other side of the Rockies, the Great Lakes steelheader would show you a box of nymphs, small streamers in the duller olives, rusty browns, grays, and greens. My personal opinion is that Great Lakes steelhead "eat" more than their western counterparts while they are in the river. In addition to the lessened physiological adjustments made during their migration in comparison to their saline western cousins, Great Lakes rivers are for the most part very fertile waters containing mayfly, stonefly, and caddis insects in abundance. This all translates to a great abundance of potential food forms for the steelhead.

Steelhead bait and bobber fishermen use Michigan "wigglers" or Hex nymphs with lethal results. The Hex Wiggle Nymph patterns imitate them well for the fly-fisher.

Simplistic patterns that imitated abundant "trout food" forms like the yarn egg and nymph became the mainstay of the 1980s. Brindle Bug style flies were the foundation for these new naturalistic patterns. Chenille palmered by hackle, seemed to appeal to the Great Lakes steelhead rainbow and thus a variation on a theme appeared. Lloyd Silvius of Eureka, California, didn't know that his Brindle Bug would start a foundation in the Great Lakes school that would continually be refined.

With this naturalistic school unfolding, our steelhead approach became more firmly based on trout nymphing techniques. Splicing lines for two handed Spey rod deliveries was not at the crux and core of our fishery like the West Coast. We for the most part were concerned with "matching the hatch," whether they are salmon, steelhead or sucker eggs, or aquatic nymphs and baitfish. Our steelhead rainbow's insatiable appetite led the way for fly development.

Perhaps one of the most important stages in the development of the Great Lakes naturalistic fly approach was a peak of articles in the late 1980s and early 1990s which appeared in *Fly Fisherman* and *American Angler* magazines. The first piece, written by Dick Pobst, noted author and founder of the Thornapple Orvis shop in Grand Rapids, Michigan, was entitled "Steelhead on the Grab." Pobst and Dick Smith documented heavy feeding of spring steelhead on black stonefly nymphs during an April hatch. Along with Pere Marquette river guides John Kluesing, Walt Grau, and the Johnson brothers, Jim and Tom, they embarked on a stomach sampling study of adult steelhead which confirmed consumption of salmon eggs, caddis larvae and stonefly nymphs. This correlates with the NYDEC Johnson study of steelhead young-of-year feeding behavior in Orwell Brook earlier mentioned.

An article by Ralph Quinn entitled "Nymphing for Steelhead" later followed with elaborate nymph patterns, featuring Oscar Felieu's "Oscar's Hex Nymph" and other variations on the stonefly caddis nymph larva motif.

The Naturalistic and Impressionistic Fusion: Today's Era of the Specialist

The creative talents and articulate insights that Great Lakes steelhead fly tiers have extracted from their interpretations of the fish's behavior when they are "on the bite" forever intrigues me. With little to no direction other than trout fishing techniques and the

West Coast writings of the Pacific masters, a specialistic application of fly patterns continues to evolve. With a renewed interest in the classic West Coast wet fly and Spey-style patterns, a greater dimension is being added to our Great Lakes heritage.

The beauty of the fusion of the naturalistic school with West Coast wet fly impressionism is that it allows the different personalities of all Great Lakes steelhead fly tiers and anglers to emerge. One can now choose how he or she wants to fish—where and how many fish need to be caught in order to satisfy the anglers' need for gratification. Fly pattern evolution through today is greatly correlated to the growing use of modern tying materials available, along with incorporating fly pattern motifs from many fly styles into single patterns which deliver maximum fly appeal to the steelhead.

Evolution of Flies: The Nymph

As traced through our history, the steelhead nymph's crude beginnings from the "body and palmered hackle" motif soon took on specific imitations to match food forms present in the Great Lakes rivers. Today stonefly, mayfly, and caddis designs are the core of the fishery. The new variations 'on-a-theme approach combines traditional and synthetic materials along with fluorescent attractor colors blended with subdued overtones of the natural.

Perhaps no mayfly nymph has received more attention that the *Hexagenia limbata* nymph. Since almost all of the Great Lakes system has abundant populations of these mayflies, the "Hex" nymph has become a standard pattern with many variations on the way it is tied and presented. From its humble emergence with the Springs Wiggler, a shellback design continues to dominate many patterns. Most shellbacks are tied with pheasant tail. Unique shellbacks use amber marabou as in the P.M. (Pere Marquette) wiggler. Other shellbacks are created from antron, swiss straw, and peacock herl. Significant to many Hex patterns and a great assortment of Great Lakes steelhead nymphs is the versatility and great use of filo-plume from the under side of pheasant grouse or partridge feathers. Layered in segments under the shell back they provide motion-without-movement simulating the undulating breathing gills of the Hex nymph. The shellback defines the abdomen and mesontum and pronotum back areas. Hackle is often used for the legs and the

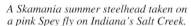

A Skamania summer steelhead taken on a pink Spey fly on Indiana's Salt Creek.

pronounced eyes are usually achieved from black bead-chain eyes or burnt brown monoifilement. Body dubbings range from dull yellows, burnt orange, cream, and tan colors. While the Pobst Michigan study did not find Hex nymphs in the adult stomach samples, I believe the imprinting to this food form comes from juvenile and smolt stages of the steelhead. Stream juveniles will experience the summer Hex hatch and biological drifting of its nymphs seeking ne burrows throughout the year. When the steelhead is downstream smolting occurs, primarily in June, they encounter massive hatches of this mayfly in downstream river lakes and estuaries. The food form is firmly imprinted in a steelhead's mind.

Jeff "Bear" Andrews is perhaps the dean of the modern Hex nymph in Michigan. His many striking designs have been mainstay of Hex patterns. Ray Schmidt of the Manistee has also had developed Hex patterns and has been an inspiration since the early 70s. Oscar Felieu's and Swisher/Richards' articulated Hex Wiggle Nymph has inspired other tiers. The P.M. Marabou Wiggler perfected on the Pere Marquette has also become a standard.

The black stonefly has perhaps seen more adaptations incorporated into it to resemble both a natural and attractor/natural. With early beginnings stemming from patterns like the Montana, Brook's, Bitch Creek, and Kaufman stonefly imitations, unique Great Lakes patterns developed. The stonefly, in its black, golden and olive varieties is extremely abundant in Great Lakes Rivers. The extreme attraction to the steelhead fly of this pattern is its color—black is highly seductive to steelhead. Also, little black stoneflies (Taniopteryx and Allocapnia) hatch occurs during the shallow water spring spawn, where the steelhead are often encountering great numbers of emerging nymphs and adults on an April afternoon.

The double tail or cercus of the nymph has traditionally been imitated by black goose biots. The circular bands of the abdomen usually incorporates larval lace or silver and gold wire. Other varieties have included red or purple wire to cut black or brown balloon strips. The curved and wide body nymph hook has been a great addition to the stonefly patterns.

Perhaps striking to the stonefly nymph design is the layered thoracic wing pads. Dark turkey tail cut in "V" segments has been the traditionally most popular. Today, various synthetic wing pad materials in a variety of natural and flourescent attraction colors are used to hint impressionism. The V-shaped legs are imitated commonly by various grades of hackle and biots along with synthetic realistic leg duplicates. The antenna is often mimicked in the same way as the tail. Black, purple, golden synthetic and blended dubbings often contain sparkle and various blended colors like Hairline's salmon/steelhead dubbings. Counter colors of hackle and dubbing are often used in the under thoracic areas. An orange or chartreuse thorax will often counter the general black body color.

The caddis larvae is a standard pattern and is mainly tied in its common green *Rhyacophila* version. Using a standard black dubbing, peacock herl, or ostrich herl head, the green body can either be natural or synthetic. Hot "disco" patterns have evolved from the various high glossy synthetics on the market which incorporate ribbing qualities. The beadhead revolution has influenced this fly design more than anything else and most patterns incorporate it often.

Suggestive nymphs such as Gartside's Sparrow combine the lucrative qualities of filo-plume, soft hackle, and various colored dubbings. Other general mayfly nymphs such as the hare's ear and pheasant tail are commonly used. Mayfly nymphs with undulating thoracic designs incorporate movement through motion marabou, saddle hackle, rabbit fur, and plucked out dubbings in an exaggerated fashion.

European nymph designers, especially the polish and czecho-slovakians, have had a modern influence on nymph designs that are excellent for the natural nymph approach to steelhead. Orvis introduced the Polish Woven Nymph—a floss interwoven concept which imitates mayfly, stonefly and caddis concepts.

Minutae plays a very important role in the Great Lakes fisheries due to the often very clear and low waters steelhead encounter. Average sizes of nymph fished are from size 6-10. However, many Lake Ontario and Lake Erie steelheaders swear by tiny size 14-18 nymphs as the mainstay in cold, clear water conditions. On my crystal clear, spring creek-like waters of the Muskegon, Manistee, and Au Sable, we have had winter fish eating size 20 shrimp and black midge larva patterns—forget about fish being landed!

The Egg Fly

Once salmonid anglers learned of the ravenous fish egg eating abilities by migrating steelhead and salmon, both West Coast and Great Lakes steelheaders have had a long love affair with colored yarn. Encoded strongly in the DNA of migrating West Coast salmonids is the overpowering urge to eat one's own or another species eggs. Whether there is some Darwinian "survival of the fittest" underlying motive to eliminate another's gene pool contribution to the future generations is not or will not fully be known.

With the egg fly's meager beginnings from the corner yarn shop to the patterned Glo Bug egg fly pioneered by Anderson, California's Bug Shop operation, the egg fly is perhaps the single most important and often used pattern in the Great Lakes. As new companies like Sierra Products introducing new yarn material like McFly foam, and Jean Guy Cote's phospherescent Uni Products egg glo yarn, virtually every color in the rainbow spectrum is now available.

Early West Coast fly patterns incorporated the importance of the round egg concept in flies such as the Double Egg Sprem fly, the Lady Godiva and the Silveris Demon. The Bug Shop's Glo Bug design made the multiple colored egg fly very versatile through the various spawning seasons.

The steelhead rainbow evolved over thousands of years on the heels of the upstream migration of salmon making the rainbow a natural connoisseur of eggs. Today's egg patterns incorporate various shapes, silhouettes, and combinations with other flashy synthetic materials.

If I had four flies to use consistently for Great Lakes steelhead, it would be these: a stonefly nymph, caddis larvae, egg patterns and a Hex nymph.

The perfectly round Glo Bug with colored dot to show the nucleus or eye-up version of the egg, is still the most seductive and widely used pattern. Tied in very small sizes to match the egg "hatch" (or larger when waters are high and off color), it is the basis for all other egg variations.

The Nuclear Roe Egg design incorporates the Glo-Bug core with an alternate color sheath over the egg as to simulate a sperm colored egg or the dual tones of an egg's appearance.

Micro and Pom-Pon eggs allow more than two colors to be incorporated on the same hook and can simulate a multiple egg batch or cluster. With an egg or eggs tied on a monofilament tag and then attached to the main hook, the cluster concept can be more aptly applied. Bob Linsenman's article in *Fly Fisherman* on Pom-Pon micro designs pioneered this art form.

The modern school of egg tying incorporates the various high-tech synthetic materials like Estaz, cactus chenille, Hi-vis antron, and Flashabou to create highly seductive and effective designs and color combinations. Egg patterns such as the Red and White Puff incorporates optic eyes in the egg. The Cactus fly, Frammus, and Salmon Flea are other multiple colored, tag ended egg type patterns. Comet eggs are egg patterns with trailing Flashabou or Zonker strips in a great array of electric colors like hot pink, purple, orange, and gold. Sucker spawn is a braided, woven series of yarn that is a cluster imitation. Its users say steelhead munch on it or it gets caught in their teeth, which make the fly so effective. Clown eggs incorporate various fluorescent colors and are usually tied very large for extremely high and off-colored waters.

Unique nymph/egg patterns tied by Ontario's James Yachetti, incorporate cactus chenille or Estaz in their abdomen along with fluorescent yarn tagged underbellies and tails.

The bottom line in egg design is an incredible array of glittering fluorescent sparkle materials and yarn that can be creatively tied as your imagination runs free. An aggressive steelhead doesn't seem to care about the various designs when it slams your egg pattern. The unique design of your pattern tends to please the originator. The basic principles of egg design that do matter are the color of eggs present, both in the freshly hatched stage or the washed-out drifting phase, and size of the eggs. Adding suggestive impressionism is the art of this fly pattern.

Classic Steelhead Wets and Speys

The origin of the classic wet steelhead fly can be traced to the Roman Army in Macedonia where a hook and red hackle caught salmonids by the bushel. Through the trout fishing legacy originated by Dame Juliania Berners on the River Avon in the 1400s, trout and Atlantic salmon patterns possessed some sort of tail or tag, a wrapped body of floss, yarn, dubbing, and hackle with some sort of wing material. Looking for greater finesse in design and inspiration for new patterns, the early West Coast purist fly fishers used the Atlantic salmon patterns of the United Kingdom to address the fickle nature of the ocean going salmonid like the steelhead. By using standard multi-colored patterns for their foundation like the Jock Scott and Lady Caroline, they delved into the world of the Spey fly and its intricacy.

With its origin dating back several centuries to the Scottish Highland of the River Spey, the designs were tied from the Spey-cock rooster. As the Spey cock became extinct, great blue heron feathers were incorporated into the designs that seemed to breathe life into the undulating hackle imitations.

In its early beginnings, the Spey fly employed earthly tones using seal fur, mallard teal, oak turkey, and widgeon. Spey flies had a hooded wing effect versus the nearly River Dee design that showed a more split-wing perspective.

In the 1920s, Roderick Haig-Brown found that the summer steelhead of British Columbia was fond of his Atlantic salmon Spey flies. The renaissance steelhead Spey pioneer Syd Glasso, fished the Olympic Penninsula streams of Washington by tying classic Speys like the Sol Duc series, the Silver, Gold and Brown Herron and the Polar Shrimp. With the Polar Shrimp design, an increased trend towards combining fluorescent colors along with the earthly tones of the classic Scottish Spey developed. These designs inspired hundreds of tiers to go forth and create beautiful patterns combining modern synthetic materials and colors with rare hackles and feathers.

The Spey-style fly combines suggestive color spectrums along with palmered hackled movement that imitates insects of all varieties, shrimp, or just plain terrestrial infusion impact for aggressive steelhead.

Since great blue herons became endangered and illegal to use, tiers went to burning and dying feathers from Lady Amherst, silver, golden and Chinese pheasants. Today goose flash feathers, larger saddle hackles, and schlappen also used. Guinea hackle is quite popular for the throat and collars.

Today, Great Lakes steelhead wets and Speys are a diverse blend of the traditional with bright fluorescent natural and synthetic materials. Perhaps the single most contemporary addition is the use of marabou feathers, which impart great undulating and quivering movement. Along with it being easy to use and wind on the hook, it combines many varied fluorescent and natural color options and is often highlighted by sparse strands of pearl and fluorescent Flashabou™. Classic and fusion Spey style tiers like Mike Yarnot and Bob Blummerich of Wisconsin, Ray Schmidt and Steve Stallard of Michigan, Larry Halyk of Ontario, and Rick Kustich of the Niagara frontier, have been forerunners in creating beautiful yet effective patterns.

The real issue with intricate and beautifully tied patterns is that they are "showpieces"—they look beautiful but don't really catch fish. Bull crap! They will hammer steelhead if you give them the respectful time they deserve to be fished. Other critics say they are very time consuming at the vise. We often become more enamored with the fly's beauty than its effective application. Show and display tying has its place and so do flies that catch steelhead. One cannot become disillusioned as to what may or may not have practical steelhead fishing applications. In an article by Rick Kustich for *Wild Steelhead and Salmon* entitled "Starting Over," he explores the time honored fly presentations of the wets and Speys and tries to realistically incorporate them into our harsh weathered environs of the Great Lakes. Kustich states, "Traditional fishing came down to a question of quality versus

Author delivers a perfect Spey cast as the tight loop penetrates the autumn fog.

Gary Phillips photo

quantity." We all know we could slam tons of fish on a Glo Bug—and that's okay—as long as perspective and appreciation for the fish remains at its highest levels. Fishing traditional means fishing aesthetically. It is more rooted in the *fishing* than the *catching*.

Finally, as our Great Lakes waters are clearing dramatically due to the zebra mussel and rivers are seeing stable flow releases from tailwaters like the Salmon, Grand, Muskegon and Manistee rivers, the need for smaller wet-fly patterns will become increasingly important. John Valk, outstanding steelhead fly tier, guide, and angler has been perfecting the small steelhead wet fly in his "Steelhead Petite Series." Tying these beautiful yet simplistic flies in sizes 6 to 12, he has embodied all of the pink, orange, black, chartreuse, and olive effective combinations. "Micro" wets are effective in drought conditions.

The Bunny Strip and Marabou Leech Invasion: The Beauty of Black and Purple

There is something magical and indescribable about the powerful, seductive qualities that an undulating, black streamer has on a steelhead. Perhaps it has the creepy, crawling "buggy" look of an insect, snake or lamprey. Or its downright evil silhouette just signals an intruding enemy. Whatever the attraction, the black streamer described as a leech, Zonker, Woolly Bugger, or Spey is a hot and reliable steelhead pattern and is here to stay. The old adage "any color will work as long as it is black" is world famous in steelhead and Atlantic salmon circles.

The hot fly box: Black, purple and blue for steelhead and Atlantic salmon

If one looks back to the early Atlantic salmon patterns like the Black Bear Green Butt, Night Hawk, and Undertaker series, black is the foundation with hints of the fluorescent. Early trout streamers like the Black Nose Dace are still terrific patterns today.

The real turning point of the "black ugly" invasion was with the Woolly Bugger. This fly can and will catch just about every gamefish species. Steelhead absolutely love a dead-drifted Bugger. With the Woolly Bugger came the Egg-Sucking Leech and other variations-on-a-theme. The steelhead Woolly Bugger incorporating marabou, chenille and palmered hackle has been tied in every size and color combination.

With the invention of Dan Byford's Zonker, the great rabbit strip fly occurred. Its popularity stems from its unique ability to pulsate, breathe, and crawl with very little motion imparted. Besides being easy to tie, they are a very cost effective and time-saving fly-tying venue to pursue.

With Tom Schumuecker's creation of the Bunny Bugger in the early 1980s, the steelhead world of fly tiers were ready to either willingly or secretly unleash their killer bunny strip patterns. Mel Kreiger, famous fly tier and fly fisher brought the Steelhead Bunny into popular spotlight. With crosscut rabbit palmered around the body and a full rabbit strip for the tail, the fly was deadly fished in black and purple. Famous Dean River guide Bob Hull of British Columbia invented the string leech—nothing more than a black or purple rabbit strip attached to black shoemaker's string with a hook and a couple of strands of blue or purple Flashabou. The bottom line was that steelhead found these rabbit patterns irresistible.

Today in the Great Lakes, rabbit strips are being used on just about any fly. They hang from the back on Comet Egg or Egg Omelet patterns. Michigan guide and tier Kevin Feenstra puts them on Hex nymph backs. Along with possum, Bunny Leeches and Buggers come in all color combinations and sizes and catches lots of steelhead.

Other Great Lakes steelhead fly tiers like John Krause on the Muskegon River in Michigan developed the Chicago Leech, a black Mohair leech with a purple Flashabou tag that is effective on summer- and winter-run steelhead—not to mention Atlantic salmon.

Since rabbit and marabou can be dyed every color of the spectrum including mottling and is very cost effective, the steelhead has obviously made its decision that the "bunny-bou" future is here to stay.

Steelhead Flymasters' Profiles

There are many talented steelhead fly fishers that have contributed their skills in developing the ever unfolding legacy of the Great Lakes. Some have written eloquently and empirically about the nuances of our sport. Others have created masterpiece fly designs. Yet many are dedicated fishing guides, anglers, biologists and conservationists who have made an impact on the steelhead angling community through their reputation as being leaders in their methods to understand the science of steelheading.

The vastness of the Great Lakes has produced talented anglers too numerous to mention. I have had the fortune to meet some of the greatest legends and master anglers. But I believe you the angler, the reader, the quiet pursuer of the art of steelheading, are perhaps the greatest testament to the art of steelheading. Each time you embark on the waters, tie on a fly, and practice your magic, you contribute to the ritualistic beauty that draws us all.

When you look at the beautiful fly patterns displayed in this book, you are looking at the personalities, the visions and artistry of the many talented fly anglers that have contributed their time and effort to make this book a reality. I am honored to present the flymasters.

Michigan

Ray Schmidt

"My background was as a trout fly fisherman. I noticed the bait and spawn anglers—then yarn guys—using fly rods with spinning reels and lead with mono. These guys just laughed at us fly anglers: 'You'll never catch a fish that way.' To me, and a lot of other people, that kind of thing just makes me dig my heels in—start scratching my head—or whatever and say, 'Wait a minute—I don't believe this and am not going to take that crap.' These fish are eating bugs, Hex nymphs, and spawn, so there must be a way we can get our flies down in these short, deep pockets and runs we have in the Midwest."

"I'm positive about the direction we're headed. We have good responsible folks in each state—steelhead guides and everyday anglers—who are saying 'Let's do this and have fun, but let's do it responsibly. Let's protect spawning gravel. Let's leave them alone while they are spawning.' These are magnificent creatures. Release them."

Quotes from *Wild Steelhead and Salmon* Magazine.

Today, Ray Schmidt is the successful fly fishing entrepeneur of Schmidt Outfitters on the Big Manistee River. In addition to his guiding, he lectures and strongly partakes in all conservation efforts.

John Kluesing

"Many of the tactics that I have had success with have been borrowed from successful trout fishing methods. The resident trout tend to keep an eye on whatever food source is most abundant at a given time of year. Steelhead also behave this way. One example would be fishing egg flies while either salmon or other steelhead are spawning. You will also find steelhead keying in on stone flies or caddis larvae when they are available in sufficient numbers. When easy pickings like this are unavailable, large attractor streamers will sometime stimulate viscious strikes."

From his guiding days at the Katmai Lodge in Alaska to his present homewaters of the Pere Marquette, Manistee, and Muskegon, John Kleusing has been guiding anglers to Great Lakes steelhead for over twenty five years.

Bob Linsenman

Thirty years ago some forgotten saint idly remarked to Bob that if he liked stream trout so much (he did), he ought to test his skills on 'those really big rainbows they call steelhead,' that he had heard of a guy who had recently caught on on the Platte River near Honor, Michigan.

A few days later, in the lower reaches of that scenic river, Bob played a leaping, dashing for many exciting minutes. Slow current and lack of snags enabled him eventually to bring the fish into the shallows on his little trout rod. I chased it around with the net for a couple more heart-stopping, advice-shouting minutes, and finally managed to fumble it into the meshes. Then we stood and stared, little realizing how this was to impact our lives.

Exerpt from his book *Great Lakes Steelhead: A Guided Tour for Fly Anglers*. Today, Bob Linsenman lives in his north woods paradise near his beloved Au Sable River. He is a prolific author and dynamic conservationist in the Great Lakes region. Bob guides steelhead fly anglers on the lower Au Sable under a strict set of rules that are not negotiable. They are: flies only, barbless hooks, no-kill, no alcohol, and a careful handling and high respect for the steelhead—the greatest freshwater game fish of them all.

His books, *Michigan Trout Streams* and *Great Lakes Fly Fishing: A Guided Tour*—both co-authored with Steve Nevala—along with *River Journal: Au Sable* and *Modern Streamers for Trophy Trout*, co-authored with Kelly Galloup, make for excellent reading.

Jeff "Bear" Andrews

"My thoughts on steelhead are simple. These are certainly one of the greatest fish that swim in freshwater. They are strong, hard fighting, often times hard to catch, and they usually win more than they lose, and that is what makes fishing for them so exciting. You never know what is going to happen, but bad weather and iced guides are worth the chance to fight one of these great silver bullets. The thought that sometime you might win makes it worth the time pursuing these great fish. Returning them back to continue their life cycle is also as important as the hunt. And taking the extra time to properly release them is also a must.

"My philosophy when it comes to steelhead flies is this. Sometimes these fish take a fly because it reminds them of the time when they were young and living in streams, so the food needs to closely resemble the natural. But then again, sometimes these fish are so used to seeing the same thing day in and day out that you have to throw something at them to maybe make them take a second look. And sometimes these fish are in just the most god-awful places that you need to tie something that is fast and suggestive. By using various natural materials with sometimes a sprinkle of flash, the end result will be satisfactory."

Jeff has been tying flies since he was 9 years old. At the age of 21 he started tying flies commercially. Bear has travelled all over the United States and Europe sharing his skill with others at various shows and fly tying events. He has also been a very active member in several conservation groups like the Federation of Fly Fishers, Trout Unlimited, and Ducks Unlimited, donating both time and his flies for their fundraising efforts. He is probably best known for his one man, 24 hour fly tying marathons "Tyathons" to raise money for the FFF Conservation Fund. To date he has done 6 solo events and been involved with 2 others raising over $60,000 for conservation work. His video, "Tying Flies for Great Lakes Steelhead" is a best seller.

Kelly Galloup

"I caught my first steelhead when I was 7 years old and my first fly caught steelhead when I was 8. I was pretty much shot from that point on. I have been chasing steel from Michigan to B.C. ever since. I began guiding when I was 16 but didn't guide steelhead till I was 20, twenty one years ago. As for my philosophy on fishing for steelhead, it is ever changing. Like most of us I began fishing steel in the spring while the fish were spawning. Later I discovered fall and winter steelhead and began to lose interest in the spring fish.

"There are a few fish regarded as highly as the steelhead as a game fish and for good reason. Few fish are as tough to figure out and to lure to the fly. For me the pursuit far outweighs the capture. My approach to patterns is simple—keep it basic. I generally prefer patterns in subtle earth tones and sparsely dressed."

Today, Kelly is the proprietor of the Troutsman Outfitters in Traverse City. He is also co-author of *Modern Streamers for Trophy Trout*. and *Spinners and Cripples*.

Dorothy Schramm

"Big fish can do something to you, but I never imagined it costing me a marriage. How could someone think they could compete with a steelhead? Twenty years ago, I thought I could fly fish, but then I went to the tributaries of Lake Superior on the Minnesota North Shore and took some lessons from steelhead, I've never been the same.

As I sit in my shop and build rods or tie flies, I worry that this fish worship will result in too much pressure on a creature that unknowingly stirs our very souls, so sometimes I am content to just haunt a river and listen for their heartbeats."

Dorothy started her steelheading in the harsh weather conditions of Minnesota's Lake Superior tributaries. She is owner of Rodsmith, a rod-building and angling-related arts company. She is a board member of the Great Lakes Council of the Federation of Fly Fishers and Flygirls.

Jim and Tom Johnson

As original owners of Pere Marquette Lodge, Jim and Tom Johnson have guided for and pursued the legendary wild steelhead of the Pere Marquette for decades. Along with others, they have perfected the art of deep-water nymphing and have created effective patterns for steelhead. Jim's love for boats has made him one of the premier designers in the Great Lakes. Aside from steelheading, Tom has competed in the World Fly Fishing Championship, guides for bonefish, and handcrafts custom knives and swords.

Walt Grau, Pere Marquette River Guide

"Being born and raised in West Michigan gave me too many good opportunities to fish for steelhead. A failed marriage and an inability to finish college were only tests to see if I really was a genuine fishing bum. I passed the tests with flying colors. I have been a guide for the last twenty years now and a full-time guide for the last fifteen. As far as understanding steelhead, things are falling into place, mainly as a result of subconscious tendencies rather than plan.

"My office is the river and while the climate control is often out of whack, I think I can learn to deal with it—I just have to do my homework."

Fred Bishop, Steelhead Fly Tier

It was not Michigan's fly-fishing waterways that initially brought him to Michigan but rather the Great Lakes themselves. Prior to beginning his career as a professional fly tier, Fred had been a commercial diver working from oil rigs in the Gulf of Mexico to the Pentwater power plant near Ludington, Michigan.

Fred's philosophy on fly tying is that no pattern is set in stone. A tier should feel free to adapt patterns, try new materials, and develop new techniques to perfect his or her tying style. Just as rivers are constantly changing, so should the fly tier be open to new ideas. Accoding to Fred, a fly tier should be prepared to try, try and try again or better yet, tie, tie, and tie again until he has matched the original. Just as patience must be mastered on the river, so too at the vise.

Kevin Feenstra, River Guide

"With a growing human population and increasing demands put on our resources, catch-and-release steelhead fishing is a necessity. As guides, I believe that we must exist as stewards of our resource. The Muskegon River and all our local rivers are seeing increased local pressure. Some of these anglers look to the guides as examples, and for this reason we must maintain the highest levels of courtesy and ethics on the water.

"I enjoy fishing with floating and sink-tip lines with flies that closely imitate naturally occuring food sources. Even the Spey type flies that I fish have color tones similar to these food sources. This means that I am willing to swing flies that imitate anything that the fish do eat, including crayfish, young salmon, and alewife."

Jeff Bacon, River Guide

"I like to take my time on the river, dissecting each run, seam, tailout. I often pick-up steelhead in water that many others have passed by. When the rivers are crowded with guide boats and anglers, I look at this as a great challenge to perfect my reading-the-water skills. I believe firmly in presenting minutae like scuds, caddis, and midge larvae to steelhead in the gin-clear, spring-creek like waters of our Michigan rivers."

Mike Bachelder

"I have a steelhead nose and can find them when most fishermen go home with no hook-ups. As for my philosophy of steelhead fishing, it is very simple. Keep your fly in the water with the right presentation. Use your guide's advice and 'lightning' will strike. And if you don't know what a pick-up is, you won't check fish! That's all there is to it."

Mike is the owner of Bachelder Spool & Fly and guides on his home waters of the Rifle River.

Sean McDonald, River Guide

Shawn takes an effective approach to steelies on a fly. He makes a few casts in every spot a steelie might possibly hang out and then moves on to target aggressive fish. He is appalled at other guides camping out in a good spot all day and waiting for fish to come to them. Favorite patterns are usually big and ugly. He is also into using heavy tippets for steelies, and keeping them out of water no more than 6 seconds. Getting a fish to grab a fly on the swing in the fall is the ultimate way to catch them.

As mentioned earlier, there are other great guides, fly designers and anglers in Michigan—too vast to mention. Fred Vargas, a master fly tier and river guide swears by bushy Hex nymphs and the "peeking" caddis. He also ties beautiful Spey flies. Veteran steelhead guides can fill pages of a directory with names like Jack Ford, John Hunter, the Rollers, Chuck Hawkins, Fred Lee, Phil Cusey, Steve Kuieck, Fred Stuber, John Kestner, John Kolhaus, Steve Fraley, Kelly Newman, Brad Snook, Steve Sallard, Mike Meneau, Bill Veurink, Brian Pitser, Ed Nemenic and many other greats.

New York

Rick Kustich

"Many Great Lakes anglers are looking for more. Our search has led us to more interesting fly patterns, as well as to techniques more closely aligned with the traditional pursuit of steelhead and salmon in their native waters. We have begun asking questions, experimenting with new flies—in essence, starting over."

"There has long been a myth that small flies are the only way to catch Great Lakes steelhead. Large, seductive flies, however, account for many fish under a range of conditions. Some are more than three inches long and tied on hooks up to 1/0. There seem to be no set rules on the color, but I have found flies with a black or purple theme to be especially effective. Black with hints of chartreuse and purple, with complements of orange, works in many types of water. I have done particularly well with olive in clear water. Of course there are times when bigger isn't better. Clear water and spooky fish can require an opposite approach—small patterns become quite effective, especially in winter and early spring. In fact, the Citation, tied in size 10 or 12 in olive or brown, was designed for the damanding spring conditions of the rivers of Michigan and Ontario. Its general appearance suggests the rich insect life which is so abundant in rivers with high water quality."

Quotes from *Wild Steelhead and Salmon Magazine.*

Rick Kustich is one of the founding fathers of books on the Great Lakes fly fishing experience. His progressive thinking and assimilation of traditional methods makes him one of the most effective modern day steelheaders. He is owner of the Oak

Orchard Fly Shop which monitors the Niagara Frontier. His brother Jerry co-authored *Flyfishing for Great Lakes Steelhead* with him and is a driving force behind this dynamic steelhead duo.

Dave Barber, Salmon River

"Our best fishing—my best fishing—happens when the barometer's on a rise, or after it has risen and stabilized. What stirs on the bites are calm periods in the day, particularly when the sun comes out in the cold winter months—which may trigger a hatch. The weather warms up just a little bit, the wind may die down, and all of a sudden the bugs come off. Stoneflies will be crawling up the sides of the banks on the snow, with midges floating into the pristine sky, just like on a trout stream. The steelhead respond tremendously."

"When the weather's truly bad, the fish don't react well at all. Nor do anglers, who have problems with guides icing up, problems feeling the drift of a well-presented fly, and problems also detecting the nice, light pick-up of the rare willing steelhead. (It's tough, too, to manage a decent cast in such inclement conditions)."
Quotes from *Wild Steelhead and Salmon Magazine.*

"In the infancy of the progressive Salmon River steelhead fishery, I began taking anglers out for 10 bucks a man in lieu of my algebra and chemistry classes at Pulaski High School. Two decades have passed since then, and for over 12 years my wife Lisa and I have been the past proprietors of an upscale fly-fishing lodge, The Fish Inn Post in Altmar, within walking distance from the fly fishing only area. Along with colleagues, we continue to set the standard on the Salmon River for guided float trips. My insatiable appetite and enthusiasm for steelhead fishing are traits that guests who have frequented the salmon River have noted for many, many years."

Dave is now the owner of Strike Silver Guide Service.

Fran Verdoliva, New York Department of Environmental Conservation Salmon River Coordinator and Steelhead Fly Fisher

"The tradition of fly fishing has always been one of limiting yourself, making it harder, by the technique. It can be a very effective management tool for species such as Atlantic salmon which are so vulnerable to flies fished on the surface or just under the surface. But the Great Lakes fly fishermen has many other factors to contend with that limits the ability to be successful at catching these fish. The non-traditional Great Lakes approach gave fly fishermen the opportunity to catch fish in extreme conditions (such as our winters) which West Coast anglers have never seen the likes of. Great Lakes fly anglers have had to fish high gradient streams with lots of narrow slots and pockets, in extreme cold, and then compete with spin fishermen which are much more efficient and effective.

"The thing to keep in mind is that there is an evolution that takes place. No matter what people say, you go fishing to catch fish. You may not care if you don't catch any, but you were still trying to catch one. As more fly fishermen become successful at catching steelhead and salmon in the Great Lakes and they fill that desire to catch a lot of fish and big fish, the evolution to challenge yourself to more difficult techniques will happen. The goal will become more to see how you can catch them, and not so much about how many and how big. The guy fishing the running line and slinky rig today can be the Spey rod and swinging Spey fly angler of tomorrow."

Bill Ingersoll

"I would say that my approach to steelhead flyfishing here comes from a great appreciation of the steelhead and its will. This appreciation is gathered by spending days upon days on the stream, learning how to read it and almost becoming a part of it.

"The most enjoyable presentation for me (when water temperature permits) is to use a floating line and long leader and to grease line or swing my fly. I use fairly small nymphs and soft hackles a lot, with streamers, wets, and Speys taking second seat most of the time. I have always enjoyed the people of the Great Lakes Region and its tremendous fishery. I have never found the need to travel elsewhere."

Being a life-long resident to the shores and tributaries of Lake Erie, Bill Ingersoll fishes and guides passionately for steelhead and owns the Chautauqua Fly Shop in Jamestown, New York.

Ontario

Larry Halyk

"How many steelhead do you need to catch before the magic starts to fade? By the mid 1980s, I had handled a lot of steelhead but was looking for something new. The predominant fly fishing approach in Ontario at that time was still either dead drift indicator fishing with nymphs and egg patterns or bottom bouncing with running line. Neither method interested me. Indicator fishing was very much like float fishing and I have been there, done that.

"By that time, I had tried my hand at Atlantic salmon fishing and had also noted that traditional swinging fly techniques were becoming the rage on the West Coast. After a few years of trial and error and information exchange with like minded individuals, I have settled on an approach that I find very rewarding. This involves variations of the traditional wet fly or surface swing. I catch far fewer fish than I once did, but it doesn't matter. Each fish hooked stands out. The take, the pull is what gives me such a blast.

"I realize that I am fishing to a much smaller segment of the run than many other anglers on the river. I'm looking for that aggressive fish that will move to take the fly. If conditions are ideal (usually fall or late spring) its even possible to take them on the surface with a waking, hitched, or even dead drift fly. This is very low percentage fishing and you have to have persistence, the rewards are worth it. One take in a day is the often best you can expect – I find myself replaying the last big surface swirl in my mind to keep me upbeat in the interval."

A fisheries biologist for the Ontario Ministry of Natural Resources (OMNR) for nearly 20 years, Larry is one of the most knowledgeable steelhead experts in Ontario. He is a passionate steelhead fly fisher and tier forever in search of new techniques and methods.

Scott Smith

"On my home rivers of Lake Superior's Canadian shore, steelhead fishing takes on some special challenges for the fly fisher. Swift, fast-gradient, freestone streams, swollen from spring runoff sometimes ten times their summer levels, call for special tactics in wading and reading water. Wild and hearty steelhead fresh from Lake Superior's cold waters can make an 8-weight fly rod seem deficient. What they lack in size, compared to their West Coast and lower Great Lake cousins, they make up for in quickness and spirit. The steelhead of Superior's northernmost shores survive in the coldest climate anywhere in the world that *Oncorhynchus mykiss* are known.

"These conditions call for special tactics: short-line nymphing techniques for pocket water, short-lived pools and undercut banks. Steelhead here are less likely to move through columns of heavy current to take a fly, so generally your presentation must be close to the bottom. Tannic-stained, tea colored water often means bright attractor patterns are in order. Indeed, most of my fly box is bursting with orange, chartreuse, and fuschia—not exactly English traditional by any means. However, over the past few years I have found a place for somber stoneflies and other nymph imitations with surprising success.

"The rivers and streams of the Ontario north-shore of Lake Superior are what I refer to as my home rivers. They are pristine, wild, rugged, and mysterious; their tea-stained pools beckon you to work them with a fly. I am in love with these rivers. To live the perfect life would be to fish every day of the northern season from April to December, plying the many streams on the north-shore never tiring of the variety of species and places to fish."

Quotes from *Wild Steelhead and Salmon Magazine.* and Scott's book *Ontario Blue-Ribbon Fly Fishing Guide* (Frank Amato Publications).

The famous northwoods "Bush Weasel," a.k.a. Scott Smith, is a prolific writer, guide, and steelhead fly fisher—not to mention one heck of a tough law enforcement officer in Ontario's Thunder Bay area.

John Valk

"My first encounter with steelhead came at the age of eight. My father and I would take weekend excursions to our favorite trout haunts. After catching a number of brook trout, we would venture to the Nottawassaga River for the second day. Two spinning rods baited with hook and worm would sit in a forked branch stuck in the bank.

"On one of these outings my father's line ripped across the surface of the water and a bright silver trout (a huge trout to an eight year old kid) bolted into the air travelling at a speed no less than 200 miles per hour. Twenty long minutes later a beautiful, silver steelhead was in the net. The fish weighed approximately six pounds, but it was incredible. I would never forget this fish or the look on my father's face.

"This look appeared again when I was ten years old. We travelled to the Beaver River of Ontario, where my father set me up on a rocky bank beside two individuals who didn't seem to mind the antics of a 10 year old kid. After I was ready and my line was cast out to the water, he left me and went slightly upstream, wading amongst the hundreds of fishermen, to a small pool. He had just made it when my line went tight in the current. I yelled and he ran towards me. The two gentlemen were shouting commands and a huge head with a bright red cheek came up through the surface of the river. I'll bet my eyes were huge (my father's sure were). After a very long sixty seconds this great fish left us for the waters of the Georgian Bay. I only saw this fish for a fraction of a second but the memory lives like this all happened yesterday, not thirty years ago! This was my introduction to steelhead. Now, thirty years later, I am a steelhead fanatic, chasing these great fish with a fly rod, continuously trying new techniques, fly patterns, even searching for them in more and more waters."

Today John Valk creates beautiful steelhead fly designs at his Grindstone Angling Outfitters in Watertown, Ontario. He was one of the first to guide for steelhead out of a McKenzie drift boat in Ontario.

James Yachetti

"My philosophy on fly fishing for steelhead is being versatile, able to fish all techniques and be effective. Fish with passion, be intense. Keep fishing challenging by handicapping yourself making it more difficult when things get too easy. I use lighter rods, lines, reels, and weight to try to achieve the same results. I feel this makes you more effective as a fly fisherman when the fishing gets real tough, and also keeps things fun and interesting. Strive for nothing less than your best effort. Be in tune with the river by using all your senses and your eyes being your most important. Fish with a plan, break down the river and methodically work every inch of water. Fishing is ¡hunting,¡ and nothing else."

Ken Geddes

For over fifteen years Ken Geddes has been fishing the Ganaraska River for its steelhead and salmon runs. In addition to guiding and instructing for Wilson's Sporting Tradition, in Toronto, he is an active member of the fly fishing community. He is president of one of Canada's largest fly fishing clubs, the Izaak Walton Fly Fishing Club, and helps facilitate its annual educational event. The Canadian Fly Fishing Forum.

Ken is also an avid fly tier and when he is not teaching or demonstrating, he enjoys tinkering with fly patterns.

Roy DeGuisti

"My techniques are definitely not as glamorous as compared to many of the West Coast techniques. The approach I use parallels the nymphing methods that I use for resident brown trout. I basically fish steelhead as if they were large resident trout. I use 9-foot leaders, a strike indicator close to the fly line, and split shots like many anglers do. What I don't like to do is use too much shot. In fact, I like to use as little as possible. What I'm looking for is a drift with neutral buoyancy, drag free and natural. I'd like to see my pattern drift like the real thing, not like an anchor. The fall season is when I truly enjoy steelhead fishing, using egg patterns when the chinooks are spawning. Sort of like matching the hatch. Other days stoneflies are the pattern of choice. In colored water I do use flourescent colored patterns and in clear water, more natural colors such as peach. Like I said, it's not glamorous but it works for me."

The St. Mary's Flymasters: Karl Vogel and John Guiliani

The swift waters of this Canadian river which joins Lake Superior and Huron demands a special breed of guide who can chase steelhead and Atlantic salmon under the most brutal weather conditions and raging water flows. Karl and John have hawk-like eyes that can spot steelhead where most mortals fail. Their consistent success and application of various clear water fly patterns and presentations give respect to this river that demands it.

Pennsylvania

John Nagy

"The tributary streams of Lake Erie are very unique. These scenic and at times remote streams are characteristically small in size and normally run low and clear. Their stream bottoms are composed mostly of eroded and broken shale , making holding lies very definable to the experienced fly fisherman.

"The confining nature of these tributaries makes Lake Erie steelhead very wary after they enter them in the fall. They become sensitive to light and seek any kind of cover they can find often holding along shale ledges or in shale cuts or troughs. As a result, they also become very conscious of current speed and drag, especially as water temperatures drop in late October. This requires the fly fisherman to refine his techniques and modify his equipment to achieve often crucial, drag-free drifts.

"The general rule for catching Lake Erie steelhead is pretty simple: Drift your fly on the stream bottom and at the same speed as the bottom current. This is the classic 'drag-free drift.' Depending on stream flows, this is most effectively accomplished by using short line nymphing techniques, such as the bottom-bouncing technique or the right-angle-floating-indicator technique."

Quote from John's book, *Steelhead Guide: Fly Fishing Techniques and Stategies for Lake Erie Steelhead.*

John Nagy is a noted author, guide and talented steelheader who has experienced guiding in Alaska. His book, cited above, is excellent and informative.

Ohio

Jerry Darkes

"Few fish excite freshwater fly fishers the way steelhead do. To me, they are as noble a fish that swims. The pursuit of these magnificent fish has become an obsession that I hope I'll never satisfy. I'm happy to admit to anyone that I am indeed a steelhead junkie.

"Steelheading is as much hunting as it is fishing. I find many parallels between the pursuit of steelhead and gamebirds and animals. We wake up at ungodly hours and endure extreme weather conditions, drink bad coffee and eat truck stop food. In order to catch these fish, they must first be located. At times we need to stalk these fish like a game animal. We need to learn and understand their movements in order to present a fly to them.

"The moment of truth arrives, much like a flock of mallards coming to the decoys with cupped wings, or a trophy buck stepping into a clearing. When you feel that tell-tale bump or tap and tighten up the fly line and the response is the characteristic double head shake before all hell breaks loose. This is what we came for and my favorite moment in steelhead fishing. The landing of the fish is secondary at this point. Best of all, if we manage to land the fish, we can release it so another angler might have the same experience.

"There is no shortcut to becoming a successful steelheader. Time spent is the only real teacher. I still learn every day I am on the water. We are constantly refining techniques and fly patterns. The education of a steelheader is a never ending process."

Jerry Darkes is one of the premier pioneers of the Great Lakes steelhead fishery. As a fly tackle manufacturer's representative, he is constantly improving techniques and methods. He has co-produced an excellent video on Lake Erie steelheading and contributes regularly to many national magazines.

Mike Bennett

"One basic philosophical consideration permeates my quest for steelhead. In my life-long study of psychology I have learned that highly successful people define success as a "process" rather than an "outcome." That is, they take great satisfaction and esteem enjoying the process of trying to get closer to something they have determined as valuable. They stay in the "process" because it feels good. Had they held an "outcome" definition of success and the outcomes were not soon realized, they would have long since given up—stopped the process. On stream this translates to the fisher taking total satisfaction out of the "process" of trying to hook a steelhead. Maintaining satisfaction and focus when not catching, this fisher will remain in "process" and catch the fish that the frustrated, not-focused "outcome" oriented fisher is still cursing on the early trip home. Enjoy the drive, the walk, the wade, the weather (whatever it may be), the presentations (good and bad), the snags (remember where they are), the lost fish, the slips and falls (wear cleats next time) and even the trophy you will release. Stay in "process," experiment with various approaches, flies and presentations. Have fun. If not, you will lose concentration, not catch fish, and call others who are catching "lucky." I don't like being called "lucky."

Mike Bennett is a prominent Lake Erie steelhead guide in addition to being known as 'Dr. Steelhead' because of his being a psychologist.

Brian Flechsig

"My philosophy of steelhead fishing may be a bit different than most and I don't think it fits the reverence that a steelhead is often given. For years I read and was told how hard a steelhead was to catch. They were so wily, so mysterious, so glamorous. Actually, I think a steelhead is a pretty brainless creature, compared to say a carp! Once you find a few flies that they will eat and know when and where to find them, they tend to be pretty easy to catch. Jim Teeny always said 'If I spot 'em I got 'em.' To a certain extent, that is true. Maybe I have been spoiled by the Lake Erie fishery and the sheer numbers of fish that we are blessed with. I do know that there is a difference between a wild fish and a hatchery fish and that might have a lot to do with it also. The one thing that I am sure of is that steelhead fishing is tons of fun and that is what is important to me most of all!"

Brian is the owner of Mad River Outfitters fly shop in Columbus, Ohio. He is the author of the *Fly Fisher's Guide to the Mad River* and has co-produced a video on Lake Erie steelheading.

Wisconsin

Mike Yarnot

"As I got deeper and deeper into steelhead flyfishing, I started to read more about steelheading on the West Coast. I began to learn about a rich tradition of fly fishing for steelhead, something the Great Lakes is devoid of, and figured that if it works on West Coast fish it should work on our fish. After my first year fly fishing with egg patterns I vowed to never use them again and now I have new techniques and flies to try. Classic hairwing wet flies and a downstream swing approach became my new passion. I spent the next year or two fishing mostly wet flies and streamer patterns and found out that West Coast flies and methods did work on Great Lakes tributaries. While the numbers of fish caught weren't as high, it didn't seem to matter. My whole philosophy was changing and numbers weren't the most important goal. I realized that I was enjoying fishing more than ever because I was catching steelhead on my flyrod the way the pioneers of the sport used to do it.

"A year or two after my introduction to West Coast steelhead techniques, I learned of a style of flies and dishing with a couple of hundred years of tradition. While it was not originated for steelhead, Speyfishing caught my attention and my steelhead fly fishing again took on a completely different direction."

Mike Yarnot is the premier Spey fly tier and fly fisher in the Great Lakes. His meticulous attention to detail in his patterns and his passion for tradition makes him a role model for the new-age Great Lakes steelheader.

Marty Kwitek, Green Bay Steelheader and Tier

"I've fished steelhead with every style conceivable, egg pattern drifting, down and across streamers, greased line with its small ties and large hooks, and of course the Spey. Now if you put that all together and put a few years of steelheading under your belt, you're going to get set into a style of fishing that suits you. I like to catch fresh, active, and aggressive fish. Most fish I catch are on the first cast to a likely holding spot. Second and third casts usually put them off. I fish up and across for the most part, getting the fly positioned for its down and across drift. I fish the cast thoroughly and move on, sometimes while the cast is playing out. Covering lots of water is important. Wade it, drift it, just make sure your first cast to a likely spot is your best. These aggressive fish act out their role as a trophy so much nicer than those that have been pulled off their beds with a hundred passes."

Wisconsin posseses many other talented steelheaders such as Bob Blumerich, John Erdstrom, George Young, Paul Schroud, and Paul Smith. Through their writings and guiding, they have continued to evolve the Wisconsin steelheading experience. In addition to great flymasters, the Great Lakes is priviledged to have the most comprehensive web site on our sport at www.stealheadsite.com. Tom Steele's site covers all the Great Lakes fisheries and has an invaluable chat forum. It covers Speycasting, rigging, conversation and has great steelhead tackle on its flydepot.com.

Chapter 10

The Tour: Great Lakes Steelhead Fisheries

Lake Superior: Beauty with Rage

Its shoreline is a spectacular vista of steep volcanic rock and sand stone cliffs where thunderous waves crash into its beaches of coral and stone colored rocks. The wilderness is unparalleled in the Great Lakes region with moose, bears and wolves being visitors to its rivers and streams. The magnificent white birch offsets the dark green of the spruce-fir-hemlock climax forest. The region's vast mineral deposits like copper and iron along with its pristine world of timber are still highly sought after, as ocean going freighters from all over the world endure brutal storms and waves to carry out precious cargo. The strong breed of Finnish, Norwegian, Welsh and Irish immigrants that populate its shores and their communities are living testaments to man's drive to settle the land and sea. French and British explorers and fur trappers intermingled with Ottawa, Ojibway, Chippewa and Pottawatomi

A classic, torrid, fast-gradient Class III Lake Superior steelhead river, the Cypress, often halts steelhead migration at fast "chute/throat" water. Steelhead use the shoreline and boulder deflection for comfort.

Scott Smith Photo

Indian nations closely. This lake is a prime example of these inland ocean basins carved out by continental ice sheets of the last glacial period. Eagles and hawks soar high above the river gorges with waterfalls as they hunt above the icy cold and perhaps most pristine waters in the world. Home to the native chars like lake trout and coaster brook trout, *Oncorhynchus mykiss* has now established itself in these harsh environs and has learned to cope with the severity of weather and water in a way nature can only produce.

The Province of Ontario and Michigan introduced McCloud river stock into the St. Mary's and Iron River in 1883 and 1889 respectively. Over the past century, the lake's steelhead rainbows have evolved to become a truly genetically unique species. They have learned to endure the steep gradient rivers with their torrid icy flows and survive through the necessity for repeat spawning. By doing so, they seed the gravel with new life, enabling future generations to attempt the unforgiving natural conditions which culls many more than it allows for survival. Natural strains of steelhead from Ontario's and Minnesota's north shore, along with Wisconsin's Bois Brule strain intermingle with stocked culturally mature strains to form a delicately balanced fishery. High gradient and variable flows from raging water as well as trickles laced with gravel characterize Lake Superior's Class III rivers.

Michigan's Upper Peninsula

Michigan's steelhead fishery of Lake Superior is carefully managed for both wild and stocked steelhead. Heavily planted Little Manistee strain steelhead have found little prosperity in the cold waters of Lake Superior and have not done as well as they do in Lake Michigan. A new focus by Michigan DNR fisheries crews is to harvest egg taking from local specific wild genetic stocks that have learned to survive these harsh waters.

Traveling east to west from Sault Ste. Marie to the Wisconsin border, the **Tahquamenon** is a scenic river best fished in its lower stretches by boat and is a "hit or miss" marginal returning steelhead stream. Its beauty is its attraction. Smaller creeks in this county such as Naomikong, Grants, Pendills, Roxbury and Halfaday are short streams best fished from the river mouth. Surf casting baitfish patterns and yarn flies is the ideal method.

In Luce county, the **Two-Hearted** (or Big Two-Hearted of Hemingway lineage) is a vast river system of branches with impending bogs and forests filled with wildlife—it has no man-made obstructions to limit steelhead upstream migration. Its East Branch and lower mainstream produce most of the steelhead activity. It has excellent runs beginning in September and is truly a great fall running river. April is prime time for the spring spawn. With plenty of gravel close to the river's mouth, a great deal of surfcasting is done.

The **Blind Sucker River** is an excellent fall fishery starting in September and lasting well into November. Good gravel in a six-mile long stretch to the first upstream dam creates spawning areas in the spring. Once again, surf fly fishing is the angler's best bet due to the inconsistent river flows.

In Alger County, the **Mosquito** and **Miners** rivers are small streams with picturesque landscapes. The Mosquito flows through Pictured Rocks National Lakeshore. The spring runs are the strongest, however they both get a good fall run in any given year. The Mosquito Falls is the natural upstream barrier and the river can be easily waded down to the lake. The **Hurricaine** River has an excellent population of wild steelhead and has spawning gravel predominantly in the middle 2 1/2 miles of water. Stream woody debris obstruction is common allowing for steelhead up to eight pounds to frequent its waters. Large pools near the mouth hold steelhead during low river flows waiting for upstream migration.

The **Sucker** River (not to be confused with the Blind Sucker) near Grand Marais is spring fed by trout streams in Lake Superior State Forest. The upper reaches of the Sucker along County Roads 716 and 711 off of Old Grand Marais offer a great hike in wilderness steelhead waters. The **Autrain, Rock** and **Laughing Whitefish** rivers round out Alger County with the Whitefish offering the better steelhead opportunities, predominantly in a spring run.

In Marquette County, the **Carp** and the **Chocolay** are the top steelheading streams. The Carp has excellent groundwater fed year-round flows and is good wading water from County Road 533 down to the lake. With excellent gravel, the river is best fished in the spring. A gorge section of the river is popular with anglers. There can be heavy crowds due to its proximity to the town of Marquette.

The **Chocolay** is a high quality steelhead stream near the town of Havey, with good access below M28 and County Road 480. Many gravel based tributary streams draw steelhead all the way up to Lake Kawbawagon. May is the peak time for the spring run. Summer Skamania steelhead were stocked in good numbers in the 1980s and mid-90s but eventually discontinued. Some natural reproducing summer runs still occur.

In Baraga County, the **Big Huron** River is perhaps the best Lake Superior Michigan tributary. At Big Eric's Bridge, the Huron splits into the East and West Branches and heavy angling pressure occurs here. The river is wadable with a mix of gravel, slate, and sand and has good access along with hot fishing at the state's campgrounds. It hosts excellent fall and spring runs of steelhead.

The Huron has seven waterfalls, however most are passable by steelhead with the exception of a section 2 1/2 miles upstream on the West Branch. In one of his classic studies on steelhead smolting in the Big Huron, Paul Seelbach of MDNR found that stocked Little Manistee strain steelhead failed to supplement the existing wild Huron fish that were dwindling in population. Stocked smolts emigrated the rivers but failed to survive in their return home accuracy. He found the date of smolting emigration to be a significant factor for survival—many of the stocked smolts left the river too early and were not able to adjust to the harsh Lake Superior environment. In the successful wild Huron steelhead population, 54% of the run were repeat spawners indicating that wild fish do better along the entire Lake Superior shoreline since they have adapted to its unique necessity to multiple spawn. By only using hatchery stock of these wild species, Lake Superior's troubled steelhead runs can rebound.

Also in Baraga County, the **Ravine, Silver, Slate**, and **Falls** rivers offer limited steelheading opportunities with perhaps the Falls River being the best. A beautiful, classic looking stream of pools and rapids, it is near the town of L'Anse and offers good access with a warmwater discharge at the mouth.

In Kewanee County, the **Gratiot** River has about nine miles of fishable steelheading water that is wadable though two low-gradient, passable falls. The spring run is the best; however, good numbers of fall fish can ascend if the water levels are high enough.

The **Ontonagan** River is perhaps another south shore jem like this Big Huron with 15 miles of steelhead bank and boat fishery water. Its spring run is heavily fished from Military Bridge to Victoria Road, lasting from mid-April through May. Other limited steelhead fisheries exist in the **Firesteel** and **Big Iron** rivers. The nearby **Union** River can produce excellent spring runs and is best fished in the surf.

Gogebic County streams either are extremely short with downed stream mouths in low flows; they also require long hikes in to wilderness picturesque areas. **The Big** and **Little Carp** are hike-in waters that offer good steelheading in the spring, boasting to fish up to six pounds. The **Black, Maple**, and **Presque Isle** tributaries are best fished at the surf.

Wisconsin's Bois Brule: A Story of Wild Steelhead and How to Manage Them

Perhaps one of the most picturesque steelhead rivers a Great Lake's angler will ever lay eyes on is the Boise Brule, (named in the French as "burnt wood"). It has hosted native runs of large, hard fighting Lake Superior steelhead for a century. Explored by French fur trappers and then settled by Finnish immigrants, the entire river is a natural, scenic wonderland in a state forest. Visited by five former angling U.S. Presidents, like Hoover, Coolidge and Eisenhower, the river is completely accessible and highly managed for its native trout, lake-run browns, and wild steelhead. Planted with McCloud strain fish in 1892, the wild fish became fully established by the 1920s. They tend to be much stockier with broader shoulders than their Lake Superior cousins.

The bittersweet story of the Brule's past and present along with the uncertainties of the future as a wild steelhead fishery, embodies all of the perplexing issues that classic steelhead rivers face. The challenges placed on fisheries biologists, concerned sportsmen groups, and tourism politics to maintain a high quality river for all to share, makes the Brule a classroom study demonstrating the fragile balance between natural consequences and man induced solutions. Here, wild steelhead, hatchery plantings, electronic lamprey weirs, fish entrapment facilities and fish habitat improvements fuse together in a complex conundrum in the hopes of making the famous wild steelhead runs of the past achieve maximum sustainable yield. Though many factors can be controlled, Mother Nature refuses to be tamed.

The camaraderie of Brule steelheaders is a serious angling fraternity made up of hardware, bait, and fly fishers. Etiquette is prolific and respect for the anglers is high. The legends of the Brule included the late Milwaukee Mike, Sven Lonkila (Greg Lonke), and Old SagAss (Guy Parker), all members of the Brule Trout Camp. Modern day writers like John Erdstrom and Dr. William Baumer have written eloquently of this Catskill-like tradition. As with all glamorous traditions and angling dynasties, doom lurked on the horizon.

In the late 1970s, the historically famous wild steelhead runs of the Brule began to decline. There was great concern and panic for this storytale fishery. The main reason for the decline during in these years was due to weak year classes caused primarily by the combination of summer floods along with cold water temperatures and a changing species composition in Lake Superior. With the tremendous fisheries management capabilities of the Wisconsin Department of Natural Resources, headed up by Dennis Pratt and Bob Dubois, a lamprey barrier/fishway was created in 1986 with a viewing observation window which contained a time-lapse video camera recording 24 hours of time into a two hour tape. They found that the numbers of returning wild steelhead varied considerably. The wild run peaked in 1989-90, when 7,905 migrated upstream, and was lowest in 1996-97, when 3,005 were documented. Since 1991-92, wild returns have decreased, averaging 51% over the last five years (3,577).

This feisty spring male hammered an orange Egg Sucking Chicago Leech during the pre-dawn hours.

The stocking of two-year-old Brule River strain smolts began in 1990 to help bolster a sagging population. It continued for five years. Percent returns from this stocking experiment were less than hoped for, with the average return at 1.6% for maiden (first time) spawners. New regulations protected all first-time spawners and repeat spawning helped increase total numbers of stocked fish in the run. In 1994-95, stocked fish made up 29% (1,567) of the total run (5,313).

A young steelhead smolt turns silver at age one, two, or three and migrates to Lake Superior, where it will spend an additional one to three years growing to maturity. But before it heads to the big lake, it must first survive the rigors of a tough stream environment. Pratt and Dubois believed that it is in the stream that the size of future runs is ultimately determined.

On the Brule, the majority of the steelhead spawning gravel is located in areas where newly hatched fry have a tough time surviving in years when high water events occur during early summer.

Ideally, spawning gravel in a trout stream should be located near the spring-fed headwaters where the water is cold and clear and stream flows are stable. Unfortunately this is not the case with the Brule. The headwater region (Highway P to Highway B) has excellent water quality, stable stream flows, and is quite productive, but lacks large amounts of gravel. In contrast, the lower river (downstream of Hwy. 2) contains the majority of the river's steelhead spawning habitat, yet this area can be very limiting to trout production because of water temperature extremes and stream flow variability. In other words, Brule River steelhead aren't spawning in ideal locations. This is one reason that runs have declined in recent years. However, when conditions are right, this section of stream is very valuable for steelhead reproduction—up to 80% of a steelhead year class can be produced.

Most steelhead spawn from early April to mid-May and fry emerge from the gravel in approximately 40 days (early to mid-June). The following two months are critical in determining year class strength and it has been found that any major increase in stream flow can hurt the survival of newly hatched fry.

Each June, DNR biologists walk various stretches of the lower river and visually count newly emerged fry. At this stage in life, steelhead are very weak swimmers and search out areas with weak currents, which are typically within 1 to 2 feet of the river bank, often behind some obstruction such as rocks, roots, or a fallen tree. Because they're confined to a small area, the fish are easily identified and counted.

Over the years, Pratt and Dubois have learned from their observations that steelhead fry survival is lowest when early summer streamflows are high and that years of low early summer flows have the best survival. Low water is not usually considered good for trout in some streams—but it is for Brule steelhead. This is because the Brule maintains ample water flows from groundwater sources upstream and normally provides ideal growing temperatures for young steelhead. It's the heavy water flow that kills these young steelhead. When an early summer rain causes the river to run high, the fry are washed away. Apparently, there's just not enough cover nearshore for the tiny fish to hide.

It's likely that the Brule had more of this crucial cover in the past. But over the years, the stream environment has changed. The lower river flows through clay soils and is surrounded by farm fields. When it rains, water rushes off these fields into the river, quickly increasing the water flow. The situation is different on the upper river, where sandy soils absorb rain before it gets to the river.

The best observed year class during the study period was in 1987, when 300,000 August fingerlings were produced. That year the Brule experienced an extremely early spring and below average summer flow rates, and no floods. As a result, conditions for young steelhead fry survival were excellent. In 1991, the other extreme occurred. That year, excellent numbers of fry were observed in June. But then the Brule experienced several successive heavy rains that caused high water throughout the summer. When river levels finally receded in August, electrofishing surveys indicated that only 64,000 fingerlings remained. Those floods devastated what would have been a strong year class. A similar heavy flood occurred in July of 1999, which ruined the fry population. Anglers are still seeing the effects of that dismal 1991 year class, as fewer large (7-year-old) fish exist.

Smolting, as stated earlier, occurs at age one, two, or three and is most prevalent in Brule steelhead at age two. Peak emigration occurs in early June. Lake Superior presents a completely new habitat for the 8-inch steelhead smolt to survive in. First of all, the vast expanse of Lake Superior's 20 million plus surface acres is infertile. Lake Superior is less than half as productive as Lake Michigan; for every ten pounds of fish that Lake Michigan produces, Lake Superior produces only four pounds. A steelhead's optimal growth temperature range is in the upper 50s to lower 60s. Lake Michigan annually has roughly two more months of water temperatures in this range than does Lake Superior.

Growth is not as rapid in Lake Superior due to the less available forage and shorter growing season. This means a smolt is less likely to survive because it grows so slowly that it remains a prey item for larger predators for a longer period of time.

Young steelhead have their best chance of survival in Lake Superior if they can grow quickly in their first few months in the lake. Smolt survival appears directly related to near shore water temperatures. During years of long and cold winters such as 1992, 1994 and 1996, Lake Superior became covered with ice and it took longer for water temperatures to rise during the spring and early summer when steelhead smolts were entering the lake. When coupled with cold summers such as those of 1992 and 1993, the lake's productivity is further reduced and delayed as a result. Dennis Pratt suspected that those two cold summers were related to the global climate phenomenon known as El Nino, in which a warming of the Pacific Ocean currents changes the jet stream patterns and led to unstable weather in the Midwest.

As a result of some dismal steelhead returns from 1993 through 1997, a fall hatchery fingerling-planting program began by stocking these small fish in cool, clean, spring-fed waters that ran fairly stable like a spring creek. Here extremely abundant aquatic and terrestrial invertebrate food sources exist to create the ideal nursery environment for the younger steelhead rainbows. By helicopter drops of fine spawning gravel in these upper spring creek stretches of the Brule to encourage more upstream steelhead spawning in the late 1990s, Pratt and Dubois's highly creative restoration practices came to fruition.

In 1998, over 11,000 steelhead ascended the Brule in a dramatic comeback. With a highly disdained and controversial 26 inch/1 fish harvest limit placed on the Brule back in 1993, the river has made a tremendous comeback form the run of 1996 where 3,600 fish ascended the river. Pratt and Dubois are living fisheries testimonials demonstrating how managers can fix something with the help and cooperation of nature and angler's attitudes.

The Brule's fall run begins about mid-September and lasts until the deep-freeze of late November/December. In the lower stretches below Highway 2, beautiful silver fish will chase a swinging marabou Spey or steelhead wet in a classic fashion in breathtaking forests and rapids. The Brule River Sportsman's Club has issued an excellent map detailing the legendary holes and runs. Some famous areas are the Mays and Lenroot Ledges for their spectacular scenic appeal. Dead End Run near Pine Tree Landing, the Grass Eddy and others dot the lower Brule.

The spring run is in full stride by the opening day of trout season and lasts well into later May.

Minnesota's North Shore

When I toured Minnesota's legendary rivers in 1999 with Minnesota DNR's experienced research biologist Tracy Close, I witnessed the term "you don't appreciate it until it's gone." The legendary famous wild steelhead runs collapsed during the past decades and forced anglers to a "no-kill" limit on steelhead. The Minnesota DNR had to build million dollar fish migration and smolt entrapment raceways to determine limiting factors that will aide them in restoring the wild runs on the Knife, French, and Baptism rivers. These rivers are Class III, steep gradient, rocky ledge rivers with waterfalls and often torrid and fluctuating waters that are precarious for steelhead survival. In a steelhead restoration plan for the north shore introduced in 1991, prepared by Close and others at the DNR, they stated, "Steelhead anglers are virtually unanimous in their opinion that steelhead stocks have declined dramatically in Minnesota." The lack of hard data, effects of stocking, and variation in spring run often make this difficult to verify, however, fishery professionals in Wisconsin, Michigan, Minnesota, and Ontario all seem to agree that steelhead in Lake Superior have declined from the high levels observed in the late 1960s and

1970s. Long term trends in creel survey data from Minnesota appear to reflect this decline for the North Shore. The two most likely explanations for a steelhead decline are increased fishing pressure and an increase of predators in Lake Superior.

Streams tributaries to Lake Superior's geographic area of Minnesota know as the North Shore typically have low fertility and flow through second growth forests. The streams have little ground water input and are subject to high spring runoff and summer floods. The steep North Shore landscape blocks upstream migration of fish with waterfalls and cascades, often only a few feet upstream from Lake Superior. Due to their low productivity, these streams have a limited carrying capacity for anadromous fish. The North Shore has a total of 63 steelhead streams, which encompass approximately 160 miles.

The Duluth Area includes 22 streams in Carlton, St. Louis, and Lake Counties, which have approximately 136 miles available to spawning steelhead. The **Knife, Nemadji,** and **Blackhoof** rivers have approximately 120 miles of stream available to steelhead and are the only major streams on Minnesota's shore, which allow migration along their entire length.

The Finland Area encompasses the northern half of Lake County and western edge of Cook County beginning at the **Split Rock** River and ending at the **Cross** River. It includes 15 streams with about 4.9 miles accessible to steelhead. Ten of these streams (1.6 miles) are marginal due to their small size and are probably not consistent producers of steelhead smolts or fishable runs of adult steelhead. Major streams include the **Split Rock, Beaver, Baptism,** and **Cross** rivers and **Palisade** Creek.

Shawn Perich battles a fish below a dam on a very short Minnesota Lake Superior tributary. These Class III streams are very short in distance and can be full or void of fish depending on timing and water levels.

The Grand Marais Area encompasses most of Cook County from the **Temperance** River northeast to the border of the Grand Portage Indian Reservation. This area includes 25 streams with about 19 miles accessible to steelhead. Fifteen of these streams (7.6 miles) are marginal due to their small size and are probably not consistent producers of steelhead smolts or fishable runs of adult steelhead. Major streams include the **Temperance, Poplar, Cascade, Devil's Track, Kadunce,** and **Flute Reed** rivers and **Kimball** Creek. There are an additional five streams in the Grand Portage Indian Reservation which have a total of about 4 miles available for steelhead. **Grand Portage** is a closed reservation and the tribe manages the streams.

In their examination and restoration efforts, Close and the DNR found that young-of-the year (YOY) steelhead must attain a critical size before over-winter survival occurs, and this critical size is variable from stream to stream. In a study by Placeh of the Minnesota DNR in 1989, he found that stonefly nymphs and midge larvae were the two principal components of the juvenile salmonid diets. He also found that the stream with the highest volume of drifting midges had the highest mid-summer fish abundance.

By studying smolting behavior, limiting factors in water quality and habitat, Close and the DNR are slowly trying to solve the restoration puzzle for their wild steelhead. By stocking and rearing natural strains, an experimental steelhead-rearing program, in cooperation with the Lake Superior Steelhead Association, was initiated in the spring of 1989. Eggs from steelhead returning to the Knife River were collected and fertilized. They were then taken to the French River Coldwater Hatchery, and reared to an average size of seven inches for stocking into both the Little Knife and French Rivers in the spring of 1990.

With the continued focus on the Knife River strain, the runs of Minnesota's North Shore are slowly coming back on this historically famous river. Other less favored rivers still receive excellent spring runs, but that have to be timed almost to the hour and day. Since these streams have very short flows (less than a mile or so) wild steelhead jump up them quickly during spate runoff conditions, drop their eggs and are gone. Look for these sleeper runs on the **Devils Track, Flute Reed, Temperance, Sucker** and **Kadunce rivers** along scenic Highway 61 to the Ontario border.

Ontario's Thunder Bay and Eastward Shoreline

This pristine wilderness is unparalleled in its beauty and is home to divergent unique wild strains of steelhead. One must now enter Jon George. Here is a steelhead biologist that speaks emphatically about his precious wild steelhead. Due to the remoteness of the rivers, in the early 1900s, steelhead were left alone to colonize and perpetuate. Today George states, *"Ontario Ministry of Natural Resources manages steelhead in Lake Superior as a wild, self-sustaining species. We enhance wild stocks by regulating the exploitation levels such as low bag limits and minimal harvest size. Any introductions are done using local wild gene pools. The existing strains are derived from original, introduced West Coast stocks. Over time unique individual stream stocks have evolved resulting in a wide variety of life history characteristics that have been expressed. Individual stream stocks maintain their uniqueness via strong homing to their place of birth. All these unique inherent life history characteristics allow individual populations to maximize themselves and should be preserved and protected at all costs. New regulations started in 1999 for the harvest of only one steelhead rainbow trout daily on the North Shore"*.

Some populations have well defined fall migrations of mature adults that over-winter and spawn early in the spring. This appears to be a strategy for populations that have to move a long distance to headwater locations. The fall migrations have a head start over spring migrants and need this strategy in order to fully seed the entire stream. The overwintering fish appear to spawn early prior to the spring migration peak. Lake Superior steelhead generally spawn from late April to the end of May. Some have been seen spawning as early as late March to as late as early July. The Steel River has wild summer run fish (perhaps the result of an original West Coast stock). This run is possibly retained due to the fact this is a large ground water system with lots of summer flow and cool water temperatures similar to rivers on the West Coast that have summer migrations. In late July and August, fresh run migrants (4 to 6 pounds) are present in the deep pools of the upper river. These fish are not to be confused with the Skamania summer runs that are genetically engineered hatchery fish.

Beginning near Thunder Bay, wild steelhead ascend the **Neebing, Mcintyre** and **Mackenzie** rivers. The McIntyre is predominantly a spring-run river in the middle of the city of Thunder Bay. It peaks around the first part of May. The McKenzie flows through a rocky canyon and has pleasant pool and pocket water, where spring steelhead are found in good numbers. Fall fish are usually able to ascend the river depending on yearly flows and rainfall.

Further eastward, the **Wolf** receives excellent fall runs and fishes well due to the heavier flows. Spring flows can often put the water out of its banks and make it unfishable. A good deal of gravel is present throughout the Wolf's system.

The larger and often turbid **Black Sturgeon** is ideal in the fall due to lower flows but can be dangerous in the spring. It is known for its larger steelhead compared with other strains. A two-handed Spey rod can be fished swinging marabou and bunny leeches when water temperatures are warm. **Portage** and **Trout** creeks and the **Coldwater** River also have wild steelhead runs into Black Bay.

The **Nipigon** River system is world famous for its gigantic world-record brook trout. It also has a good run of summer steelhead and resident and migratory rainbows. The summer steelhead rainbows take dries and are awesome fighters due to optimal water conditions. This is truly a spectacular fishery.

In the Rossport area, a sleepy fishing village nestled in a bay is a quaint tourist destination, with charming lodging like the historic Rossport Inn. This area is home to two outstanding wild steelhead rivers: The **Jackpine** and **Cypress**. While guided by author/writer Scott Smith, author of *Ontario Blue-Ribbon Fly Fishing Guide* (Frank Amato Publications), we backpacked into the upper Cypress for coaster brook trout and early fall steelhead. The remoteness and beauty of this river that runs through rock ledges and waterfalls amazed me. Its color is highly tannic from cedar swamps and mineral deposits. The Cypress perhaps has the best run of steelhead on the North Shore, due to its repeat spawner steelhead profile. It can be fished comfortably down from Highway 17 as long as flows are low in the fall for its autumn steelhead. Spring runoff can unleash the waters from Hell.

The **Jackpine** is another outstanding steelhead river that rages in the spring and continually cuts through the rocky moraine, and providing life-nourishing gravel to repeat spawning steelhead. The spring runs occur from mid-April until June with aerial minded steelhead using the great flow of the river to their advantage once hooked.

The **Steel** River, which empties into Terrace Bay, is one of my favorites. Not only does it have breathtaking cliffs and wildlife, it is perhaps the most beautiful and austere river in the Great Lakes basin with wild steelhead present at all times of the year. Peak spawning is from April through June along with fall runs in October and November. It has a unique wild summer run. When I hiked into the middle section of the river with Scott Smith to the Hospital Pool, I was awestruck by the river's surroundings. Here summer steelhead are known to take the dry fly like British Columbia fish. Some Atlantic salmon reproduction is occurring on the Steel and is being further investigated. **Special note:** When you go on a trip with Scott Smith make sure you are in great shape. Those hike-in backpack trips are grueling but well worth it! As you travel further east towards Wawa, the wide flowing **Michipicoton** receives excellent fall and spring runs, but is unique in its wild summer strain of fish. This is a fine western style river with classic riffle, pool, and tailout water. Eric CiCarlo, a local steelhead guru, fishes nymphs and sculpin patterns with great success. The summer steelhead will eat lots of caddis and can be quite selective at times.

The St. Mary's River, actually a river channel or strait connecting Superior with Huron, receives massive runs of steelhead from Lake Huron in the fall period from October through November. Its spring run peaks around the middle of May through the third week of June. Large shouldered brutes up to 18 pounds can be taken while wading the rapids off the berm wall in Sault Ste. Marie. Wading can be treacherous so wear cleats and use a wading staff. The nearby Garden River also gets fall and spring steelhead and is a little known secret destination.

Lake Michigan's Steelhead Paradise

The water and rivers of Lake Michigan are perhaps the greatest steelhead fisheries in the world. With its meandering shoreline of sandy dunes and beaches, along with scenic bays and inlets like the Grand Traverse, unique microclimates allow great wineries and orchard productions to prosper. The steep dunes of the lake, such as the famous Sleeping Bear National Lake Shoreline, are reminiscent of wind blown sands left by the immense glaciers that carved the lake's basin 15,000 years ago. Along with its beautiful port towns and fishing villages adorned with piers and historic lighthouses, it is home to large metropolitan cities like Chicago and the industrial shoreline of Indian and Wisconsin.

Since the 1880's introduction of steelhead into Lake Michigan's Boyne, Paw Paw, and Kalamazoo rivers, the Lake Michigan steelhead dynasty took off in full force and never looked

Master steelheader Steve Stallard casts to fish on the hallowed wild steelhead water of Michigan's Little Manistee River. Fresh pines and the soil of budding wildflowers permeate the air with the refreshing smell of a northwoods spring.

back. Today's modern Lake Michigan steelhead fishery is a carefully balanced ecosystem which utilizes the wild, self-sustaining fishery of Michigan's fabled spring-fed rivers and tailwaters to exist with the heavily stocked waters of Indiana, Illinois and Wisconsin. With millions of steelhead produced each year due to optimum spawning areas, great forage food opportunities and large sophisticated hatchery systems, Lake Michigan is truly a steelhead factory.

Truly unique to the state of Michigan's shoreline are large, river estuary lake basins, that encompass vast areas. Muskegon Lake, White Lake, Manistee Lake, and others provide ideal smolt sanctuary habitat and allow gradual staging of returning adults. Also Lake Michigan's "not too cold, not too warm" water allows for greater growth rates and bigger sizes of the steelhead.

Michigan's silver lined "century circle," has rivers with unique ecosystems of moderate gradient waters, constant spring-fed flows, and spawning gravel and nursery waters. The rivers of Michigan's northwest lake basin are some of the most unique systems in the world. Along with larger, gravel-laden tailwaters like the Muskegon, and Manistee, managed under stable flow regulations, things could not be more perfect for Michigan's Little Manistee strain winter run steelhead.

Beginning in the lower southwest corner of the state, the **St. Joseph** River is a marvel of political cooperation between states and environmental agencies to produce a world class steelhead fishery. With a fifteen million dollar cooperative program known as the St. Joseph River Interstate Anadromous Fish Project, which took 12 years to complete, five fish ladders from Michigan to South Bend, Indiana bring summer Skamania and Michigan winter strain fish through the entire system. With over a half- million steelhead being stocked with excellent returns, it has one of the highest angler catch rates for steelhead in North America (1 fish per 19 minutes of angler hours.)

The real appeal of the St. Joseph is the summer run Skamania strain stocked by Indiana. Beginning in June and lasting through September, approximately 40,000 summer steelhead between 8 and 26 pounds ascend the river. These beastly, ferocious, leaping fighters can only be compared to Atlantic *Salmon* or tarpon. Excellent angling exists during the summer along the river and creek mouths of the Pipestone, Lemon, McCoy, Dowagiac, Judy and Brandywine creeks. Below the dam at Berrien Springs large numbers of both summer and winter run fish congregate near the shore and islands, fish ladder and hydrogates. Excellent spawning gravel areas exist at the Sportsman's Club area in the lower river, below the dam at Niles, the Dowagiac River and at the Leeper Park area of South Bend. You can virtually hook a steelhead any day, 365 days a year on the St. Joe. The **Dowagiac** River, starting at the dam at Pucker Street in Niles, works like a pristine northern river with beautiful riffle, pocket, pool and tailout structure. The river runs cold in the summer and attracts summer steelhead in good numbers.

Proceeding up the coast, the **Paw Paw**, a tributary of the St. Joe, the **Black** in South Haven, and the **Kalamazoo** up to the Allegan dam host good runs of winter Little Manistee strain steelhead from fall to early spring.

The **Grand** River, whose rushing waters flow through the heart of the city of Grand Rapids, receives heavy runs beginning in September and lasting until late May. The fish ladder at the Sixth Street Dam in downtown congregates fish and fishermen who wade and boat these waters. The **Rogue** River is a beautiful trout and steelhead river where some natural reproduction of steelhead occurs. A Grand tributary, it is a classic steelhead river with riffle-pool-tailout design. West River, Packard, Childsdale and Jericho Roads are good access points, as is the dam at

Rockford. Steelhead also enter other creeks like the **Flat** and **Prairie** systems as they proceed all the way to Lansing.

North of Grand Rapids towards Newaygo is the world famous **Muskegon** River. It was back in the early 1900s that along the banks of the Paris fish hatchery experimental strains of West Coast steelhead were dumped into its waters. It was here that natural reproduction was first documented in Lake Michigan tributaries.

For more than 70 miles, steelhead, both wild and planted, swim up to Croton Dam, which is not passable. With the river's new "stable flow, run-of-the-river status" natural reproduction is vastly occurring. From Newaygo to Croton, the river is laced with gravel and its aquatic insect life is diverse. Steelhead up to twenty pounds are common on this classic looking, western-style river, where a two-handed Spey rod works well. Its crystal clear waters and vegetation look like a giant spring creek. Starting at the impassable barrier of Croton Dam, good fall and winter holding pools exists from the dam to the DNR Pine access and Calvary Riffle slightly below. At Carmichael Flats and below to the first high clay banks, good holding pools and spawning gravel can be found.

At the Thornapple DNR access, good spawning gravel is found along with spring-fed holding pools found along the High Rollaway access down to Devil's Hole. From Cottonwood Flats to **Bigalow** Creek (an important fish spawning sanctuary) productive fall and winter holding water is found. The Henning Park access, with Riverfront Park and New Bridge DNR access, has prime winter holding water all the way down to the Old Women's Bend access off of Felch Road and Mystery Creek access off of River Road.

Good winter steelheading pools exist from Bridgeton down to Maple Island. From **Cedar** Creek (another major steelhead spawning tributary) down to the North Causeway in Muskegon, heavy logging stumps line the runs and make bottom drift fishind difficult. Please note that from Thornapple access down to Lake Michigan, the river is a trophy trout/steelhead managed fishery with 3 fish a day over 15 inches.

Just a brief drive north is the **White** River. With its North Branch and a heavy gravel laden, picturesque setting up to the dam at Hesparia, excellent fall, winter and spring runs of wild and planted fish can be found in this highly productive river. The Garfield Road and the Taylor Bridge access points are your best bets. The nearby **Pentwater** River also hosts excellent runs of winter and spring Little Manistee strain fish, especially at the mouth of Pentwater Lake.

One of the greatest steelhead rivers in the world is a short distance north—the **Pere Marquette**. Hosting incredible runs of McCloud origin fish since the early 1900s, the Pere Marquette produces hundreds of thousands of wild steelhead yearly through its gravel-laced, spring-fed mainstream, Middle branch and Little South branches—with existing smaller feeder streams. Extremely wary and selective, its steelhead are incredible fighters and magnificent looking fish. The "PM" has a 7-mile catch-and-release flies-only stretch which is heavily fished in the spring. Its fall run occurs from October through December. In the lower stretches from Gleason's Landing to Scottville it is primarily a drift boat fishery (for reference, see my *River Journal: Pere Marquette*). The steelhead in the "flies only" water see a lot of pressure—fish tiny patterns on light tippets. Good areas to wade can be found along the Rainbow Club's water at Lumberjack access off of 72nd

Michigan rivers like the Muskegon, Manistee and St. Mary's often have excellent spring runs of spawning steelhead well into Memorial Day Weekend when the weather is warmer. Thanks to the cold water coming from the tailwater impoundments and Lake Superior, water temperatures remain ideal for steelhead, despite the heat on the St. Mary's.

Street, along with the Fisherman's Trail access at the junction of the Baldwin River.

From Green Cottage, through Wadell's riffles down through the clay banks, Canon Ranch and PM Rod and Gun Club, outstanding spawning gravel and holding pockets can be found. Prime fall holding pools exist from Rainbow Rapids down through Lower Branch Bridge and on to Walhalla.

Further up along the hallowed coast is the **Little Manistee**. This is the river where the historic research by Paul Seelbach took place on steelhead behavior. This river's unique genetic strain provides the weir egg-taking operation for its genetic contribution to Michigan's hatchery system. Prime fall, winter and spring runs can be found. The area from Six Mile to Nine Mile Road is a great place to prospect for steelhead, with the Johnson's Bridge area being the upstream boundary for fall and spring steelheading.

Opposite of the smaller brached Little Manistee, the **Big Manistee** receives winter and summer Skamania steelhead all year long. From Tippy Dam in Wellston, famous runs and pools like the "Sawdust Hole," Tunk Hole, Suicide Bend, School Bus Run, and others provide hot steelheading. Bear Creek, a good tributary, also attracts good numbers of fish along with cold water tributaries like the Pine which attracts summer steelhead during hot weather periods. Gin-clear waters require light leaders and small flies since the fish see plenty of pressure. Drift boats float from Tippy Dam down to High Bridge which is the most popular stretch. From High Bridge down, one can often have secluded and less populated crowds. Ray Schmidt is the master of the mighty Manistee and he and his outfitters are located in Wellston.

North towards Frankfort and Benzonia, the **Betsie** is another hallowed, mid-sized river with a mix of wild and hatchery fish. The old Homestead Dam is passable by fish and allows steelhead to go upstream to cold feeder creeks for natural reproduction. Good late fall/winter runs occur on the Betsie through December. Most angling occurs at the Homestead Dam and below Highway U.S. 31 by drift boats.

Towards Honor, the crystal clear waters of the **Platte** are noted for their historic coho runs. Yet its wild steelhead are silvery and opaque and blend in perfectly with their natural surroundings. The fish are very skittish due to lack of cover. Good numbers of fall fish can be found from M22 down along with spring fish after the April 1st opener downstream and upstream from Haze road.

The **Boardman**, which flows through Traverse City, has a good fall, winter, and spring run fishery predominantly of hatchery stock up to the dam in town. Further through the Traverse district the **Boyne** and **Jordan** rivers get excellent fall and spring runs running into Lake Charlevoix and can provide great fall steelheading during the less crowded times of deer season. Its spring runs seem to run later into May and if you hit it just right, you can have these rivers to yourself.

Along the Sleeping Bear Leelanau Penninsula, small streams such as the **Crystal** and the **Carp** can get a fast "flash" run of steelhead where timing is everything.

Beginning in Mackinac County, and proceeding along the lake's north shore through Michigan's Upper Peninsula, the **Carp** River is perhaps the best noted steelhead fishery in a remote setting, with many miles of fishable water accessible from M 123 and Ozark Road. Mainly a spring run river, some late fall steelhead ascend its beautiful surroundings. The Cut, Brevost, Paquin and Davenport tributary streams offer hit-and-miss fall and spring runs based on water flows. Surf fishing is often more reliable.

In Schoolcraft County in the Upper Penninsula, the **Manistique** is a short stretch of big steelhead water with good fall and a spring runs. Primarily a boat fishery in the lower river, the upper sections are swift. Most of the action occurs by the dam spillway and paper mill near the town of Manistique. In Delta County, the DAYS River which empties into Little Bay De Noc is a great stream with a perfect gradient and excellent runs lined with gravel. In a classic riffle-pool-tailout structure, it has good fall and spring runs. County roads 529, 430, M-35 and U.S. 2 are access points. Other Bay De Noc streams that host flashy spring runs are the **Sturgeon, Whitefish, Rapid** and **Tacoosh** rivers.

Finally, as we exit Michigan's shoreline in Menomonee County, also in the U.P., we find the short mile and a half **Menominee** River below the dam. This is primarily an excellent fall fishery since it lacks sufficient spring spawning habitat.

Wisconsin's Prolific West Coast

Wisconsin's progressive management approach to its steelhead fishery began in earnest in the 1980s, with a classification system for steelhead rivers and strains stocked. Since many of the rivers are dammed, upstream migration for reproduction is limited except for a few streams. With excellent stocked smolt survival due to the favorable waters of Lake Michigan and with abundant food sources and water temperatures, Wisconsin has created a world class fishery utilized by many sportsmen from the Midwest's heavily populated cities.

Wisconsin's main emphasis is to stock strains and improve return to angler harvest (since natural reproduction is limited by often warmer and silt-laden waters). With excellent returns on harvest from 12 to 23%, Wisconsin continues to fine tune it's fishery with the development of the Besadny Anadromous weir and trapping facilities on the Kewanee River. The facility monitors returns of steelhead, collects basic biological information on the strains, and has a floy (little plastic string tagging) program to determine movement and migration.

Wisconsin today utilizes a careful balance of three strains. The Skamania summer strain from the Washougal River in Washington runs from June through the fall. The Chambers Creek strain is another Washington State transplant and runs from October through April. The Ganaraska

As two steelhead prepare their spawning redd on Michigan's Platte River, an angler takes time to watch nature's powerful drive to procreate.

Ontario strain is a spring runner with peak occurrence form March through May. With these three strains, a 365-day fishery has been created.

To stock the various strains Wisconsin devised a Class I and II system for their streams. Class I streams generally are heavier in flow, wider, and can support year round angling. They contain little to no obstructions at their mouths. They also possess good upstream access and migration to certain impassable barriers and dams. These streams also have sufficient winter flows and depth to support the overwintering capacity to carry Skamania and Chambers's Creek strains.

Class II rivers are often short with minimal flows and frequently have downed river mouths blocked with sand in low summer, fall and winter months. They seem to have the best flows during spring runoff and are ideally suited to the spring running Ganaraska strain.

Concentrating on the Class I waters beginning in the Green Bay area is the **Peshtigo** River. The dam in the village of Peshtigo has the greatest concentration of angling where deep holes gradually tailout to shallow gravel. Much of the spring spawning run ends up here along Highway 41. From the dam downstream about 100 feet is a Wisconsin DNR Fish Sanctuary closed to fishing from March 1 through May 15 to protect spawning populations. Below this is nice gravelly, fast moving water with some beautiful stretches for wading.

The **Oconto** River, a half-hour drive north of Green Bay, is one of the more picturesque and as close to a "wilderness-like" setting on Wisconsin's west shore. Good access is from the upstream impassable dam at Stiles in Highway 41 for 13 miles. Flowing through a beautiful forest of cedar, birch and pine, one can launch a drift boat or canoe and float form Stiles dam down to the boat launch at Hgwy J for a 4-mile trip. The Highway 141 bridge is popular with fly anglers and has received some excellent Wisconsin DNR boulder habitat stream improvement to attract steelhead to these shallower, riffle-strewn areas. Susie's Rapids, within the city of Oconto is a new DNR shore access popular for its spring attraction due to excellent spawning riffles. The dam at Stiles regulates under minimal flow restraints.

The **Ahnapee** River at the dam in Forestville is heavily fished. Angling also occurs near Algoma. The river is generally wide and shallow, with a soft sandy bottom.

One of the premier and heaviest stocked steelhead rivers is the **Kewaunee**. There are no dam obsturctions in the rivers for 22 miles, including tributaries of the Scarboro, Little Scarboro, and Casco Creeks. Natural reproduction of steelhead has been documented and does occur in this river. Since the Besadny Brood stock facility for steelhead exists here near Foot Bridge, anglers cannot fish from Highway F to 500 feet above the facility. Popular angling areas are from Highway F downstream to Highway C. Fly fishers particularly like the scenic waters upstream from the DNR facility at Clyde's Hill Bridge and at the 3rd Highway C crossing. The upper reaches have classic riffle, pool-tailout waters whereas the lower section is wider and slower.

The **East Twin** River is accessible to steelhead for 11 miles up to the dam at Michicot. Angling mainly takes place here downstream to the Fire Station. The East Twin is narrower than the other Class I streams. The West Twin has six miles of water upstream to the dam at Shoto where shallow rocky pockets and riffles attract wading anglers.

The **Manitowac** River is one of the premier steelhead fly fishing rivers in the area. Approximately 41 miles of river, including the scenic Branch River tributary, is open to the steelhead migration. Upstream 21.5 miles on the main river, the Clarks Mill Dam and the Cato Falls area is popular angling water. The Manitowac has a steep gradient at Clarks Mills, forming excellent riffle, pool, and gravelly runs. The **Branch** River is best accessed at Damore and South Union Road bridges. In the lower Manitowoc, the county parks system is popular with fly fishers. Some very shallow riffles exist about 6 miles up from the lake at Highway 43. If the river is having an exceptionally low drought year, upstream access by steelhead is limited.

The **Sheboygan** River flows passable for steelhead from the lower dam at Kohler for 8 miles. Private access is available on the Kohler estate. The Black Wolf Run Golf Course is also popular with anglers. It is a pleasant rocky substrate river with some long pocket/pool waters. Good access is also available at highway PP.

Since the removal of the North Avenue dam upriver of the city, the **Milwaukee** River allows steelhead to breach smaller dams and ledges and swim up to the second dam in Graften, which is also slated for removal. The Milwaukee is a wider, heavier flowing river, which attracts good numbers of steelhead and crowds at peak run times. Most angling occurs between the old North Avenue dam to the Kletzach Park spillway. The DNR has been working to create more habitats for salmonids by adding boulder and cracked cement to create holding water on the Milwaukee above the Estabrook Park dam where good spawning gravel exists.

Perhaps the most popular, the most crowded, and the most controversial river is the **Root**. Stocked heavily with all salmonids from the Horlick Dam in Racine downstream six miles to the lake, it can be a madhouse of fish and fishermen when the run is on. A new brood stock egg-taking facility at Lincoln Park does not allow anglers to fish 200 feet above or below the area. The Root stocks 105,000 Skamania, Chambers and Ganaraska strains with excellent returns. There are good access to riffles, runs and pools (with the exception of a private golf course). When the run is on, be prepared for elbow to elbow synchronized casting. Due to the congestion, short-line nymphing and egg presentations are best. No room here for Spey casting!

Several other sleeper Class II waters exist like **Whitefish Bay, Stoney**, **Hubbards**, **Reibolts**, and **Heins** creeks of Door County. **Silver** Creek in Kewaunee County, the Pigeon in Sheyboygan County, and the **Oak** and **Kinnickinnic** creeks in Milwaukee County also get good runs of spring Ganaraska strain fish. Don't forget the excellent surf fishing around the warm water discharge and power plants around along the Wisconsin/Illinois lakefront area.

Indiana's Skamania Coast

Though only 40 miles long, the shoreline of Indiana's southern industrial shore and national dunes lakeshore sees a tremendous amount of steelhead smolts migrating to the big lake from its rather short and small tributary streams. Thanks to the vision of Indiana's Department of Natural Resources to bring the Skamania summer steelhead from Washington State in the early 1970s, Indiana has claim to one of the finest summer steelhead fisheries in the world. Approximately 200,000 Skamania summer and Little Manistee winter strain fished are planted in each of the tributary mouths as healthy nine inch fish which quickly smolt adding greatly to the Lake Michigan offshore steelhead fishery. Along with Illinois' planting of 50,000 Skamania along its Chicago shoreline, the homing returns to the southern shore are strong.

When you first look at Indiana's Trail, Little Calumet, and Salt Creeks, your first impression is "My, how could such huge fish hold in these muddy, catfish ditches?" However when you put your hand in the water on a sweltering hot July day, your fingertips will get a little chilled. Due to the vast, limestone

Steve Stallard photo

*The author chases a "freight train" steelhead
down a Lake Huron Georgian Bay stream.*

Miles Chance photo

*Keeping summer steelhead out of the logjam-filled
Lake Michigan Indian tributaries requires a short stiff
9-weight rod, heavy 1X tippets and a lot of heaving.*

groundwater supply of the region, cool springs allow these 20 pound plus Skamania harbingers with hell raising, bronco-busting acrobatics to perform so well. Few people know that the Great Lakes and All World Freshwater Tackle Record for steelhead stands at 31 pounds 4 ounces, taken on Lake Michigan. The fish was an 8 to 10 year old Skamania stocked by Indiana.

Proceeding along the shoreline from Chicago, the **Little Calumet** system is the first tributary stocked located near Burns Harbor. The headwaters flow through the National Dunes Lakeshore heron rookery containing a beautiful small stream frequently fished by anglers. For the most part it flows parallel to Route 20. The most popular access is at the Main Gate area of the Bethlehem Steel Plant down to where it empties into Burns Ditch.

Salt Creek, a tributary that flows cool due to underground springs, attracts great numbers of steelhead from Valporaiso down to its confluence with the "Little Cal." Imagination Glen Park and Route 20 are good access points.

Trail Creek, located in Michigan City, receives year round runs of summer and winter steelhead with good access. A DNR access at Trail Creek Forks on Route 20 and the Johnson Road areas are your best bets. I've built a custom 7ft., 9 weight rod to handle these 20 pound brutes in tight brushy quarters. These creeks average between 10 and 20 feet in width with very heavy woody debris. To handle these huge fish, heavy tippets and stiff rods are advised.

Lake Huron:
Wilderness with Civilization

The vast expanse of this second largest Great Lake is surrounded by pristine northwoods beauty, contrasted with cultured farmlands and villages to the south. Its northern steelhead rivers and streams offer many miles of unspoiled beauty with sufficient gradient; in contrast, low-lying southern agriculture areas are impacted by smaller tributaries. With a tremendous network of inlets and islands like the Georgian Bay, ideal forage feeding grounds and habitat exist for steelhead with a great diversity of water temperatures and currents favored by these wandering, nomadic fish.

Laying claim to being the first Great Lake stocked with steelhead in 1876, occurring in the Au Sable River of Michigan, Lake Huron continues to produce healthy runs of wild and hatchery fish with broad shoulders and aggressive fighting capabilities.

Ontario's Georgian Bay
and Eastern Shore

Here the north shore wilderness of Superior continues into white limestone cliffs and a dense forest landscape of the Georgian Bay District. I recall summers spent with my family vacationing at our cottage at Wasaga beach near the Nottawasaga River. I remember picking wild mushrooms in the sandy forested soils of pines and other exotic northern hardwoods. The aromatic smoke-filled campfire nights were enchanting as my body basked in the invigorating chilly nights, while wolve and coyotes hauntingly cried in the distance. I look back to the many fishless days of the trout opener, chasing the giant rainbow, often when the rivers were frigid and raged coffee brown from runoff. When I finally seduced my first wild Georgian Bay steelhead in my teens, its beauty and its fullness of body captivated me. Today, these rivers are still managed as in years past for their wild bounty.

Larry Halyk, noted Ontario Ministry of Natural Resources steelhead biologist fly fisher, and fly tier knows the rivers of Lake Huron and Georgian Bay and has graciously introduced and assisted in my knowledge of them. Along with the OMNR biologists like David Reid and Fred Dobbs who monitor and closely study the Ontario Lake Huron fishery, they have detailed the vast resource the fishery has to offer.

Returning adult rainbow trout were documented in tributaries of the Nottawasaga River on the Canadian side of the lake as early as 1903. In spite of these early reports, however, the emergence of introduced rainbow trout as an important gamefish seemed to coincide with the collapse of native lake trout stocks, which started in the 1940s and was complete by the mid-1950s. Prior to the decline in lake trout numbers, competition with this dominant top predator species was probably responsible for maintaining rainbow trout numbers at a low level.

The elimination of lake trout from the Lake Huron ecosystem by the mid-1950s, may have provided an opportunity for rainbow trout populations to expand in size. The onset of effective lamprey control in the late 1960s permitted steelhead rainbow trout populations to expand to the carrying capacity of the Lake Huron Ecosystem, limited only by the availability and accessibility of spawning and nursery habitats in the tributary streams. Fish ladder construction between 1963 and 1980 was an important factor in providing access to new spawning and early-rearing habitats for increasing the production of young steelhead rainbow trout. The elimination of biological and physical constraints on the fish starting in the late 1960s leading to the development of strong steelhead populations throughout Lake Huron. At this time, Southern Georgian Bay may have supported the largest populations of wild steelhead located anywhere in the Great Lakes Basin.

The emergence of strong steelhead populations in the late 1960s led to the development of a large sportfishery targeting this species. Although the most intensive sport-fishing effort seemed to occur on the regular opening of the stream trout season in late April, stream fishing for early-migrating fish during the fall months also became popular. Steelhead populations seemed to be strong even when faced with pressure from increasing angler harvest impacts.

Starting in the late 1980s, a decline in Southern Georgian Bay steelhead was observed by anglers and also by conservation officers and biologists working for the OMNR. The perceived decline of the fish populations in Southern Georgian Bay lead to the implementation of rainbow trout population assessment program by the Ontario Ministry of Natural Resources (MNR), starting in 1993.

Most Lake Huron/Georgian Bay steelhead are wild. This is especially true of the Georgian Bay side. Some stocking by OMNR and clubs (Ontario Steelheaders, Maitland Valley Anglers, Nine Mile Steelheaders) takes place in Lake Huron streams (Saugeen, Maitland, Bayfield, Nine Mile) and in the Sydenham River.

The steelhead here tend to average 6-8 pounds with fish over 10 pounds fairly common and fish well into the teens caught every season. Every once in a while, you hear of fish over 20 pounds, but these are rare. The Ontario record steelhead (over 29 pounds) came from Wasaga Beach at the mouth of the Nottawasaga River in the 1970s.

The major steelhead producing tributaries are located along the Lake Huron Shoreline from Goderich to Sauble Beach, and along the Georgian Bay Shoreline from Wiarton to Wasaga Beach. Southern Lake Huron (Lambton County near Sarnia and Grand Bend) has too many agricultural impacts to produce many wild fish and the eastern and northern shoreline of Georgian Bay has physiological limitations that do not allow these tributaries to maintain temperatures, baseflow, and gravel substrate conditions suitable for steelhead production.

The headwaters of all the good steelhead tributaries have one thing in common: abundant groundwater which maintains baseflow and temperatures that permit steelhead juveniles (smolts) an ideal year-round environment. Many of these headwater streams still have pretty good brook trout fishing. The lower reaches of many of the larger tributaries (Saugeen, Maitland, Nottawasaga, and Beaver) are warm and are therefore marginal trout habitat at best. This means that the steelhead runs generally start when waters cool in September and continue through the fall and winter, right up to late May during a late spring.

The limestone soils and agricultural nature of these watersheds result in a rich invertebrate foodbase for juvenile steelhead.

Guide John Guilliani points to porpoising Atlantic salmon on the St. Mary's River as Steve Stallard riffle-hitches a Thugmeister tube fly to elicit an explosive surface strike.

All of the major mayfly and stonefly groups are well represented in the headwater areas occupied by steelhead, caddis are abundant in the lower reaches of these streams. Small black stoneflies are so effective in the early season that even many float fishermen favor stonefly imitations to fresh roe at this time. A generalized mayfly nymph imitation such as hare's ear is always a good choice.

Most of the tributaries can be characterized (at least in the lower reaches where most of the steelhead fly fishing takes place) as being broad and open with a good mix of riffles and pools with gravel, boulder, and bedrock bottoms—in other words, ideal fly water. Because they are so open, wind can sometimes be a factor. In generaly, these rivers are fairly easy to read by those familiar with the usual places that steelhead hold. Larger rivers such as the Saugeen and Maitland are big water—care should be taken when wading, especially when the water is up (which also coincides when the fish are in).

Summer steelhead are present in some tributaries but not in numbers that can support a major fishery. Through the mid-late 1980s, Michigan was experimenting with summer steelhead stocking in its Lake Michigan and Huron tribs (primarily Skamania strain obtained from Washington via Indiana). Strays from the Au Sable River Michigan planting would show up in the Maitland and Saugeen Rivers in late July and through August (probably less than 200-300 fish per river). These provided a small but interesting fishery for those of us willing to put in enough hours. Michigan reduced, then eliminated its Lake Huron stocking of Skamania steelhead by the early 1990s and as a result, the summer steelhead run on Lake Huron rivers has dwindled to only a few token fish.

The Sydenham Sportsman's Club still maintains a Skamania stocking program (about 15,000 yearlings stocked annually) in the Owen Sound area of Georgian Bay. These fish show up mainly in the open lake and shoreline fishery and do not produce a lot of sport in the tributaries, save for modest runs of stray fish in the Bighead, Beaver, and Nottawasaga Rivers.

Starting at the southern end of Lake Huron and working up the **Bayfield** River to Georgian Bay, is a short to medium-sized river (about 50 feet wide in the lower reaches) that is located a short distance south of the Maitland. The lowest 6 miles are fairly high gradient with plenty of juicy boulder studded runs and pockets. In the fall, this river fishes best a day or two after a major freshet and is best avoided during dry periods. The steelhead run is probably a 50:50 mix of stocked and wild fish.

The **Maitland** River is one of the most scenic rivers in the lower Great Lakes. It is a big river, comparable in size to the Saugeen. The big difference is that it is generally very shallow and so fish are reluctant to enter during low flows.

The main river of the Maitland (excluding tribs) is open to December 31 downstream from Hwy. 4 in Wingham. This is over 31 miles of river and most of it is ideal fly water—broad and open with many runs perfect for swinging a fly. There are no dams in this section that would tend to stack fish so the fish are scattered. It can run very low early in the fall and as a result, steelheading is inconsistent until the big rains come in late October or early November. The steelhead run is a mix of wild and stocked fish.

Nine Mile (Lucknow) River is a small to medium-sized river that is similar in character to the Bayfield. It is located just north of the Maitland. Like the Bayfiled, it's a good alternative to the Maitland after a hard rain. There is a small dam and fish ladder located less than 1/4 mile up from the mouth. When the water is high and the run is in, the stretch below the dam is a zoo, with gear fishermen lining both banks. A lot of fish are caught, but the scene is ugly. Avoid this stretch unless you like crowds or are looking for entertainment. Most of the steelhead in

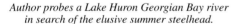
Author probes a Lake Huron Georgian Bay river in search of the elusive summer steelhead.

the Nine Mile are wild and the run size averages an estimated 2 to 5 thousand fish. An impressive run for such a small river.

The **Saugeen** is the largest and best known steelhead river in the province. Its reputation and popularity are well deserved. For its size, the Saugeen does not support a huge steelhead run. The total run size is probably in the neighborhood of 5-10,000 fish. What makes the Saugeen so attractive to many is its freestone character. Riffles, pools, and runs in just the right amount—and plenty of flowing water for a fresh steelhead when hooked. Denny's Dam is located about 2 miles upstream of the mouth. About 99% of the fishing pressure takes place on this lower stretch, most of which is open year round. There is a well-maintained campsite here run by the Ontario Steelheaders. After the salmon are done by early November, mostly seasoned steelheaders are here. The Saugeen gets both spring and fall steelhead runs and on mild winters, with good fishing continuing all winter long. You can usually count on some fish being at the "first rapids" on the lower river by Labor Day. The upper river is underutilized—hardly anyone fishes it. Like the Maitland, this stretch of river will offer big rewards to those patient enough to learn its secrets. There are miles and miles of beautiful water here that go virtually unfished. This is an untapped fishery waiting to be discovered.

The **Sauble** is a low-gradient river except for the stretch in the vicinity of Sauble Falls. It has a reputation for running clear when all other rivers around are unfishable. Its sand bottom and gentle gradient give this river a character similar to Michigan streams such as the Betsie or Little Manistee. Only a couple tributaries are suitable nursery streams so the steelhead run is not large. When conditions are right, however, good numbers of fish are taken.

The **Bighead** is a real gem. All its fish are wild and very strong. These are very broad shouldered fish that just don't stop fighting. The river is open to December 31 in St. Vincent Township. The lowest 3 miles flows though a beautiful valley that has a western flavor to it. This section is mainly boulder studded pocket water that is ideal for an upstream "high sticking" nymph technique. Upstream of St. Vincent Township, the river branches into many small nursery streams that provide ideal conditions for spawning and rearing of steelhead. Flows vary widely on the Bighead. Since the Bighead basin drains very hilly country, flows increase dramatically after a good rain as it swells to true river size. The time to be on the Bighead is just as the water clears enough to see your fly in 8-10 inches of water.

The **Beaver** River in Thornbury is very popular with Toronto area anglers since it is less than an hour away from the Greater Toronto Area. The 1/4 mile stretch from the Thornbury Mill Dam down to the lake can be shoulder to shoulder when the runs are in. This stream is just south of the Bighead River and has a slightly greater baseflow. Since its flows are greater, it can attract a few steelhead and salmon even during dry periods. The River is attractive enough with pocket water stretches and easy to read runs and pools. There is a lock type fishway at the Thornbury Dam. Only a fraction of the steelhead run makes it above this dam. The river is only open in the fall below the Thournbury Dam. Upstream of the Thornbury all the way to Kimberly are miles of attractive water. This water deserves attention in the spring after opening day, yet is lightly fished.

Compared to most other Lake Huron Rivers, the **Nottawasaga** is a tough river to read and to fish. Its steelhead generally run much earlier in the fall than most other rivers.

Some of the fish can be very large. The upper Nottaqwasaga and its many tributaries (Pine, Boyne, Mad) are located on the Niagara Escarpment and are excellent steelhead nursery streams. These tributaries add up to one of the largest steelhead runs in the province. Since the river is long and the fish have a long way to go to reach spawning grounds, a large proportion of the Nottawasaga run takes place in the early fall. The Nottawasaga is known for its September and October runs of aggressive fish. The river is open year round all the way up to mouth of the Boyne River. Fly fishermen are best to concentrate in the lower river in the vicinity of the Wasaga Beach Provincial Park and near the top end of the open section in the vicinity of the village of Baxter.

Michigan's Eastern Shore

Once, the eastern shore of Lake Huron was a vast forest of white pine, wildlife, and fish in abundance along with the prosperous and healthy Indian tribes of the Huron, Ojibway, and Ottawa. The early intermingling of the tribes and the French and British proved disastrous and came full circle in the War of 1812. Along with the scavenging of the land by the "Lumber Barons" who build Detroit, today the land is gently healing with jackpine and second growth forests. Its rivers still run clean and abundantly while golf courses outnumber fast food restaurants all the way to the Mackinac Straits.

Traveling from the southern most Michigan town of Port Huron past Bay City, the first major steelhead water of significance is the **Rifle**. It is a classic looking trout stream that drains good runs of decent-sized Lake Huron fish. Its clear water often makes fish quite spooky. Access is available in the upper river at country roads 18, 16, 19 and 10 along with M-55 and the Rifle River Trail in southern Ogenaw County. Good fall runs appear after the salmon, especially with mild weather and good flows. This is Mike Bachelder's river. Mike, of Bachelder Spool and Fly, uses tiny nymphs and drifts the lower river with intimate knowledge of the fishery.

The **East Branch of the Augres** has excellent riffle, pocket, and pool steelhead water with a good gravel and sand bottom averaging 20 feet in width. The most productive fishing occurs from M-55 downstream to Turtle Road. Other access points are at Alabaster and Sand Lake Roads. The river gets an excellent spring run while fall runs are dependent on water flows.

A deep-bodied, red-cheeked male steelhead that devoured a clear McKenzie Egg on Michigan's Au Sable River.

The legendary **Au Sable** River is noted for its large, deep-bodied wild steelhead of ground zero genetic importance dating to 1876. With 17 miles of water up to Foote Dam, it is primarily a driftboat fishery due to deep water; only limited wading is allowed. When low, it can run extremely clear with small nymphs needed to entice wary steelhead. With run-of-the-river stable flows, the future is bright for the lower Au Sable's wild fish. The Au Sable flows gin clear, requiring fine tippets and tiny nymph and egg patterns. Small Speys in black, purple, and pink work well also.

Bob Linsenman, acclaimed Michigan author and guide, knows the Au Sable better than anyone. He is the guardian and steward of this fine historic river which he detailed beautifully in his books *Great Lakes Steelhead* and the *River Journal: Au Sable*.

To complement the Au Sable's legendary wild runs, the MDNR has started an adipose clip/micro-tagging study to understand the migration and significance of hatchery produced fish to the Au Sable fishery.

The **Black** River in Alcoma County is a small, remote stream that has a beautiful strain of wild steelhead. The lower reaches are a bank and wadable fishery at Lakeshore and Black River roads. The upper stretches must be hiked in or canoed.

The **Ocqueoc** River in Presque Isle country is a gem of a little steelhead stream that is fly fished and wadable from Oqueoc Falls Highway down. This riffle and pocket classic stream has a gravel and sand bottom with migrating steelhead up to 15 pounds. When timed perfectly, it is possible to have the stream and plenty of fresh chrome fish to yourself.

Other smaller and variable flow streams that produce limited ihit-or-missî spring runs based on conditions are the **Cheboygan, Thunder Bay, Devil's, Pine, Swan** and **Maple** rivers, scattered between Mackinaw City and Oscoda. The locals know these tributaries well and the absence or abundance of cars parked at the bridge access points will tell you if the run is on or off.

Lake Erie:
The Unfolding New Steelhead Dynasty

It was only back in the 1960s that Lake Erie was officially proclaimed "dead." With industrial pollution running rampant and unchecked from the smokestack filled cities of Detroit, Cleveland and Buffalo, the water was a cesspool. I vividly recall these days growing up in Niagara Falls; we often travelled to visit my Uncle Mike who lived in Dunkirk, New York and worked for the Niagara Mohawk Power Company. When he took us on walks along the beach, the stench from the sewer colored waters and dying fish was enough to make you gag—we often carried handkerchiefs to cover our nose and mouths. Along with heavy, toxic, agricultural runoff from both American and Canadian farms producing fertile waters for algae and other undesirable vegetation and their decomposition which stripped the water of oxygen, what few fish remained, were gulping for air and suffocating to death. Ohio's heavily polluted Cuyahoga River "caught on fire" due to its toxic make-up. Today, chrome silver steelhead ascend its waters in abundance.

With the demise of the indigenous lake trout, blue-pike, and whitefish due to the introduction of lamprey predators from the Welland Canal, the initial planting of steelhead rainbows in the Michigan, Pennsylvania, Ohio and New York tributaries of Lake Erie in the 1880s somehow barely survived the onslaught of exotic predators, commercial fishing, and massive phosphate pollution. With regular stockings by individual states and the Province of Ontario from the 1970s to the 80s, a few self-sustaining "steelhead rainbow populations" began to take hold in the cooler trout waters of New York, Pennsylvania, and the Ontario Long Point streams.

John Nagy photo

The magnificent Cattaragus Creek of Lake Erie's New York shoreline. This is a classic Class I steelhead river that flows through the magnificent Zoar Valley with ideal riffle, pocket, pool and tailout characteristics, along with increasing natural reproduction.

In the 1970s, as a result of severe EPA fines for pollution, coupled with a U.S. and Canadian agreement to reduce man-made toxic waste and phosphates in all the Great Lakes, began Lake Erie healing quite. Today, a new exotic species, zebra mussels, filter millions of gallons of water each day and Lake Erie depth visibility now can run down to 40 feet. With all of these changes taking place the lake became an ideal habitat for steelhead.

Lake Erie is shallow and much warmer when compared to the other Great Lakes. It is basically broken down into three basins. The eastern basin, which runs from Buffalo to a north/south line extending from Ontario's Long Point to Pennsylvania's Presque Isle, is the deepest and coldest, averaging 80 feet deep with a maximum depth of 210 feet. The central basin from Cedar Point, Ohio east averages 61 feet with a maximum depth of 81 feet. West of Cedar Point, the lake is very shallow averaging about 28 feet. The total lake's water retention turnover time can be as little as 2 1/2 years.

Since steelhead prefer slightly warmer and surface oriented habitats which are more fertile from a food standpoint, the lake has quickly become a steelhead utopia. Insect hatches like the Hexagenia mayflies thrive in mind-boggling numbers, along with smelt, gizzard shad, shiners, and now the goby. With a gradual downward trend in the once prolific walleye, the future of Lake Erie clearly favors the steelhead.

Lake Erie steelhead once averaged four to six pounds. But with the increase in forage base, slow declines in its chief smolt predator, the walleye, and introduction of larger strains like the Little Manistee steelhead, fish from 12 to 16 pounds are now being caught more readily.

Today, close to two million steelhead are stocked by Ohio, Pennsylvania, and New York, with good natural reproduction existing in several New York and Ontario streams. On a per unit basis, Lake Erie is the most heavily stocked steelhead lake in the Great Lakes. This accounts for the bizarre 50 to 70 hook-up days on Pennsylvania and Ohio tributaries when conditions and the run is ideal. With its healthy future Erie is well worth checking out by the fly rod steelheader.

Ohio's Buckeye Bonanza

When I first heard reports of large runs of fall and spring fish with in the double digits—hook-ups, I was skeptical. On a late fall/early winter December trip to the Chagrin River within site of Cleveland's skyline, Brian Fleishig, owner of Mad River Outfitters fly shop and guide Mike Bennett showed me the steelhead mecca. With over 70 hook-ups of mint silver 6- to 13-pound, broad-shouldered Little Manistee torpedoes by 11:00 am, I was a believer in the Buckeye steelhead miracle. With fish aggressively taking tiny size 16 to 18 bead head nymphs on 5X tippets in gin clear waters, I was amazed how things had changed since my boyhood adventures along this once shoreline of "scum."

According to Kevin Kayle, Ohio's steelhead expert with the Division of Wildlife, the new era of Ohio's steelhead rainbow fishery started when they began stocking rainbow trout in Lake Erie tributaries in 1974 in Rocky River. The program had an auspicious beginning with 5,000 fingerling domestic rainbow trout from Ohio's London State Fish Hatchery. During the 1970s and early 1980s, fingerling rainbow trout were stocked intermittently across a number of Ohio tributaries to Lake Erie. Four primary steelhead stocking streams remain today: the Rocky River on Cleveland's west side, the Chagrin River in a suburban area east of Cleveland, the Grand River in Lake and Ashtabula counties east of Cleveland, and Conneaut Creek in Ashtabula County near the Pennsylvania border.

A total of 266,383 steelhead trout yearlings were stocked in 1998. Stocking of surplus London-strain yearlings was completed in February in the Rocky (13,408), Chagrin (3,136), and Grand (6,992) rivers. These steelhead averaged 279 mm (11.0 inches) at the time of stocking. Stocking of yearling Little Manistee River strain steelhead trout was completed during March through April 1998 in the Rocky (42,291), Chagrin (50,884), and Grand (47,576) Rivers and Conneaut Creek (54,030).

The Ohio Division of Wildlife has begun to implement changes and improvements to the Castalia State Fish Hatchery. The revamped facility will become home to the Division of Wildlife steelhead trout program in 1999, and could meet target program demands for 400,000 steelhead trout averaging 175-225 mm (7-9 inches).

While a typical Manistee strain fish can measure 25 inches after two summers in Lake Erie, the average weight is close to 5-6 pounds. Well over 10% of their fish are three-summer fish, which average 28 inches and 8-9 pounds. It is common to see Manistees in the 9- to 11-pound range every December-March.

Ohio's London and Manistee strains exhibit different runs in that the Manistees start to run a few weeks later in the fall (mid October) and run far later into the spring (late April) than the Londons. After early May, most fish have migrated to the central basin of Lake Erie, where they spend the summer eating rainbow smelt, alewives, shiner, gizzard shad, and aquatic and terrestrial insects. Forage is abundant in Lake Erie's central basin.

Juvenile assessment in Ohio streams will begin again during summer 1999 after a five-year hiatus. Steelhead reproduction has been documented in several Ohio streams. Several tributaries to Conneaut Creek and the Chagrin River produce consistent, but small year classes. Occasional year classes again small, are produced in tributaries to the Grand River and Whitman Creek in Ashtabula County.

Starting from the western basin, the **Rocky** River is a heavily stocked stream 5 miles west of Cleveland in the town that bears its name from the river. As with all Ohio rivers, watching the flow and conditions of these variable-running waters is important to time the run. Since the streams run through rocky shale slate, they accumulate runoff quickly. Any good precipitation or snowmelt will trigger a fall or spring run in good numbers. Thanks to an excellent Cleveland Metro Park system, good access is available at the Morely Rockcliff, Horse, and Cedar Point Fords. Valley Parkway, Lorraine, Detroit, and Brookpark roads are also excellent spots. The East Branch is accessible through the Rocky River Reservation Metro Parks at Purple and Spafford roads, with Valley Parkway being the best. The West Branch fishes well at Bagley Road.

Brian Fleischig and Mike Bennett hold up a fat and healthy Lake Erie steelhead on Ohio's Cargin River. This stocked fish is from Michigan's wild Little Manistee River strain. With the abundant aquatic life and crystal-clear waters of Erie, the lake has turned into a steelhead mecca.

The spate-driven, shale-ledged 16 Mile Creek of Pennsylvania's Lake Erie shoreline. "Steelhead Alley,"
near the city of Erie, has dozens of steelhead streams with lots of steelhead and lots of anglers.

The bigger and more diverse **Chagrin** has excellent room to throw a two-handed rod and gives the angler more space particularly around Woodland City Park, Chagrin River Park, and Daniel's Park.

The **Grand** and **Conneaut** offer more of a remote setting compared to the urban fisheries of the Rocky and Chagrin. On the Grand, good access is at 535 County Road, Painsville City Park, Masons Landing, Metro Park, and Indian Point Metro Park.

The Conneaut at the eastern tip of Ohio near Ashtabula gets spectacular runs of both Ohio and Pennsylvania fish and has a classic riffle-pool-tailout stream character. Access is good along Old Main Road, Route 7, Blue Bell Park, and at Kingsburg, State, Horton, and Wetmore Roads.

Though not stocked, shorter and more variable "hit-or-miss" action occurs when fish stocked from the "big four" hop up and stray other tributaries. Going from west to east, the **Vermillion** River, **Mckinley**, **Arcola**, **Wheeler**, **Cowles**, **Indian**, **Wittmans** and **Turkey** creeks get sporadic runs based on flows.

Pennsylvania

With a monumental stocking of close to 1 million steelhead by the Pennsylvania Fish Commission on short but tributary-laced Erie shoreline, incredible action can be found based on timing. Using a domesticated Lake Erie rainbow of Washington State origin for its egg taking program, these Heinz 57 steelhead have adjusted to the Lake Erie environment well. Since "Pennsylvania strain" steelhead are early running and spawning fish, some mixing with Washington State summer run strains may have contributed dominant genes. By varying the egg-taking cycle to specific individual

runs occurring from September through April, the Pennsylvania Fish Commission can mix up the genetics.

Elk Creek is one of the most heavily fished and receives great runs of steelhead. With bedrock bottoms and a few gravel areas, fish and fishermen tend to congregate at deeper holes near gravel. It can contain medium to heavy flows particularly in winter and spring runoffs so careful wading is advised. It flows through slate rock gorges, farmland and small towns giving it a nice character.

A winter steelheader probes a trestle pool
on Lake Erie's Elk Creek in Pennsylvania.

Access is at Route 5, Whitman's, Tamery, and Sterrotania roads along with Guard Boro Park and Old Route 20.

Walnut Creek, though somewhat smaller, is a heavily stocked and fished steelhead river. From Manchester Road down to the lake, along with Route 5, Route 20, Old Rte. 832 and Zimmerly Road, good access can be found. **Twenty Mile** Creek can have more desolate, scenic beauty while more privacy can be had from the Waterfall near Route 5 to the lake. **Sixteen Mile** Creek and Peck Run also have waterfalls above Route 5. By basically using Route 5 as your guideline, Twenty Mile, **Eight Mile** and **Raccoon** creeks can also be fished.

A "must-buy" if you plan to visit the Lake Erie tributaries is a helpful book by noted Pennsylvania steelhead guide and author John Nagy entitled Steelhead Guide:—*Fly Fishing Techniques and Strategies for Lake Erie Steelhead*. It has everything you want to know about the area with its whims and characteristics of the rivers.

New York's Orchard and Winery Coast

The beautiful eastern basin features the gateway coast to the Niagara Frontier, rich in its vast expanse of fruit farms and wine growing areas. Some excellent boutique wineries extend from the Erie coast all the way through the fabled Finger Lakes district. With its porous soil, along with lake effect precipitation often producing monumental winter blizzards, the Route 5 and New York State Thruway is often closed due to heavy snowfall when the lake effect machine forgets to turn off.

This area is home to the Concord grape, and many other Great Lakes varietals like the Chancellor and Niagara. Welch's Grape Juice, the staple of yesterday's youth, is near the banks of Chataqua Creek, a fine steelhead stream.

Streams here generally are called creeks and have two distinct characteristics. The majority are small tributaries with good gradients that cut through shale and slate bedrock with good supplies of gravel to attract steelhead. The large **Cattaragus** Creek system cuts through a large rocky moraine valley and has numerous tributaries that produce wild steelhead. The "Cat" is similar to a western style river with rolling hills, gravel, and boulder laden runs and pools with excellent groundwater supplies from its upper trout water origins.

New York began its steelhead rainbow introductions in 1899 on the Cattaragus by releasing fingerling and yearling in its upper tributaries. The current steelhead program is increasing in scope and popularity as ideal Lake Erie habitat for the fish continues to improve. According to Bill Culligan, NYDEC Supervisory Aquatic Biologist, 228,000 yearling fish are stocked in nine different streams. The New York program relies totally on Washington State's Chambers Creek strain with egg taking done on Lake Ontario. With the Cattaragus system beginning to provide substantial natural reproduction, the search is on in other tributaries to document natural stocks as water conditions and habitat improves.

Fish start to show in the Lake Erie tributaries by mid-October with peak fall runs occurring by late November. During winter melt-off, fish will run the smaller tributaries during any given river spate. Spring runs last until mid-May. New York's Lake Erie steelhead take advantage of the excellent rainbow smelt and aquatic and terrestrial food sources abundant in the fertile eastern basin.

Beginning along the coastline near the Pennsylvania border is **Chataqua** Creek, which receives excellent runs from October through April. Water flows are essential for these steeper gradient streams where shale and slate ledges will hinder upstream migration, especially near Route 5. North and South Gale Streets and

Route 20 are also popular access. **Canadway** Creek is similar in character in that it requires good flows for the runs to begin. Routes 5 and 20 along with Madison and Willow Roads are places to hunt for steelhead when the timing is right. **Beaver, Silver,** and **Walnut** creeks are also short tributaries that receive good seasonal runs, especially in the spring when snow melt and rains occur. The latter two are stocked by the NYDEC and access is in the Routes 5/20 corridor.

The **Cattaragus** (the "Cat") Creek is the most significant in regard to natural reproduction and beautiful steelhead system on Lake Erie or perhaps in the entire Great Lakes basin. Flowing through gentle rolling hills, valleys, farmland and small rocky gorges, its character is suited for the classic steelhead wet fly presentation on a two-handed rod. Its wide rock and gravel banks allow good room for a backcast and the ability for an angler to beach land a fish. The Cattaragus has great potential for wild steelhead production eminating from spring fed tributaries like **Derby Brook, Spooner,** and the **Clear** creek systems which have had natural reproduction documented since the early 1900s.

The Cat runs approximately forty miles from its mouth at Silver Creek to the dam in Springville. Flowing through the upper Zoar Valley the river features a rolling landscape of hills, hardwoods, and wildlife in abundance. Some gorge areas are as high as three hundred feet. With a rocky gravel bottom, classic riffle-pool-tailout holding water is in abundance. From Gowanda down it runs throughout he Cattaragus Indian Reservation where a separate license is needed to fish.

Since the Cattaragus drains a major river valley system, its runoff can be severe during heavy flows and can shift and change the riverine character due to its gravel, sand, soil, and clay structure. It becomes discolored quickly and can remain mocha colored for weeks due to the significant tributary drainage. When the river subsides during the late fall and spring, the fishing can be phenomenal as steelhead take up classic lies and go on the bite. A local map will point to the many access sites available along its mainstream and tributaries.

Close to Buffalo, the **18 Mile** Creek system is very popular with the urbanites and cuts through some steep rocky ledges. Water flows vary greatly with conditions and can be often low in the fall. During these times most of the action occurs near the mouth of Lake Erie from Route 5 and Lakeshore Road. Route 20, South Creek, North Creek, Lakeview, and Versailles Roads provide access. Blyey, Belknap, Jennings, and Church roads along with Route 62 can access the 18 Mile Creek's South Branch. **Buffalo** and **Cayuga** creeks also receive steelhead stockings and are urban fisheries near the city of Buffalo and its quiet suburbs. If your timing is right on with the spate conditions, you could have excellent action mainly in the late winter through spring runoff periods.

Ontario's North Shore

According to Larry Halyk, steelhead expert for the OMNR, Lake Erie streams with the exception of the Grand River, are predominantly wild stocks and are located in the Norfold sand plain in the Long Point Bay area. As a result, groundwater and spring seepage is abundant on the sand plain and the streams run cool, clear, and are relatively stable.

These tributaries reached a low ebb in the 1960s and 70s when unregulated dam construction and severe sedimentation from poor agricultural land use practices took their toll on wild fish production. Since then, improved agricultural practices, active stream rehabilitation, and dam removal/fishway construction projects have resulted in improved wild steelhead and migratory brown trout runs on many of these streams.

The Grand River of Lake Erie's Ontario shore is quickly becoming an excellent steelhead fishery, with many smaller one- to two-pound fish taking dry flies during August and September in the lower river. These are the waters of steelhead experts John Valk and Larry Halyk.

Lake Erie tributaries drain rich limestone based gravels and sands, resulting in fertile spring creek conditions on most streams. Caddis and mayflies are abundant, and because of this and ideal temperatures, the trout grow fast. Stoneflies are present but not terribly abundant. The average Great Lakes stream takes 2 years to produce a smolt that migrates down to the lake. Some Lake Erie tributaries can do it in one.

Caddis are especially abundant on the Grand River tributaries. This could be why Grand steelhead seem to have an affinity for a swinging Spey or soft hackle or even a waking fly. Perhaps these flies trigger some memory of a caddis pupa moving across the water column on its way to hatching.

Big Creek is the largest stream flowing into Long Point Bay. Historically Big Creek was the biggest steelhead producer on Lake Erie. During the late 1950s and early 1960s, Big Creek rivaled the Owen Sound area of Georgian Bay as the mecca for a small but dedicated group of steelhead pioneers in the province. Since then, Big Creek has fallen on hard times but it appears poised to make a comeback.

Currently, there is a year round open season on the lower 27 miles of Big Creek from the village of Lyndoch down to Long Point Bay. An additional 10 km upstream of that (to Highway 3 in Delhi) is open to December 31. The best water for fly fishing is the 6 mile section in the Delhi area. Here, the stream is 40-50 feet wide with riffles and pools and a sand and gravel bottom—very similar in appearance to Michigan streams such as the Betsie, Rifle, or Platte. Because the stream rarely floods, there is thick undergrowth right to the stream edge and therefore casting can be tight. Below Lyndoch the stream opens up, but is much more difficult to wade, read, and fish because of its low gradient and uniformly deep U-shaped channel.

Most of the steelhead running Big Creek in the "good old days" spawned in high quality nursery streams in the Delhi area—North Creek and Stoney Creek. The current steelhead run in Big Creek is estimated to be in the vicinity of one or two thousand fish. Electrofishing studies conducted by OMNR in 1998 indicated that juvenile steelhead numbers in the Big Creek system have increased dramatically over what they were five years ago. There is no reason not to expect a doubling of the Big Creek steelhead run over the next few years as a result of these improvements.

The **Grand** is the largest tributary on the Canadian side of Lake Erie. Its upper reaches in the Fergus and Elora area are well known as trophy brown trout fishery. The lower reaches downstream of Brantford provide excellent fishing for smallmouth bass and walleye, but steelhead are taking over center stage.

The Grand River is well over 125 miles long. The makeup of the Grand River watershed is that sand and gravel deposits located upstream of Brantford; they contain abundant groundwater which feed streams suitable for trout production. Until the late 1980s, steelhead and salmon migrating up the Grand were blocked at the Lorne Dam in Brantford and were therefore prevented from entering suitable nursery streams. All this changed in 1989 when the Lorne Dam was removed. Now steelhead have access to Whiteman's Creek and other excellent nursery streams on the Grand and Nith Rivers.

The Grand River is stocked with steelhead and the origin of its steelhead run is unknown. A genetic study of Lake Erie steelhead currently being conducted by OMNR may shed some light on this. Apparently, the Grand River with its big flow has the ability to attract fish from other rivers, so the predominantly wild run is probably supplemented by stray fish from U.S. stocking programs and perhaps other Ontario streams.

Currently, there are three dams located on the lower Grand River that steelhead must pass over before they get to the spawning streams. The lowest is located in Dunnville about 6 km upstream of the lake. This is a low head dam that is easily scaled. The Wilkes Dam is located in Brantford approximately 62 miles from the lake. Like the Dunnville Dam, this one is easily jumped under virtually all river flow conditions. The Wilkes Dam marks the upstream boundary of the extended fall season for steelhead on the Grand.

The Caledonia Dam, located 50 km from the lake, is the first true barrier to challenge upstream migrants. The dam is about 10 feet high with fishladders. During extremely low or high flow or during cold water conditions, the fish will stack below the Caledonia Dam. This section has moderate depth pools that are suitable for fly fishing, but it must be said that suspended clay particles and algae often create murky conditions, especially during the early fall and late spring. The Grand supports both spring and fall steelhead runs but the fall season is of special interest because a higher than normal percentage of the fish tend to be early fall runners. There are usually at least a few steelhead at the Caledonia Dam (50 km up from the lake) by Labor Day. Because temperatures are ideal at this time, the angler has an excellent shot at taking an aggressive fish on a swinging or ever waking fly.

Whitman's is a high-quality trout stream that flows into the Grand River a mile upstream of the Wilkes Dam, near Brantford. Whittman's a very pretty stream—although it's small (40-50 feet) it is fairly open with enough gravel bars and sweeping bends to cast a fly line.

Because Whitman's Creek is now a fish sanctuary from October 1 to opening day in April to protect spawning and staging browns and steelhead, there are no fall steelheading opportunities. Depending on how late the spring is, there can be a fair number of spawning and drop-back steelhead around on opening day and for a few weeks afterwords.

The **Nith** River is a medium-sized river that enters the Grand in Paris, about 125 km upstream of Lake Erie. Like the main Grand, the Nith has several small tributaries that are now cranking out wild steelhead and the runs are building. The lower reach from the village of Ayr downstream to Paris is a pleasant mix of riffles, pools and boulder studded runs. The only downside is that it often a bit offcolor due to intensive farming in its upper reaches.

Other Streams

There are other Lake Erie streams that support wild steelhead, but these are not really large enough for pleasant fly rodding. These include **Young** Creek, **Fishers** Creek, and **Potters Normandie** Creek. These streams are located a few kilometers from each other in the Turkey Point area and flow into Long Point Bay. These streams provide excellent surf casting options in the late fall and spring by using marabou smelt patterns.

Lake Ontario's Atlantic Gateway

The cold, deep, waters of the the smallest Great Lake, are ideally suited to raising large and healthy steelhead. As with Lake Michigan and Huron, Lake Ontario produces fish with big girths, which grow rapidly with the lake's forage base and biological interchange with ecosystems like the St. Lawrence and Atlantic Ocean.

Ontario's rivers and streams are varied in scope. The north and south shore have gentle farmland and low gradient waters with gravel and varied seasonal flows. This contrasts the brawling **Niagara** and classic steelhead river structure of New York's **Salmon** River watershed. Just as Lake Michigan's Little Manistee wild strain has been widely used for stocking purposes, Ontario has produced the Ganaraska strain from the river that carries its name. Lake Ontario steelhead are fished and sought out heavily by the large populated northeastern cities of North America. The Salmon River of New York probably attracts more salmonid anglers than any river in the world.

New York's Empire Shoreline

Beginning in the Niagara Frontier and stretching to Watertown and the St. Lawrence Seaway, New York manages several dozen rivers and streams. Chamber's Creek strain and summer Skamania steelhead nicely intermingle with natural wild strains from primarily the Salmon River tributaries and the Tug Hill plateau system. Initial plantings of steelhead started in 1878 into Caledonia Spring Creek and Genesee River tributaries. The Altmar Fish Hatchery and broodstock facility on the Salmon River is the driving force for creating a world class steelhead fishery in New York.

The thundering **Niagara** River receives significant runs of fall, winter, and spring steelhead migrations. It is a dangerous, high volume white water, carved through an ancient gorge with unparalleled beauty. For all practical purposes, the Niagara is a channel rather than a true river, draining Lake Erie into Ontario. Millenniums of gushing water have carved the Niagara bedrock gorge and created huge whirlpools and whitewater that invite steelhead and tourists. As a natural "wonder of the world," the famous "honeymoon capital" is a great family destination to combine sightseeing and entertainment with fishing.

In the upper two miles, the majestic Niagara is steep, ferocious, and inaccessible until it hits "the whirlpool." Here, a long descent of steps takes the adventurous angler down to a swirling expanse of water where "deep water express" shooting heads of 600 grains are often used to penetrate holding lies. Fluctuating water releases from the Niagara Mohawk Power Plant can raise the river six feet in a given morning. Steep gorge banks and brush limit your backcasts. This is the ideal two-handed Spey-rod river.

The lower Niagara is predominantly a boat fishery where fly anglers can drift egg patterns with pencil lead and shooting line as they drift through runs ranging from 12 to 25 feet deep. White Spey and bunny leeches tied with Flashabou and a hint of pink resemble the great concentration of baitfish the Niagara receives. Holding lies are often found close to shore near rocky strewn tailouts and current deflecting ledges. Additional shore access exists

Dave Barber—an expert guide, writer and former owner of the Fish Inn Post on New York's Salmon River off Lake Ontario's Tug Hill plateau—holds up a beautiful Chambers Creek strain steelhead as his trusty golden retriever looks on approvingly.

Dave Barber photo

at the Devil's Hole Park and near the Art Park Performing Arts Center. The water below the Queenston Bridge is a little slower and more conducive to steelhead presentation. Fall runs peak around November through December. Fish ascend the Niagara all winter with a good crop of chrome females hitting the river in February and early March—fish will linger in the Niagara usually through late May. An occasional summer run steelhead is caught during cooler summers.

The size and fight of a Niagara steelhead is well worth pursuing. When these fish charge downstream with thousands of cubic feet per second water to their advantage, the chase is breathtaking. When conditions are ideal and water levels dropping, you could have spectacular multiple hook-ups on the Niagara when fresh, aggressive fish are present in good numbers. Famous steelhead book author and guide, Rick Kustich, is master of the Niagara. Owner of the Oak Orchard Fly Shop in Williamsville, New York, he creatively pursues the Niagara River steelhead with his beautifully designed Spey flies. Rick likes the month of February for fat, chrome, aggressive fish.

Proceeding east along the shoreline of orchards and wine country, **18 Mile** and **Olcott** creeks offer 2 miles of fishing to Burt Dam. From the Railroad Trestle to the dam, steelhead will be fresh and stacked thickly when the water flows are good. **12 Mile** Creek at Wilson has a sand bar problem at the mouth and is mostly a surf fishery.

The author gets dumped on by a Tug Hill plateau lake-effect snow squall on New York's South Sandy Creek off Lake Ontario.

Keg Creek, a few miles east of 18 Mile has some wild reproduction but is dependent on flows for favorable fish passage. A bridged river mouth forms during low flows.

A major steelhead and lake-run brown fishery exists at **Oak Orchard** Creek. From below the impassable barrier of the Waterport Dam, the river has fluctuating releases of water through a narrow, swift gorge. The river becomes wader friendly concentrating fly water for about a mile. When runs are on, the crowds can be very heavy, especially during October when lake-run browns up to 15 pounds make their spawning runs. Steelhead usually ascend the Oak Orchard at the tail end of the brown run in late October and will migrate all winter if adequate flows exist. Egg patterns are most popular for these fresh-run chromers. In the lower, slow pools early fall fish will attack black and purple Speys and bunny leeches along with the bright attractor colors of orange and pink. When water levels are low, tiny flies or narrow diameter tippets are a must.

Nearby **Johnson's** Creek has about six miles of fishable water to the Lindenville impassable barrier. This moderate sized creek gets good pressure during peak fall and spring runs—a public fishing site exists at Blood Road. Many of its fish are strays from Oak Orchard and its moderate flows have good gravel to attract fish.

Sandy Creek in Monroe/Orleans County has twelve to fifteen miles of water that gets fall and spring steelhead runs. The river gets its flow from the Erie Barge Canal and is quite stable except for major spates.

The **Genesee** River at Rochester has a significant winter fishery below the lower falls in this urban setting located off of Seth Green Drive. Even during low flows the "Genny" will attract good numbers of fall and winter fish eager to hit egg patterns and black and purple Speys in its pocket and pool water.

Irondequoit Creek has about twelve miles of river which supports wild steelhead and stream trout populations. Its spring-fed, cool groundwater flows from East Rochester to Mendon. **Maxwell** Creek in Wayne County has about a half-mile of public water to the impassable barrier and can attract good numbers of steelhead in the spring when flows are good. **Red** and **Nine Mile** creeks also get bursts of fish during the spring run.

The **Big Oswego** River gets some massive runs of fish in its three mile drift boat fishery up to Varich Dam. It is fast and deep water, with large rocky runs and drains the full array of salmonids out of the lake. Steelhead fishing starts at the tail end of the

salmon run and brown trout spawn when aggressive steelhead target the bounty of the egg hatch. Once caviar is all gone, baitfish imitations work well all winter to spring when nymphs and egg patterns return to the bite. It is a great urban fishery.

As we enter Pulaski, the fabled Salmon River is a magnificent system of main river and tributaries that is carefully managed by Les Wedge and Fran Verdoliva of the New York Department of Environmental Conservation. Due to the massive crowds and drift boats during peak times, it is amazing how many people can fish this river at the same time.

With the new era of stable releases by Niagara Mohawk Power Authority from the dam, cool consistent flows will allow greater natural reproduction and an increase in populations of summer steelhead and Atlantic salmon.

From the Lighhouse Hill Reservoir dam at Altmar, thirteen miles of fishing exists to the lake. Two fly fishing only, catch-and-release sections exist upstream of the Altmar Bridge. Famous pools such as the School House, Old Trestle, and Compactor Pool line this beautiful, classic flowing river that allows all fly fishing presentations and methods to be imparted. The Dougleston Salmon Run is private water on a fee accessible basis. Dave Barber, Salmon River guide, author, and former lodge owner of the Fish Inn Post in Altmar, is an extremely knowledgeable and experimental steelhead fly fisherman who has the very small nymph and slinky technique down to a science. With the new lower and clear flows, tiny nymphs, and egg patterns are the key. Swinging wets and Speys for fall- and summer-running steelhead is ideal in the upper pockets and pools near Altmar.

The upper flies-only water above the Altmar Hatchery is some of the most beautiful steelhead water in the Great Lakes. Fast rapids, pools and pocket water cascade through rocky cliffs and boulders giving this area a hint of British Columbia ambience. It is a great place to swing a Spey fly on a two-handed rod for summer Skamania steelhead and Atlantic salmon with its high dissolved oxygen levels in the summer months. The fish hit hard here and are acrobatic performers in the challenge of the current.

The Salmon has many moods and seasons and will become a 365-day-a-year destination for steelheaders due to the new flows. When I drifted the river with Dave Barber during the hot summer of 1999 in search of summer steelhead and Atlantic salmon,

Probing the Salmon River for summer Skamania steelhead and Atlantic salmon (the new "boys of summer" fishery that is yet to be understood and utilized) the future is bright!

I could not get over how underutilized the summer fishery was - we had the entire river to ourselves while Skamania steelhead and Atlantic salmon up to fifteen pounds played with our Spey-rod presentations. NYDEC public fishing water is located all the way down the river system with the exception of Douglaston. The *Salmon*'s tributaries of Orwell Creek and Trout Brook produce excellent spring runs and wild steelhead recruitment.

To the north along the shoreline, the **North** and **South Sandy** creeks are classic steelhead streams with excellent riffle-pool-tailout water that draw good numbers of fall through spring steelhead in its heavily-laden gravel waters. It also has the potential for wild steelhead reproduction with its cool water groundwater and excellent oxygenated runs, and pocke/boulder water.

Other fine runs of spring steelhead exist on the **Stony, Lindsey, Skinner,** and **Grindstone** creeks which all depend on good flows to get flashes of chrome fish out and up from the lake quickly. Fall runs are dependent on stream flows although mild temperatures will draw fish upstream well into December.

Ontario's Provincial Shoreline

The north shoreline tributaries vary in character from the larger headwater systems of the Credit River to the smaller and very steelhead rich rivers like the Wilmot. Its most productive wild steelhead waters drain the limestone, porous soils of the Oak Ridge Moraine running eastward of Toronto. With spring creek-like waters feeding the main tributaries, excellent gravel and moderate gradients create good spawning gravel and nursery waters.

West of Toronto, along the Niagara Encampment, the streams and rivers are a mix of hatchery stocks and wild fish. With good source groundwater flows sometimes running through steep gradients followed by wider and warmer lower estuarian environments, they are more weather influenced in terms of water spates and flows. Major agricultural areas with abundant fruit farms are intertwined with a resurgence of wineries. Tourist opportunities exist along the Province's shoreline like Niagara-on-the-Lake and the exciting cosmopolitan city of Toronto.

Starting at the mighty **Niagara** previously described, the predominantly boat fishery can be accessed at the Whirlpool on the Niagara Parkway, the Queenston sand docks, and at the Canadian hydro plant where warm discharge attracts salmonids. This area is a year-round fishery, attracting browns, lakers, steelhead, and salmon.

The true Niagara character is a giant tailwater—fluctuating and changing holding and taking lies with many fish often within a rollcast distance. The river attracts "stray" fish from all of the Lake Ontario tributaries due to its heavy discharge. There are two true channels or Great Lakes drainage systems: the St. Mary's and the Niagara. When fish are in, they are hot on the grab. They are not selective and will hammer just about any well-presented egg pattern, baitfish streamer, or big black and purple ugly streamer.

Small, brief tributaries in the wine country district from Niagara Falls to Hamilton offer primarily surf activity due to drowned river mouths.

After passing through Hamilton from the Niagara, **Bronte** Creek is the first major steelhead stream, which is fished heavily during peak times. It is a true spate river, depending on flows for steelhead migration. Between Highway J and the QEW is a hot spot along with the Lowville Park system near Waterdown.

When in Toronto, you can combine a world class city with urban steelheading on the **Credit** River. Once an historic river for Atlantic salmon and still stocked heavily by the OMNR to hopefully restore this native species, the Credit can be "hot" when the water levels favor migration. Its classic steelhead profile of throat-pocket, tailout character makes this an ideal candidate for the wet fly swing. In the city of Mississauga in Erindale Park, steelheaders

enjoy some excellent water- though it's often crowded. From Highway J to the QEW the river is open year round and hosts good numbers of fish through mild winters.

The **Rouge** River near Scarborough sustains an egg-taking conservation group partnership facility for steelhead stocking production. The most popular section is the upstream site of Markham, where a fish ladder is in production to allow upstream migration for another 20 miles. Fly anglers are fond of the Rouge Park system when the spring runs are on.

The once legendary Atlantic salmon **Humber** River, this urban Toronto fishery receives heavy plantings of approximately 25,000 steelhead at East Branch Mill Road and at King Vaughn Line. Flowing from its branches at Woodbridge and Weston, it slows through York and attracts heavy angling pressure during the spring run. The nearby **Duffins** Creek, from 401 Highway could have some excellent steelheading if you could miss the crowds and time the water levels. Though not a steelhead stocked stream, it receives strays from the others and has a very limited wild self-sustaining population.

Sleeper streams that are stocked with steelhead and fish well after a spate runoff are the **Don** and **Highland** creeks. In the Oak Ridges area are **Bowmanville** and **Soper** creeks. With classic, small stream gradient and woody debris structure, it greatly resembles the Michigan streams of the Little Manistee. From the town of Hampton down to Bowmanville, fly anglers use Glo-Bugs and nymphs to target its skittish, migrating wild fish.

The **Wilmot** is a diamond of a small stream spring run fishery. Massive runs of steelhead ascend the snow and rain runoff water in this glacial-till and gravel-laced stream. The numbers of wild spring run fish are increasing. The fishing parking lot at Highway 2 is where to start your adventure.

The **Ganaraska** is the Little Manistee of Ontario. Its ideal limestone springs, abundant gravel nursery waters, and aquatic insect populations make it one of the blue-ribbon wild-steelhead destinations of the Great Lakes. With a fish ladder completed back in the mid-1970s over Corbett Dam, excellent upstream spawning areas were open to the fish. John Bowlby of the OMNR is the northshore steelhead biologist who both fly fishes and scientifically monitors the "Ganie" to determine the health and abundance of its wild steelhead. He closely monitors the repeat spawning index of returning adults and has recorded repeat spawning rates at high levels from 40% to as high as 80% of the returning adult population. The Spring Run of rainbow trout peaked in 1989 when more than 18,000 returned to spawn. In more recent years, the spring run has declined to about 10,000 steelhead rainbow trout.

This decline appears to be related to an increase in the size and age of first spawning. Apparently, channel improvements in the Ganaraska River during the early 1980s may have made it easier for larger fish to move upstream. Data collected at Ganaraska Fishway show that angling harvest has not had a large impact on the size of rainbow trout run.

Steelhead usually start moving through the Ganaraska Fishway during the last week of March or first week of April. The peak run usually occurs during the second or third week of April, and typically the run is over by the end of April.

When the run is in full swing, the steelhead pour through the fishway at Port Hope in big numbers. The lower section of the river can be quite shallow with bedrock ledges and during low water conditions the Ganie's big steelhead (20 pounds plus) will stack up near the mouth.

The ideal spawning gravel and rifle-pool-tailout water above the fishway is a combination of private water for lease to anglers and several conservation areas which see hordes of anglers. It definitely pays to have private access obtained through landowners' permission. They don't take too kindly to trespassers—trust me!

Chapter 11

Atlantic Salmon of the Great Lakes

Though our subject matter is steelhead, there is perhaps no other fish that behaves and fights as similarly or is as highly sought after by the fly fisher than *Salmo salar*—the leaper. Wealthy anglers travel the world from Iceland's Laxa Adaldal to Russia's Ponoi, paying top dollar to battle with these explosive, jumping, regal fish. Fisheries managers of the Great Lakes have spent considerable time and effort to create or restore Atlantic salmon fisheries with mostly limited success at best. Several thriving Atlantic fisheries exist in the Great Lakes and can only get better in the future.

By the time European settlements (1700 and 1800s) came to Lake Ontario, the settlers found incredible numbers of Atlantic salmon present in almost all of the New York and Canadian tributaries of the lake. In an excellent abstract entitled Early History of Atlantic Salmon in New York, the late Dwight A. Webster, Professor of Fishery Science at Cornell University, documented the early abundance of the fish.

In 164, Jesuit Fathers Le Mercier and La Moyne ascended Lake Ontario's Oswego River and met Oneida Indians spearing

The unmistakable kype-jaw and bluish-green cheek plate of a mature Atlantic salmon.

the Atlantics by the thousands. *"With their canoes filled with fresh salmon.one of our men caught twenty large salmon, and on the way up the river our people killed thirty other salmon with spears and paddles. There were so many of them that they were struck without difficulty."*

In 1817, a dam was built on the Genesee River at Rochester, which flows into Lake Ontario. Thousands of salmon were clubbed to death, mangled with spears and pitchforks, in mass, frenzied, seal-like slaughters. Accounts of hauling Atlantic salmon from Lake Ontario's tributaries in the 1800s are frightening:

"In October, 1836, two men took (on the Salmon River at Pulaski) two hundred and thirty Salmon between 8 p.m. and 12, with spears and fire-jacks, and after 12 till morning two other men in the same skiff took two hundred odd, the average weight of the entire lot being fourteen and three quarters pounds. We have had fifteen hundred fresh salmon in the fish-house at one time. When a freshet occurred in June a few would always come up, and sometimes a few early in the spring. Any time from June till winter when there was a freshet they were sure to come. The principal time, however, was in fall, during September, October and November. Twelve skiffs in one night have taken an average of three hundered salmon each."

In the many diaries kept by early settlers, their testaments to the great numbers of fish prior to their extinction in the late 1800s can be accounted:

"It was nothing uncommon for teams fording the rivers and creeks at night to kill salmon with their hoofs. An older settler living in the town of Hannibal told Mr. Ingersoll that one night while driving across Three-Mile Creek the salmon ran against his horses' feet in such numbers that the horses took fright and plunged throughout the water, killing one large salmon outright and injuring two others so that they were captured. The farmers living near the smaller creeks easily supplied their families with salmon caught by means of pitchforks." (Smith, 1892:196)

"My father and Uncle Asa for a number of years could catch every fall from 15 to 20 barrels of salmon They would come up the creek sometimes as early as September and would be very fat The largest that I ever saw caught in Salmon Creek weighed 32 pounds and the largest I ever saw was caught in Salmon River; it weighed 42 pounds after it was dressed and was sold for $1.00" (Simpson, 1949:176)

"Salmon were so abundant that men stood on the log across Salmon Creek and speared them with pitchforks in the 'fish shoal'. Women often caught a salmon with their hands or in their aprons." (Simpson, 1949:154)

"Forty years ago the salmon fisheries on this (Salmon) river brought more money to the people than all the machinery now on the river." (written by a Mr. Cross and quoted by Goode, 1884:474)

On the Ontario side, similar accounts came from the Credit and Humber Rivers with many others from west of Toronto to the Bay of Quinte. By the 1830s Atlantic Salmon were already dramatically reduced. In 1896, the species was declared extinct in Lake Ontario.

It has been suggested that Atlantic salmon were lost from Lake Ontario primarily because of dams and mills, and secondarily because of heavy exploitation during spawning runs. Settlement brought many changes to the Lake Ontario shores. Dams for saw and grist-mills were built which prevented upstream spawning migrations and also caused increased water temperatures. Logging and land clearing for agriculture resulted in soil erosion and the resulting siltation of streams and the nearshore environment. The lack of forest cover was also identified as causing changes in stream temperatures. Refuse from the mills and tanneries further degraded the habitat.

With the Pacific salmon introduction and explosion of the 1870s in Lake Ontario, the 1980s brought about a creative

A perfect Atlantic salmon taken on a rainbow smelt streamer pattern.

willingness by fisheries managers to look at restoring indigenous species. The Atlantic salmon was high on the list of priority.

Fran Verdoliva, a very talented steelhead and salmon fly fisherman, one time Salmon River guide, and now the NYEC's Fisheries Coordinator for the Salmon River, is passionate about the pursuit to restore the Atlantic in Lake Ontario. He has shared with me the history of the program and its future. Verdoliva states, *"A number of attempts starting in the late 1860s, stocking native strains of Lake Ontario salmon, and later introducing land-locked and sea run strains, all resulted in failure to restore the lake's native salmon. Periodic attempts were made throughout the 20th century to reintroduce the species. All have resulted in further failure. With the successful introduction of Pacific salmon from the 1970s on, it was hoped that improved lake and tributary conditions might eventually lead to reintroducing Atlantics as part of a diverse salmonid fishery make up of chinook, coho, steelhead, brown trout, and lake trout."*

The first attempts were initiated in three small, high quality tributaries of the lake in 1983. Fifty thousand smolts were stocked between the three streams with the hope that adults returning would reproduce successfully, showing the possibility for maintaining self-sustaining populations. Summer runs of adults occurred in all three tributaries, and naturally reproduced young of year Atlantics were found. Poaching was high, and it was felt that numbers of naturally reproduced salmon were not high enough to warrant continuation of the program in these streams after 1987.

The program then changed to a put, grow, and limited take policy for Atlantics, and if naturally reproducing fish occurred it was a bonus. Stocking levels increased to 200,000 smolts per year, with an anticipated catch of 10,000 adults a year. Stocking levels never reached the goals and through the mid 1990s, despite the greater number stocked, catches actually declined. Fewer Atlantics were being caught from the larger stockings than when the stocking policy was 50,000. The best-recorded catch was a little over a thousand Atlantics in the open water boat fishery.

The stocking policy was again changed in 1995 to reflect the poor results of previous efforts. Stockings were reduced to 80,000 to 100,000 per year. Only three streams would be stocked. These included the Black River (50,000), Oak Orchard Creek (20,000), and the Salmon River (30,000). The policy is to provide a presence of this native species in the fishery with the opportunity to possibly catch a trophy. Limits are set at one Atlantic per day with a minimum 25-inch size limit. This also allows the continuing monitoring of the species for possible future efforts at rehabilitation.

The Salmon River was included in the stocking program of Atlantics to help create a diversified salmonid fishery that would include besides Atlantics, a summer component made up of Skamania summer run steelhead and resident brown trout. This was being done to help offset the perceived loss of revenue that would result when snagging for Pacific salmon was made illegal in 1995. Also, licensing of the hydro facilities on the Salmon River was initiated with resulting minimum flow requirements year around. This was hoped to produce conditions conducive to salmonid natural reproduction in the main stem of the river and conditions allowing adult salmonids to survive during the summer months. With the Salmon River's strong flows and rock/boulder water, the sucker shaped pectoral fins of juvenile salmon can hold the fish on the bottom in main flows where other salmonids cannot habitate.

Angler Pat O'Boyle with a magnificent 18-pound Atlantic salmon taken on a Midge Larvae Lace Bead Nymph on the St. Mary's River.

Starting in 1996, the Salmon River received its first yearly stocking of 30,000 Little Clear Land-locked strain smolts from the NYSDEC Adirondack LLS Hatchery. The Little Clear strain is a mix of Grand Lake, Sebago, and Gullspang strain salmon. Four new, circular rearing tanks were also for Atlantics. Presently, the Salmon River's allotment of Atlantics for stocking are brought from the Adirondack Hatchery as fingerlings and then raised in the curricular tanks.

Other projects working with Atlantics on the Salmon River are being done in cooperation with the United States Geological Survey at Tunison Labs and with the Environmental School of Forestry at Syracuse. These projects are researching competitive interactions between Atlantics and introduced salmonids, especially steelhead, in the tributaries of the Salmon River. The possibility of juvenile habitat for Atlantics in the mainsteam of the river with minimum flows is also being studied. 100,000 Lake Memphamagog landlocked fry were stocked by the Environmental School of Forestry in 1999 in the main stream as part of this study. Tunison Labs also stocked sea run Penobscot fry in Orwell and Trout Brooks, both tribs with drought conditions most of the summer.

A freak summer flash flood of 9,000 cfs in the river also threw a monkey wrench into the equation. Although it is still early in the study, one result showed despite the extreme conditions, Atlantic salmon fry were found in the main river. This may suggest that the main stem is too warm for juvenile steelhead survival. If that is the case, the main stem of the Salmon River may provide a unique opportunity for Atlantic salmon colonization. Natural reproduction of steelhead is probably best suited for the Salmon River's smaller feeder tributaries. It should also be noted that the main stem of the Salmon River is producing large numbers of wild chinook as a result of the minimum flows, providing good winter conditions for survival of eggs and fry. The same winter conditions in the river should benefit Atlantics also.

In 1998 and 1999, broodstock Atlantic salmon were stocked in the Salmon River to provide fishing opportunity, introduce the species to anglers, and to monitor adult survival during the summer months. This program was very successful. Adults have survived very well in the river and catches of these tagged fish have been very good.

The biggest obstacle presently to adult survival of Atlantics in the lake, is the reproductive problems associated with a thiamin deficiency found in Atlantics from eating alewives. Alewives are high in the enzyme thiaminase, which reduces thiamine, resulting in reproductive failure. If adult returns can not be accomplished, or if the fish are incapable of reproducing, then the Atlantic program is ultimately doomed to failure.

On a positive note, the summer of 1998 saw the first big returns of Atlantics to the Salmon River. Numerous accounts of Atlantics being caught were made. Regional Fisheries Manager Les Wedge caught a dime bright Atlantic of about 9 pounds on May 24 while fishing a streamer fly in the upper fly section. Fran Verdoliva and Charles Biaas hooked seven Atlantics between 6 and 10 pounds on streamers on May 29, 1998. A 19.5-pound Atlantic was caught in the September, 1998. The summer of 1999, despite the drought, brought numerous accounts of lake run Atlantics. Some stocked smolts have also taken up residence in the river and have reached sizes of up to 17 inches in just a few years.

Despite these accounts, Verdoliva states we can never go back to what once was. The native lake Ontario Atlantic salmon went extinct a little over a hundred years ago in 1898. Wouldn't it be wonderful, as we enter the next century, if there was a chance to bring the Atlantic salmon back to the river for which it was named. The Salmon River of Lake Ontairo offers the greatest chance to reintroduce, reestablish, and maybe in the future, restore this magnificent species.

Ontario's greatest hope for restoration lies in the Credit River, a larger tributary which is ideally suited due to its high rock cover and low fine sediment. According to OMNR Lake Ontario biologist Jim Bowbly, Atlantic egg survival is good where brown trout do well since they frequent similar spawning areas with lower autumn and early winter flows. There has been documentation of wild Atlantic salmon already seen on the Credit, with the potential for a promising future.

The St. Mary's Dynasty

Perhaps the greatest Atlantic salmon success story is on the banks of the St. Mary's River, which connects Lake Superior and Huron. "It all begins with some of the cleanest water on Earth—Lake Superior," expressed Bill Gregory, one-time President of Sault Edison Power, and founding father and landlord of Lake Superior State University's Aquatic Research Laboratory housed in his hydroelectric plant. "The water teems with plankton—the life-giving food source for all salmonids. That's why Atlantic salmon do so well here."

Prior to the onset of the Lake Ontario restoration attempts, Atlantic salmon were stocked in Lake Michigan. It was a half-hearted attempt to introduce the species. Small stocking numbers, lack of return data, inferior strains, and anglers not being able to tell the difference between an open-water brown and an Atlantic salmon doomed the effort. Michigan did continue, however, to pursue the program in cold, deep inland glacial lakes where even today, some still carry a wild reproducing stock. A healthy Atlantic salmon program is back in full swing on Torch Lake near Traverse City, Michigan.

But things were brewing in Sault St. Marie, on an academic, secular level. After Dr. Gale Gleason's discovery of the massive plankton-carrying capacity of the St. Mary's waters, for the first time in Michigan fish culturing history, whitefish were raised from egg to well over 12 inches in a hatchery environment. He accomplished this by the kind permission of Sault Edison Power which allowed him the use of one of the unused penstocks at the 1,300 foot hydroelectric plant. President Bill Gregory and Vice Chairman Robert C. Kline were his staunch supporters.

In February, 1986, Bill Gregory was relaxing and enjoying a libation at Gale Gleason's comfortable home on the St. Mary's. The phone rang. Gale received news that the first shipment of Atlantic salmon eggs was being flown from Bangor, Maine to Traverse City, Michigan, and would arrive at noon the next day. On the spot, they made a decision to drive the next day to Traverse City airport, pick up the eggs (which were packed in ice), and bring them up to the aquatic lab. The evening was clear and bright when they made their decision. Gale and Gregory left in their Suburban at 7 a.m. the next morning. The weather was miserable. Cars were going off the road in partial whiteout conditions. Nonetheless, they made it to Traverse City in time to receive the shipment of eggs, turned right around and headed home for Sault Ste. Marie. The salmon eggs were in their hatching trays by 6 P.M. that evening.

In June 1987, with much publicized fanfare and a televised event featuring officials from the Department of Commerce, members of the Soo Area Sportsmen's Club, Lake Superior State University, and others, the first Atlantic salmon were released in the St. Mary's River. At that time, one could only wonder what would happen. Would the fish return? Would they survive? Would they provide a viable fishery if they did?

The Atlantic salmon program got off to a great start with the first return of mature fish exactly two years later in June,

1989. As anglers began tying into these battling, acrobatic denizens, the reputation of the St. Mary's Atlantic salmon fishery and the aquatic lab grew. Publicity began spreading to all corners of the state. In 1992, Gregory was recognized as Fisheries Conservationist of the Year by the Michigan United Conservation Clubs.

Today, the salmon program is thriving thanks to Roger Greil. Lake Superior State University in conjunction with the Michigan DNR and lab students, release about 50,000 Grand Lake strain salmon yearlings every year. They track their returns by offering prizes to anglers who return a Floy tag or fish head to the lab. They currently estimate a 5 percent return on the stocked fish, well above the Great Lakes norm. Each spring they electrofish the rapids and have documented an increase in natural reproduction.

Once in the big lakes, the Atlantics are fortunate to have fertile grazing grounds in the vicinity of Georgian Bay in Lake Huron. Here, cold water, massive schools of baitfish, and good structure contribute to quick weight-gain. One of the biggest problems with creating such a fishery is the great tendency of sea-origin fish to roam and travel. Thus far, the aquatic lab have received fish tags from Atlantic salmon caught by anglers from the Niagara Gorge to Lake Ontario. Roger Greil continues to be the master of Atlantic Salmon in the Great Lakes.

Personalities of Steelhead and Atlantics

Steelhead and Atlantics fight the same, both being avid tail walkers, cartwheeling leapers, and hard driving fish, there are some differences. Atlantics like fast water and hold above a rock. Steelhead will hold behind boulders and obstructions in slower currents. Normally steelhead won't travel more than three to four feet to take a fly—Atlantics are more aggressive, often swimming so fast to your fly they'll crash into the side of the boat. That is, when the mood hits them.

To be "on the bite" is much more prevalent for steelhead than the often "moody" and "sulking" Atlantic. Atlantics also need more time to hold on to the fly and a slower hookset. Steelhead spit quickly and you have to hit the hook quick and hard. The initial personality of a hook-set and fighting Atlantic or steelhead is an explosion.

The Lake Ontario Fisheries partnership with New York is firmly committed to restoring its indigenous stock of Atlantic salmon. The "leaper" has found a thriving home in the Lake Huron-St. Mary's River system; the future looks bright for this admirable sporting fish which so nicely complements the steelhead.

Tactics for Great Lakes Atlantics

Atlantic salmon of the Great Lakes, due once again to their potanadromous movement, behave much more opportunistically once they run their natal rivers. Though they are still selective, "moody," and wary like their saline cousins, they show a greater interest to "eat" and will do so all the way to the spawning bed. When Great Lakes Atlantics first arrive in their natal rivers, they still have a strong tendancy to attack baitfish streamers. Patterns that simulate smelt, herring, and other baitfish work well (see color fly plates).

Once established in the river, they will show curiosity to sculpin, mayfly, stonefly and caddis aquatic insects. When the heavy Hexagenia limbata hatch occurs, they will eat them on the surface like trout.

Though traditional Atlantic salmon classic patterns work early in the run, it is best to stick with Muddler Minnow patterns and nymphs. Bead-head pheasant tails, caddis and midge larvae, and scud patterns account for many fish. As the fish approach spawning, they show a strong liking for pink and chartruese egg patterns.

Chapter 12

The Future

In the inland oceans of the Great Lakes, the steelhead rainbow trout has flourished and prospered in its relativley short century and a quarter time span. When I fished, photographed and traversed the entire coastline of the Great Lakes, I found a great diversity in river ecosystems, management programs, valued perception and appreciation for the steelhead fishery by the various states and Province of Ontario. As of this writing, I am very pleased to have witnessed in all the fisheries management plans, a great future vision and a progressive thinking approach to enhancing all steelhead fisheries - both hatchery maintained and wild reproducing stocks. With a greater empahsis and appreciation for establishing and preserving wild steelhead populations and habitat, along with a careful intermixing of hatchery fish from established gene pools, the Great Lakes steelhead fishery has been manicured and fine tuned to consistently produce some of the greatest steelhead fishing in the world. This did not come about by haphazard or chance. By working closely with the lakes natural capacity of cold, clear water and abundant food and riverine habitats, dedicated fisheries biologists have managed fisheries for the highest quality sustainable yield to please anglers, and yet be guardians of the fragile natural and man-induced elements that can quickly decimate a quality fishery.

With a great deal of politics and public pressure to produce bigger and better steelhead runs, fisheries personnel have endured public and peer attacks for their often dogged stance on certain management programs geared towards understanding limiting factors and sustainable yield that nature and man can create in a steelhead fishery. As steelhead fishermen, we rarely stop to think of how these non-indigenous rainbows came here, or why the fishing is often so damn good or at times dismal. We quite often get caught up in the "taking" end of the sport—greed is a common human quality that can run rampant if unchecked. In this new millenium of uncertainty, we must become "givers"—stewards of the resource, to appreciate and preserve what we have. It is time to give thanks and praise for the hundreds of dedicated steelhead biologists and fisheries managers that have created and guarded this world class fishery. We must try to work together in harmony and understand the unique ecosystem of every Great Lakes river and stream. As opposed to arguing and self gratifying bickering over management programs, we as anglers should become interactive as partners in management, and allow a positive flow of ideas and concerns to be reasonably sorted out for a healthy outcome.

Steelhead of the Great Lakes have withstood over a century of natural hardships and have adjusted well, with many wild genetically unique populations like the Little Manistee strain, the Ganaraska and many others in Lake Superior, Erie and Huron. Aside from the lamprey, adult steelhead of the Great Lakes have no other chief predator in their food chain hierarchy but man. When the storied wild runs of the very ecologically fragile Lake Superior steelhead of Wisconsin's Bois Brule River drastically declined in the early 1990s, the Wisconisin DNR management team was faced with a public relations nightmare. The DNR program, headed by Dennis Pratt, did an outstanding job of communicating and educating the steelhead anglers (who were used to the "good old days") how to cope with the current problem. Dennis Pratt, in public press announcement plainly said, "You steelhead fishermen are the chief problem and obstacle to restoring the wild runs of the Bois Brule—period." Being as blunt as he was, bickering mouths were silenced quickly.

Yes, believe it or not, we are the problem. As a result of greed, relentless bombardment casting over fish on spawning gravel, use of high-tech tackle, GPS, fish finders, and more, we are the greatest threat to the steelhead's future survival. Unless we change our focus from numbers, size, and self-serving pompous gratification, we will lose our fisheries in a similar fashion to the catastrophic collapse of the West Coast steelhead dynasty of the late 1900s. Famed West Coast steelheader Bob York, a.k.a. Steelhead Bob, thinks North American steelhead are doomed because "North American man is too stupid to do anything about it! Steelhead and politics don't mix."

As a result of sportsmen's dollars and what seems like a never satisfied angling public, including charter guides, lodge owners, and tourist towns, fisheries managers are caught between "a rock and a hard place." In environmental politics, the trend has been to work retroactively—fix something once it is broken. As nature has continually shown, the outcome is either catastrophic or the solution far from what is desired.

Nowhere was this more painfully obvious than when I met with Tracy Close of the Minnesota DNR French River Research Station on the North Shore of Lake Superior. Here over the past decades, the once hallowed wild steelhead populations of the Knife, French, and Baptism rivers came to a spiralling crash due to greed, overharvesting, ecosystem changes, and a lack of appreciation for the resource. Today, Minnesota is the only Great Lakes state to have catch-and-release status for its steelhead. It seems we have to wait for the "well to run dry" before we come up with progressive management solutions. The MDNR has built a multi-million dollar fish entrapment facility to measure and record every migrating adult and emigrating smolt in order to understand limiting factors and restore the once-fabled runs.

In extremely abundant steelhead ecosystems like Lake Michigan, Erie, and Ontario, we are infatuated by numbers of fish hooked or landed. This is a damaging practice that must cease. This degrading, self-serving mentality turns these aesthetically precious fish into something we take for granted.

Our desecration of nature is often thoughtless. A national newspaper article, reported on a minor league baseball team in California called the "Sacramento Steelhead." The team was having a problem with fans throwing dead steelhead on the infield, in some sort of wacky "off the wall" autonomous fan behavior. This baffles the mind in a state that is on the verge of making its steelhead federally endangered and threatened.

As a steelhead fly fisher and guide who makes a living on the river, I see countless atrocities to these fish. I frequently pull treble hooks out of the tails and backs of beautiful steelhead that someone has attempted to snag. One summer I saw over a hundred dead Skamania steelhead lying in carnage on a small tributary bank with shotgun shot in their sides because somebody got mad at the world and decided to go down to the creek and shoot fish. Other sickening stories, such as the episode where a female spawning steelhead was caught on the Little Manistee and then tied alive and swinging to a rock on a gravel bed to entice more courting males which were caught immediately and killed. This begs me to question "have we lost our minds?" These undesirable behaviors exist when man is presented with 'excess." Fist fights over prime spawning gravel, casting over other people's lines, racing ferociously to beat another angler to the hot spot are common events in this often taken-too-seriously steelhead world.

Our culture has too often bred an angler that takes his sport seriously, too seriously. This competitive, lethal, stalking monster often sadly approaches the sport like they do their jobs and the stock market. Always a winner, always in a hurry, always in search of the trophy. I think back to a brief period when I was younger and burned this sort of torch. When I fell from my conquering horse, I fell hard. Man was not meant to endure such an outlandish pace. Our complicated society has created walking "exposed nerve" anglers pretending to enjoy the outdoors. I see very few smiling faces on the stream anymore. Jovial chit-chat is limited to the seriousness of the pursuit. I beg all in this new century to stop, to take a deep breath and discover ourselves again as children. In our youth we were mesmerized by grasshoppers and butterflies, pine cones, the sound of rushing water, and the frolicking of ducks along the stream. There was a sense of awe and excitement when we saw a silver steelhead swimming upriver. We spent fruitless hours trying to catch them. These were precious times that age can sour.

Ray Schmidt of Michigan's Manistee River is optimistic about the future. "Barring no unforseen natural catastrophic disaster, I think we're going in the right direction." "I'm seeing people starting to pay attention to our methods, our ecology, our beautiful fish." The next generation of anglers have been versed in conservation, in caring for the planet, much more so than our forefathers that raped the forests and streams.

The Great Lakes is one of the most magnificent coldwater frontiers in the world. Despite global warming, El Niño, La Niña, droughts, and changing climatic factors, it will take millenia to destroy this optimal enviroment for *Oncorhynchus mykiss*. In this new age, we must all vow to take a hard look at ourselves, and search for the silver lining, that innocence that first brought us to the sport. By slowly pacing ourselves when we use the rivers, soaking in all the natural beauty around us, we will appreciate what nature and God has given us. As steelheaders, we should walk in humble footsteps, enjoying every breath, every day that brings the gift of health, which allows us to pursue these magnificent fish hopefully for eternity.

For those of us that give back, protect, and honor the resource, there has to be a steelhead heaven.

I hope you and I get to go there.

Winter steelheading can be brutal. Tough weather conditions, changing barometric pressure and unfavorably cold waters can keep fish "off the bite." Often a whole day passes without a hook-up. Yet, at the magic hour of dusk, when the waters are warmest and the air is calm, a magic chrome steelhead reveals itself and is landed. The author, wearing his guide hat, knows the anxiety of getting skunked and exuberantly kisses the steelhead that "saved the day!" To preserve our Great Lakes legacy, we must embrace each steelhead as a gift from their creator and appreciate the sporting magic they give us.

Plate 1

Bear's Head Banger Stone, Hex Style

Bear-Hawk Hex

Bear's Hex

Bear's Head Banger Hex

Feenstra's Super Hex Wiggle Nymph

Bishop Hex Wiggle Double-Jointed

Schmidt's Hex Nymph

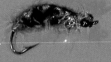

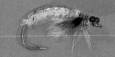

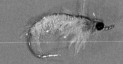

Bacon's Scud-Back Hex, Mutt Series

Bacon's Coyote Filo Hex, Mutt Series

Bacon's Rainbow Scud Back Hex, Mutt Series

Bacon's Lite-Brite Scud-Back Hex, Mutt Series

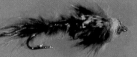

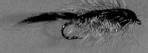

Empie's Antron Hex

Rubber Tail Olive/Amber Hex (Roller)

Mottled Turkey Back Hex

Tied Down Hex/Caddis

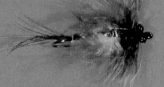

Amber Mottled P.M. Wiggler

Bishop's Beaded P.M. Wiggler

P.M. Wiggler Blonde

Runyon's Wild Swiss Straw Hex

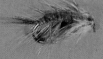

Vargas Strip Nymph

Graba's Rabbit Back Hex

Heneveld's Hex

Geddes Latex Wiggler

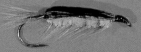

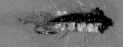

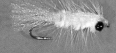

Spring's Wiggler (Low Water)

Spring's Wiggler (Cold Water)

Schmidt's Antron Bug Stone

Schmidt's Antron Bug Hex

Plate 2

Schmidt's Caddis Larvae

Reid's Crinkle Head Caddis

Runyon's Amnesia Caddis

Valk's Bead Head Caddis

Viagra Caddis

Barber's Micro Caddis

Czech Mate (Orvis)

Feenstra's Super Caddis

Bachelder's Caddis

Barber's Rhyacophila

Bacon's Peeking Cased Scud Caddis

Vogel's St. Mary's Caddis

Vargas Peeking Caddis

Johnson's P.M. Caddis

Fred's Disco Caddis

Steve's Bead Head Brer Possum

Galloup's Reverse Caddis

Bear's P.M. Caddis

Bear's Rubber Legged Caddis

Gartside Sparkle Sparrow

Bishop Double Sparrow

Tan Sparrow

Bishop's Steelhead Bee

Dusty's Fuzzbuster

Bear's Turkey Tail

Bear's Pheasant Tail

Galloup's Bead-Butt Hare's Ear

Galloup's Traditional Hare's Ear

Ingersoll's Steely Stone Yellow & Brown

Ingersoll's Steely Stone Orange & Brown

Ingersoll's Peacock & Possum

Traditional Pheasant Tail

Schmidt's PCP Nymph

Geddes Bead Head Mayfly

Smith's Nympho

Theo's Gold Bead Bomber

Rummel's Woolly Worm

Bead Head Prince

Bennet's Erie Sparkle Maggot

Bear's Ironhead Cock-tail

Geddes Green Butt

Valk's Red Squirrel Mayfly

Valk's Olive Mayfly

Valk's Pheasant Tail

Valk's March Brown

Valk's Hendrickson

Valk's Bead Head Pheasant Tail

Plate 3

Barber's Micro Mayfly Stone

Barber's Micro Pearl Grizzly

Barber's Micro Natural

Barber's Dark Olive Caddis

Barber's Antron Micro Gnat

Barber's Baetis

Bacon's Amber Lite-Brite Scud

Bacon's Bead Head Mysis Scud

Bacon's Dark Gray Scud

Bacon's Copper Back Scud

Steelhead Buzzer Midge

Bead Head Brassie

Red Pheasant Tail

Bachelor's Baby Rat

Walle's Soft Hackle Hare's Ear

Yachetti's Golden Pearl

Yachetti's Steelhead Sac-Fry

Yachetti's Pink Sac-Fry

Yachetti's Micro Black & Purple Wet

Yachetti's Micro Signal Light

Yachetti's Micro Reverse Signal Light

Yachetti's Purple Peril Wet

Vogel's October Caddis

Nagy's Neon Stone

Dorothy's Grizzly & Brown

Dorothy's Badger

Skamania Bee

Deep Brown Pheasant Stone

D. King's Hare's Ear

Mini-Bugger

Bead Head Mohair White Leech

Troutsman Turkey Bugger

Troutsman Egg Sculpin Leech

Yachetti's Black & Purple Zonker

Yachetti's White Zonker

Yachetti's Electric Purple Spey

Bishop's Egg Sucking Fish

Schmidt's Steelhead Woolly Bugger

Schmidt's Egg Sucking Leech

Plate 4

**Bacon's Larva
Lace Stone**   **Bacon's Larva Lace
Flash Back Stone**   **Darkes
Simple Stone**   **Darkes
Purple Jesus**   **Mike's Stone**

**Black Pheasant Tail
Flash Back Stone**   **Barber's
Chartreuse
Head Stone**   **Barber's Natural Stone
Chartreuse Thorax**   **Barber's Jet Black
Chartreuse Stone**

**Schmidt's
Stone**   **Geddes
Black Stone**   **Geddes
Montana Stone**   **Bachelder's
Stone**

——————————— *Valk's Krystal Stonefly Series* ———————————

Spring Stone   **Creepy Stone**   **Bishop's Rubber
Molded Stone**   **Kaufmann's Stone**

Claret Stone

Purple Estaz Stone

Manistee Red Stone

**Black Bead Stone,
Rubber Legs**   **Bead Head Stone,
Rubber Legs**

Plate 5

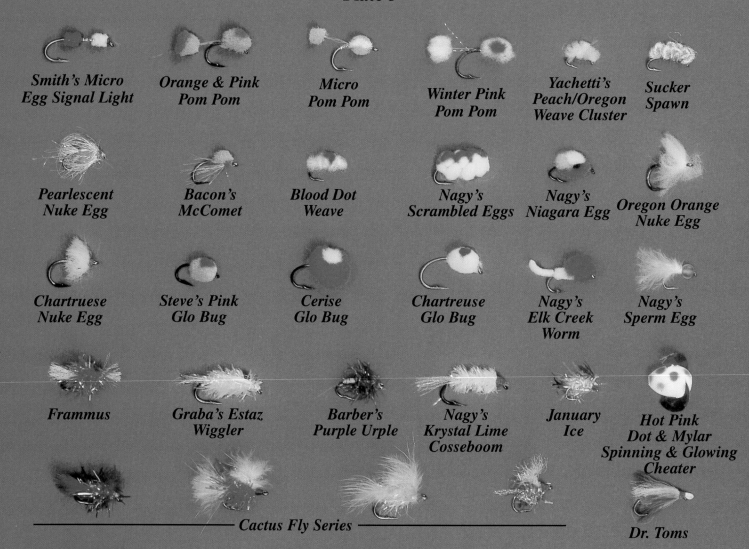

Smith's Micro Egg Signal Light

Orange & Pink Pom Pom

Micro Pom Pom

Winter Pink Pom Pom

Yachetti's Peach/Oregon Weave Cluster

Sucker Spawn

Pearlescent Nuke Egg

Bacon's McComet

Blood Dot Weave

Nagy's Scrambled Eggs

Nagy's Niagara Egg

Oregon Orange Nuke Egg

Chartruese Nuke Egg

Steve's Pink Glo Bug

Cerise Glo Bug

Chartreuse Glo Bug

Nagy's Elk Creek Worm

Nagy's Sperm Egg

Frammus

Graba's Estaz Wiggler

Barber's Purple Urple

Nagy's Krystal Lime Cosseboom

January Ice

Hot Pink Dot & Mylar Spinning & Glowing Cheater

————————————————— *Cactus Fly Series* —————————————————

Dr. Toms

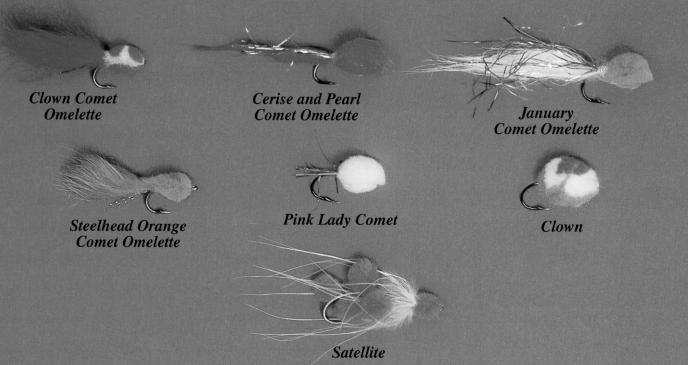

Clown Comet Omelette

Cerise and Pearl Comet Omelette

January Comet Omelette

Steelhead Orange Comet Omelette

Pink Lady Comet

Clown

Satellite

Plate 6

Valk's Steelhead Skate Series

Gray Wulff

Light Hendrickson

Dark Hendrickson

Irresistible

Green Buck Bug

Royal Wulff

Orange Bomber

Irresistible Wulff

Steelhead Cicada

Steelhead Bee

Smith's Coaster Skating Diver

Gray Drake

Shewey's Spawning Purple

Kaufmann's Freight Train (Modified)

Rainbow Spey

Peacock Gold Spey

Copper Guinea Spey

Low Water McMillin's Winter Hope

Blue Charm (Modified)

Red Butt Skunk

Undertaker

Stallard Maggot Spey

Spirit River Mighty Minnow Rainbow Trout

Plate 7

*Kustich's Purple
Bunny Spey*

Kustich's Devil's Advocate

*Kustich's Purple &
Orange Marabou Spey*

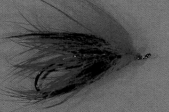

*Kustich's Purple
October*

*Kustich's
Catnip*

*Kustich's
Citation*

*Halyk's Orange & Black
Reverse Akroyd*

*Halyk's Orange & Black
Reverse Akroyd*

Halyk's October Spey

Bear's Skamaniator

Bush Weasel Spey

*Schmidt's Spey
Green-Butt*

*Schmidt's Natural
Spey Red Butt*

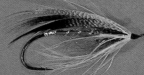

Graba's Spey

*Vogel's
St. Mary's Spey*

*Graba's Low
Water Spey*

Plate 8

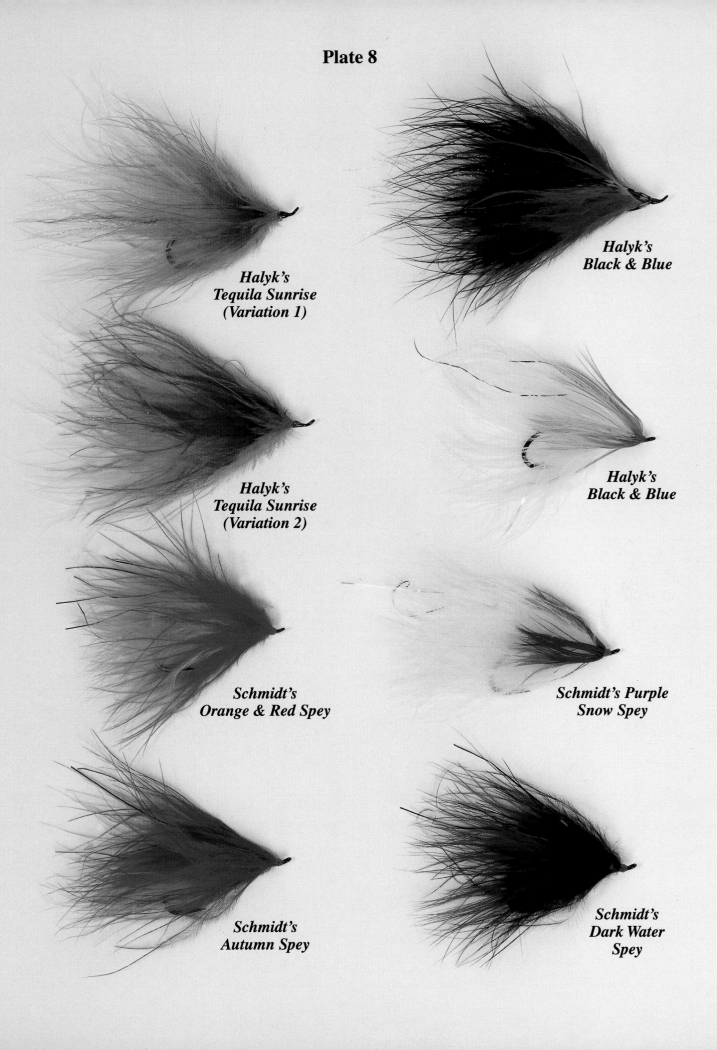

*Halyk's
Tequila Sunrise
(Variation 1)*

*Halyk's
Black & Blue*

*Halyk's
Tequila Sunrise
(Variation 2)*

*Halyk's
Black & Blue*

*Schmidt's
Orange & Red Spey*

*Schmidt's Purple
Snow Spey*

*Schmidt's
Autumn Spey*

*Schmidt's
Dark Water
Spey*

Plate 9

**Yarnot's Steelhead
Ackroyd**

**Yarnot's Wild
Turkey Orange**

**Yarnot's Purple
and Orange**

Yarnot's Emerald Eagle

**Yarnot's Steelhead
Stinger, Black**

**Yarnot's Steelhead
Stinger, Orange**

Stallard's Thugmeister

Purple Guinea Spey

Plate 10

Valk's Steelhead Petite Series

Valk's Steelhead Petite Series

Valk's Beadhead Squirrels

Valk's Beadhead Squirrels

Krause's Chicago Leech

Krause's Chicago Egg Sucking Leech

Smith's Chartreuse Fire Fly

Geddes Alexandra

Geddes Thunder Creek Steelhead

Egg Sucking Leech Purple Head

Electric Candy Cane

Feenstra's Emulator Possum

Feenstra's Emulator Olive Rabbit

Thugmeister Leech

Darkes Rabbit Strip Spey

Clouser Leech

Plate 11

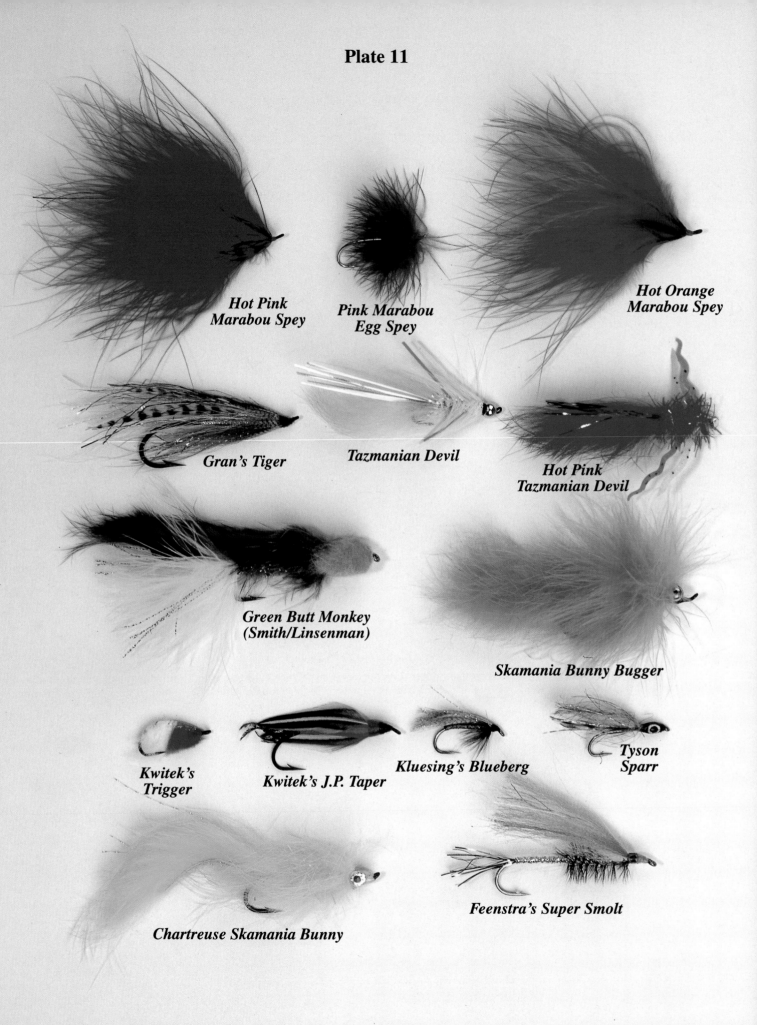

Hot Pink Marabou Spey

Pink Marabou Egg Spey

Hot Orange Marabou Spey

Gran's Tiger

Tazmanian Devil

Hot Pink Tazmanian Devil

Green Butt Monkey (Smith/Linsenman)

Skamania Bunny Bugger

Kwitek's Trigger

Kwitek's J.P. Taper

Kluesing's Blueberg

Tyson Sparr

Chartreuse Skamania Bunny

Feenstra's Super Smolt

Plate 12

Skinny Pete
"Peacock & Gray"

C-4-See-Me-Smelt

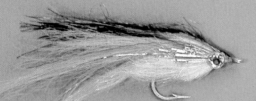

C-4-See-Me-Alewife

Ultra Hair Clocker
"Clearly Canadian"

Ultra Ghost

Skinny Pete
Angel Hair & Gray

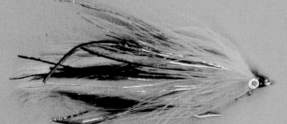

Reid's Boliciever

Sea Habit Bucktail

Bunny Foo Foo
Chinchilla and Blue-Peacock

Skinny Pete
"Peacock and Blue"

Plate 13

Angel Hair Ghost

Bunny Bendback

Shmoo

Woolly Smelt

WTF

Woolly Smelt
(Low Water)

Waker Alewife

B-17® Rainbow Smelt

FLY PLATE 1
NYMPHS - *HEXAGENIA* IMITATIONS

Row 1 - Left to Right
Bear's Hex
Hook: Daiichi 1270
Thread: 8/0 Tan Uni Thread
Tail: 3 Emu Fibers
Back: Pheasant Tail (Treated with Flex Seal)
Gills: After Shaft from pheasant
Ribbing: Mono thread or fine gold wire
Abdomen: Sulpher squirrels blend (Spirit River)
Wing Case: Pheasant tail folded (Treated with flex)
Hackle: Tan hen saddle
Thorax: Sulpher squirrel blend
Eyes: Ex-small mono eyes

Bear's Head Banger Stone, Hex Style
Hook: Daiichi 1270
Thread: 8/0 Black Uni thread
Tail: Chartreuse micro egg yarn
Gills: Black after shaft
Back: Turkey tail treated with (flex seal) and folded
Abdomen: Black squirrel blend dubbing
Wingcase: Turkey tail folded and treated (with flex seal)
Legs: Black hen saddle
Eyes: Ex-small mono eyes

Bear-Hawk Hex
Hook: Daiichi 1270
Thread: 8/0 Tan Uni thread
Tail: Pheasant maribou
Back: Pheasant tail fold and treated with (flex seal)
Gills: Aftershaft collared
Abdomen: Sulpher squirrel blend
Wing Cases: Pheasant tail folded and (treated with flex seal)
Hackle: Tan hen saddle
Eyes: Ex-small black mono eyes

Bear's Head Banger Hex
Hook: Daiichi 1270
Thread: 8/0 Tan Uni thread
Tail: Steelhead orange micro yarn
Gills: Pheasant after shaft collared
Back: Pheasant tail folded and (treated with flex seal)
Abdomen: Sulpher squirrel blend
Thorax: Sulpher squirrel blend
Hackle: Tan hen saddle
Eyes: Ex-small mono eyes

Row 2 - Left to Right
Feenstra's Super Hex Wiggle Nymph
Hook, Rear: Straight Eye Streamer, 4XL (Tiemco 9395)
Hook, Front: Tiemco 105 Egg Hook or Scud hook as substitute
Rear Hook Dressing:
Tail: Clump of Australian possum
Body: Dirty yellow, tan, or olive dubbing, with two clumps of Australian possum mixed in
Front Hook Dressing:
Connection: 15-20 lb. Maxima, looped through the eye of rear hook, bound to front hook with thread and a drop of Zap a Gap
Over Tail: Clump of Australian possum
Wing Case: Brown Antron
Hackle: Grizzly hen or olive/grizzly hen, tied in and pulled forward with wingcase over body
Body: Dirty yellow, tan, or olive nymph dubbing
Eyes: Black mono craft eyes

Bishop's Double-Jointed Wiggler Hex
Back Hook: Daiichi 1560, size 6
Thread: Brown
Tail/Wing Casing: Golden pheasant tail
Gills: Gray filo plume
Ribbing: Fine gold wire
Body: Cream
Front Hook: TMC 105, size 8
Thread: Brown
Wing Casing: Golden pheasant tail, flex-coated
Body: Cream
Hackles: Two hen pheasant to size
Eyes: Brunt mono-filament, preferred 20 lb. or above

Schmidt's Hex Nymph
Hook: Tiemco 200R or Partridge CS54 size 6 (weighted)
Thread: 3/0 light orange
Eyes: Burned black mono
Tail: Pheasant tail central fibers
Shell Back: Pheasant tail central fibers
Rib: Fine copper wire
Body: Golden stone Awesome ëPossum w/ 20% Hex Antron dubbing blended in
Wing Case: Pheasant tail central fibers (treated w/ Flex-seal of Flexament)
Thorax: Same as body
Legs: Partridge or hen saddle

Row 3
Bacon's Scud Back Hex, Mutt Series
Hook: Daiichi 1150
Thread: Gray
Back: Dyed plastic Amber latex Bodi-Stretch (Spirit River)
Ribbing: Copper wire
Abdomen: Filo Plume pheasant after shaft
Thorax: Estaz pearl olive with claret scud dubbing mix
Eyes: Black mono craft

Bacon's Coyote Filo Hex, Mutt Series
Hook: Daiichi 1530
Thread: Gray
Tail: Amber Antron with light fox
Back: Fluff of dark fox
Body: Rainbow scud dubbing
Collar: Filo plume pheasant after shaft
Head: Rainbow scud dubbing
Eyes: Black mono craft

Bacon's Rainbow Scud Back Hex, Mutt Series
Hook: Daiichi 1150
Thread: Gray
Back: Bodi-Stretch Clear
Ribbing: Mono
Body: Rainbow sow scud dubbing
Collar: Filo plume pheasant after shaft
Head: Lite bright dubbing blue/green
Eyes: Black mono craft

Bacon's Lite Brite Scud Back Hex, Mutt Series
Hook: Daiichi 1150
Thread: Gray
Back: Amber Bodi-Stretch
Ribbing: Copper
Body: Pearl Pink and Green Lite Brite
Thorax: Filo pheasant after shaft
Eyes: Black mono craft

Row 4
Empie's Antron Hex
Hook: Daiichi 1530
Thread: Cream
Tail: Three strips of pheasant tail inserted through tan Antron and tied off at tip
Body: Yellow or cream Antron
Back: Tan Antron
Collar/Thorax: Tan mottled saddle hackle
Eyes: Blakc mono core

Rubber Tailed Olive/Amber Hex (Roller)
Hook: Daiichi 1270
Thread: Black
Tail: Black rubber legs
Back: Pheasant tail
Wing Case Body: Dirty olive or squirrel
Abdomen: Burnt Orange filo plume after shaft
Thorax: Paltered brown hackle

Mottled Turkey Back Hex
Hook: Daiichi 1270
Thread: Cream
Tail: Pheasant tail and filo plume after shaft
Body: Cream Antron
Back: Pheasant tail
Rib: Copper wire
Gills: Filo plume pheasant after shaft
Collar: Mottled burnt orange turkey butt marabou
Back: Folded mottled turkey (stone fly style)
Eyes: Black mono craft

Tied Down Caddis/Hex
Hook: Mustad 38941
Thread: Orange
Tail & Back: Black squirrel tail
Body: Burnt or hot orange Antron
Hackle: Palmered Grizzly Hackle

Row 5
Amber P.M. Wiggler
Hook: Daiichi 1530 size 6
Thread: Tan
Tail & Back: Amber mottled marabou
Ribbing: Black ostrich herl
Body: Tan Antron
Eyes: Black mono craft

Bishop's Beaded P.M. Wiggler
Hook: Daiichi 1530 size 6
Thread: Primrose
Tail: Marabou, ginger
Over Body: Marabou, ginger
Ribbing: Ostrich herl, ginger
Body: Four orange glass beads
Eyes: Plastic bead chain, black 2.5 mm

P.M Wiggler - Blonde
Hook: Daiichi 1530 6-10
Thread: Cream
Tail & Back: Tan/Blonde marabou
Ribbing: White ostrich herl
Body: Cream Antron
Eyes: Black mono craft

Runyon's Wild Swiss Straw Hex
Hook: Daiichi 1270
Thread: Brown
Tail: Clump of pheasant tail
Back & Wing Case: Grayish Swiss straw
Ribbing: Gold wire
Body: Cream Antron
Thorax: Thick stands of filo plume from under breast of pheasant breast with palmered brown saddle hackle
Eyes: Black mono craft

Row 6 - Left to Right
Vargas Strip Nymph
Hook: Daiichi 1530
Thread: Cream
Tail, Abdomen , Gills (all one): Hide strip of tan Australian opossum
Thorax: Cream white dubbing
Back: peacock Krystal flash
Legs: Tan vernille, shaped with heated needle
Eyes: Silver bead chain

Graba's Rabbit Back Hex
Hook: Daiichi 1530
Thread: Black

Tail: Brown Hackle
Body: Amber SLF dubbing
Rib: Copper
Raised Back: Natural rabbit
Collar: Burnt orange/brown saddle hackle
Wing Case: Brown Swiss straw

Heneveld's Hex
Hook: Daiichi 1530
Thread: Amber
Tail: 3 Striped quills: amber, or pheasant tail
Body: Wrapped amber/olive Antron on extended tail wrapped on heavy mono
Gills: Filo plume undershaft pheasant feather
Wing Case: Striped amber quills, cemented
Legs: Stripped amber quills cemented or Spirit River's Legs-on-a-Stick

Geddes Latex Wiggler
Hook: Daiichi 1120
Thread: Brown
Tail: Pheasant tail
Body: Dark Amber latex with palmered brown hackle
Head & Throat: Filo plume pheasant under shaft feathers

Row 7 - Left to Right

Spring's Wiggler (Cold Water) Nicholson
Hook: Daiichi 1720
Thread: Black
Tail & Back: Amber/Black squirrel
Body: Orange chenille
Hackle: Ginger palmered

C&D: Schmidt's Antron Bug
Hook: Tiemco #9395 or Tiemco #3761 size 6
Thread: 3/0 waxed mono cord to match body color
Eyes: 3mm black plastic bead chain
Tail: Antron yarn, dark brown for stone and hex; cream for shrimp (white)
Hackle: Furnace saddle hackle for stone and hex; ginger for shrimp (white)
Body: Medium chenille, black for stone, tan for hex, white for shrimp (white)
ShellBack: Same as tail

FLY PLATE 2
Nymphs, Caddis, Stonefly, Various

Row 1 - Left to Right

Schmidt's Caddis Larva
Hook: Tiemco #2457 size 8 or equivalent
Thread: 3/0 waxed mono cord (black)
Rib: Gold or copper Krystal Flash
Body: Micro Chenille colors to simulate larva; caddis green, chartreuse, olive etc.
Thorax: Peacock herl

Ried's Crinkle Head Caddis
Hook: Daiichi 1560
Thread: Black
Body: Hairline's sparkle caddis dubbing
Head: Peacock herl spiked with black Krystal Flash

Runyon's Amnesia Caddis
Hook: Daiichi 1120
Thread: Black or white (depending on how bright you want the body)
Body: Green amnesia shooting line
Head: Black ostrich

Valk's Bead Head Caddis
Hook: Daiichi 1270
Thread: Brown
Body: Kelly green dubbing or micro chenille
Rib: Copper

Head: Brown dubbing with gold bead
Under Thorax: Olive rabbit hair

Viagara Caddis
Hook: Daiichi 1510
Thread: Black
Tail & Body: Erect piece of green vernille burnt on tip
Thorax: Black dubbing

Barber's Micro Caddis
Hook: Daiichi 1120
Thread: Black
Body: Olive Antron
Rib: Copper wire
Head: Black dubbing

Row 2 - Left to Right

Czech Mate (Orvis)
Hook: Daiichi 1120
Thread: Black
Back: Amber green latex or bodi-stretch
Rib: Gold wire
Body: Natural hare's ear
Thorax: Chartreuse Antron or chartreuse bead with hare's ear dubbing plucked out for legs

Feentra's Super Caddis Larva
Hook: Daiichi 1120
Thread: Black
Head: Gold bead
Body: Phosphorescent green Kreinik metallic braid or green phosphorescent Flashabou, wrapped in segments up the hook
Rib: Copper wire, wrapped between segments
Thorax: Peacock herl or Australian possum

Bachelder's Caddis
Hook: Daiichi 1120
Thread: Black
Body: Very bright chartreuse Flex-Floss (Spirit River)
Head: Peacock herl

Barber's Rhyacophila Caddis
Hook: Daiichi 2151 size 10
Thread: Olive
Body: Light olive dubbing
Rib: Light olive floss or thread
Head: Black dubbing

Bacon's Peeking Cased Scud Caddis, Mutt Series
Hook: Daiichi 1120
Thread: Black
Back: Clear bodi-stretch or scud back
Tail: Black ostrich
Abdomen: Tan dubbing
Rib: Mono
Thorax: Sparkle caddis green dubbing
Head: Black ostrich

Vogel's St. Mary's Caddis
Hook: Daiichi 1120
Thread: Black
Body: Highlander green dubbing
Rib: Copper wire
Collar: Brown mottled soft hackle from Hungarian partridge

Row 3 - Left to Right

Vargas Peeking Caddis
Hook: Daiichi 1720
Tag: Black Krystal Flash with several strands plucked out then cemented with gold glass bead added
Body: Weighted wire on hook shank, dubbing is a mixture of various lite-brite colors blended with dark gray.

Johnson's P.M. Caddis
Hook: Daiichi 1530
Thread: Gray
Body: Highlander green dubbing
Collar: Woodduck or teal feathers
Head: Natural Hare's Ear

Fred's Disco Caddis
Hook: TMC 2457, size 6, 8, 10
Thread: Primrose
Abdomen: Frostbite, highlander green
Head: Crystal dubbing, olive brown

Steve's Bead Head Brer Possum
Hook: Daiichi 1530 or Tiemco 2302
Sizes: 12-16
Thread: Tan 6/0 * Gold bead to fit hook size
Tag: Kreinik medium braid, glow-in-the-dark green
Abdomen: Kreinik medium or small braid ñ copper or brown trout with light opossum, twist tightly
Collar: Light opossum guard hairs

Galloup's Reverse Caddis
Hook: Daiichi 1720
Tail: Black rabbit plucked ñout
Abdomen: Chartreuse micro chenille or dubbing
Main Body/Thorax: Fine brown ostrich or brown dubbing palmered with brown hackle and clipped tight to body

Row 4 - Left to Right

Bear's Rubber Legged Caddis
Hook: Daiichi 1120
Thread: 8/0 Grey UNI thread
Head: Gold bead
Body: Jan Simans dubbing brush
Legs: Extra fine gray rubber legs
Collar: Pheasant after shaft

Gartside Sparkle Sparrow
Hook: Daiichi 1530, size 6, 8, 10
Thread: Primrose
Tail: Male pheasant marabou
Body: Crystal dubbing, caddis green
Hackle: Male saddle hackle
Over Hackle: Filo plume

Bishop Double Sparrow
Hook: Daiichi 2050, size 5
Thread: Primrose
Tail: Male pheasant marabou
First Body: Crystal dubbing, caddis green
First Hackle: Male pheasant saddle, natural
Second Body: Crystal dubbing, caddis green
Second Hackle: Large male pheasant saddle, natural

Tan Sparrow
Hook: Daiichi 1530
Thread: Tan
Tail: Filo plume from pheasant undershaft feather
Body: Amber/tan Antron
Collar: Hungarian partridge soft hackle
Head: Filo plume undershaft feather

Bishop's Steelhead Bee
Hook: Daiichi 1530
Thread: Amber
Body: Amber/Orange sparkle dubbing or lite-brite
Ribbing: Amber ostrich
Collar: Mottled partridge soft hackle or mottled saddle hackle
Head: Filo plume pheasant with amber ostrich herl

Row 5 - Left to Right

Dusty's Fuzz Buster (Olive)
Hook: Daiichi 1710

Thread: 8/0 Olive UNI thread
Tail: Olive chicken marabou
Back: Pheasant Tail (Treated with Flex Seal)
Ribbing: Fine silver wire
Abdomen: olive ostrich herl
Wing Case: Pheasant tail folded (treated with Flex Seal)
Thorax: Olive hen saddle collared forward

Bear's Turkey Tail

Hook: Daiichi 1710
Thread: 8/0 Black Uni thread
Tail: Turkey tail
Ribbing: Fine silver wire
Abdomen: Turkey tail
Wing Case: Turkey tail treated with (Flex Seal) and folded
Thorax: Peacick herl
Hackle: Black pheasant rump collared, followed by black aftershaft collared
Eyes: Ex-small Black mono eyes

Bear's Pheasant Tail

Hook: Daiichi 1120
Thread: Tan 8/0 Uni thread
Tail: Pheasant tail
Ribbing: Fine gold wire
Abdomen: Pheasant tail
Wing Case: Pheasant tail (treated with Flex Seal) and folded
Thorax: Peacock herl
Hackle: Pheasant rump collar followed by aftershaft collar
Eyes: Ex-small black mono eyes

Galloup's Bead-Butt Hare's Ear

Hook: Daiichi 1270
Thread: Red
Tail: Australian opossum or fox hide hare
Butt: Gold bead
Body: Amber hare's ear
Rib: Gold wire
Thorax: Plucked-out fox hair
Wing Case: Mottled turkey feather

Galloup's Traditional Hare's Ear

Hook: Daiichi 2421
Thread: Red
Tail: Pheasant tail
Body: Natural light hare's ear
Ribbing: Gold thread
Legs: Hungarian partridge soft hackle
Wing Case: Mottled turkey feather

Row 6 - Left to Right

A & B Ingersoll's Steely Stone Nymph

Hook: TMC 5263 (3 XL) sizes 8-16 or 7999 sizes 8-12
Thread: Dansville 6/0 Fl. Orange/chartreuse
Tail: Quills from ringneck pheasant hen wings, (substitute grouse or partridge) leading flight feathers
Rib: UNI-floss rust/bright yellow 1x
Abdomen: Haretron dubbing dark brown #16 (both)
Thorax: Haretron dubbing burnt orange #17/yellow #9
Wing Case: Secondary feathers (soft hackle) from ringnecked pheasant hen wings (substitute grouse or partridge to create mottled look under the pearl Flashabou, - 9 to 12 strands approx. (not too much, allow hen pheasant to peek through, length of hook shank)
Legs: Tips of hen pheasant wingcase split to sides and tie back over
Shoulder: Same as thorax
Beads: Copper for orange & brown, gold for bright yellow and brown

C. Ingersoll's Peacock & Possum Soft Hackle

Hook: TMC 7999 size 8-12 3769

Thread: Black 6/0
Tail: Dark brown hen hackle
Rib: Copper wire
Abdomen: Arizona synthetic peacock natural
Thorax: Arizona crystal possum
Collar: Dark brown hen hackle 1 1/2 times the hook gap tied sparse

D. Traditional Pheasant Tail

Hook: Daiichi 1120
Thread: Brown
Tail, Body, and Wing Case: Strands of natural pheasant tail tied in at tail, wrapped forward and overlaid for wing case
Thorax: Peacock herl

E. Schmidt's PCP Nymph (pheasant, copper, peacock)

Hook: Tiemco #2457 size 8 or 10
Thread: 3/0 waxed mono cord (dark brown)
Tail: Ring-necked pheasant tail central fibers
Rib: Fine copper wire
Body: Ring-necked pheasant tail central fibers
Thorax: Peacock herl

Geddes Bead Head Mayfly

Hook: Daiichi 1120
Head: Copper bead
Tail: Teal flank
Body: Natural amber hare's ear
Ribbing: Copper wire
Collar: Brown saddle hackle

Row 7 - Left to Right

Smith's Nympho

Hook: Tiemco 200R sizes 8-10
Thread: Orange UNI thread 6/0
Tail: Golden pheasant crest
Rib: Gold oval tinsel
Body: Chartreuse Steelhead dubbing
Wing Case: Six strands of peacock herl
Thorax: Orange or fuchsia Hairline's Steelhead Dubbing, pick out fibers to resemble legs
Commented: Tied to the same proportions as a Gold-Ribbed Hare's Ear Nymph

Theo's Gold Bead Bomber

Hook: Daiichi 1530 or Tiemco 3761
Sizes: 10-16
Thread: Black 6/0 *Gold bead to fit hook size
Tail: Golden pheasant tippets and red wool yarn
Rib: Gold wire, fine
Body: Peacock
Legs: Black Hackle

Rummel's Woolly Worm

Hook: Daiichi 1530
Sizes: 10-14
Thread: Black 6/0
Tail: Red Yarn Tag
Body: Medium variegated chenille orange/black
Hackle: Micro-barb saddle feather-grizzly

Bead Head Prince Nymph

Hook: Daiichi 1530
Thread: Black
Head: Gold bead
Tail: Brown goose biot
Rib: Gold tinsel
Body: Peacock herl
Hackle: Brown
Wings: White goose biots

Bennet's Erie Sparkle Maggot

Hook: Tiemco 2457
Sizes: 12-18
Thread: Black 6/0
*Gold bead either brass or tungsten to fit hook size and

preference
Body: White or pearl Flashabou dubbing or Lite Brite dubbed tight
Thorax: Peacock herl, 2-3 wraps tight behind the bead

Bear's Ironhead Cock-Tail

Hook: Daiichi 1530
Thread: 8/0 Tan UNI thread
Tail: Pheasant marabou
Body: Peacock
Back: Folded pheasant tail (treated with Flex Seal)
Wingcase: Fold pheasant tail (treated with Flex-Seal)
Legs: Collared pheasant rump

Row 8 - Left to Right

Geddes Green Butt

Hook: Daiichi 1530
Thread: Black
Tail: Red hackle
Tag: Chartreuse chenille
Body: Black chenille
Rib: Silver tinsel
Collar: Black saddle hackle or schlappen
Overwing: White Antron or calf-tail

Valk's Red Squirrel Mayfly

Hook: Mustad 9671
Thread: Black
Tail: Black hackle tips
Body: Red squirrel or Antron
Rib: Gold tinsel
Wing Case: Brown saddle hackle or pheasant tail with tips plucked out for legs

Valk's Olive Mayfly

Hook: Mustad 9671
Thread: Olive
Tail: Pheasant tail
Body: Olive dubbing
Rib: Amber Antron
Legs: Ginger saddle hackle
Wing Case: Gray hackle

Valk's Pheasant Tail

Hook: Mustad 9671
Thread: Brown
Tail, Body, & Wing Case: Pheasant tail
Ribbing: Copper wire
Thorax: Peacock herl
Legs: Pheasant tail fibers plucked out from wing case

Valk's March Brown

Hook: Mustad 9671
Thread: Black
Tail: Teal
Body: Cream Antron
Rib: Amber Antron
Legs: Teal
Wing Case: Gray hackle

Valk's Hendrickson

Hook: Mustad 9671
Thread: Black
Tail: Teal, wood duck
Body: Dark brown/claret dubbing with interlude or yellow or chartreuse dubbing followed by brown/claret dubbing
Wing Case: Black hackle

Valk's Beadhead Pheasant Tail

Hook: Daiichi 1120
Thread: Brown
Head: Copper bead
Tail, Body & Wing Case: Pheasant tail
Rib: Copper wire

Fly Plate 3

NYMPHS - NATURALS, ATTRACTORS, BUGGERS

Barber's Micro Mayfly/Stone
Hook: Daiichi 1510 #18
Thread: Black
Tail: Black gook biots
Body: Black dubbing
Rib: Red or copper wire
Head: Black dubbing or black clipped ostrich

Barber's Micro Pearl Grizzly
Hook: Daiichi 1530 #16
Thread: Black
Body: Fine dark brown ostrich
Thorax: Pear Lite-Brite or Antron
Collar: Grizzly hackle

Barber's Micro Natural
Hook: Daiichi 1530 #16
Thread: Black
Body: Fine dark brown ostrich clipped tight
Collar: Grizzly hackle

Barber's Dark Olive Caddis
Hook: Daiichi 1120
Thread: Black
Body: Dark olive dubbing, very fine taper building up
Thorax: Peacock herl

Barber's Antron Micro Gnat
Hook: Daiichi 1530 #16
Thread: Black
Tail: Black hackle
Body: Black dubbing
Overwing: White or pearl Antron
Underwing: Black hackle

Barber's Baetis
Hook: Daiichi 2421 #12
Thread: Black
Tail: Mallard or teal
Body: Dark olive
Rib: Copper wire
Throat: Hungarian partridge
Wing Case: Black stipped ostrich herl

Row 2 - Left to Right

Bacon's Amber/Lite-Brite Scud
Hook: Daiichi x510
Thread: Tan
Back: Amber Bodi-Stretch
Rib: Mono
Body: Blue-green Lite Brite
Antennae: Wood duck

Bacon's Bead Head Mysis Scud
Hook: Daiichi 1120
Head: Black or silver bead
Back: Pink or amber Bodi-Stretch
Ribbing: Silver tinsel
Body: Light pink and white rabbit blend plucked out

Bacon's Dark Gray Scud
Hook: Daiichi 1120
Thread: Black
Tail Tips: Antron clear
Back: Amber Bodi-Stretch
Body: Dark gray rabbit or Antron
Head: Tuff of green/blue Lite-Brite

Bacon's Copper Back Scud
Hook: Daiichi 1120
Thread: Tan
Back: Amber Bodi-Stretch

Rib: Heavy copper wire
Body: Pearl and green (blue Lite-Brite)

Steelhead Buzzer Midge
Hook: Daiichi 1120 #16
Thread: Black
Body: Black thread
Ribbing: Silver tinsel
Wing: Clear Antron
Head: Sparkle hare's ear

Bead Head Brassie
Hook: Daiichi 1120 #16
Head: Brass bead
Body: Copper
Thorax: Peacock herl

Red Pheasant Tail
Hook: Daiichi 1530
Thread: Black
Tail: Pheasant tail
Body & Thorax: Peacock herl
Ribbing: Red wire
Wing Case: Pheasant tail fibers

Row 3 - Left to Right

Bachelder's Baby Rat
Hook: Daiichi 2451 #8
Thread: Black
Tail: Two black rubber legs
Body: Multiple wraps of filo plume underfeather of pheasant with an additional pair of rubber legs coming out near thorax

B. Dick Walle's Soft Hackle Hare's Ear
Hook: Mustad 3906 B
Thread: Olive
Body: Sparkle hare's ear dubbing
Rib: Gold tinsel
Collar: Hungarian partridge soft hackle

Yachetti's Golden Pearl
Hook: Daiichi 1530
Thread: Tan
Tail: Mallard, wood duck
Body: Cream Antron
Rib: fine gold tinsel
Wing Case: Pearlescent Mylar tinsel
Legs: Mallard, wood duck

Yachetti's Steelhead Sac-Fry
Hook: Daiichi 1530
Thread: White
Tail: White hackle
Abdomen: Uni Glo Yarn floss
Egg Sac: Steelhead orange Glo-bug
Wing Case: Uni Glo Yarn floss
Thorax: Pearl Estaz cropped tight

Yachetti's Pink Sac-Fry
Hook: Daiichi 1530 #16
Thread: White
Tail: White hackle
Abdomen: Light pink or white floss
Egg Sac: Pink yarn
Thorax: White pearl Estaz cropped
Wing Case: Uni Glo Yarn floss

Yachetti's Micro Black and Purple Wet
Hook: Daiichi 1530 #14
Thread: Black
Tail: Black squirrel
Body: Electric purple Lite-Brite or Krystal dubbing
Collar: Black saddle hackle

Row 5 - Left to Right

Yachetti's Micro Signal Light
Hook: Daiichi 1530
Thread: Orange
Tail: Black squirrel
Tag: Chartreuse thread or floss

Yachetti's Micro Reverse Signal Light
Hook: Daiichi 1530
Thread: Chartreuse
Tail: Black squirrel
Tag: Chartreuse thread or floss
Body: Hot orange dubbing or micro chenille
Collar: Black saddle hackle

Yachetti's Purple Pearl Wet
Hook: Daiichi 1530
Thread: Black
Tail: Electric purple Lite-Brite
Body: Pearl/purple Krystal flash
Wings: Purple rabbit hair with a touch of purple Lite-Brite

Vogel's October Caddis
Hook: Mustad 94840
Thread: Orange
Body: Burnt orange floss or dubbing
Hackle Rib: Palmered ginger
Wing: Deer hair

Nagy's Neon Stone
Hook: Mustad 9671
Thread: Red
Tail: Red Hackle
Body: Chartreuse chenille
Thorax Hackle: Red palmered
Wing Case: Red Antron or Glo Yarn

Row 5 - Left to Right

Dorothy's Grizzly & Brown
Hook: Daiichi 1530 size 8
Thread: Green
Body: 2 strands peacock herl
Hackle: Soft grizzly wet hackle palmered Spey style to front
Hackle: Brown, 4 wraps in front of grizzly

Dorothy's Badger
Hook: Daiichi 1530 size 8
Thread: Black
Tail: Badger hackle tips
Body: Badger hackle palmered forward
Eyes: Black craft beads
Head: Red steelhead yarn tied top & bottom

Skamania Bee
Hook: Daiichi 1530
Thread: Black
Body: Alternating bands of chartreuse and black Estaz
Legs: Metallic chartreuse "grizzly" legs of rubber

Deed Brown Pheasant Stone
Hook: Daiichi 1530
Tail: Dark brown pheasant tail
Body: Dark brown dyed pheasant tail
Rib: Gold tinsel
Thorax: Peacock herl
Hackle: Deed brown saddle hackle
Wing Case: Dark brown pheasant tail

D. King's Hare's Ear
Hook: Mustad 3971
Thread: Gray
Tail: Calf tail, black/white
Body: Hare's ear
Rib: Gold tinsel
Thorax: Plucked out hare's ear
Wing Case: Black guinea
Antennae: Plucked out black guinea

Mini-Bugger

Hook: Mustad 3399A
Thread: Black
Tail: Black marabou with black Krystal Flash
Body: Black chenille
Hackle: Palmered black hackle

Bead Head Mohair White Leech

Hook: Daiichi 2220
Thread: White
Tail: White marabou, rabbit, Super Hair or hackle with pearl Flashabou
Body: Wrapped white mohair
Head: Silver bead

Troutsman Turkey Bugger

Hook: Daiichi 2421
Thread: Red
Tail: Mottled amber turkey butt marabou
Body: Amber ostrich herl with turkey filoplume undershaft
Hackle: Brown palmered across body
Head: Black hare's ear, ostrich or hackle

Troutsman Egg Sculpin Leech

Hook: Daiichi 2421
Thread: Black
Tail: Black marabou
Body: Black chenille
Hackle: Palmered black
Head: Spun black deer hair in sculpin v-shape
Under-head: Tuft of steelhead orange Glo Yarn

Row 7 - Left to Right

Yachetti's Black and Purple Zonker

Hook: Daiichi 2220
Thread: Black
Upper Body: Black rabbit Zonker with electric purple Flashabou
Body: Pearl silver tubing
Underwing: Black rabbit hair

Yachetti's White Zonker

Hook: Daiichi 2220
Thread: White
Upper Body: White rabbit Zonker with pearl Flashabou
Body: Pearl silver tubing
Underwing: White rabbit

Yachetti's Electric Spey

Hook: Daiichi 2421
Thread: Black
Body: Rainbow Krenick tinsel
Collar: Purple rabbit with electric purple Flashabou spun Spey style

Bishop's Egg Sucking Fish

Hook: TMC 2457, size 6
Thread: Red
Tail: Grizzly marabou
Thorax: Lite-Brite, pearl
Wing Back: Grizzly marabou
Gills: Red ostrich herl
Eyes: Black beads, 2.5 mm
Egg: Clear orange glass bead

Row 8 - Left to Right

Schmidt's Steelhead Woolly Bugger

Hook: Tiemco #3761 or Daiichi #1530 size 6
Thread: 3/0 waxed mono cord (black)
Tail: Black marabou with peacock Krystal Flash
Rib: Copper wire (optional)
Body: Peacock herl
Hackle: Furnace saddle hackle

Schmidt's Egg Sucking Leech

Hook: Tiemco #3761, size 4 and 6
Thread: 3/0 waxed mono cord
Egg: Orange craft store pompom or medium chenille
Tail: Black marabou with gold Krystal Flash
Rib: Copper wire
Body: Peacock herl
Hackle: Black saddle hackle
Collar: Black dubbing

FLY PLATE 4
NYMPHS - STONEFLY VARIATIONS

Row 1 - Left to Right

Bacon's Larva Lace Stone

Hook: Daiichi 1510
Thread: Black
Tail: Black goose biot
Body: Black ostrich
Rib: Black Larva Lace
Thorax: Black hackle
Antennae: Black goose biot

Bacon's Larva Lace Flashback Stone

Hook: Daiichi 15510
Thread: Black
Tail: Black goose biot
Body: Black ostrich
Rib: Black Larva Lace
Thorax: Black hackle
Wing Case: Pearl, blue, green Flashabou or Mylar
Antennae: Black goose biot

Darkes Simple Stone

Hook: Daiichi 1530
Weight: Lead wire tied on each side of hook shank or a black bead head
Tail: Black or brown goose biots
Rib: Copper wire or strand of pearl Krystal Flash
Abdomen: Black or brown hare's ear blend spun on thread
Thorax: Black or brown hare's ear blend spun into a dubbing loop to simulate legs
Wingcase: Turkey quill section, folded over top

Darkes Purple Jesus

Hook: Daiichi 1530 sizes 10-16
Weight: Black bead head
Tail: Black goose biots
Rib: Strand of pearl Krystal Flash
Body: Purple Brite-Blend, Psuedo Seal, or similar dubbing material
Collar: Black ostrich herl

Mike's Stone

Hook: Tiemco 5263, sizes 10-12
Thread: Black UNI Thread 6/0
Tail: Black goose biots (pair)
Rib: Black balloon strip
Body: Brown dubbing
Wingcase: Turkey quill
Legs: Grouse
Throrax: Ostrich herl
Antennae: Black goose biots (optional)
Comments: Quill and grouse tied in the "over the thorax & legs" technique as per Randall Kaufmann's *Fly Tier's Nymph Manual.*

Row 2, Left to Right

Pheasant Tail Flash Back Stones

Hook: Daiichi 1530
Thread: Black
Tail: Black hackle
Body: Black dyed pheasant tail
Wing Case: Pearlescent flashabou or Fly Flash
Thorax: Black hackle

Barber's Chartreuse Head Stone

Hook: Daiichi 1530
Thread: Black
Tail: Black moose mane or deer hair
Body: Black Antron
Rib: Copper wire
Head: Tuft of chartreuse Glo Yarn (any color)

Barber's Natural Stone, Chartreuse Thorax

Hook: Daiichi 2421 #12
Thread: Black
Tail: Black goose biots
Body: Black antron
Rib: Gold tinsel
Thorax: Chartreuse yarn or floss
Hackle: Badger
Wingcase: Mottled turkey (Note: substitute any color yarn or floss for thorax)

Barber's Jet Black Chartreuse Stone

Hook: Daiichi 2421 #12
Thread: Black
Tail: Black hair
Body: Black Antron
Rib: Copper wire
Wing Case: Dark duck or pheasant fibers
Thorax: Chartreuse yarn or floss
Hackle: Black saddle

Row 3 - Left to Right

Schmidt's Stone

Hook: Daiichi #2151 size 2 or 4 (weighted)
Thread: 3/0 waxed mono cord (dark Brown)
Shell back: Mottled turkey tail fibers (treated with Flex-seal or Flexament)
Tail: Goose biots, dark brown
Rib: Copper wire
Body: Kaufmann's Blend, brown stone, mixed 50/50 with Awesome 'Possum, dark stone
Wing Cases: Mottled turkey tail fibers (treated)
Thorax: Same as body
Legs: Hen saddle

Geddes Black Stone

Hook: Daiichi 2441
Thread: Black
Tail: Black goose biot
Abdomen: Black Antron
WingCase: Dark brown pheasant tail
Thorax: Claret hazel brown dubbing

Geddes Montana Stone

Hook: Mustad 9671
Thread: Black
Tail: Black goose biots
Body: Black chenille
Thorax: Yellow chenille
Hackle: Palmered grizzley

Bachelder's Stone

Hook: Daiichi 1530
Thread: Black
Tail: Black goose biots
Body: Tapered black Antron
Wing Case: Folded mottled turkey
Thorax: Tuft of white Antron with palmered black hackle

Row 4 - Left to Right

Valk's Krystal Stone Fly Series

Flies A, B, C, D, E
Hook: Daiichi 1720
Tail: Black, white, goose biots
Body: Black, white, brown, purple dubbing
Ribbing: Silver or electric blue tinsel
Thorax: Peacock herl with grizzly hackle palmered

Wing Case: Krystal Flash in electric blue, pearl, electric green, electric purple

Row 5 - Left to Right

Spring Stone
Hook: Tiemco 5263, sizes 4-10
Thread: Black Uni-thread 6/0
Tail: Red fox squirrel tail
Rib: Gold oval tinsel
Body: Black chenille
Wing Case: Red fox squirrel tail
Thorax: Black chenille
Legs: Brown neck hackle palmered
Antennae: Red fox squirrel tail

Creepy Stone
Hook: Mustad 37160
Thread: Black
Body: Black Antron
Wing Case: Mottled turkey
Legs: Very long back ring-necked pheasant plucked out wildly for undulation

Bishop's Molded Rubber Stone
Hook: Daiichi 1530
Thread: Black
Body: Pre-molded Traun River black stone, leg and tails cut from poured mold, white feathers filoplume underneath

Kaufmann's Stone
Hook: Mustad 9575
Thread: Black
Tail: Black goose fibers
Rib: Black swannundase
Body: Kauffmann's stone dubbing (Hareline) or 50% black rabbit and 50% claret, amber, orange, rust, brown, blue and ginger goat fur
Wing Case: Folded dark turkey tail
Antennae: Black goose biots

Row 6 - Left to Right

Claret Stone
Hook: Daiichi 1530
Thread: Black
Tail: Amber goose biots
Body: Sparkle claret dubbing
Rib: Purple mylar strip
Wing Case: Black turkey
Hackle: Ginger palmered

Purple Estaz Stone
Hook: Daiichi 1130
Thread: Black
Tail: Amber goose biot
Body: Sparkle black steelhead salmon dubbing (hairline)
Rib: Pearl Krystal Flash
Wing Case: Pearl Holographic Flashabou
Thorax: Purple Estaz

Manistee Red Stone
Hook: Daiichi 1730
Thread: Black
Tail: Pheasant tail
Body: Black Larva Lace
Rib: Red tinsel
Wing Case: Black Swiss straw
Throrax: Peacock herl
Hackle: Black palmered

Row 7 - Left to Right

Black Bead Stone Rubber Legs
Hook: Daiichi 1270
Thread: Black
Tail: Black rubber legs

Body: Black beads
Wing Case: Black Swiss straw
Thorax: Palmered black marabou
Antennae: Black rubber legs

Bead Head Stone, Rubber Legs
Hook: Daiichi 1550
Thread: Black thread
Body: Black partridge SLF dubbing
Rib: Copper wire
Thorax: Black hackle with 4 rubber legs
Head: Gold head
Antennae: 2 rubber legs

Fly Plate 5
Egg Patterns

Row 1 - Left to Right

Smith's Micro-Egg Signal Light
Hook: Daiichi 1530
Thread: Red
Back Egg: Red chenille

Orange & Pink Pom-Pom
Hook: Daiichi 1530 or x510
Thread: Pink or orange Kevlar hot pink UNI Stretch
Main Egg: Orange McFly Foam or steelhead orange Glo Bug yarn, cerise dot
Trailer Egg: Same yarn tied on mono and cemeted or super-glued yarn shop pom-poms may be used and colored
Tail: Pear Flashabou

McRoe Pom-Pom
Hook: Daiichi 1530 or x510
Thread: Pink or orange Kevlar, hot pink UNI Stretch
Main Egg: McFly Foam McRoe color with hint of January Pink
Tag: Pearlescent braid
Trailer Egg: Same colors tied on heavy mono and glued

Winter Pink Pom-Pom
Hook: Daiichi 1510 or x510
Thread: Pink, orange Kevlar or Uni stretch hot pink
Main Egg: McFly Foam January pink with cerise eye
Trailer Egg: Same colors tied & glued on heavy mono
Tail: Pink Krystal Flash

Yachetti's Peach/Oregon Weave Cluster
Hook: Daiichi 1510 or 1120
Thread: UNI Stretch hot pink
Cluster: Tiny twisted and looped yarn pieces of Oregon Cheese and Apricot/Peach Glo Bug yarn

Sucker Spawn
Hook: Heavy wet-fly or curved scud hook. Sizes 8-14
Body: Any 2- or 3-ply yarn is usable. Sparkle yarn or Angora yarns are the most productive. Cream, orange, pink and chartreuse are popular colors. Blue, purple, and yellow will also work
Thread: Danville momocord or 6/0 depending on hook size. Color can match or contrast body color. Don't be afraid to experiment with color combinations.
Step 1: Separate a length of yarn into individual plies. Tie the yarn down the length of the hook shank so that it extends back from the rear of the hook.
Step 2: Bring the yarn forward so that it forms a small loop at the rear of the hook. Secure the yarn with 2 turns of thread.
Step 3: Pull the loose yarn up and back, advance the thread directly in front of the yarn.
Step 4: From another small loop of yarn directly in front of the first loop. Tie down again with 2 turns of thread. Pick up the excess yarn and advance the thread in front.

Step 5: Repeat the procedure for forming yarn loops forward down the length of the hook. *It is very important to make the loops as close together as possible.* When you reach the front of the hook, tie down the excess yarn to the front and trim.
Step 6: From a small head and whip finish. Trim the thread and go fishing!

Row 2 - Left to Right

Pearlescent Nuke Egg
Hook: Daiichi 1510
Thread: Stretch hot pink
Egg: McFly Foam pink or cerise
Sheath: Pearlescent Flashabou strips tied in at tail and overlapped towards the head

Bacon's McComet
Hook: Daiichi 1120
Thread: UNI stretch hot pink
Egg: McFly Foam Illiamna Pink or McRoe
Under-Tail: Pearlescent Flashabou

Blood Dot Weave
Hook: Daiichi 1120
Thread: UNI stretch hot pink
Body: Weaved McFly Foam January pink with cerise dot

Nagy's Scambled Eggs
Hook: Daiichi 1510
Thread: Uni stretch hot pink
Body: Weave of chartreuse and flame Glo-Bug yarn

Nagy's Niagara Egg
Hook: Daiichi 1510
Thread: Uni stretch hot pink or Kevlar
Bottom of Egg: Flame Glo-Bug yarn
Top of Egg: Light Blue and Chartreuse Glo-Bug yarn with a tiny strand of black yarn for eye, or waterproof marker for eye (note: key to all yarn layering is to stack them together when tying them down with thread in order to their preferred appearance)

Oregon Orange Nuke Egg
Hook: Daiichi 1510
Thread: Chartreuse
Hook: Daiichi x510
Nuke Egg: Tangerine McFly Foam
Sheath: Oregon Cheese Glo-Bug yarn

Row 3 - Left to Right

Chartreuse Nuke Egg
Hook: Daiichi x510
Thread: Uni Stretch hot pink
Nuke Egg: Tangerine orange McFly Foam
Sheath: Glo Bug chartreuse

Steve's Pink Glo Bug
Hook: Daiichi 2570
Thread: Pink Kevlar
Egg: Glo Bug salmon egg color with flame yarn dot

Cerise Glo Bug
Hook: Mustad 4250
Thread: Pink Kevlar
Egg: Cerise Glo-Bug with flame dot

Chartreuse Glo Bug
Hook: Daiichi 1120
Thread: Fluorescent Kevlar
Egg: Chartreuse yarn with flame dot

Nagy's Eld Creek Worm
Hook: Daiichi 1510
Thread: Kevlar
Tail & Body: Chartreuse micro chenille burned at the tip

Egg: Cerise Glo-Bug

Nagy's Sperm Egg
Hook: Daiichi 1510
Tail: White marabou
Head: Orange plastic bead

Row 4 - Left to Right

Frammus
Hook: Daiichi 1510
Back Tag: Chartreuse antron
Body: Hot pink Estaz
Front Tag: Chartreuse antron

Graba's Estaz Wiggler
Hook: Daiichi 1510
Tail & Back: Chartreuse Antron
Body: Chartreuse Estaz

Barber's Purple Urple
Hook: Daiichi x510
Tag: Chartreuse floss
Thorax: Purple Estaz or Cactus Chenille

Nagy's Krystal Line Cosseboom
Hook: Mustad 1530
Thread: Uni Stretch hot pink or red
Tail: Pearl Flashabou
Body: Chartreuse Krystal chenille
Head: Thick wrap of red thread

January Ice
Hook: Daiichi 1120
Tail: Metallic red Flashabou
Body: White Estaz
Wing: Metallic red Flashabou

(Hot Pink Dot, Mylar Spinning, and Glowing Cheater Contact Beau-Mac Enterprises, Auburn, Washington (253) 939-8607)

Row 5 - Left to Right

Flies A, B, C, and D are:

Cactus Fly Series
Hook: Tierce 105, size 6-10
Thread: Orange Uni-thread 6/0
Tail: Tuft of colored filoplume or marabou the length of the hook gape
Body: Cactus Chenille
Wing: Tuft of colored filoplume or marabou the same length as the tail
Comments: Polypropylene yarn may be substituted for filoplume or marabou.

Dr. Tom's
Hook: Daiichi 1530
Thread: Hot pink
Body: Orange chenille
Hackle: Palmered orange
Shell Back & Wing: Chartreuse antron

Row 6 - Left to Right

Clown Comet Omlette
Hook: Daiichi 1530
Thread: Kevlar
Tail: Hot pink rabbit strip with electric red Krystal Flash
Egg: McFly Foam Ripple and January pink intermixed strands of yarn

Cerise and Pearl Comet Omlette
Hook: Daiichi 1530

Thread: Kevlar
Tail: White marabou
Tag: Pearl braid
Egg: Cerise Glo-Bug

January Comet Omlette
Hook: Daiichi 1530
Thread: Kevlar
Tail: White marabou
Tag: Pearl braid
Egg: McFly Foam pink

Row 7 - Left to Right

Steelhead Orange Comet Omlette
Hook: Daiichi 1530
Thread: Orange Kevlar
Tail: Hot orange rabbit strip with orange Krystal Flash
Egg: Glo-Bug steelhead orange or McFly Foam, tangerine with flame dot

Pink Lady Comet
Hook: Daiichi 1150
Thread: Kevlar
Tail: Electric red Flashabou
Egg Bottom: Glo Bug baby pink
Egg Top: Chartreuse Glo Bug

Clown
Hook: Daiichi 1150
Thread: Kevlar
Egg: Strands of orange, chartreuse and pink McFly Foam or Glo-Bug yarn to individual specifications

Row 8

Satellite
Hook: Daiichi 2050, size 5
Thread: Primrose
Hackle: White marabou
Eggs: Glo-Bug yarn, colors egg, chartreuse, steelhead orange, flame
Note: Tie five eggs on separate monofilament lines, different lengths. Attach behind eye. One wrap of white marabou behind thread wraps. Tie six eggs to cover thread wraps.

FLY PLATE 6
DRIES, BOMBERS, WETS

Row 1 - Left to Right

Valk's Steelhead Skater Series

Gray Wulff
Hook: Daiichi 1170
Thread: Gray
Tail: Deer hair
Body: Dark gray dubbing
Wings: Deer hair
Hackle: Dark dun

Light Hendrickson
Hook: Daiichi 1170
Thread: Gray
Tail: Dun hackle
Body: Tan Antron
Wings: Wood duck
Hackle: Dark dun

Dark Hendrickson
Hook: Daiichi 1170
Thread: Amber
Tail: Dun hackle
Body: Gray Antron/rabbit

Wing: Wood duck
Hackle: Dark dun

Irresistible
Hook: Daiichi 1170
Thread: Gray
Tail: Deer hair
Body: Spun deer hair clipped tight
Wings: Deer hair
Hackle: Dark dun

Green Buck Bug
Hook: Daiichi 2421
Thread: Black
Tail: Ginger hackle
Tag: Amber Antron
Body: Spun green deer hair
Hackle: Palmered brown

Row 2 - Left to Right

Royal Wulff
Hook: Daiichi 2421
Thread: Black
Tail: Deer hair
Butt: Peacock herl
Body: Red floss
Shoulder: Peacock herl
Wings: White calf tail
Hackle: Palmered brown

Orange Bomber
Hook: Daiichi 1750
Thread: Grey
Tail: Orange calf tail
Body: Deer hair spun and cropped tight
Hackle: Palmered orange

Irresistible Wulff
Hook: Daiichi 1750
Thread: Black
Tail: Squirrel tail
Body: Spun deer hair cropped tight
Body Hackle: Palmered grizzly
Wings: Deer hair
Thorax hackle: Grizzly

Row 3 - Left to Right

Steelhead Cicada
Hook: Mustad 9671
Thread: Kevlar
Body: Orange-dyed deer hair with bands of black deer-hair wings
Wings: Orange-dyed deer hair
Head: Spun orange deer hair cropped round

Steelhead Bee
Hook: Daiichi 2571
Thread: Kevlar
Body: Black and yellow bands of spun deer hair cropped oval
Wings: Natural deer hair

Smith's Coastal Skating Diver
Hook: Daiichi 1250
Thread: Kevlar
Tail: Orange and yellow hackle with pearl Flashabou
Body: Ornage Estaz
Head: Spun yellow and amber brown deer hair cropped sculpin/diver style
Eyes: Prismatic black

Gray Drake Spinner (Stuber Tie)
Hook: Daiichi 1170
Thread: Black
Body: Gray Deer hair
Rib: Black thread

Wings: Light dun hackle with organza veil material

Row 4 - Left to Right

Shewey's Spawning Purple
Hook: Daiichi 2441
Thread: Black
Tag: Silver
Body: Orange floss
Wing: Purple marabou
Collar: Teal flank

Kaufmann's Freight Train (modified)
Hook: Daiichi 2441
Thread: Black
Tag: Gold
Abdomen: Orange floss
Rib: Heavy gold
Thorax: Black ostrich
Overwing: White calf tail
Underwing and Collar: Purple saddle hackle

Rainbow Spey
Hook: Daiichi 2161
Thread: Black
Body: Krenick rainbow
Thorax: Red partridge SLF dubbing
Collar: Heron/pheasant Spey hackle or substitute

Row 5 - Left to Right

Peacock Gold Spey
Hook: Daiichi 2161
Thread: Black
Body: Copper tinsel or wire, heavy
Thorax: Peacock herl
Collar: Heron/pheasant Spey hackle or substitute

Copper Guinea Spey
Hook: Daiichi 2161
Body: Copper tinsel or Flashabou
Thorax: Peacock herl
Collar Wing: Black guinea

Low Water McMillan's Winter's Hope
Hook: Daiichi 2421
Thread: Red
Body: Silver tinsel
Throat: Purple and blue hackle
Wing: Yellow and orange calf tail

Row 6 - Left to Right

Blue Charm (variation)
Hook: Daiichi 2421
Thread: Black
Body: Black floss
Rib: Silver wire
Throat: Blue guinea
Wing: Yellow, red and black bucktail, polar bear or synthetic hair

Red Butt Skunk
Hook: Daiichi 2421
Thread: Black
Tail: Black calf tail
Tag: Red floss
Body: Black floss or partridge SLF dubbing
Rib: Silver
Wing: Black bucktail
Throat: Black hackle

Undertaker
Hook: Daiichi 2421
Thread: Black
Tag: Gold tinsel chartreuse and orange floss
Body: Peacock herl
Wing: Black bucktail

Throat: Black hackle

Row 7 - Left to Right

Stallard Maggot Spey
Hook: Daiichi 2161
Thread: Black
Body: Bare hook
Thorax: Amber Antron
Collar: Heron/pheasant spey hackle or substitute

Spirit River Mighty Minnow Rainbow Trout
Hook: Daiichi 2220
Thread: Cream
Body: Pearl Lite-Brite
Wing: Spirit River's Lite-Brite, Spectra Splash Mylar, Crystal Splash in pearl, red, green and blue
Underwing: Same material in blue
Eyes: Black mono craft

FLY PLATE 7
NEW AGE SPEYS AND CLASSICS

Row 1 - Left to Right

Kustich's Purple Bunny Spey
Hook: Daiichi 2051
Thread: Purple
Body: SLF Purple Haze
Rib: Small round copper
Wing: Purple rabbit strip fastened Matuka-style with rib
Hackle: Large purple schlappen
Collar: Purple jumbo guinea

Kustich's Devil's Advocate
Hook: Daiichi 2051
Thread: Red
Tag: Orange Uni-stretch
Body: Polar Pearl Lite Brite cut and dubbed
Hackle: White Hareline select marabou Spey hackle
Collar: Natural jumbo guinea

Kustich's Purple & Orange Marabou Spey
Hook: Daiichi 2051
Thread: Purple
Tag: Silver tinsel
Body: Purple Steelhead and Salmon Dubbin'
Rib: Silver tinsel
Hackle: Purple over orange Hareline select marabou spey hackle
Collar: Purple jumbo guinea

Row 2 - Left to Right

Kustich's Purple October
Hook: Daiichi 2051
Thread: Purple
Rib: Silver tinsel
Body: Purple steelhead & salmon dubbin'
1st Hackle: Purple burnt goose
2nd Hackle: Orange-Dyed pheasant rump
Collar: Purple guinea
Wing: Purple arctic fox

Kustich's Catnip
Hook: Daiichi 2421
Thread: Red
Tag: Silver tinsel
Body: Orange Hairline Steelhead & Salmon Dubbiní
Hackle: Orange Hoffman soft hackle
Wing: Yellow calf tail

Kustich's Citation
Hook: Daiichi 2421
Thread: Olive
Tail: Natural hen neck fibers
SLF: Summer duck

Rib: Small round copper wire
Hackle: Natural hen neck
Wing: Filoplume from natural pheasant rump

Row 3 - Left to Right

Halyk's Orange and Black Reverse Akroyd
Hook: Daiichi 2051
Thread: Black
Tag: Silver
Body: Orange seal or SLF Dubbing
Rib: Gold
Thorax: Black seal
Hackle: Black saddle or schlappen
Wing: Deer hair
Collar: Teal

Halyk's Orange and Black Reverse Akroyd Low Water
Hook: Daiichi 2051
Thread: Black
Tag: Silver
Body: Orange seal or SLF Dubbing
Rib: Gold
Thorax: Black seal
Hackle: Black saddle or schlappen
Wing: Mottled Turkey
Collar: Teal

Halyk's October Spey
Hook: Daiichi 2051
Thread: Amber
Tag: Gold
Body: Rear orange floss; upper, amber SLF dubbing
Rib: Heavy gold wire
Body hackle: Palmered brown saddle hackle
Wing: Deer hair
Collar: Orange-dyed guinea feathers

Row 4 - Left to Right

Bear's Skamaniator
Hook: Daiichi 2441
Thread: 8/0 Black UNI Thread
Tail: Purple marabou with a few wisps of purple flash
Body: 3 purple schlappen feathers collared up hook shank

Bush Weasel Spey
Hook: Daiichi 2421
Thread: 8/0 black UNI Thread
Tag: Fine silver mylar (size 12)
Body: Medium black chenille
Ribbing: Fine silver tinsel (size 12)
Hackle: Black schlappen palmered
Wing: Teal flank
Throat: Teal flank
Collar: Black schlappen

Schmidt's Spey, Green Butt
Hook: Daiichi 2161 size 1 or 2
Tag: Ultra chenille (micro) green or red
Rib: Gold or copper Krystal Flash
Body hackle: Pheasant rump
Body: Kaufman Blend dubbing (dark stone)
Collar hackle: Black pheasant rump

Row 5 - Left to Right

Schmidt's Natural Spey, Red Butt
Same as above except
Tag: Ultra chenille red
Collar Hackle: Natural pheasant rump

Graba's Spey
Hook: Daiichi 2421
Thread: Black
Tag: Rainbow holographic
Body: Floss

Rib: Silver
Thorax: Purple Partridge SLF
Wing: Teal
Collar: White/Black mottled marabou

Vogel's St. Mary's Spey

Hook: Daiichi 2161
Thread: Amber
Tag: Holographic tinsel
Body: Partridge SLF dubbing olive
Rib: Holographic tinsel
Hackle: Oliver saddle or Spey hackle palmered from butt through body

Graba's Low Water Spey

Hook: Daiichi 2421
Thread: Black
Body: Electric blue Flashabou
Thorax: Pink floss
Collar: Purple saddle hackle
Wing: Pearlescent Krystal Flash

FLY PLATE 8
MARABOU SPEYS

Row 1 - Left to Right

Halyk's Tequila Sunrise (Variation 1)
Hook: Daiichi 2441
Thread: Black
Tail: Red bucktail with pearl Krystal Flash
Body: Palmered yellow, orange and blue marabou

Halyk's Black and Blue
Hook: Daiichi 2441
Tail: Pear Krystal Flash
Body: Black, purple and blue marabou
Collar: Blue-dyed guinea

Row 2 - Left to Right

Halyk's Tequila Sunrise (variation 2)
Hook: Daiichi 2441
Thread: Red
Tail: Pear Krystal Flash
Body: Yellow, orange, red and blue palmered marabou

Schmidt's Chartreuse Kingfisher Spey
Hook: Daiichi 2441
Thread: Red
Body: Chartreuse marabou tied as above
Flash: 4 strands pearl and 2 strands red Flashabou
Collar: Kingfisher blue marabou or schlappen
Head: As above

Row 3 - Left to Right

Schmidt's Orange & Red Spey
Hook: Daiichi 2441
Thread: UNI Stretch hot pink
Body: Orange marabou tied as above
Flash: 6 strands of red Flashabou
Collar: Red marabou as above
Head: As above

Schmidt's Purple Snow Spey
Hook: Daiichi 2441
Thread: UNI Stretch hot pink
Body: White marabou tied as above
Flash: 4 strands white and 2 strands of purple Flashabou
Collar: Purple marabou as above
Head: As above

Row 4 - Left to Right

Schmidt's Autumn Spey
Hook: TMC 7999 sized to your liking, I prefer 1/0
Thread: Bright red or cherry 3/0 monocord or single-strand floss
Body: 1 orange, 1 cherry red marabou plume, barbells stripped off one side. Start with the orange at the halfway point on the hook shank. Palmer forward. Tie in the cherry red at the orange end point and palmer forward.
Flash: 4 red and 2 purple strands of Flashabou, tied on top, cut off the same length as the marabou
Collar: 1 purple marabou, stripped and wound at head
Head: Bright red

Schmidt's Dark Water Spey
Hook: TMC 7999 sized to your liking, I prefer 1/0
Thread: Bright red or cherry 3/0 monocord or single-strand floss
Body: Red marabou, purple marabou tied as Autumn Spey above
Flash: 4 purple and 2 red Flashabou
Collar: Black marabou as above
Head: Bright red

FLY PLATE 9
CLASSIC SPEYS AND WETS

Row 1 - Left to Right

Yarnot's Steelhead Akroyd
Hook: Daiichi 2051/Alec Jackson spey 3/0
Tag: Small flat silver tinsel
Tail: Claret golden pheasant crest
Butt: Black ostrich herl
Body: Rear 1/2: Claret seal fur
      Front 1/2: Black floss
Rib: Medium flat gold over seal fur, medium silver over floss
Joint: Black ostrich herl between seal & floss
Hackle: Claret neck hackle over seal fur, black heron substitute over floss
Collar: Teal
Cheeks: Jungle cock
Wing: Claret goose
Head: Black 12/0 thread

Yarnot's Wild Turkey Orange
Hook: Daiichi 2051/Alec Jackson Spey size 1.5, 3/0
Tag: Small flat gold tinsel
Body: Rear 1/2: Flo orange floss
      Front 1/2: Hot orange seal fur
Rib: Medium flat gold tinsel, small oval gold tinsel
Hackle: Wild turkey marabou wound over orange seal
Collar: Orange mallard flank
Wing: Strips of hot orange swan or goose
Head: Orange 12/0 thread

Row 2 - Left to Right

Yarnot's Purple & Orange
Hook: Daiichi 2051/Alce Jackson spey 1.5, 3/0
Tag: Small flat gold tinsel
Body: Rear 1/2: Fluo. Orange floss
      Front 1/2: Purple steel
Rib: Rear 1/2: Small flat gold tinsel
      Front 1/2: Medium flat copper tinsel, small oval silver tinsel
Hackle: Marabou dyed orange with purple tips
Collar: Purple mallard flank
Wing: Strips of purple turkey tail
Head: Black 12/0 thread

Yarnot's Emerald Eagle
Hook: Daiichi 2051/Alec Jackson spey size 1.5, 3/0
Tag: Small flat silver tinsel
Body: Rear 1/2: Chartreuse floss

Front 1/2: Black seal fur
Rib: Medium embossed silver tinsel, small oval silver tinsel
Counter Rib: Fine oval gold tinsel
Hackle: Marabou dyed green with black tips wound over black seal
Collar: Black mallard flank
Wing: Strips of black goose or swan
Head: Black 12/0 thread

Row 3 - Left to Right

Yarnot's Steelhead Stinger, Black
Hook: Daiichi 2051/Alec Jackson spey 5, 3
Body: Rear 1/2: Small flat silver tinsel
      Front 1/2: Black seal fur
Collar: Black neck hackle
Wing: Arctic fox
Head: Black 12/0 thread

Yarnot's Steelhead Stinger, Orange
Hook: Daiichi 2051/Alec Jackson spey 5, 3
Tag: Small flat gold tinsel
Body: Rear 1/2: Fluorescent orange floss
      Front 1/2: Fluorescent orange seal fur
Collar: Red and orange neck hackle wound together
Wing: Arctic fox
Head: Orange 12/0 thread

Row 4 - Left to Right

Stallard's Thugmeister Spey
Hook: Daiichi 2051
Thread: Black
Tag: Silver
Shoulder: One wrap of black chenille
Thorax: Electric blue Flashabou
Wing: Layers of black hackle tips, black and electric blue Krystal Flash, silver Flashabou and purple marabou
Throat: Purple saddle hackle

Purple Guinea Spey
Hook: 2441
Thread: Black
Body: Purple Krenick braid
Thorax: Peacock herl
Underwing: Black hackle tips
Collar: Purple saddle and black guinea hackle

FLY PLATE 10
PETITE SPEYS, LEECHES, ZONKERS

Row 1 - Left to Right
Valk's Steelhead Petite Series
Flies A, B, C and D Dressing is:
Hook: Kamasan B. 220 black
Thread: Black
Bodies: Uni stretch in wine, purple, black, blue, orange and olive
Tag & Rib: Flat gold or silver tinsel
Thorax: Peacock herl
Wing: Antron yarn cut to half of hook shank in clear, chartreuse, yellow and olive
Collar: Hoffman Chickabou soft hackle in colors pink, purple, black, blue, grizzly and olive

Row 2 - Left to Right

Flies A and B same Dressing as above
Flies C and D are: Valk's Bead Head Squirrels
Hook: Kamasan B 220 nymph
Thread: Black
Bead: Gold
Tail: Squirrel natural, orange and black
Rib: Gold oval
Body: Ultra chenille in chartreuse, orange, and purple
Overwing: Squirrel tail in natural, black and orange

Collar: Hoffman Chickabou soft hackle in olive grizzly, white, purple and burnt orange

Row 3 - Left to Right

Flies A and B - (Same dressing as above)

Krause's Chicago Leech
Hook: Daiichi 1720
Thread: Black
Tail: Electric purple Flashabou with strands of black marabou
Body: Wrapped black mohair
Head: Black Cyclops bead

Krause's Egg Sucking Chicago Leech
(Same dressing as above except for ball of hot orange dubbing for the head)

Row 4 - Left to Right

Smith's Chartreuse Fire Fly
Hook: Daiichi 1530
Thread: Black
Body: Ultra chenille, chartreuse
Collar: Black marabou
Head: Chartreuse plastic bead

Geddes Alexandra
Hook: Daiichi 2421
Thread: Black
Tail: Flame red marabou
Body: Silver
Wing: Peacock herl
Throat: Black hackle

Geddes Thunder Creek Steelhead
Hook: Daiichi 1530
Thread: Red
Body: Silver tinsel
Wing: Strand of pink Super Hair topped with reddish-orange deer hair
Throat: White calf tail
Head: Red and white hair overlapped in a ball and cemented with prismatic eyes added

Egg Sucking Leech, Purple Head
Hook: Daiichi 1530
Thread: Black
Tail: Black marabou
Body: Black chenille
Rib: Black palmered hackle
Head: Purple hareline sparkle steelhead/salmon dubbing

Row 5 - Left to Right

Electric Candy Cane
Hook: Daiichi 2441
Thread: Black
Tail: Black marabou
Body: Bands of black chenille hot red Edge-Brite with silver tinsel under the Edge-Brite to make it glow. Black rubber legs tied in at each color change
Hackle: Black schlappen palmered throughout body

Flies B and C: Feenstra's EMUlator (A crayfish imitation) Variations 1 and 2
Hook: 4-6XL Streamer hook, weighted as desired (Tiemco 9395 works fine)
Antennae: Two pheasant tail sections
Claws/Tail: Two small strips of Australian possum or olive rabbit-strip sections
Body: One insect green and one olive emu feather wound forward simultaneously
Head: A clump of Australian possum or muskrat tied around the front of the hook as a head

Row 6 - Left to Right

Thugmeister Leech
Hook: Daiichi 2131
Thread: Black
Head: Gold bead
Tail: Black rabbit stud
Body: Cross-cut purple Zonker strip
Wing: Electric purple Flashabou

Darkes Rabbit Strip Spey, Emerald Shiner
Hook: Alec Jackson Spey, Size 5
Tail: White rabbit strip
Body: Pearl-n-green Lite Brite dubbing
Wing: Olive Flashabou with olive rabbit strip over top
Collar: Olive Hoffman Chickabou or schlappen hackle
Eyes: Jungle cock (optional)

Row 7

Clouser's Leech
Hook: Daiichi 1750
Thread: Black
Tail: Big tuft of black marabou with reddish-amber Flashabou
Body: Black chenille
Hackle: Black saddle or schlappen
Head: Wrapped black chenille or spun black deer hair, cropped tight
Eyes: Red and black prismatic

FLY PLATE 11

MARABOU SPEYS, STREAMERS, WETS

Row 1 - Left to Right

Hot Pink Marabou Spey
Hook: Daiichi 2051
Thread: Uni stretch hot pink
Tag: Gold tinsel
Thorax: Hot pink Estaz
Hackle: Hot pink and cerise marabou palmered with electric pink Flashabou
Collar: Red guinea feather

Pink Marabou Egg Spey
Hook: Daiichi 2135
Thread: Black
Thorax: Black chenille
Hackle: Cerise pink mottled mini marabou

Hot Orange Marabou Spey
Hook: Daiichi 2051
Thread: Uni Stretch hot pink
Tag: Gold tinsel
Thorax: Orange Estaz
Hackle: Orange and flame orange marabou with orange/gold Flashabou
Collar: Hot orange or pink guinea feather

Row 2 - Left to Right

Grau's Tiger
Hook: Daiichi 2441
Thread: Black
Body: Gold tinsel braid
Overwing: Layer of yellow bucktail, dyed green grizzly hackle tips, dyed green bucktail, green Flashabou and pearl Krystal Flash
Throat: Red bucktail, orange bucktail, red and orange Krystal Flash
Collar: Dyed green partridge feather

Tazmanian Devil
Hook: Daiichi 2131

Thread: Black
Tail: Chartreuse bunny strip with orange/gold Flashabou
Body: Chartreuse Estaz with orange and chartreuse Holla-hoop Rubber Legs (from Bass Pro shops)
Hackle: Chartreuse saddle hackle
Head: Gold bead

Hot Pink Tazmanian Devil
Hook: Daiichi 1530
Thread: Uni Stretch hot pink
Tail: Hot pink bunny strip with electric red Flashabou
Body: Hot pink Estaz with Holla-hoop thunder bolt spotted rubber legs in orange and chartreuse (Bass Pro shops)

Row 3 - Left to Right

Green Butt Monkey (Smith/Linsenman)
Hook: Daiichi 2220
Thread: Uni thread 3/0
Tail: Chartreuse marabou, gold Krystal Flash
Body: Gold tinsel chenille over a lead underwrap
Wings: Rusty brown rabbit strip
Throat: Red yarn
Collar: Pheasant rump
Head: Four to six chunks of cigar-sized tan ram's wool (white ram's wool dyed in Linsenman black coffee) Wool is tied on tightly, teased with a needle, then trimmed in oval shape

Skamania Bunny Bugger
Hook: Daiichi 2441
Thread: Black
Tail: Orange Zonker strip
Body hackle: Hot pink and blue palmered marabou
Eyes: Silver bead chain

Row 4 - Left to Right

Kwitek's Trigger
Hook: Partridge 218
Thread: Hot red
Back: Clear scud back
Rib: Copper wire
Lower body: Chartreuse Spirit River yak streamer hair, Fly Fur or Antron
Upper body: Same but in flame orange

Kwitek's J.P. Taper
Hook: Partridge CS2
Thread: Black
Tail: Peacock strands
Body: Multiple tapered turns of orange flat waxed nylon to build up density and weight
Side flanks: Jungle cock hackle
Throat: Red flat waxed nylon
Head: Deep build-up of black thread

Kluesing's Blueberg
Hook: Daiichi 1530
Thread: Black
Body: Electric blue Flashabou
Overwing: Woodduck flank with pearl purple Krystal Flash
Throat: Brown hackle

Tyson Sparr
Hook: Daiichi 1530
Thread: Black
Body: Silver tinsel
Wing: White Fun Fur and blue/green Lite-Brite
Side flanks: Yellow dyed grizzly hackle
Head: Build up of black thread
Eyes: Round circles painted with white waterproof paint

Row 5 - Left to Right

Chartreuse Skamania Bunny

Hook: Daiichi 2441
Thread: Chartreuse
Tail: Chartreuse bunny strip, chartreuse Krystal Flash
Body: Chartreuse Estaz with chartreuse crosscut rabbit
Eyes: Prismatic

Feenstra's Super Smolt

Hook: 4-7XL streamer hook, sizes 2-8
Thread: Uni-mono
Tail: Sunburst Flashabou
Body: Silver Diamond Braid
Hackle: Black or grizzly saddle, tied in halfway up the body and palmered forward to front of hook
Wing: (Three Parts)
Clump of white arctic fox tail (marabou OK)
3-6 strands sunburst Flashabou
Topping: Clump of blue Antron (SAAP fibers from Dan Bailey's)
Head/Eyes: 1/8 red and black stick-on eyes, bound with mono thread and lacquered.

FLY PLATE 12

SURF AND LOWER ESTUARY BAITFISH STREAMERS

Matt Reid's Great Lakes Baitfish Series

Row 1 - Left to Right

Skinny Pete (P&G)

Hook: Mustad 79666S, size 1-2/0
Tail: 2 Hackle feathers (gray)
Body: Braided pearl mylar
Wing: Peacock herl and light blue sparkle flash. Pearl saltwater Flashabou side
Cheek: Mallard flank
Eyes: Stick on prismatic
*Hard head or Softex over eyes and head

C-4-See-Me-Smelt

Hook: Tiemco 300 size 2-4
Tail: White SLF
Body: Pearl Lite Brite
Under wing: Gray SLF over peacock Krystal Flash
Wing: Ice blue Angel Hair
Cheek: Silver pheasant
Throat: Red SLF
Eyes: Stick on prismatic
*Hard head or softex over eyes and head

Row 2 - Left to Right

C-4-See-Me-Alewife

Hook: Tiemco B115 size 2-4
Tail: Gray SLF
Body: Stacked holographic tinsel
Underwing: Gray SLF/pearl Flashabou
Wing: Blue Angel Hair
Throat & underside: White SLF

Ultra Hair Clouser

Hook: Tiemco 8115
Body/Wing: Seafoam green Ultra Hair over clear. Pearl Sparkle Flash
Wing: Peacock ultra hair
Eyes: Pearl dumbell

Row 3 - Left to Right

Ultra Ghost

Hook: Tiemco 8115 size 4-2
Wing: Peacock herl over gray Ultra Hair
Cheek: Silver pheasant
Eyes: Stick-on prismatic

Skinny Pete (A&G)

Hook: Mustak 79666S size 1-2/0
Tail: 2 hackle feathers (gray)
Wing: Peacock Angel Hair over pearl Angel Hair
Cheeks: Silver pheasant
Eyes: Stick-on prismatic

Row 4- Left to Right

Reid's Bouciever

Hook: Tiemco 8115 size 2-4
Tail: Two webby hackle feathers, gray
Wing: Peacock herl and blue Flashabou, pearl Flashabou
Collar: Ice blue marabou over pink marabou
Eyes: Stick-on prismatic
*Nikki's favorite

Seahabit Bucktail

Hook: Tiemco 8115 size 4-1
*Layered pink/white bucktail, silver holographic tinsel
Wing: Peacock herl and blue Flashabou

Row 5 - Left to Right

Bunny Foo Foo

Hook: Tiemco 7999 size 1/0
Tail: Chinchilla bunny
Body: Chinchilla bunny rainbow Krystal Flash
Wing: Peacock herl layered with light blue Sparkle Flash

Skinny Pete (P&B)

Hook: Mustad 79666S size 1/2/0
Tail: 2 hackle feathers (blue)
Body: Braided pearl mylar
Wing: Peacock herl over pink Krystal Flash, pearl saltwater Flashabou side
Throat: White marabou
Cheek: Mallard flank
Eyes: Stick-on prismatic

FLY PLATE 13

SURF AND LOWER ESTUARY BAITFISH STREAMERS

Matt Reid's Great Lakes Baitfish Series

Row 1

Angel Hair Ghost

Hook: Tiemco 8115
Tail: Pearl Flashabou
Body: Braided mylar
Wing: Peacock angel hair, over ice blue angel hair, over pearl Flashabou,over (2) gray hackle feathers
Cheek: Silver pheasant
Throat: White sheep wool
Eyes: Stick-on prismatic
*Hard head or Softex over eyes and head

Row 2 - Left to Right

Bunny Bendback

Hook: Tiemco 8115 (slight upward bend ° in size 1 behind eyes)
Tail: Bunny white
Wing: Peacock Angel Hair over peacock Krystal flash over silver bunny strip
*Trim off at hook bend
Underside: Pearl Flashabou over white sheep wool
Throat: Red SLF veiled under white sheep wool
Eyes: Stick-on prismatic

Shmoo

Hook: Tiemco 8115 size 2

Wing: Holographic tinsel over white deer hair over pink Krystal Flash
Collar: Palmered white bunny
Eyes: Stick-on prismatic

Row 3 - Left to Right

Wooly Smelt

Hook: Tiemco 811S size
Tail: 4 Gray schlappen feathers
Wing: Layered sheep wool with Krystal flash (mix colors)
Underwing: Layered sheep wool with pearl Flashabou
Throat: Red SLF veiled under white sheep wool
Eyes: Stick on prismatic

WTF

Hook: Tiemco 811S size 4
Wing: Seafoam green ultra tail
Underwing: Yellow ultra hair
Sides: Grizzly hackle feathers
Eyes: Small bead chain

Row 4 - Left to Right

Wooly Smelt (low water)

Hook: Tiemco 811S size
Tail: Trimmed hackle sections glued into a length of pearl braided mylar
Body: Pearl Estaz
Wing: Layered sheep wool with Krystal Flash, grays, olives
Underside: Layered sheep wool with Krystal Flash, white, pearl
Eyes: Stick-on prismatic

Waker Alewife

Hook: Tiemco 8089 size 2
Tail: Seafoam green Ultra Hair over generous holographic tinsel over clear Ultra Hair
Wing: Black Ultra Hair over generous holographic tinsel
Soft collar: Black marabou (top) white marabou (bottom)
Head: Stacked and trimmed deer hair colored with permanent markers, black over gray sides
Eyes: Stick-on prismatic

Row 5

B-17 Rainbow Smelt

Package kit assembly available from:
B-17 Fly Tackle Limited
9164 Brady
Redford, Michigan 48239
(313) 255-2838